International Handbook of E-learning, Volume 2

The *International Handbook of E-learning, Volume 2* provides a comprehensive compendium of implementation and practice in all aspects of e-learning, one of the most significant ongoing global developments in the entire field of education. Covering the integration, challenges, implications, and context-appropriate use of open education networks, blended learning, mobile technologies, social media, and other platforms in a variety of unique international settings, these thirty contributions illustrate the wide-ranging applications and solutions made possible by this rapidly growing new paradigm. Case studies are driven by empirical research and attention to cultural specificity, while future research needs are discussed in relation to both confirmed practice and recent changes in the field. The book will be of interest to anyone seeking to create and sustain meaningful, supportive learning environments within today's anytime, anywhere framework, from teachers, administrators, and policy makers to corporate and government trainers.

Dr. Mohamed Ally is Professor in the Centre for Distance Education and Researcher in the Technology Enhanced Knowledge Research Institute (TEKRI) at Athabasca University, Canada. He previously served as Director of the Centre of Distance Education at Athabasca University, Canada's Open University. He is Past President of the International Federation of Training and Development Organizations (IFTDO) and a Founding Director of the International Association of Mobile Learning (IamLearn).

Dr. Badrul H. Khan is the founder of McWeadon Education, a professional development institution. He previously served as Founding Director of the Educational Technology Leadership (ETL) graduate cohort program at The George Washington University, Founding Director of the Educational Technology (ET) graduate program at the University of Texas, Brownsville, and Instructional Designer and Evaluation Specialist in the School of Medicine at Indiana University, Indianapolis. Professor Khan has the credit of first coining the phrase "web-based instruction" and popularizing the concept through his bestselling 1997 book *Web-Based Instruction*, which paved the way for the new field of e-learning.

The Routledge International Handbook Series

International Handbook of E-learning, Volume 2

Implementation and Case Studies

Edited by
Mohamed Ally and Badrul H. Khan

NEW YORK AND LONDON

First published 2015
by Routledge
711 Third Avenue, New York, NY 10017

and by Routledge
2 Park Square, Milton Park, Abingdon, Oxon OX14 4RN

Routledge is an imprint of the Taylor & Francis Group, an informa business

© 2015 Taylor & Francis

Library of Congress Cataloging-in-Publication Data
International handbook of E-learning / edited by Badrul H. Khan,
    Mohamed Ally.
        volumes cm. — (The Routledge international handbook series)
    Includes bibliographical references and index.
    Contents: v. 1.   Theoretical perspectives and research —
v. 2.   Implementation and case studies.
    1. Internet in education.   2. Internet in education—Case studies.
3. Web-based instruction.   4. Web-based instruction—Case studies.
5. Distance education—Computer-assisted instruction.   6. Distance
education—Computer-assisted instruction—Case studies.   I. Khan,
Badrul H. (Badrul Huda), 1958– editor of compilation.   II. Ally, Mohamed,
editor of compilation.
    LB1044.87.I5564 2015
    371.33′44678—dc23
    2014033703

ISBN: 978-1-138-79372-9 (hbk)
ISBN: 978-1-315-76090-2 (ebk)

Typeset in Bembo
by Apex CoVantage, LLC

Printed and bound in the United States of America
by Edwards Brothers Malloy on sustainably sourced paper

Contents

Contents

Preface

The field of e-learning has matured significantly since I first started to work on the *Web-Based Instruction* book in 1995 (Educational Technology Publications). Its enormous acceptance worldwide has resulted in invitations to speak in different parts of the world. Through these experiences, I have learned about online learning initiatives globally, have had the privilege of meeting many researchers and practitioners, and can say that, in my humble opinion, among all emerging and new disciplines, e-learning is the fastest and the most recognized internationally. I always felt that there was a tremendous need for someone to compile the diversity of experiences, applications, and practices of e-learning from different parts of the world. This endeavor of putting together the two volumes of the *International Handbook of E-Learning* is the result. After developing the proposal for the handbook, I realized that by myself I could not accomplish the huge task of putting it together. The first individual I thought of who could greatly contribute to the handbook is none other than Professor Mohamed Ally, an expert in mobile learning with whom I worked on several global e-learning projects, including "ICT and E-learning in the Middle East," a special May–June 2010 issue of *Educational Technology*. I am very pleased to have him as my partner in this endeavor.

Badrul H. Khan

In both volumes of the international handbook, we tried to include e-learning theoretical practices, research, and case studies from different parts of the world. Some authors are not native speakers of English, therefore their presentation of materials in their respective chapters may appear different. We tried to keep their original expression and did not attempt to modify them. This allows the reader to get the essence of what is happening in different parts of the world. Diversity is an integral part of e-learning, and this handbook is not any different in that sense. I am delighted to be co-editing both volumes of the international handbook with Dr. Badrul H. Khan, who is a world leader in the field of e-learning. He has published many books and papers in the field of e-learning, and his books have been translated into many languages.

Mohamed Ally

Foreword

This compendium of 57 chapters in the two volumes is presented as an international handbook of e-learning even though a majority of the authors are from Canada and the US. Does this matter? When I served as a senior official of UNESCO, which brings together nearly 200 member states, we required a greater diversity and spread of country participation before calling a project 'international.'

The essential point, however, is not the variety of national flags on the papers, but whether, taken as a whole, the contributions in these volumes give a genuinely international perspective on e-learning. I give credit to the editors for even attempting to pull together a global picture of such a fast-moving field. The effort is worthwhile because, in their long journey into e-learning, most institutions have only reached the foothills, so any hints about how to surmount the challenges of the climb ahead are useful. In his annual surveys of e-learning in North America, for example, Tony Bates judged that it was only in 2013 that most institutions engaging in e-learning began to do so with an acceptable degree of competence. This means that the enterprise is now ready for lift-off, which makes this book timely.

As is all too common in writing on educational technology, most of the authors implicitly assume that e-learning began with the Internet and focus on comparing e-learning with class-room instruction. While classroom teaching will indeed be the more familiar environment for most readers, it is also important to situate e-learning within the long tradition of distance education that goes back decades, centuries, or even millennia, depending on one's reading of history.

Those who forget the past can be condemned to relive it, which explains why Bates found that institutions were taking so long to get up to speed in e-learning. In his book *Harmonizing Global Education: From Genghis Khan to Facebook*, Jon Baggeley opined that Asia does e-learning better than the West. This is because traditional distance education co-exists alongside e-learning in Asian countries, and the lessons from the older body of research on distance learning have not yet been forgotten.

Whether e-learning has made the techniques of distance learning converge on a common approach is an important question. Thirty years ago, the US interpreted distance education rather differently from most of the rest of the world, including, interestingly, Canada. In the US, simultaneous remote classroom instruction through video links was all the rage, whereas in other countries distance learning usually meant independent study through multimedia with tutorial support. This in turn reflected much older differences in approaches to teaching: an emphasis on tutorials and seminars in Europe and a focus on classroom teaching in America.

The Internet unquestionably brought these approaches together, and, for a time in the 1990s, the virtues of 'asynchronous' communication were lauded everywhere. Although the continuing advance of technology now makes it possible to blend synchronous and asynchronous learning in a great variety of ways, it is fascinating to see how differences in approach persist. Massive open online courses (MOOCs) are a striking example (see Chapter 4 in the *International Handbook of*

E-learning, Volume 1). The early Canadian MOOCs, circa 2008, were based on multidirectional discussions and multiple exchanges of open educational resources among learners, whereas the later US MOOCs, circa 2012, used unidirectional video for what was essentially a remote-classroom approach, although it was delivered asynchronously. MOOCs have diversified greatly since those 'early' days. Like many other innovations, they began in universities but may find their major application in professional training and at other levels of education.

The main conclusion that I take from the frenzy that greeted MOOCs is the (very old) lesson that purpose and process are more important than technology. As they breathlessly proclaimed MOOCs to be a revolution in higher education, the news media forgot two facts. First, history shows that higher education develops by evolution, not revolution. Second, and more importantly, the most important power that societies give to their universities is the authority to award degrees and credentials.

Open educational resources and MOOCs are important contributions to the e-learning space, but it is vital for the future that e-learning focuses on the more challenging task of creating courses and programs that include serious student assessment leading to credible credentials. The criticism that too much assessment in e-learning uses trivial multiple-choice questions is equally valid for much traditional campus instruction, but that is not a sufficient excuse. Fortunately, groundbreaking work is being done in various places, such as the UK Open University's Knowledge Media Institute, to harness technology to the development of assessments that are both relevant and academically challenging.

This is the dynamic and exciting world that is the focus of this handbook, an enormous endeavor compiled by Badrul H. Khan and Mohamed Ally, two eminent scholars and practitioners of e-learning. I am sure that, by dipping into the variety of articles that it contains, all those who are charged with improving the quality and impact of e-learning in their institutions will find much to inspire and guide them.

Sir John Daniel
2014-08-16

Acknowledgments

We would like to thank the following reviewers of the chapters:

Abed Salem, Adolfo Tanzi Neto, Ahmed Ali, Alex Sergay, Alice Stefaniak, Amanda Funk, Amy Scott, Andrea Bosshard, Antonia Jokelova, Arifa Garman, Barbara Smith, Carlos R. Morales, Carmen Winter, Chetan Bhatt, Chris Heizer, Cindy Poore-Pariseau, Dale Mueller, Daniel Strozzi, Dave Hallmon, Dave Hildebrandt, Deyu Hu, Didem Tufan, Dustin Summey, Ellen Taricani, Emre Sezgin, Glen Gatin, Harold Jeffrey Rosen, Ida L. Rodgers, James Braman, Jennifer B. Staley, Jeremy Schwehm, Jerry Pon, Jill P. Viers, Jillian Wojcik, Kathy Jackson, Kim A. Hosler, Kim Jamison, Konstantinos Kalemis, Lisette Reyes-Paulino, Ludwika Goodson, Manuela Rodrigues, Margaret Wherry, Martin Addison, Mary Ann Remnet, Mauri Collins, Mike Menchaca, Muhammad Sabri bin Sahrir, Nicola Ritter, Nicole Dalton, Nirupama Akella, Noam Ebner, Nor Aziah Alias, Norma Ortiz Rodriguez, Pam Jimison, Patrick Devey, Patrizia Maria Margherita Ghislandi, Peter Young, Robyn Defelice, Rosemary Talab, Sabrina Leone, Shaira Ali, Shelagh McGrath, Sheri Anderson, Vrinda Narayanan, William Diehl, and Zoaib Mirza.

We also want to thank Alex and colleagues of Routledge, who worked with us to publish this handbook.

About the Editors

Dr. Mohamed Ally is professor in the Centre for Distance Education and Researcher in the Technology Enhanced Knowledge Research Institute (TEKRI) at Athabasca University in Canada. He was director of the Centre of Distance Education at Athabasca University, Canada's Open University. He obtained his PhD from the University of Alberta, Canada. His current areas of research include mobile learning, e-learning, distance education, and use of emerging learning technologies in education and training. Dr. Ally is Past President of the International Federation of Training and Development Organizations (IFTDO) and is one of the founding directors of the International Association of Mobile Learning (IamLearn). He recently edited seven books on the use of emerging technologies in education. His book "Mobile Learning: Transforming the Delivery of Education and Training" won the Charles A. Wedemeyer Award for significant contribution to distance education. Dr. Ally has presented keynote speeches, workshops, and papers in many countries.

Dr. Badrul H. Khan is a world-renowned educator, author, speaker, and consultant in the field of distance education. He has 20 years of experience in developing and managing distance education programs. Professor Khan has the credit of first coining the phrase *web-based instruction* and popularizing the concept through his 1997 bestselling *Web-Based Instruction* book that *paved* the *way* for the new field of e-learning. In recognition of his unique contribution to the field of e-learning coupled with his services to worldwide e-learning communities, Egyptian E-Learning University Council on August 13, 2012, appointed Dr. Badrul Khan as an honorary distinguished professor of e-learning.

His *Managing E-Learning* book has been translated into 14 languages. He contributed to the development of US virtual education policies organized by the White House Office of Science and Technology Policy and the Naval Postgraduate School, the National Educational Technology Plan by the US Department of Education, and the Review of Joint Professional Military Education organized by the Joint Chiefs of Staff. He served as contributing and consulting editor of nine prestigious international learning journals and magazines. He is a past president of the International Division of the Association for Educational and Communication Technology (AECT). He authored and coauthored 11 books/manuals and over 100 papers in the field of e-learning and distance learning. He delivered keynote speeches in more than 50 international e-learning and distance learning conferences.

He is the founder of McWeadon Education (a professional-development institution). He previously served as the founding director of the Educational Technology Leadership (ETL) graduate cohort program at The George Washington University; the founding director of the Educational Technology (ET) graduate program at the University of Texas, Brownsville; and an instructional designer and evaluation specialist in the School of Medicine at Indiana University, Indianapolis. Dr. Khan has served as a consultant to distance education, learning development, and human resource development projects at: (a) the World Bank, (b) the US Federal Government, (c) the Asian Development Bank, and (d) various academic institutions and corporations in the US and throughout the world. For more info, please visit his personal website: http://BadrulKhan.com/

Contributing Authors

Fayiz M. Aldhafeeri is an associate professor and associate dean for research, consultations, and training at Kuwait University. He was the director of the Education Technology Center at Kuwait University. Dr. Aldhafeeri received a distinguished teaching award from Kuwait University in 2004, presented by the Crown Prince of the State of Kuwait. He has published several research studies and reports in the area of e-learning and educational technologies in education and training and authored many books in the field of educational technology, including *Computer Applications in Education, Educational Technology: Theory and Practice*, and *Methods of Teaching Computer*. He presented specialized radio programs, such as the Information Technology Series and Language of the Age show, which were done on Here Is Kuwait Radio. He has presented at several international, regional, and local conferences. He has also designed and conducted more than 100 training, consultation, and supervision programs for various educational and corporate institutions inside and outside Kuwait in the following areas: courseware design/instructional design, presentation skills, training program evaluation techniques, training program delivery techniques, needs assessment techniques, training analysis techniques, successful and effective training, leadership skills, and educational communication and technology.

Ali Al-Musawi obtained his PhD on learning resources and technology centers in 1995 from Southampton University, UK. He works for the Sultan Qaboos University since 1985. At present, he is an associate professor at the Instructional and Learning Technologies Department at the College of Education. He has published several journal research articles, chapters in reviewed books, and papers and contributed in many conferences, symposia, and workshops. He conducted and compiled several national, regional, and Arab studies and reports. He wrote a book on cooperative learning in 1992, contributed in writing another in 2003, and published a book on learning resources and technology centers in 2004. He also translated, with others, two books on e-learning strategies and instructional multimedia to Arabic in 2005 and 2010. Dr. Ali has several activities in fields of instructional skills development, study skills, instructional design, and web-based design; his interests include Arabic poetry; he published two anthologies in addition to other hand-written ones.

Rasha AlOkaily is an English language instructor at the University of Sharjah and IT committee chair of the English Language Center. She holds an MA degree in applied linguistics from SOAS, University of London. Her main area of interest is in educational technology and teacher training. She has conducted various teacher training sessions on the use of technology in education in coordination with the Ministry of Education as well as within the University of Sharjah.

Khalid Al-Shahrani currently works at academic relations at the King Abdullah University of Science and Technology (KAUST), Jeddah–Saudi Arabia. Previously, he held positions of assistant professor and lecturer at the Saudi Naval Academy between 2003 and 2013, in which he taught English in face-to-face and blended learning environments. His research interests include e-learning and blended learning in higher education, teaching English to speakers of other languages (TESOL), and capacity building in higher education.

Joni de Almeida Amorim is a postdoctoral fellow in Computer Science at the University of Skövde (HiS), in collaboration with the Saab Group, Sweden. He is also a researcher at Universidade de São Paulo (USP), Brazil, and Universidade Estadual de Campinas (UNICAMP), Brazil. Dr. Amorim has experience as a consultant on project management and as a teacher on topics such as multimedia production and distance education.

Sten F. Andler is professor of computer science at the University of Skövde (HiS), Sweden. He is the program manager for the Information Fusion Research Program, Sweden. Dr. Andler was dean of research 1998–2000, HiS, Sweden. His previous affiliation was at IBM, USA. Dr. Andler is the group leader for the Distributed Real-Time Systems (DRTS) research group, HiS, Sweden.

Tanim Ashraf has been working in BBC Media Action's Bangladesh office for the last two and a half years. Currently, he works on BBC Janala, an award-winning, multiplatform project that aims to improve the English skills of 25 million adult Bangladeshis by 2017. He has been closely involved with the product development and impact evaluation of BBC Janala's media products. He graduated from Jahangirnagar University, Bangladesh, with a degree in business administration.

Susan Bainbridge has been an educator and administrator for the past 40 years. She began her teaching career in Ontario and then spent 12 years in the Northwest Territories and Yukon as a teacher and school principal. She has spent the past 6 years in the UAE as lead faculty–academic programs with the higher colleges of technology in Ras Al Khaimah, teaching business and liberal studies. She taught in the Lower Mainland of British Columbia for 10 years, where she helped to set up Rick Hansen Secondary School with state-of-the-art facilities for special needs students. Susan then moved to Japan and was director of education for a chain of English schools in the Tohoku region for more than a decade. She spent a couple of years in Seoul, South Korea, as director of MapleBear English Immersion Preschools, a joint venture with CECN and Telus Korea.

Elena Barberà has a doctorate in psychology from the University of Barcelona (1995). She received an extraordinary award for her doctoral thesis. She is currently director of research for the eLearn Center and doctoral program faculty chair in ICT and education of the Open University of Catalonia in Barcelona (Spain). She is also an adjunct professor for the international doctorate in Nova Southeastern University in Florida (USA). Her research activity is specialized in the area of educational psychology, a field in which she has several publications, conferences, and educational courses, relating in particular to knowledge-construction processes and educational interaction in e-learning environments, evaluating educational quality and assessing learning, distance learning using ICT, and teaching and learning strategies. As head of the EDUS (Distance School and University Education) research group, which is linked to the eLearn Center, she participates in various national and international projects related to electronic learning, assessment processes, and the time factor in e-learning. She is an external and independent evaluator of research projects promoted by the European Union (e-learning program) and collaborates with international organizations in developing knowledge by organizing congresses and international awards as a member of scientific committees.

Lisa Marie Blaschke is program director of the Master of Distance Education and E-Learning (MDE) graduate program at Carl von Ossietzky Universität Oldenburg, Germany. She is also an associate professor at University of Maryland University College, the MDE partner institution. Lisa is an executive committee member of the European Distance Education and E-Learning Network (EDEN) and an EDEN Fellow. Her research interests are in the areas of lifelong and self-determined learning (heutagogy) and the pedagogical application of Web 2.0 technologies. Before rejoining academia in 2006, Lisa worked for an international software company, leading and implementing enterprise-wide knowledge management and training solutions. She lives with her family in Germany at the edge of the Odenwald forest.

Jane E. Brindley is a clinical psychologist and a faculty member in the Department of Educational and Counselling Psychology and Special Education at the University of British Columbia. The focus of her research is adult learner engagement, motivation and support. She has designed and written courses for online and flexible delivery, taught in an international online graduate program in distance education and e-learning, and worked as a distance education consultant and trainer in Canada and internationally. She has written numerous articles and book chapters including *Researching Tutoring and Learner Support* (an open-source research methods manual for practitioners), *Learning on the Information Highway: A Learner's Guide to the Technologies* (co-author), and was lead editor for *Learner Support in Open, Distance and Online Learning*. She lives in Vancouver, Canada.

Len Cairns is associate dean (engagement and international) in the faculty of education, Monash University, Australia. Len has been a teacher educator since the early 1970s and has taught at the University of Sydney as well as Monash. He has been a visiting scholar at a number of European and USA universities and currently teaches leadership (school and organizational). Len taught extensively in many distance education programs for over 20 years and researches workplace learning, capability development, and aspects of leadership. His involvement in online and blended learning has continued to adapt and change as technology and student-centered work has become more of a norm. Len's fascination with the Internet commenced when he saw the prototype "Mosaic" demonstrated at the University of Illinois in the early 1990s.

Lorenzo Cantoni graduated in philosophy and holds a PhD in education and linguistics. He is full professor at the Università della Svizzera italiana (University of Lugano, Switzerland), Faculty of Communication Sciences, where he is also director of the Institute for Communication Technologies and dean of the faculty. Lorenzo Cantoni is scientific director of the laboratories Webatelier.net, NewMinE: New Media in Education Lab, and eLab: eLearning Lab. His research interests include where communication, education, and new media overlap, ranging from computer-mediated communication to usability, from e-learning to e-tourism, from ICT4D to e-government.

Edméa Oliveira dos Santos is a professor of the Graduate Program in Education at the State University of Rio de Janeiro, Faculty of Education, Rio de Janeiro, Brazil, and is leader of the Teaching and Cyberculture research group. She has a master's degree and PhD in Education from Federal University of Bahia, Brazil. She is a member of the Laboratory of Image of State University of Rio de Janeiro and a member of GT 16 of Education and Communication and the Association of Researchers in Cyberculture. She operates in the initial and continuing formation of teachers and researchers.

Giovanni Farias is an electronic engineer, with a master's degree in computing science and post-baccalaureate diploma in distance education management. After teaching in public and private universities in Brazil, he began working with distance education in 1997, becoming a Moodle Certified Partner in 2006. He provides pedagogical and technical services for Brazilian corporations, universities, federal government departments and ministries, federal and state courts, and schools. He has already deployed dozens of distance education operations and trained hundreds of professionals in the use of technology applied to online education. Since 2011 he has been studying in the doctor of education program of the Athabasca University, Canada. He has been researching the use of learning management systems and social network systems for online education purposes and on the use of open educational resources in mobile learning.

Hans W. Giessen studied at Free University of Berlin, Saarland University, Saarbrücken, and Université de Metz, France. He holds a PhD and a habilitation degree from Saarland University, has been working in the media sector at Saarbrücken and Luxembourg, and is now with the faculty of Saarland University. He has written several publications in German, English, and French, and some of them have been translated into other languages, such as Russian and Dutch. He has been teaching in Germany, France, the UK, Estonia, and Poland.

Edith Gotesman is a teacher of English with a PhD in computer assisted instruction. Her interest is in the use of assistive technology in order to help students with learning disabilities. She has presented at national and international conferences and is researching the impact of assistive technology on the reading outcomes of college students with dyslexia. She also teaches English for academic purposes and the use of assistive technology to college students and teachers.

Yasemin Gülbahar is currently the chairman of Department of Informatics and coordinator at The Distance Education Center at Ankara University. Having graduated from the Middle East Technical University of Ankara with a BS degree in mathematics, an MS degree in science education, and a PhD in computer education and instructional technology, she has skills as an instructional designer and a programmer. Dr. Gülbahar worked for Middle East Technical University as a programmer for Computer Center for six years and as a teaching assistant in the Faculty of Education for four years. After getting her PhD, Dr. Gülbahar worked at Başkent University as a faculty member for nine years. She has been working at Ankara University since 2011. Her areas of expertise include e-learning, mobile learning, instructional design, adult learning, technology planning, technology integration, project management, and web-based programming.

Per M. Gustavsson is currently a principal research scientist in information security at Combitech, Sweden; at Command and Control Systems at the Centre of Excellence in C4I, George Mason University (GMU), USA; and at the Swedish National Defence College (SNDC), Sweden.

Sri Harijati joined the Indonesia Open University (Universitas Terbuka) in 1988 and became the academic staff in the Faculty of Mathematic and Natural Sciences at UT. She has undergraduate and doctoral degrees from the Bogor Agricultural University, Indonesia, and a master's degree from the University of Victoria, Canada. She has served as head of the Community Service Center, at the Institute for Research and Community Services–UT. Currently, she is serving as assistant director of academic affairs at UT's graduate program. In accordance with her duties at graduate program, she focused on the provision of materials and process of distance learning that meet the needs of students. Also, she is interested in developing e-learning at UT, especially increasing the competence of online tutors at UT graduate programs.

Carolyne Jacobs is joint head of technology enhanced learning at the University of Portsmouth in the UK. Dr. Jacobs has worked in education for over 20 years. She has taught in adult and higher education from predegree to the postgraduate level. In addition, she has managed a number of local, national, and international online learning projects and is currently managing a range of institution-wide projects at the University of Portsmouth. Qualifications include a BSc in economics, an MSc in information systems, and a doctorate from the University of Brighton, on the impact of social networking on student integration into university life.

Shekh Mohammad Mahbubul Kadir has been working for BBC Media Action for about two years. He currently heads the interactive web and mobile team across several media for development projects, all of which aim to improve the lives of people in Bangladesh in areas such as education, health, governance, and climate. Mr. Kadir has deep technology knowledge across diverse industries, such as telecoms and ICT, and broad management experience of more than eight years. Previously, he worked for Grameenphone (Telenor), Bangladesh's largest telecom operator, and GPIT, Bangladesh's largest IT company. He completed his BSc at the University of Dhaka in computer science and engineering.

Hiroshi Kawahara is president and dean of the Faculty of Information Technology and Business at Cyber University in Fukuoka, Japan. When Softbank Corp. founded Cyber University in 2007 as Japan's first full-online four-year university, he joined as a professor in multimedia technologies and management of technologies. Prior to his academic career at Cyber University, he had been chief technology officer at various start-up companies in the Softbank group, where technologies played major roles in creating new business models. At Cyber University, he continued his role of applying leading-edge technologies to full on-demand learning practice, and delivered Cyber University's mobile-based and cloud-based e-learning platform not only to academic institutions but also to industries. Hiroshi has a BS in physics from Humboldt State University in California, and a ScD in ocean engineering from Massachusetts Institute of Technology.

Terry Kidd is a seasoned faculty and administrator with more than 10 years of experience. He holds multiple degrees, most notably, a research doctorate (PhD) from Texas A&M University (College Station, TX). Dr. Kidd has published five books and 15 peer-reviewed articles in top-tiered journals, including the *Journal of Educational Media and Hypermedia, International Journal of E-Learning, Journal of Science Education and Technology,* and *Education and Information Technology,* to name a few. As a researcher, Dr. Kidd focuses on the socio-ecological aspects of people, environment, and digital media and technology use, with the goal of improving theory, practice, and policy for the design and implementation of new learning, work, and social spaces. Dr. Kidd has also been quoted on Amazon.com, featured on ABC News as an expert on the social and ethical ramifications of computer hacking in higher education, and has been recently nominated to present at the Oxford Round Table in the UK.

Andreas König is head of the Center for Education and New Learning at the Zurich University of Applied Sciences in Switzerland. He is a lecturer for human resource management, his main teaching areas being technology-enhanced learning, human resource development, organizational development, and leadership, and his main research activities concern the organizational and social impact of technology-enhanced learning. Newer publications question the relationship between management and leadership of higher educational institutions and the systemic impact of technology-enhanced learning. Current research topics are learning and Web 2.0 technologies as seen from a sociological perspective, asking for mutual interdependencies of technology and society. Andreas König holds a PhD and a master of arts in cultural anthropology. His academic career brought him into research and lecturing positions at the universities of Berlin and Seville. Formerly, he worked as program director for an IT training and development corporation. He gained further business experience from five years of consulting for large retail stores of the Metro Group and its branches, where he introduced new learning technologies and trained leaders in intercultural management.

Ashok Paul Kumar is currently working as research officer within the English in Action project. He completed his master's in development studies from University of Dhaka and has experience of working in the development sector, especially doing monitoring. His current research interests include the use of technology in education.

Angela Kwan is the learning manager at the Commonwealth of Learning, where she leads the eLearning for International Organisations initiative (eLIO). The initiative helps large international organizations to increase and accelerate their human capital enhancement through distance and technology-mediated learning programs. For a decade, she has designed, deployed, and delivered customized e-learning programs for employees of the United Nations system, development banks, and humanitarian organizations. She is focused on giving employees based in remote and isolated offices in the deep field the same quality of learning available to those in urban headquarters. Prior to immigrating to Canada, Angela was head of administration at the Open Learning Institute of Hong Kong (now Open University). She holds a BA (Hons) from the Chinese University of Hong Kong, a postgraduate diploma in education administration from the University of Birmingham, and an MBA from the University of Leicester, UK.

Mary Lane-Kelso is an assistant professor and head of instructional and learning technologies department at Sultan Qaboos University, Oman. She designs, develops, and instructs educational technology courses for preservice teachers and graduates. She also researches, develops, and evaluates grants with community schools/districts in the United States. She conducts needs assessments, surveys, and programmatic research, and consults with faculty on educational technology issues, such as universal design, constructivist pedagogy, the National Council for Accreditation of Teacher Education (NCATE) accreditation, and global engagement. She leads faculty workshops/seminars for on-campus faculty and presents at workshops and conferences concerning educational technology issues.

Claude Martel holds a PhD in educational technology from Concordia University and is a well-established practitioner and educator in the Canadian training and education community. He has been in the forefront in the development of human performance technology practices and the implementation of distance education technology in large corporations and educational institutions. Over the last 25 years, he has held senior roles in large organizations, such as Pratt and Whitney Canada, Telus, Hydro-Québec, and DMR (Fujitsu) Consulting. He has also worked as a national and international HPT consultant, providing expertise and support to national and international organizations, including the Airport Council International (ACI) and the International Civil Aviation Organization (ICAO). He is also a founding member and former president of multiple training and education associations, such as the eLearning Alliance, the Quebec chapter of the Canadian Society of Training and Development (CSTD), and he is the current chairman of the Canadian eLearning Enterprise Alliance (CeLEA), the national association of e-learning producers. In addition, he has managed over 60 projects and has implemented HR, communication, and training technologies solutions in more than 30 large organizations.

Jon Mason is director of e-learning at the Centre for School Leadership, Learning and Development at Charles Darwin University in Australia. Prior to taking on this role, he worked for an extended period in international ICT standards development, initially as the founding co-chair of the Dublin Core Education Working Group but more generally within the e-learning domain, including the IMS Global Learning Consortium and the IEEE Learning Technology Standards Committee, while also serving as Australian head of delegation to ISO/IEC JTC 1/SC36 on behalf of Standards Australia. He has master's degrees in knowledge management and cognitive science. He is actively engaged in research activities at Charles Darwin University and is completing a PhD at Queensland University of Technology, focused on inquiry-based learning and knowledge modelling.

Sayaka Matsumoto is a lecturer in the Faculty of Information Technology and Business at Cyber University, a four-year online university in Japan. She has a PhD in human informatics from Nagoya University. Her specialty is in "socio-informatics"; after the Tohoku earthquake in 2011, she has joined the disaster recovery support team of the Society of Socio-Informatics and has been taking a part in building systems to digitize the photo albums damaged in the disaster areas, and returning them to the owners. At Cyber University, she teaches website production, and multimedia presentation courses. Her current research focuses on survey and design of web systems that are useful for the public for daily usage and learning.

Shelagh A. McGrath is an accomplished learning and development consultant. She holds a master of distance education from Athabasca University and a bachelor of arts with honors from St. Francis Xavier University. Shelagh is a professional learning consultant, working with organizations to implement and support learning solutions, including virtual and technology-based approaches. Her successes include the implementation of learning and development departments for several large companies, a "corporate university" for the Canadian Credit Union system, and large-scale global learning system implementations, including blended solutions. Her personal passion is the furthering of virtual learning simulation and augmented reality.

Sanjaya Mishra joined COL as director of the Commonwealth Educational Media Centre for Asia (CEMCA) on July 1, 2012. Dr. Mishra is a leading scholar in open, distance, and online learning in Asia. Most recently, he was program specialist (ICT in Education, Science and Culture) at UNESCO, Paris. Dr. Mishra has over 18 years of experience in design, development, and management of open and distance learning programs. With a blend of academic and professional qualifications in library and information science, distance education, television production, and training and development, he has been promoting the use of educational multimedia, e-learning and the use of open educational resources (OER) and open access to scientific information around the world, in particular, Asia. During his service in different capacities at the Indira Gandhi National Open University (IGNOU), among many innovative activities and programs, he developed the successful OER-based one-year postgraduate diploma in e-learning. As a staff developer and trainer, Dr. Mishra has received the ISTD-Vivekanand National Award for Excellence in Human Resource Development and Training in 2007, and has facilitated over 100 training sessions in over 12 countries. He has contributed over 200 publications as books, chapters, journal papers, conference presentations, book reviews, and distance learning materials. Most recently, at UNESCO, he facilitated the adoption of open access to scientific information and research. Dr. Mishra has also previously served as assistant regional director of one of IGNOU's regional centers and as a program officer at CEMCA (2001–2003).

Miwako Nogimori is an assistant professor in the Faculty of Information Technology and Business at Cyber University, a full-online four-year university in Japan. She has a master's degree in education and has studied in the doctoral program at the Ontario Institute for Studies of Education of the University of Toronto. At Cyber University she also works as a staff member in the Office of Academic Administration, which is responsible for maintaining the University's academic standards in collaboration with the faculty. Her research interests include interaction and motivation in online education, curriculum and pedagogical design, diversity and equity in education, and education for humanity and social awareness.

Dewi Padmo's career at the Indonesia Open University (Universitas Terbuka) started in 1987 as a lecturer in the Faculty of Teacher–UT. In 1991, she got her master of arts in educational technology at Concordia University, Montreal, Canada. Upon her return to Universitas Terbuka (UT), in Indonesia, in 1992, she was appointed as head of the Multimedia Production Center–UT, and served the center for two terms until 1998. Following from her work at the Center for Multi-Media Production, Padmo had an opportunity to become an assistant of vice rector for academic affairs in 1998, then served as head of the Institute of Research in 2005. Padmo got her doctor of philosophy in instructional systems degree at Florida State University, USA, in 2012. Upon returning to Indonesia in mid-2012, Dewi was assigned by the rector as head of the Institute for Research and Community Services of Universitas Terbuka.

Hitendra Pillay works at Queensland University of Technology in Australia (QUT). His interest in the nature and development of knowledge and systems theory has led to a diverse academic research portfolio that includes areas such as distributed/social cognition and learning, adult and community education, industry-based training, and technology-based learning. Professor Pillay also has extensive expertise in macro and micro aspects of social-sector reform in developing countries using technology. Drawing on his academic research and social-sector development work, his current research interest is on synthesizing the fragmented research agendas into more holistic and cross-disciplinary models of knowledge creation, innovation, and global development.

Troy Priest is the senior mobile learning specialist in the Center for Educational Innovation at Zayed University in the United Arab Emirates, where he spearheads the ongoing, one-to-one mobile learning initiative within the university. Troy joined Zayed University in 2001, and previously he has taught in Korea and the United States before coming to the UAE. His responsibilities as the university's senior mobile learning specialist include the planning and development of teacher training in the use of innovative mobile learning pedagogies; overseeing the development of course materials mediated through the mobile devices; working with and advising stakeholders on all aspects of the implementation of mobile devices; and pursuing best practices regarding the use of mobile technology. Troy's research interests include best practices in mobile technology pedagogy and project-based assessments.

Anthony Ralston currently works at the United Nations High Commission for Refugees at the Global Learning Centre, Budapest, Hungary. He is the unit head for design and development and is involved in online global training and education for UNHCR staff worldwide. In addition, he is also an associate faculty member at Royal Roads University, Victoria, in the School of Education and Technology and also runs a consulting business that is involved in designing online and mobile learning programs. Anthony speaks regularly on topics such as online and mobile learning at the Association of Canadian Community Colleges (ACCC), the Canadian Network for

Innovation in Education (CNIE), and UNESCO. His master's of professional education degree at Deakin University, Australia, encompassed educational leadership, online and distance learning, and, specifically, the implementation of online and mobile learning. He holds a postgraduate certificate in education (EdD) from the University of Nottingham, England. He is completing his studies through Athabasca University (EdD) and is researching mobile learning in international settings for humanitarian workers.

Emanuele Rapetti graduated in education at the Catholic University of the Sacred Heart in Milan with a master thesis on media education. He holds a PhD in communication sciences (Università della Svizzera italiana–Lugano, Switzerland); his research work was titled "LoDE— Learners of the Digital Era: From the Analysis of the Current Debate to an Empirical Study Emphasizing the Learners' Perspective." He is currently a researcher in education at the CeRi-Form (Centro Studi e Ricerche sulle Politiche della Formazione) of the Catholic University in Milan. His research interests are pedagogy, digital pedagogy, education, e-learning, educational evaluation, and research methodology.

Izabel de Moraes Sarmento Rego is a researcher on educational technology. Currently, she is a PhD candidate at Universidade Estadual de Campinas (UNICAMP), Brazil, researching mobile learning at the Language Studies Institute. She has a master's degree in applied linguistics and a bachelor's degree in Spanish language. Also, she works managing distance learning courses for vocational education and teacher continuing education at Serviço Nacional de Aprendizagem Industrial (SENAI-SP), Brazil. In this company, she recently developed a research project about mobile learning for vocational education. She has experience as a consultant on different projects in foreign-languages teaching.

Martha Robinson received her master of distance education from Athabasca University in Canada, and her bachelor of education in secondary school education from the University of Alberta, Canada. She has worked on teaching and training, curriculum development, resource development and evaluation, and instructional design for individualized learning and distance learning. She has published articles on culture and e-learning in Qatar, and received Best Paper recognition for her work titled "Transition to E-learning in a Gulf Arab Country."

Margarida Romero holds a European PhD in psychology from UMR CNRS (France) and the Autonomous University of Barcelona (extraordinary PhD award in psychology). She is assistant professor in educational technology in Université Laval (Canada) and research associate at Universitat Oberta de Catalunya (Spain). She was awarded third prize for Technology Transfer from the EU Network of Excellence Kaleidoscope in 2007, and first prize in the Artificial Intelligence French Association Award in 2006. Her research is focused on collaborative learning, game-based learning, and the time factor in e-learning. She has published 16 peer-reviewed papers and 32 conference proceedings, and has participated in seven research projects funded by the European Commission. She has taught in French higher education institutions (Institut Universitaire de Nimes 2005–2007, Centre National d'Arts et Métiers 2007–2008, Limoges University Virtual Campus 2003–2012) and Spanish universities (Universitat Ramon Llull Blanquerna and ESADE 2008–2013, Universitat Oberta de Catalunya 2008–2013, Universitat Autònoma de Barcelona 2008–2013). As a consultant, she has assisted the European Commission in the evaluation of the LLL proposals for the EACEA (2007), the EC e-government program (2007), Eurostars Eureka (2008–2012), and the National Centre of Science of Kazakhstan (2012–2013).

Tatiana Stofella Sodré Rossini is a doctoral student of the graduate program in education at State University of Rio de Janeiro, Faculty of Education, Rio de Janeiro, Brazil, a member of the Teaching and Cyberculture research group, and has a master's degree in education and a PhD in systems engineering from the University Estácio de Sá, Rio de Janeiro, Brazil.

Sanjib Saha is the head of research working in the governance, climate change, reproductive, maternal, and neonatal health and multimedia English teaching program, BBC Janala at BBC Media Action, where he has been working since 2006. Sanjib is interested in a range of issues related to governance, health, English learning, and media in the developing world. At present, he manages a large research team in the Bangladesh office and oversees all research activities related to projects' formative and impact assessment. Sanjib has the expertise of both quantitative and qualitative techniques in his research and has a special interest in studies that have media implications in governance, health, and education. Prior to working in BBC Media Action, Sanjib was a journalist and worked in several media organizations in Bangladesh. He completed his master's and bachelor's degrees in anthropology from the University of Dhaka.

Mohammed Samaka is an associate professor of computer science in the Department of Computer Science and Engineering (CSE), College of Engineering, at Qatar University. He obtained his PhD and master's degrees from Loughborough University in England and a postgraduate diploma in computing from Dundee University in Scotland. He obtained his bachelor of mathematics degree from Baghdad University. His current areas of research include wireless software architecture and technology, mobile applications and services, networking, e-learning, and computing curricula development.

Kevin Schoepp is the director of educational effectiveness at Zayed University and has just completed a year as the founding director for the Center for Educational Innovation. His role in educational effectiveness includes program review, learning outcomes assessment, and accreditation. He has also been one of the lead participants in the university's mobile learning initiative. He has recently presented at the ABET symposium and has published in *Assessment Update,* one of the leading practitioner journals in higher education assessment. He has a doctorate in higher education leadership and a master's degree in educational technology from the University of Calgary, and he has an undergraduate and master's degree from the University of Alberta. His current research interests are in the development of effective and sustainable assessment and accreditation processes, creating a culture of assessment to foster continuous improvement, and the pedagogical implications of integrating mobile learning devices into the higher education classroom.

Robina Shaheen is a senior research fellow at the Open University (UK) and head of research and quality assurance for the Dfid-funded project 'English in Action' in Bangladesh. She chaired the preconference workshop "mLearning solutions for international development: Rethinking what's possible," at the 11th World Conference on Mobile and Contextual Learning in Helsinki in October, 2012, as well as presenting in the main conference. Dr. Shaheen completed her PhD (education) from the University of Birmingham in 2010. Prior to this she worked within the NGO sector before joining the International Labor Organization, working on child labor elimination, and then UNICEF and the National Commission for Human Development (Pakistan), where she managed large-scale education projects aimed at enhancing access and quality of primary education in Pakistan. She has undertaken evaluation and consultancy projects for AusAID, NORAD, and the Higher Education Academy. She has taught on a range of undergraduate and postgraduate courses, including research methods, human resource management, thinking skills and creative leadership, and is an associate of the Higher Education Academy, UK.

Ramesh C. Sharma has a PhD in education (in the area of educational technology) and a master's degree in computer applications (MCA). He is working as regional director of Indira Gandhi National Open University (IGNOU), India. From July 2009 until June 2011, he was the director of the Institute of Distance and Continuing Education (IDCE) at the University of Guyana, Guyana, South America, to lead distance education activities in the country. He had been a member of an advisory group on human resources development for the United Nations Conference on Trade and Development (UNCTAD). The UNCTAD is one of the main UN bodies devoted to a development-friendly integration of developing countries into the world economy. He has also worked with UNDP for its Enhanced Public Trust, Security and Inclusion (EPTSI) project, Volunteer Service Overseas (VSO), and as a United Nations Volunteer (UNV) to develop suitable educational opportunities for communities and youth. He has been involved in the planning, design and development of teaching and learning materials for Indira Gandhi National Open University; M P Bhoj Open University, Bhopal; Vardhman Mahaveer Open University, Kota; and Maharshi Dayanand University, India. These are premier institutes of India. He is the co-editor of the *Asian Journal of Distance Education* (www.ASIANJDE.org) and country editor for India for the *British Journal of Educational Technology*. He sits on the editorial advisory board of many journals, including *International Review of Research in Open and Distance Learning*, an online journal published by Athabasca University, Canada; *International Journal of Distance Education Technologies*, published by IGI-Global, USA; and *Indian Journal of Open Learning,* published by IGNOU. He was also on the editorial advisory board of *Distance Education,* published by the Taylor & Francis Group.

Salys Sultan is a PhD candidate and assistant lecturer in the Department of Computing and Information Technology at University of the West Indies, St. Augustine Campus. She has a European master's degree in informatics from RWTH Aachen, Germany, and the University of Trento, Italy. She holds a bachelor's degree (first class honors) in computer science and management from the University of the West Indies, Trinidad and Tobago. Her current research interests include modeling and design of mobile applications, computer supported ubiquitous learning, and advanced technology in education. In the classroom, Salys uses a blended learning approach. She uses and customizes a learning management system for the online component of the courses she manages. Her PhD thesis surrounds the use of mobile technologies for the delivery of diabetes self-management education for persons living with Type 2 diabetes in Trinidad and Tobago.

Carlo M. Trentadue is a fourth-year student at the University of Toronto, specializing in English, history and media communications. Carlo graduated in 2013 and is applying for the masters of information program at the iSchool in Toronto (University of Toronto), focusing on the relationship between culture and technology.

Katherine (Kassy) M. Tyler is an instructional designer at the Joint Special Operations University located at MacDill Air Force Base in Tampa, Florida. Dr. Tyler's work focuses on designing relevant educational instruction and planning curriculum for the special operations forces community. A graduate of the University of West Florida and Troy State University, she earned her EdD in curriculum and instruction in 2010 from the University of West Florida. She was on the instructional design staff at UWF's Academic Technology Center and served as the director of the Navy College Office at Naval Support Activity Souda Bay, Crete, Greece.

Michael Walimbwa is an assistant lecturer at the Department of Foundations and Curriculum Studies, College of Education and External Studies, Makerere University. He has two master of education degrees (information and communication technology) from Makerere University and the University of Cape Town, respectively. He likes to work with learning technologies and is currently engaged in researching learning technologies and resource-constrained initial teacher education institutions at the University of Cape Town, South Africa.

Mary Wilson is a researcher and instructional designer with a longstanding interest in online learning. She works independently as a corporate training consultant. Her work includes design and facilitation of soft-skills training, coaching and professional development for training department staff, and design of corporate training initiatives. She has worked with the Commonwealth of Learning's eLearning for International Organizations (eLIO) initiative since 2003, first as a tutor and more recently as an instructional designer/course writer and coach for new tutors. She holds an MA in educational studies from the University of British Columbia, where her research was on design for interaction in online courses. Her PhD, from Simon Fraser University, was a metastudy of instructional development initiatives for university faculty. Her ongoing research interests include workplace learning, learning in the community and citizen science.

Opening Digital Learning for Deeper Inquiry

Jon Mason and Hitendra Pillay

Introduction

Advancements in learning technologies are being driven from an increasing diversity of domains of practice and research. Through identifying the evolution of e-learning and its transformation to digital learning from various historical standpoints, this chapter highlights that contemporary development within the field of e-learning points to opportunities for technological innovation and practical implementation of e-learning that provides support and scaffolding for inquiry. Discussion is first focused on the issue of terminology and the broad semantics associated with e-learning. The fact that this term has been widely adopted and defined in diverse ways, however, is not necessarily an academic problem to be solved—certainly not here. One of the themes this chapter is concerned with is the broad range of semantics associated with the word *open*. In the latest edition of the Australian Macquarie Dictionary, for example, there are well over 80 different meanings listed. Such breadth also brings high utility.

Historical perspectives on the evolution of the theory and practice of e-learning are also presented to show that this field can be accurately described as *emergent*. Because of the scale of the development and diversity of inputs, there is not one history of e-learning. History is always a combination of facts and interpretations contextualized by time and changing circumstances. For example, when the web was first invented, there was an abundance of literature that emphasized the revolutionary nature of hypertext and hypermedia (Landow, 1991). Yet, in the contemporary setting the discourse has moved on, and hypertext is rarely mentioned—whether it is highlighting the revolutionary nature of digital technology itself (as in the Australian Government's Digital Education Revolution policy launched in 2008) or a particular facet, as in the literature associated with mobile learning, where *mobility* refers to the learner, the technology, and the learning itself (El-Hussein & Cronje, 2010; Oller, 2012; Sharples, Taylor, & Vavoula, 2007).

The theme of openness in education is given emphasis in this chapter for the reason that it provides an informative case study on the social response to the evolving digital infrastructure that supports learning (OECD, 2007). Opportunities for the "open agenda" to move forward into new territory are identified, and by corollary, therefore, also point to opportunities for digital technology to likewise develop (Leeson & Mason, 2007). Of course, while *openness* is valued highly in the education sector, it is not the only driver of change or innovation with ICT that matters (see Figure 1.1). Social media continues to shape the nature of much engagement online and the late 20th-century mantra that "content is king" is giving way to a fresh focus on so-called 21st-century skills, where content is co-constructed by users and is often transient, and competencies such as digital literacy, critical thinking, and problem solving are seen as more important (Griffin, McGaw, & Care, 2012). Oller (2012) argued that the big shift in e-learning theory and practice is currently being driven by mobile technologies, where the so-called natural user interface (NUI) enabled by handheld devices is surpassing the windows-icon-mouse-pointer (WIMP) paradigm of the personal computer era. Meanwhile, discourses on sense-making and developments in knowledge management and knowledge-sharing infrastructures continue to inform the theory and practice of e-learning (see, for example, papers published in *Knowledge Management and e-Learning—an International Journal*). While acknowledging all these trends as significant the open agenda is highlighted for two other reasons:

1. It is an agenda that is deeply embedded within the history of the Internet and web, and can be seen to reflect this broader development in its own historical progression; and,
2. it provides suitable context for a frontier ready for further technological innovation: the stimulation and support of questioning online through *open* inquiry-based learning.

Within this setting, research into *why*-questioning is then highlighted to emphasize that, despite all the technologies and tools already available, a frontier for tool development focused on inquiry-based learning is yet to be adequately explored. This is the case largely because *why*-questioning, while so important during inquiry, presents numerous technical challenges for digital tool development. Why? Because the semantics involved typically involve ambiguity, dialogue, or further inquiry. Investigation into *why*-questioning reveals that the object it seeks is typically *explanatory content*. Such content is not straightforward to discover through conventional search engines because they are calibrated to retrieve information based upon factual data and sequential logic. While content that can be characterized as such thus presents challenges for learning technology design, it also presents opportunities for innovative technology to support and stimulate reasoning skills and deep inquiry.

E-learning and Digital Learning

A review of the literature associated with digital learning shows it to be inextricably linked to e-learning, a term which reveals a wide domain of usage and conception. It is therefore important to make explicit what is meant by this term as it has been appropriated by diverse communities of practice since it first appeared in mainstream discourse around 1998–1999 (CIPD, 2008; Cross, 2004; Garrison & Anderson, 2003). *Digital learning* is a more recent term and arguably has broader long-term utility in that it comfortably describes learning via all kinds of technology devices that are built primarily for other purposes—such as games for entertainment or navigation through GPS.

Without embracing the term *digital learning* recent research aimed at developing an "inclusive definition of e-learning" and conceptual framework that supports it (Sangrà et al., 2012) identifies four broad categories of definitions: technology driven, delivery-system oriented, communication oriented, and educational-paradigm oriented. This research was itself based on literature dating from 2005 and supplemented by a Delphi survey of international experts. This time constraint is perhaps limiting, however, because it is arguable that in the period 2002–2005 a number of other definitions already had high acceptance among practitioners and policy makers—for example:

1. For the OECD, e-learning refers to "the use of information and communications technology (ICT) to enhance and/or support learning in tertiary education" (OECD, 2005, p. 11).
2. For the UK Department for Education and Skills, "if someone is learning in a way that uses information and communications technologies (ICT), they are using e-learning" (DfES, 2003).

But we are now well into the second decade of the 21st century, and it is clear that e-learning is a term that may be subsumed into *digital learning*—this is further highlighted by the appearance of a fairly awkward term, *mobile learning*, that is essentially e-learning through mobile (typically hand-held) devices. However, there is a significant body of literature devoted to e-learning and this term can signify both a theoretical discourse and a range of activities that take place in many contexts—formal and informal, within educational institutions and workplace settings, or elsewhere "any time any place," as the saying goes. Adopters of the term include corporate training associations, professional associations, academic web enthusiasts, government policy makers, software vendors, standards development organizations, and military organizations, just to name a few (Mason, 2005, p. 320). There are distinctions according to context. For example, Bates (2004, p. 275) identified key differences between postsecondary education and corporate settings—the latter being more concerned with the broader context of knowledge management and the former focused on learning and research. In an attempt to broaden philosophical perspective, Friesen (2009, p. 20) put the case for "re-thinking e-learning research" and argued for a "reconceptualization of e-learning as an inter- and cross-disciplinary endeavor." Conceptualizing in even broader terms, Cooper (2010) argued that its scope of activity is best understood as "emergent" and therefore subject to analyses that highlight perspectives on "complexity." Others prefer to use the related terminology "online learning" to frame the challenges of "integrating technology into classroom instruction" (Tomei & Morris, 2011). For the purposes of this chapter, however, *e-learning* is considered as being transformed to *digital learning* and defined as *learning that is facilitated by engagement with ICT*. Figure 1.1 summarizes some of the historical inputs that have shaped this evolution.

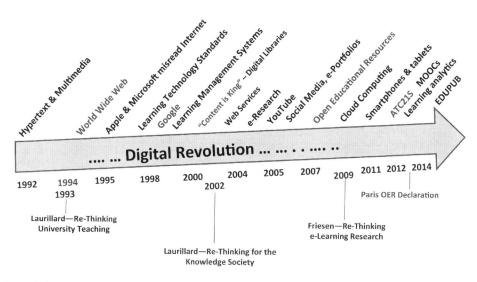

Figure 1.1 A Snapshot of Digital Learning Inputs

In tracking the evolution of e-learning as it progresses to open digital learning, both multidisciplinary and "transdisciplinary" research is required because the perspectives required typically involve what has been termed "Mode 2 knowledge production" (Manathunga, Lant, & Mellick, 2006, p. 365). This approach is necessary in order to span the relevant inputs enabling digital learning as well as to identify opportunities for future development. It is also arguably the case that the conceptual boundaries that define e-learning as an academic discipline are also emergent (Cooper, 2010)—as the term can describe both formal and informal learning enabled by ICT, and the ubiquitous nature of learning seems to blur the traditional conceptual boundaries thus creating confusion among digital learning practitioners. The following discussion on key historical developments is therefore intended to highlight the key drivers of digital learning over time.

Historical Perspectives

A recognition that the educational potential of existing, emerging, and future developments in digital technologies is applicable beyond formal schooling is now commonly discussed in many diverse settings (daily newspapers, school curriculum support materials, political party policy documents, workplace human resource departments, standards-setting bodies, academic literature, and in higher education strategic planning). This has come about largely since the invention of the World Wide Web, although prior to this the potential of educational technology was recognized at various other historical moments (such as with the inventions of radio, television, personal computers, and digital media). Not only has evolution of the World Wide Web taken place within a short period of time accompanied by rapid innovation, it has been transformative, representing a global revolution in the production, distribution, and access to information and communications (Benkler, 2006; Castells, 1996, 2001). For instance, the shift from analogue TV to digital is transforming that tool as a complex and multilayered educational tool.

A number of commentators have consequently attempted to classify the evolution of the World Wide Web in terms of its impact upon learning. Taylor (2001), for instance, began visioning "fifth generation distance education" around 2001–2002 as an "intelligent flexible learning model"—it was student-centric in conception but impacted significantly the organizational structures and readiness for institutions concerned. In 2005, Siemens proposed a new learning theory called "connectivism," motivated principally by the impact of the proliferation of networked ICT applications and the limitations of dominant learning theories (behaviorism, cognitivism, and constructivism) to explain and support the scope of interactions of a learner and the nature of distributed, networked knowledge.

A distinguishing characteristic of Siemens' theory is the prominent role of networks in creating connections between disparate learning sources and entities. Because there exist important antecedents to this theory—such as connectionism within the field of artificial intelligence (McClelland & Rumelhart, 1986); actor-network theory (Latour, 1987); the sociological analysis of Castells (1996); and even the foresight of Bush (1945)—there is plenty of debate as to whether connectivism actually represents a new learning theory (Kop & Hill, 2008). Nonetheless, it is certainly the case that its articulation has gained significant worldwide attention and contributes to the understanding of digital learning.

It is worthwhile adding here that while the term *e-learning* may not have been coined until 1998, learning with much of the educational technologies in the decade up until then could likewise be characterized as e-learning. It is therefore important to acknowledge that neither e-learning nor digital learning began when these terms were introduced. The capabilities that already existed in early phases of development were just described by different terms that gave emphasis to a particular approach—for example, Computer Based Training (CBT), Computer

Assisted Learning (CAL), Computer Managed Learning (CML), Computer Managed Instruction (CMI), Interactive Multimedia (IMM), Computer Mediated Communication (CMC), and Computer Supported Collaborative Learning (CSCL). It is also interesting that CSCL is a term that still has widespread usage while many of the others have fallen by the wayside.

Broadening historical perspective by looking into the roots of *open* movements provides further context for how digital learning may develop into the future with "the emergence of new kinds of open participatory learning ecosystems" (Seely Brown & Adler, 2008, p. 32; Conole, 2013).

Open Agendas

For at least a century terminology associated with "openness" has been used in educational and social contexts (see Table 1.1 for a summary). An analysis of this usage, particularly since the beginnings of the Internet, reveals that the semantics are dominated by themes associated with *access, intellectual property, benefit to the public domain, sharing,* and *technical interoperability.* Each of these five themes has been important in shaping the Internet and World Wide Web. But what is most interesting about each of these themes is that none directly touch upon the semantics associated with "open learning," a term with roots attributed to Montessori (1967/1949), Dewey (1910), and Piaget (1966) in which "openness" was used to describe a pedagogical approach that facilitates independent, inquiry-based, and self-determined learning or "productive inquiry" (Brügelmann, 1975; Lillard, 2005; Piaget, 1966; Seely Brown & Adler, 2008, p. 24). The summary information in Table 1.1 therefore provides further context to the historical snapshot depicting the evolution of digital learning in Figure 1.1.

Table 1.1 Openness, Society, and Learning

Term	Associated Meaning	Origins
Open learning	Independent, inquiry-based, and self-determined learning	John Dewey (1910) Maria Montessori (circa 1911)
Open society	Democratic governance, transparent government, and respect for human rights	Henri Bergson (1932) & Karl Popper (1945/1971) Advocated by George Soros with formation of Open Society Institute (1993)
Open architecture	Extensible infrastructure (of the Internet)	1969 (ARPANET) International Organization for Standardization (ISO) Open Systems Interconnection (OSI) Model (ISO/IEC 7498–1:1994)
Open university	No academic prerequisites to entry; use of ICT including radio and broadcast television for distance learning and e-learning	1971 (UK Open University)
Open standard	Indicates that the process of development is transparent; the standard promotes *interoperability;* is publicly available; but intellectual property may be preserved	Mid-1980s
Open license	Typically noncommercial access to content and/or software	Richard Stallman and the GNU Project (1983) Developed by Creative Commons (2001)

(Continued)

5

Table 1.1 (Continued)

Term	Associated Meaning	Origins
Open source	Shared *intellectual input* into the development of software with specific but royalty-free licensing requirements	The term appeared in 1998 but roots of sharing software code date back to the beginnings of the Internet
Open knowledge initiative (OKI)	Interoperability specifications	Massachusetts Institute of Technology (2001) (Thorne et al., 2002)
Open courseware (OCW)	Free access to structured, quality courses and content	Massachusetts Institute of Technology (2002)
Open access	Royalty-free publication and dissemination of content (typically academic research)	The Berlin Declaration on Open Access to Knowledge in the Sciences and Humanities (2003) arXiv.org influential (1999)
Open content	Content that can be freely used and modified by others	David Wiley (1998)
Open scholarship	Sharing intellectual endeavor and outputs	Can be traced to origins of arXiv.org with repository initiatives such as the Los Alamos National Laboratory
Open educational resources (OER)	Educational resources (content, digital tools, and standards) developed for free public access and use.	The term OER emerged in 2005 but content developed specifically for the public good or the "public commons" has been happening for centuries
Open government	Using contemporary digital technologies to interact with very accessible Government departments	Emerged in wake of Web 2.0 as Government 2.0 but also arguably has origins in Open Society movement
Open teaching	Being explicit and transparent about teaching methodologies	Diana Laurillard (2008)
Massive online open courses (MOOCs)	Online learning involving large numbers of participants.	2008. George Siemens and Stephen Downes deliver online course called "Connectivism and Connective Knowledge"
Open data	Linked closely with Open Government; key drivers are public benefit and public ownership of publicly-funded data collection	2010. Can also be linked back to the Open Archives Initiative (2000) and the protocol for exposing metadata records for reuse
Open digital learning	Digital Learning that combines meanings associated with OER together with emergent dimensions, such as inquiry, assessment, participation, and dialogue	Emerging now Builds on OER with "new kinds of open participatory learning ecosystems" (Seely Brown & Adler, 2008)

By conceiving of *inquiry-based learning* in terms of *openness*, then, a number of questions arise:

- *What does this look like when facilitated by digital technology?*
- *Do the digital tools currently available adequately scaffold open inquiry?*
- *What is the scope for development of digital tools that will promote open inquiry?*

Answers to these questions are pointed to in the following sections focused on questioning online and the role of *why*-questioning in particular.

Questioning Online

Questioning is a fundamental activity of learning, yet the digital tools that might promote it in self-directed, online learning contexts are quite limited—if interactive dialogue made possible by social media is excluded. This limitation is most readily seen in search and query technologies, which are typically calibrated to parse coded information and data created from factual information reducible to semantics that Mason has described as the "primitives of information discovery: *who, what, when, and where*" (Mason, 2008). There are of course other primitive questions such as *how* and *if* but from an information science perspective they can be seen to be concerned with procedural or rule-based information. Another way of describing this limitation of the inquiry tools currently available is that they lack sophisticated inference engines that can handle the ambiguities of natural language and, in particular, the ambiguities and functions of *why*-questioning (Verbene, 2010).

While learning can clearly take place without questioning—for example, through basic information-seeking, repetition, and memorization—it is through questioning that high level cognitive functions such as inquiry, reflection, dialogue, reasoning, analysis, and knowledge construction take place (Mason, 2011). Thus, Glaser (1984, p. 93) observed that "establishing a cognitive basis for a pedagogy that fosters thinking and reasoning in school learning has been continuously expressed by educators and researchers at least since John Dewey." Consistent with this perspective, socio-cultural philosophers of education, Freire and Faundez, have argued for the need for a "pedagogy of asking questions" that gives emphasis to questioning as something valuable in itself, where an answer may not even be relevant: "Thinking about questions that may not always or immediately arrive to an answer are the roots of change" (Freire & Faundez, 1989, p. 37). More recently, Rothstein and Santana (2011) have developed this view in advocating the use of the *Question Formulation Technique* as a means to encourage students to ask their own questions), while Thomas and Seely Brown identified the emergence of a "new culture of learning" as a consequence of relentless innovation with ICT:

> We propose reversing the order of things. What if, for example, questions were more important than answers? What if the key to learning were not the application of techniques but their invention? What if students were asking questions about things that really mattered to them?
> *(Thomas & Seely Brown, 2011, p. 81)*

To simplify the argument and to connect it to the underlying theme of this chapter, a metaphor can be made by describing the difference between *closed* questions (that seek yes/no or fact-based responses) and *open* questions (that seek to probe deeper, stimulate dialogue, and promote curiosity). *But what are the digital tools that promote open questioning?* Apart from research and development into natural language search technology which is primarily concerned with automated question answering the most effective current tools are social or collaborative in nature, such as wikis, online forums, and MOOCs (Butin, 2012).

Why-Questions as a Key

To bring a sharper focus to the challenge of opening digital learning to deeper inquiry the development of tools that specifically scaffold *why*-questioning looks to be a promising frontier that warrants further investigation (Verberne, 2010; Mason, 2012). There are compelling reasons for this—reasons that are best reviewed in aggregate:

1. Technologies that support *information-seeking* are ubiquitous and available at the fingertips of anyone with a smartphone or other mobile technology—but they are not sufficient for scaffolding deeper inquiry.

2. Information-seeking is typically *a first step to inquiry* and a key activity of learning. Importantly, information-seeking only seeks a clear or factual answer to a search query.

3. In direct contrast to the primitive questions of information discovery—*who, what, when,* and *where*—*why* is a term that has ambiguous semantics. As such, it presents problems for data mining tools and search engines.

4. Inquiry instigated by *why*-questioning typically seeks a plausible *explanation, a rationale,* or *elaboration* as a response, not just information. As such, it is instrumental in stimulating or continuing a dialogue or interaction with other humans or devices. Importantly, *why*-questioning does not necessarily seek factual answers.

5. To *ask* why is to make sense of something. Thus, sense-making tools (textual and visual) may prove to be more effective than the dominant search paradigm of information-seeking when adequate responses to *why*-questioning are sought.

6. To *learn* why involves processes of reasoning, meaning-making, acquisition of knowledge, and the development of understanding. Thus, tools that directly support these processes would be useful for digital learning.

7. To *explain* why can invoke reasoning, storytelling, and reflection upon motivation, purpose, and context—all activities so important to metacognition and deeper learning. *Explaining why* can demonstrate understanding or lack of it. Thus, tools that support the development of explanatory techniques would be useful for digital learning.

Conclusion

This chapter presented the evolution of *e-learning*, which is currently at a phase where it may be subsumed into *digital learning*, a term that has emerged to describe a broader, more inclusive set of digital technologies and contexts for learning—and perhaps not so fraught with debates about definition. The short history presented here can be seen in terms of changes in key technologies and theories over two decades; however, digging deeper into history also reveals the importance of the influence of open movements and suggests that more dimensions of openness—beyond *access, intellectual property, public benefit, sharing* and *technical interoperability*—may also shape future innovations in digital technology. One such dimension looks as though it may involve digital tools that will directly scaffold and support prolonged and productive inquiry, and particularly inquiry that is instigated by questions of *why* and supports the 21st-century digital demands of productive citizens.

References

Bates, T. (2004). The promise and myths of e-learning in post-secondary education. In M. Castells (Ed.), *The network society: A cross-cultural perspective* (pp. 271–292). Cheltenham, UK: Edward Elgar. Retrieved from http://www.tonybates.ca/wp-content/uploads/2008/07/castell4.pdf

Benkler, Y. (2006). *The wealth of networks: How social production transforms markets and freedom.* New Haven, CT: Yale University Press.

Brügelmann, H. (1975). Open curricula—A paradox? *Cambridge Journal of Education, 1*(5), 12–20.

Bush, V. (1945). As we may think. *The Atlantic Monthly, 176*(1), 101–108. Retrieved from http://www.w3c.it/talks/2012/lpw/bush_aswemaythink.pdf

Butin, D. (2012, June). What MIT should have done. *eLearn,* Article 3. New York, NY: ACM. doi:10.1145/2241156.2263018

Castells, M. (1996). *The rise of the network society—The information age: Economy, society and culture* (Vol. 1). Oxford, UK: Blackwell.

Castells, M. (2001). *The Internet galaxy—Reflections on the Internet, business, and society.* New York, NY: Oxford University Press.

CIPD (2008). *E-learning: Progress and prospects* (Chartered Institute of Personnel and Development, UK, Factsheet). Retrieved from http://www.cipd.co.uk/subjects/lrnanddev/elearning/elearnprog.htm

Conole, G. (2013). Open, social and participatory media. In J. M. Spector & S. LaJoie (Eds.), *Designing for learning in an open world: Explorations in the learning sciences, instructional systems and performance technologies,* (Chapter 4, pp. 47–63). New York, NY: Springer.

Cooper, A. R. (2010). Key challenges in the design of learning technology standards: Observations and proposals. *International Journal of IT Standards and Standardization Research, 8*(2), 20–29.

Cross, J. (2004). *A history of eLearning: The future of eLearning.* Internet Time Group. Retrieved from http://www.scribd.com/doc/12913198/History-Future-of-eLearning-On-the-Horizon

Dewey, J. (1910). *How we think: Restatement of the relation of reflective thinking to the educative process.* Republished edition, 2008. New York, NY: Cosimo Books.

DfES. (2003). *Toward a unified e-Learning strategy.* UK Department for Education and Skills. Available at https://www.education.gov.uk/consultations/downloadableDocs/towards%20a%20unified%20e-learning%20strategy.pdf

El-Hussein, M.O.M., & Cronje, J. C. (2010). Defining mobile learning in the higher education landscape. *Educational Technology & Society, 13*(3), 12–21. Retrieved from http://www.ifets.info/journals/13_3/3.pdf

Freire, P., & Faundez, A. (1989). *Learning to question: A pedagogy of liberation.* New York, NY: Continuum.

Friesen, N. (2009). *Counterpoints: Studies in the Postmodern Theory of Education* (Vol. 333): *Re-thinking e-Learning research: Foundations, methods, and practices.* New York, NY: Peter Lang Publishing.

Garrison, D. R., & Anderson, T. (2003). *E-learning in the 21st century: A framework for research and practice.* New York: Routledge/Falmer.

Glaser, R. (1984). Education and thinking: The role of knowledge. *American Psychologist, 39*(2), 93–104. doi:10.1037/0003-066X.39.2.93

Griffin, P., McGaw, B., & Care, E. (Eds.). (2012). *Assessment and teaching of 21st century skills.* London, UK: Springer.

Kop, R., & Hill, A. (2008). Connectivism: Learning theory of the future or vestige of the past? *International Review of Research in Open and Distance Learning, 9*(3), 1–13. Retrieved from http://www.irrodl.org/index.php/irrodl/article/view/523

Landow, G. (1991). *Hypertext: The convergence of contemporary critical theory and technology.* Baltimore, MD: Johns Hopkins University Press.

Latour, B. (1987). *Science in action: How to follow scientists and engineers through society.* Milton Keynes: Open University Press.

Laurillard, D. (2008). Open teaching: The key to sustainable and effective open education. In Toru Iiyoshi & M. S. Vijay Kumar (Eds.), *Opening up education: The collective advancement of education through open technology, open content, and open knowledge.* Cambridge, MA: MIT Press.

Leeson, J., & Mason, J. (2007). The open agenda and organisational alignment. *Supplementary Proceedings, the 15th International Conference on Computers in Education, 1,* 189 194. Retrieved from http://www.intercog.net/publications/20071105_ICCE_Leeson_Mason.pdf

Lillard, A. (2005). *Montessori: The science behind the genius,* New York, NY: Oxford University Press.

Manathunga, C., Lant, P. & Mellick, G. (2006). Imagining an interdisciplinary doctoral Pedagogy. *Teaching in Higher Education, 11*(3), 365–379.

Mason, J. (2005). From e-learning to e-knowledge. In R. Madanmohan (Ed.), *Knowledge management tools and techniques* (pp. 320–328). London: Elsevier.

Mason, J. (2008). A model for sense-making: Exploring *why* in the context of learning and knowing. *The 16th International Conference on Computers in Education, Taipei* (Vol. 1, pp. 545–549). Retrieved from http://www.apsce.net/ICCE2008/papers/ICCE2008-paper286.pdf

Mason, J. (2011). Cognitive engagement and questioning online. In A. Mendez–Vilas (Ed.), *Education in a technological world: Communicating current and emerging research and technological efforts.* Formatex. Retrieved from http://www.formatex.info/ict/book/90-99.pdf

Mason, J. (2012). Theorizing *why* in e-Learning—A frontier for cognitive engagement. In D. Sampson, J. M. Spector, D. Ifenthaler, & P. Isaias (Eds.), *Proceedings of the IADIS International Conference on Cognition and Exploratory Learning* (CELDA 2012, pp. 57–64). Retrieved from http://files.eric.ed.gov/fulltext/ED542651.pdf

McClelland, J. L., Rumelhart, D. E., & the PDP Research Group. (1986). *Parallel distributed processing: Explorations in the microstructure of cognition. Volume 2: Psychological and biological models.* Cambridge, MA: MIT Press.

Montessori, M. (1967). *The absorbent mind* (C. Claremont, Trans.). New York, NY: Dell Publishing. (Original work published 1949)

OECD. (2005). *E-learning in tertiary education: where do we stand?* Centre for Educational research and Innovation, Organization for Economic Cooperation and Development. Retrieved from http://www.oecd.org/innovation/researchandknowledgemanagement/34899903.pdf

OECD. (2007). *Giving knowledge for free: The emergence of open educational resources.* Centre for Educational Research and Innovation, Organization for Economic Cooperation and Development. Retrieved from http://www.oecd.org/edu/ceri/givingknowledgeforfreetheemergenceofopeneducationalresources.htm

Oller, R. (2012). *The future of mobile learning.* EDUCAUSE Center for Applied Research. Retrieved from http://net.educause.edu/ir/library/pdf/ERB1204.pdf

Piaget, J. (1966). *The child's conception of physical causality.* London, UK: Routledge and Kegan Paul.

Popper, K. (1945). *The open society and its enemies* (Vol. 1). Princeton, NJ: Princeton University Press. (Reprinted 1971)

Rothstein, D., & Santana, L. (2011). *Make just one change: Teach students to ask their own questions.* Cambridge, MA: Harvard Education Press.

Sangrà, A., Vlachopoulos, D., & Cabrera, N. (2012). Building an inclusive definition of e-learning: An approach to the conceptual framework. *International Review of Research in Open and Distance Learning, 13*(2), 145–159. Retrieved from http://www.irrodl.org/index.php/irrodl/article/view/1161

Seely Brown, J., & Adler, R. P. (2008). Minds on fire—Open education, the long tail, and learning 2.0. *Educause Review, 43*(1), 17–32. Retrieved from http://net.educause.edu/ir/library/pdf/ERM0811.pdf

Sharples, M., Taylor, J., & Vavoula, G. (2007). A theory of learning for the mobile age. In R. Andrews, & C. Haythornthwaite (Eds.), *The sage handbook of e-learning research* (pp. 221–248). London, UK: SAGE Publications. doi:10.4135/9781848607859.n10

Taylor, J. C. (2001). Fifth generation distance education. *e-Journal of Instructional Science and Technology (e-JIST), 4*(1), 1–14.

Thomas, D., & Seely Brown, J. (2011). *A new culture of learning—Cultivating the imagination for a world of constant change.* Lexington, KY: CreateSpace.

Thorne, S., Shubert, C., & Merriman, J. (2002). *OKI Architecture.* MIT. Retrieved from http://web.mit.edu/oki/learn/whtpapers/ArchitecturalOverview.pdf

Tomei, L. A., & Morris, R. (2011). Top technologies for integrating online instruction. *International Journal of Online Pedagogy and Course Design, 1*(1), 12–28.

Verbene, S. (2010). *In search of the why: Developing a system for answering why-questions.* Nijmegen, The Netherlands: Radboud Universiteit. Retrieved from http://repository.ubn.ru.nl/handle/2066/76174

2

Using Social Media in the Online Classroom

Lisa Marie Blaschke and Jane Brindley

Introduction

Millions of individuals communicate through social media such as Facebook, LinkedIn, and Twitter every day. Social media applications have become the tools of choice for messaging and marketing as well as personal socializing. More recently, social media tools are being recognized for their usefulness in the classroom, whether virtual or campus based. McCrea (2013), in *Campus Technology*, identified the recognition of the value of social media for learning as one of the top six trends in higher education.

Social media applications are proving to be an excellent fit with current and emerging pedagogies that call for engagement, active learning, and collaborative problem solving. Current educational practice extends beyond acquisition of disciplinary knowledge, emphasizing acquisition of skills necessary for self-directed lifelong learning and adaptation to rapidly changing contexts that characterize the world in which learners will live and work. Acquisition of capabilities such as critical thinking and complex analysis, communication and presentation, research and management of learning resources, collaboration with peers, digital literacy, and self-knowledge and reflective practice can be aided significantly by the effective use of social media for learning tasks.

Prensky (2010) used an analogy that compares the relationship between critical skill development and the choice of technology tools for teaching as the matching of nouns to verbs. In his analogy, the nouns (tools we have available to us) change over time, but the verbs (skills critical to lifelong learning) remain fairly constant. As with any other tool, each social media application has unique affordances that are suited to particular tasks (Bates & Sangrà, 2011). For example, wikis have proven to be very effective tools for collaborative work, whereas electronic learning journals can be excellent spaces for individual reflection (Blaschke & Brindley, 2011).

The challenge for the educator is to choose social media tools appropriate to the learning task or particular skill development, and embed them in courses and the curriculum in active and meaningful ways so that learners embrace them because they are useful, effective for the purpose, and engaging. This chapter addresses that challenge by defining social media and explaining its various forms, affordances, and applications that engage learners and improve learning outcomes. Considerations for course design, and the challenges and implications of social media use are also discussed in the context of exploring the potential of social media to create more democratic, collaborative, and dynamic learning spaces.

Social Media Defined

The term *social media* is often used interchangeably with Web 2.0, although in reality social media have actually been designed using the technology platform called Web 2.0. Kaplan & Haenlein (2010) defined social media as a "group of Internet-based applications that build on the ideological and technological foundations of Web 2.0, and that allow the creation and exchange of User Generated Content" (p. 61). Social software tools is another term used synonymously with social media, defined by Anderson (2005) as "networked tools that support and encourage individuals to learn together while retaining individual control over their time, space, presence, activity, identity and relationship" (p. 4). A simpler definition comes from Tadros (2011), who wrote "Social media are any media that help integrate technology into the lives of people for the purpose of communication" (p. 85).

Bates and Sangrà (2011) emphasized the participatory and democratic aspects of social media, defining them as "Web 2.0 tools (that) empower the end user to access, create, disseminate, and share information easily in a user-friendly open environment" (p. 34).

The Internet offers a vast source and variety of content but with social media, the user can go beyond being a consumer of content to communicating and collaborating with other users and creating and co-creating content. It is this user-centered aspect of social media that makes it particularly well suited for use in teaching and learning.

Social Media's Pedagogical Benefits and Affordances

Social media offer a variety of pedagogical benefits and affordances. First and foremost, social media are learner-centered, allowing students to connect with others and to become active rather than passive participants in the learning experience (Klamma et al, 2007, as cited in Crompton, 2012; Crompton, 2012). The learner-centered environment provided by social media extends the boundaries of the physical classroom, giving students opportunities to learn from the world (Harris & Rea, 2009). Affordances of social media include the opportunity to discover and share information, perform inquiries, be creative and authentic, reflect, construct knowledge, create dialogues, connect, interact, organize, and engage in collaborative learning (Conole, 2012; McLoughlin & Lee, 2008). A recent NMC Horizon Report (Johnson, Adams, & Cummins, 2012) found that

> the world of work is increasingly collaborative, driving changes in the way student projects are structured. As more and more employers are valuing collaboration as a critical skill, silos both in the workplace and at school are being abandoned in favour of collective intelligence. To facilitate more teamwork and group communication, projects rely on tools like wikis, Google Docs, Skype, and online forums. Projects are increasingly evaluated by educators not just on the overall outcome, but also on the success of the group dynamic.
>
> *(p. 14)*

Social media's shared spaces provide a place where students can learn the collaborative process by working on a project from beginning to end, assess their individual strengths and weaknesses against those of peers, and work to improve the latter while completing a task by pooling complementary strengths. Communication and interaction, essential to online teaching and learning (Conrad, 2013), can be facilitated and enhanced using the affordances of shared spaces and social networking, for example, through peer critiquing and feedback and information sharing. The distributed authorship capabilities of social media further support individual and shared user-generated content and knowledge construction (Griesemer, 2012, p. 9).

Use of social media can help create a sense of increased accessibility and availability of the instructor, peers, and course content (Griesemer, 2012, p. 9). There is also evidence to suggest that embedding social media tools within courses supports skill development that can lead to learner capability (capacity to use skills with confidence in a variety of situations), as well as stimulate cognitive skills such as critical thinking and reflection on content and one's individual learning process (Blaschke & Brindley, 2011; Blaschke, Porto, & Kurtz, 2010; Griesemer, 2012). Price & Wright (2012) have also found that the use of social media can support and improve the efficiency of the research process cycle, from visualizing a research problem and collecting and organizing resources to developing, managing, and evaluating research content.

Given the widespread use of social media and social networking for communication and archiving, it makes sense that these tools are being "appropriated and repurposed" for teaching and learning, particularly as many of them are uniquely suited to specific learning tasks and processes (Hemmi, Bayne, & Land, 2009, p. 19).

A Classification Scheme for Social Media

Social media tools are in a state of constant change. With new media rapidly appearing on the technological landscape, a static definition or classification system for social media is elusive. In the 2013 Horizon report, Johnson et al. wrote the following:

> **Complexity is the new reality**. One of the main challenges of implementing new pedagogies, learning models, and technologies in higher education is the realization of how interconnected they all are. Games, for example, often overlap with natural user interfaces as well as social media with social networks, and learning analytics are increasingly associated with adaptive learning platforms. Even as we acknowledge that topics continuously converge, morph, and evolve, we need the proper language to accurately discuss and define them.
>
> *(p. 15)*

Despite the challenges of classifying new technologies, it is necessary to create a framework and a commonly understood language for discussion. For the purposes of this chapter, we have chosen to align our discussion most closely with a slightly modified version of the classification scheme offered by Kaplan and Haenlein (2010). They categorize social media according to levels of self presentation and disclosure, social presence, and media richness. Here, we are more concerned about classification by affordances to support specific kinds of learning. Accordingly, we have renamed their *blog* category as *individual showcase projects* to include all technology tools that can be used for this purpose. A brief description of each category is provided below.

- *Collaborative projects*: Students work together, engaged in activities such as problem solving and carrying out research with the goal of constructing and developing new knowledge by creating content together.
- *Individual showcase projects*: These projects are primarily used to present ideas and concepts, and to document and curate other types of content such as progression toward a goal, achievements, or important resources, using social media as the platform.
- *Content/information sharing communities*: In this category, students share information and learning resources with others using a variety of media.

- *Social networking*: Students use social networking for making and sustaining connections with family, colleagues, and other students. Students create personalized profiles, invite their contacts to connect with them, and then use the site for e-mailing and instant messaging.
- *Virtual game worlds*: With this form of social media, students create avatars that interact with other avatars in a virtual gaming environment.
- *Virtual social worlds*: Much like virtual game worlds, virtual social worlds allow more freedom and students can "choose their behavior more freely and essentially live a virtual life similar to their real life" (Kaplan & Haenlein, 2010, p. 64).

Matching Social Media Tools to Skill Development

Prensky's (2010) simple analogy comparing the relationship between nouns and verbs to the relationship between technology tools and critical skills provides a framework for effectively matching social media tools to learning activities. In his analogy, verbs are the essential skills of learning (e.g., researching, analyzing, reflecting, communicating, collaborating) that do not change very much over time. Nouns are the technology tools that students use to develop skills and competencies. Unlike the verbs of learning, nouns (tools) are constantly evolving.

Table 2.1 is Prensky's (2010) framework adapted to the social media classification scheme from Kaplan and Haenlein (2010). The categories of social media (column 1) are used to classify various social media tools (column 3), which are matched to the critical learning skills that these are best suited to support (column 2). The list of skills that are displayed in column 2 in Table 2.1 was identified based on the literature reviewed for this chapter. These competencies

Table 2.1 Skills (Verbs) and Tools (Nouns) by Social Media Type

Classification	Skills (Verbs)	Tools (Nouns)
Collaborative projects	Collaborate; communicate (write, read, discuss, interact); construct knowledge (individual and group); socialize; navigate; negotiate; solve problems; think deeply, critically, and logically; reflect; evaluate	Wikis, Google Docs, brainstorming tools (e.g., mindmaps), mashups, Dropbox, Box.net
Individual showcase projects	Design and create; think critically, deeply, and logically; share knowledge; share experience; give advice; express yourself	Blogs, e-portfolios
Social networking	Communicate (read, write, discuss, interact); collaborate; search; explore; listen; connect; share; think critically; reflect; support others; build community; promote (self); exchange	Twitter, LinkedIn, Facebook, social tagging (e.g., Flickr, Pinterest), Cloudworks
Content/ information sharing communities	Communicate (read, write, discuss, interact); collaborate; search; inquire; compare; combine; think critically; reflect; observe; share; build community; promote (self); distribute	YouTube, Diigo, Twitter, LinkedIn, news aggregators (RSS), Evernote
Virtual game worlds	Connect; collaborate; navigate; play; communicate (read, write, discuss, interact); explore; analyze and solve problems; think critically; compete; program; model; innovate; plan; simulate	Minecraft, alternate reality games (ARGs), massively multiplayer online games (MMO), and global social awareness games
Virtual social worlds	Explore; observe; experiment; discover; model; predict; solve problems; innovate; plan; simulate	Simulations, Second Life

Adapted from Prensky, 2010.

are most commonly cited as being essential for lifelong learning, innovation, a knowledge-based economy, and/or the 21st-century workplace.

Social Media and Its Uses

The metaphor of nouns (tools) and verbs (skills), applied within the social media context, allows us to incorporate social media into the online classroom by considering the affordances of the social media category (column 1), the skills or competencies that we want students to acquire within a learning activity (column 2), and the tools that help us to achieve our learning goals (column 3). The next sections discuss each of the social media categories shown in Table 2.1 and their specific pedagogical affordances.

Collaborative Projects

Web 2.0 tools provide much greater capacity than an LMS for both synchronous and asynchronous student–student interaction and collaboration. At the same time, complex problems and issues in higher education and the workplace call for multidisciplinary and cross-functional team approaches. Employers place a high value on collaborative skills and ability to work in teams using a variety of online collaboration tools (Johnson et al., 2012; Johnson, Levine, Smith, & Stone, 2010). Collaborative tools such as wikis and Google Apps are particularly well suited to support student–student collaboration, promote discussion and dialogue, and help bring more balance to the teacher–student relationship (Johnson et al., 2012). Collaborative projects help aid in the development of negotiation skills, support student collaboration and interaction, and are easily and centrally accessible in shared virtual spaces (Harris & Rea, 2009). They can be used for constructing knowledge both individually and in groups, evaluating peer contributions, problem solving, understanding concepts and their complexities, engaging students in classroom tasks, and promoting deeper thinking and reflection on ideas and concepts through observation (Harris & Rea, 2009).

Individual Showcase Projects

Individual showcase projects, such as blogs and e-portfolios, are particularly useful for developing skills of self-expression, and with their capacity for different levels of access can also accommodate dialogue. Pedagogical benefits include supporting reflective thinking, development of metacognitive skills, and sharing of knowledge and experience. Individual showcase projects can be used for communicating ideas, inspiring reflective thinking, and documenting and curating content. They can also be used to make connections, provide advice, make announcements, or used as a living record of progress and achievements, such as an e-portfolio (Harris & Rea, 2009). For example, students can use blogs or wikis as a form of reflective learning journal (Blaschke & Brindley, 2011; Conole & Alevizou, 2010), as well as an e-portfolio showcasing a student's work for purposes of assessment and/or employment (Porto, Blaschke, & Kurtz, 2010).

Social Networking

Social networking supports interaction among participants in a community and has become more popular within academia, as "scientists and researchers use social media to keep their communities informed of new developments" (Johnson et al., 2013, p. 14). Pedagogical benefits of social networking include increased student engagement and interaction, collaboration, and peer support

(Conole, 2012; Conole & Alevizou, 2010; Rodriguez, 2011). Networking can be used for creating communities, making connections with peers, broadcasting and self-promotion, sharing information and resources, exchanging ideas, back channeling, gathering viewpoints through surveys, and for research purposes (Conole, 2012; Conole & Alevizou, 2010). One example of using social networking for research is the use of Twitter to follow specific trends within a field of study, thus conducting active research while observing development of the trend. An example of a social networking site used for the exchange of instructional ideas is Cloudworks (http://cloudworks.ac.uk/).

Content/Information Sharing Communities

Online communities allow learners and educators to share user-generated content, resources, and information with each other and can offer pedagogical benefits, such as supporting self-directed and inquiry-based learning, collaboration, and interaction among students (Conole, 2012). Instructors can use these resources as course-content supplementary material to provide additional guidance to students as a form of scaffolding (Harris & Rea, 2009). Information sharing communities can also be used to distribute a variety of multimedia, such as presentations (e.g., SlideShare), lectures (e.g., YouTube), and images (e.g., Flickr and Pinterest) and to disseminate these using different channels (Conole, 2012).

Virtual Game Worlds

Use of virtual game worlds for learning is steadily on the rise. Johnson et al. (2013) report that game-based learning supports "cognitive development and the fostering of soft skills among learners, such as collaboration, communication, problem-solving, and critical thinking" (p. 2). Their NMC report goes on to describe game-based learning as goal oriented, social, and offering real-world and relevant simulation. Games used for pedagogical purposes have the capacity to support learning objectives and incorporate instructional aspects, such as assessing student performance and providing feedback (Hays, 2005). Minecraft (https://minecraft.net/) is an example of an online video game where gamers (individually or with others) use blocks to build virtual worlds that can be used in learning contexts. For example, Minecraft has been used by students who work together to create a virtual community and, through the process, learn about city planning, environmental issues, and project management (Dunn, 2013). Other examples of virtual games for learning include UNESCO's games for change (http://www.gamesforchange.org/) and the United Nations' global social awareness games, such as Stop Disasters (http://www.stopdisastersgame.org/en/home.html) and Free Rice (http://freerice.com/#/english-vocabulary/1467).

Virtual Social Worlds

The final category of social media is virtual social worlds, the most well known being Second Life (www.secondlife.com). Pedagogical benefits of a virtual social world are the constructivist approaches applied with the virtual environment "such as discovery learning, learning through trial and error, problem-based learning, scenario-based learning and authentic learning" (Kirriemuir, 2008, as cited in Conole & Alevizou, 2010, p. 83). Use of virtual social worlds for learning has been found to motivate students by allowing them to create simulations, apply knowledge within this context, and have access to this greater community from which to learn (Harris & Rea, 2009). It should be noted that virtual social worlds often require extensive technical support and hardware, are frequently associated with a steep learning curve, and require instructors to adapt to shared control of the learning environment and be prepared to deal with unforeseen situations, such as harassment (Harris & Rea, 2009). Ways in which virtual social worlds can be used in the classroom include engaging in group work (socializing and collaborating); planning projects; conducting research; creating and testing models, such as simulations; problem solving; developing tools; performing presentations; establishing an institutional presence; providing support for a course; and encouraging multidisciplinary collaborations across departments (Harris & Rea, 2009; Kirriemuir, 2007).

Design Considerations

Incorporating social media into the online classroom requires careful planning by the instructor and application of good instructional design practice. It is essential that a design approach that emphasizes the effective pedagogical use of the media be identified and applied. Instructors take on a significant designer role as "architects of classroom experiences, balancing the development of multiple literacies and designing a learning environment where appropriate computer-based cognitive tools are applied imaginatively to collaborative, student-focused, reflective, problem-based approaches to learning" (Kimber & Wyatt-Smith, 2006, p. 28). Some examples of design approaches follow.

In the holistic, contextual approach to design presented by Kimber and Wyatt-Smith (2006), the instructor is designated as designer of learning activities, while students are responsible for creating a digital representation of their knowledge, either individually or with other students. Kimber and Wyatt-Smith (2006) argued that the more active a student is in the learning activity and the more reflection that the student undertakes while completing the activity, the more engaged she or he becomes in the learning activity, thus increasing the opportunity for development of higher order thinking skills that lead to transformative learning—a finding further supported by social media research by Blaschke, Porto, and Kurtz (2010).

Similar to this approach is the backwards design approach (Wiggins & McTighe, 2005), in which the instructor again adopts the role of designer, focusing first upon identifying the desired learning outcomes—both knowledge and skills. Once these outcomes have been identified, the instructor then works backward to design a learning path with individual and collaborative activities that will support the realization of these outcomes. Technology tools are chosen based on their capacity to support the learning activities.

Conole (2012) offers another approach, in which the instructor maps the affordances of a specific technology to learning activities so that the activity is supported by the affordances of the technology chosen to perform the activity. In this process, the instructor 1) defines the goal (or vision) of the learning activity (or intervention), 2) identifies the media resources for supporting the activity, 3) creates a sequential process for the learning activity, and then 4) tests and evaluates the activity in terms of its effectiveness and makes adjustments as needed (Conole, 2012).

Yet another holistic approach is that of a learner-centered framework, described by Luckin (2010) as an Ecology of Resources model and design framework. Within this framework, the learner is characterized "in terms of the interactions that form a learner's context" and in each interaction, the learner engages with specific resources incorporated to support the learner in the learning activity (p. 115). To apply this design approach, a team of designers conducts a three-step process, involving repeated iterations: 1) identify resources that can be used to support the learning activity (an Ecology of Resources model), 2) map how these resources relate to the learning activity and each other and to learner needs (learner context), and 3) scaffold the activity so that it supports the learning process (Luckin, 2010).

Challenges and Implications of Using Social Media in the Online Classroom

Online learning harnesses the power of the Internet, multimedia resources, and social media tools to create a rich learning environment, free of time and place constraints—and is transforming teaching and learning in many contexts. Web-based technologies are *disruptive* in that they open educational access to many new students and put much greater control in the hands of the learner, providing full access to peers and an almost infinite set of learning resources. Web-based technologies are also disruptive in challenging traditions of higher education. At the same time, only one-third of higher education faculty (34%) use social media for teaching purposes in the classroom, and mostly in a passive way (e.g., for viewing purposes; Moran, Seaman, & Tinti-Kane, 2012). There is resistance to incorporating new technologies in teaching for a variety of reasons.

The shift in control of the learning process from teacher to learner can be seen as positive but also threatening to faculty autonomy. Acquisition of instructional design and technology skills and managing a classroom that never closes are not necessarily seen as attractive by faculty focused on disciplinary research and already concerned about increasing workloads. Lack of time and interest, inability to see the added value, privacy issues, lack of funding and/or incentives, lack of skills, a perception that that there is too strong of an institutional emphasis on technology (versus pedagogy), and lack of institutional support are all cited as reasons why faculty are reluctant to embrace new technologies (Conole, 2010, as cited in Conole & Alevizou, 2010; Rodriguez, 2011).

Bates and Sangrà (2011) emphasized that faculty workloads, reward systems, and training are issues that must be addressed in order to facilitate integration of new technologies in teaching, and since 2008 each annual NMC Horizon Report has identified a growing demand for digital literacy skills, a demand that is expanding within and across disciplines, placing greater pressure on educators and institutions to adapt (Johnson et al., 2010; Johnston, Smith, Willis, Levine, & Haywood, 2011; Johnson et al., 2012; Johnson et al., 2013). Training is particularly important for teaching with social media tools that evolve quickly and are used not to broadcast content but rather must be embedded meaningfully in learning activities for their capacity to be realized.

Tadros (2011) noted a number of challenges related to using technology for teaching, including lack of tech-savviness (learners and educators), lack of access to technology, digital divide between tech-savvy educators and those who are not, fear of loss of control in the classroom, and challenges of keeping up with continuous change. Harris and Rea (2009) cited additional concerns about pedagogical use of social media as inaccessibility of technology, assessment difficulties, online sabotage/vandalism, plagiarism, and student discomfort with degree of openness (pp. 141–142).

Moran, Seaman, and Tinti-Kane (2012) identified barriers to the use of social media that include possibly a lack of integrity of student submissions, privacy concerns, little or no integration of social media tools with LMS, time required for learning and using tools, and lack of institutional support. (The authors note that since their similar study, conducted in 2011, these barriers have decreased somewhat across all categories, particularly "time required for use" and "institutional support.") Conole (2012) considered additional challenges that include extensive development and support time, complexity of use, production costs, difficulties with assessment (e.g., complexity and time involved in tracking activity and assessing individual level of competency achievement in collaborative projects), and need for digital literacy skills.

In addition to the concerns from an institutional perspective, learners may have significant concerns about privacy (Rodriguez, 2011). Once learners move out of institutionally protected spaces to ones owned and managed by another provider, privacy of any conversations or documents created is governed by that provider. A related issue is the potential for plagiarism when work is created and becomes available on the web. For example, students may post work samples in e-portfolios that include completed and graded assignments. These can be easily accessed and copied by other students depending upon the level of privacy provided.

Conclusion

It is evident that there are a number of challenges that must be addressed in order to integrate social media tools into teaching, learning, and assessment. A significant investment of time and energy is required by both teacher and learner to use social media effectively; issues of privacy and intellectual property must be addressed to protect individuals and institutions; and institutions must make an investment in infrastructure as well as address the issues of faculty workloads, reward systems, and training.

Despite these challenges, we cannot ignore the unique opportunities that social media offer to maximize learning and to develop critical lifelong learning skills in more open, collaborative, and dynamic learning spaces. Social media changes how everyone—from educators, students, scientists, and researchers to the general public—creates new knowledge, organizes and shares content and resources, and interacts and collaborates, and "it is clear that social media has found significant traction in almost every education sector" (Johnson et al., 2013, p. 14).

Harnessing the power of social media tools for pedagogical purposes requires careful and creative planning and design of courses, matching learning objectives to learning activities, and applying technologies according to their affordances. Prensky's (2010) nouns–verbs (tools–skills) analogy offers an accessible way of thinking about how social media tools can be used for supporting skill development within the context of an instructional design model. This chapter provides guidance and a framework for educators whose roles have shifted considerably to include learning design as well as disciplinary expertise in creating effective dynamic online learning environments.

References

Anderson, T. (2005). *Distance learning: Social software's killer app?* Paper presented at the ODLAA 2004 Conference, Adelaide, Australia. Retrieved from http://auspace.athabascau.ca/bitstream/2149/2328/1/distance_learning.pdf

Bates, A. W., & Sangrà, A. (2011). *Managing technology in higher education: Strategies for transforming teaching and learning.* San Francisco, CA: Jossey-Bass.

Blaschke, L., & Brindley, J. (2011). Establishing a foundation for reflective practice: A case study of learning journal use. *European Journal of Open, Distance, and E-learning (EURODL),* Special Issue. Retrieved from http://www.eurodl.org/materials/special/2011/Blaschke_Brindley.pdf

Blaschke, L., Porto, S., & Kurtz, G. (2010, October 25–27). *Assessing the added value of Web 2.0 tools for e-learning: The MDE experience.* European Distance and E-learning Network (EDEN) Research Workshop, Budapest, Hungary.

Conole, G. (2012). *Designing for learning in an open world: Explorations in the learning sciences, instructional systems and performance technologies.* New York, NY: Springer.

Conole, G., & Alevizou, P. (2010). *A literature review of the use of Web 2.0 tools in higher education.* Higher Education Academy, UK. Retrieved from http://www.heacademy.ac.uk/assets/EvidenceNEt/Conole_Alevizou_2010.pdf

Conrad, D. (2013). Interaction and communication in online learning communities: Toward an engaged and flexible future. In O. Zawacki-Richter & T. Anderson (Eds.), *Online distance education—Towards a research agenda* (pp. 381–402). Athabasca, Edmonton, Canada: Athabasca University Press.

Crompton, H. (2012). How Web 2.0 is changing the way students learn: The Darwikinism and folksonomy revolution. *eleed, 8.* urn:nbn:de:0009-5-32405. Retrieved from https://eleed.campussource.de/archive/8/3240

Dunn, J. (2013, January 18). Swedish school now has a mandatory Minecraft class. *Edudemic.* Retrieved from http://edudemic.com/2013/01/this-swedish-school-now-has-a-mandatory-minecraft-class/

Griesemer, J. (2012). Using social media to enhance students' learning experiences. *Quality Approaches to Higher Education, 3*(1), 8–11.

Harris, A., & Rea, A. (2009). Web 2.0 and virtual world technologies: A growing impact on IS education. *Journal of Information Systems Education, 20*(2), 137–144. doi:1755224731. Retrieved from http://www.unf.edu/uploadedFiles/aa/acadaffairs/provost/VirtualWorld_Technologies.pdf

Hays, R. T. (2005). *The effectiveness of instructional games: A literature review and discussion* (Tech. Rep. 2005–004, Naval Air Warfare Center, Training Systems Division). Retrieved from http://www.dtic.mil/cgi-bin/GetTRDoc?AD=ADA441935%26Location

Hemmi, A., Bayne, S., & Land, R. (2009). The appropriation and repurposing of social technologies in higher education. *Journal of Computer Assisted Learning, 25*, 19–30.

Johnson, L., Adams, S., & Cummins, M. (2012). *The NMC Horizon Report: 2012 higher education edition.* Austin, TX: The New Media Consortium. Retrieved from http://net.educause.edu/ir/library/pdf/hr2012.pdf

Johnson, L., Adams Becker, S., Cummins, M., Estrada, V., Freeman, A., & Ludgate, H. (2013). *NMC horizon report: 2013 higher education edition.* Austin, TX: The New Media Consortium. Retrieved from http://www.nmc.org/system/files/pubs/1360189731/2013-horizon-report-HE.pdf

Johnson, L., Levine, A., Smith, R., & Stone, S. (2010). *The 2010 horizon report.* Austin, TX: The New Media Consortium. Retrieved from http://www.nmc.org/pdf/2010-horizon-report.pdf

Johnson, L., Smith, R., Willis, H., Levine, A., & Haywood, K. (2011). *The 2011 horizon report.* Austin, TX: The New Media Consortium. Retrieved from http://www.nmc.org/system/files/pubs/1316814265/2011-Horizon-Report%282%29.pdf

Kaplan, A. M., & Haenlein, M. (2010). Users of the world unite! The challenges and opportunities of social media. *Business Horizons, 53,* 59–68. doi:10.1016/j.bushor.2009.09.003. Permalink: http://ezproxy.umuc.edu/login?url=http://search.ebscohost.com/login.aspx?direct=true&db=edselp&AN=S000768 1309001232&site=eds-live&scope=site

Kimber, K., & Wyatt-Smith, C. (2006). Using and creating knowledge with new technologies: A case for students-as-designers. *Language, Media and Technology, 31*(1), 19–34. Permalink: http://ezproxy.umuc.edu/login?url=http://search.ebscohost.com/login.aspx?direct=true&db=eric&AN=EJ734502&site=eds-live&scope=site (Requested and received from UMUC Library)

Kirriemuir, J. (2007). The second life of UK academics. *Ariadne* [Web magazine]. Retrieved from http://www.ariadne.ac.uk/issue53/kirriemuir

Luckin, R. (2010). *Re-designing learning contexts: Technology-rich, learner-centred ecologies.* New York, NY: Routledge.

McCrea, B. (2013, January 15). Higher ed tech trends to watch in 2013. *Campus Technology.* Retrieved from http://campustechnology.com/Articles/2013/01/15/6-Higher-Ed-Tech-Trends-To-Watch-in-2013.aspx?=CTNU&m=2&Page=1

McLoughlin, C., & Lee, M. J. W. (2008, November 30–December 3). *Mapping the digital terrain: New media and social software as catalysts for pedagogical change.* Proceedings from Ascilite, Melbourne, Australia. Retrieved from http://www.ascilite.org.au/conferences/melbourne08/procs/mcloughlin.pdf

Moran, M., Seaman, J., & Tinti-Kane, H. (2012*). Blogs, wikis, podcasts and Facebook: How today's higher education faculty use social media.* Pearson Learning Solutions and Babson Survey Research Group. Retrieved from http://www.pearsonlearningsolutions.com/higher-education/social-media-survey.php

Porto, S.C.S., Blaschke, L. M., & Kurtz, G. (2010). Assessing the added value of Web 2.0 tools: The MDE experience. In C. Wankel (Ed.), *Educating educators with social media* (pp. 107–134). Bingley, UK: Emerald Group.

Prensky, M. (2010). *Teaching digital natives: Partnering for real learning.* Thousand Oaks, CA: Corwin Press.

Price, G. P., & Wright, V. H. (2012). Aligning web-based tools to the research process cycle: A resource for collaborative research projects. *Journal of Interactive Online Learning, 11*(3), 121–127. Retrieved from http://www.ncolr.org/jiol/issues/pdf/11.3.3.pdf

Rodriguez, J. E. (2011). Social media use in higher education: Key areas to consider for educators. *Journal of Online Learning and Teaching, 7*(4). Retrieved from http://jolt.merlot.org/vol7no4/rodriguez_1211.htm

Tadros, M. (2011). A social media approach to higher education. In C. Wankel (Ed.), *Educating educators with social media.* Bingley, UK: Emerald Group.

Wiggins, G., & McTighe, J. (2005). *Understanding by design.* Alexandria, VA: ASCD.

3

The Integration of Educational Technology in Education and in the Workplace

An Organizational Perspective

Claude Martel

Introduction

For the last two decades, researchers and practitioners have been exploring the potential of digital educational technologies in both schools and the workplace. Some of the early research offered fairly mixed results (Clark & Mayer, 2008). Many of these early studies were mainly focused on the usability, efficiency, and reliability of these new learning environments compared to their classroom counterpart (Oncu & Cakir, 2011). The major question investigated in these exploratory experiments was "can we really effectively learn with these technologies?"

Shortly after the turn of the millennium, a series of landmark studies shifted the research perspective about digital educational technology solutions (Tamim, Bernard, Borokhovski, Abrami, & Schmid, 2011). One such study was the meta-analysis published by a team of Concordia University researchers (Bernard et al., 2004). This study synthesized the results obtained by 232 studies comparing classroom and online delivery of instructional material. The breakthrough conclusion obtained showed that there was no significant difference on achievement, attitude, and retention measures between learning in the classroom and learning from the technological/distance learning solutions. This type of result redirected the attention of many researchers from "can we learn with these technologies?" to "how can we use and integrate these technologies in education and in the workplace?" (Bernard et al., 2009).

In the following discussion, we will use the term *digital learning,* referring to the full spectrum of education and training solutions offered in the educational technology and distance education fields. This reflects the current globalization trend in education and training, where associations, educational institutions, and corporations are gradually grouping their educational/training offerings in large-scale online delivery organizations. Some of these ventures will be presented in this chapter.

Acceleration of Digital Learning Ventures

It is also during the first decade of the 21st century that we see a worldwide acceleration in the use of digital learning solutions (ASTD, 2012; UNESCO, 2012). The number of educational institutions using online learning and the number of students taking credited online courses has steadily grown over the last 9 years—some years reaching double-digit growth (Allen & Seaman, 2011). In a 2011 survey from the Babson Research Group, more than 2,500 United States universities and educational institutions are now offering online courses. They reported more than 6.1 million students taking at least one online class during fall 2010 in the United States; a 10.1% increase over the previous year (Allen & Seaman, 2011).

The credibility of online learning has also continued to increase. In 2011, 67% of academic professionals in the United States rated online education as the same or superior to face-to-face instruction; a slow but steady increase over the previous 8 years (Allen & Seaman, 2011). According to a 2011 review of the digital learning market (Adkins, 2013), until recently, the online learning market was largely composed of corporate ventures and developing economies. This has changed, as the market is now one of rapid adoption in all the buyer segments. The largest growth is in developing economies like India and China, but the demand for specialized skills has also grown significantly in the US, Europe, and India, as shown below:

- In the US, the University of Phoenix has experienced 22.3% growth from 2008 to 2009; 16.8% growth from 2009 to 2010. Over 325,000 students were enrolled in online classes in 2012 (Apollo Group, 2013).
- According to the European Association of Distance Teaching Universities, about 500 European institutions provide short courses or entire programs at a distance. Student enrollment increased by 15%–20% in 2012, making online education a serious educational alternative in Europe.
- The Indira Gandhi National Open University (IGNOU) has dramatically increased enrollment since offering a distance e-learning mode and now serves over 4.2 million students in India and 36 other countries. IGNOU is currently the largest distance education institution in the world.

In his analysis on the worldwide market for self-paced e-learning, Adkins (2013) reported that the countries with the highest growth rates for digital learning were Vietnam, Malaysia, Romania, Azerbaijan, Thailand, Kenya, Slovakia, the Philippines, India, and China. They were all above 30%, which is four times the worldwide aggregate growth rate for online learning adoption. During the same period, there were dozens of countries with growth rates over 15%; they include Indonesia, Nigeria, Qatar, Oman, Poland, Russia, Tunisia, the Czech Republic, Tanzania, Brazil, Columbia, Bolivia, Hungary, Croatia, Bulgaria, Georgia, and Ukraine. Even if there is a worldwide growth in the adoption of digital learning solutions, the growth is more important in regions that do not have a sufficient "brick and mortar" infrastructure to answer their national demand in education (UNESCO, 2012).

In the following sections, we will look at different models of digital learning that are emerging. We will then look at the importance of modeling digital learning solutions to determine how they can better fit the growing needs of this more global and digital world.

A New Generation of Digital Learning Solutions

Even before the information revolution, scholars voiced their concerns about the limitation of the existing education model. Visionary thinkers like Clark Kerr (2001), former president of the UC system, foresaw the need for educational institutions to outgrow their physical and geographical boundaries. He coined the concept of "multiversity" to describe an educational world where universities collaborate across geographical borders. While Kerr's (2001) insights focused on American universities, the concept of multiversity is currently being used to transform individual universities as well as national educational systems (Fallis, 2007).

In the last decade, there has been a proliferation of new education and training models that have been supported by online and digital technologies (Faviero, 2012). Here are a few of the key models that have appeared:

a) **Large-scale distance education institutions**. From the beginning, distance education targeted niche needs from the geographically disperse to the highly specialized. In the last decade, distance education has gone beyond this niche mission to reach a mainstream status. In the developed countries, distance education institutions like the UK's Open University (250,000 students) or the University of Phoenix (225,000 students) in the United States have steadily grown to surpass the enrollments of their brick-and-mortar equivalent. In developing countries, distance education institutions have grown to become a significant method of delivering education to the general population. In India, the Indira Gandhi National Open University is the host to more than 4.2 million students. Currently, China is home to more than 70 different online colleges and universities with a few already showing enrollments of over a million students. These numbers are likely to grow in the coming years in order to meet the demand for skilled labor in China (ICEF, 2012). In the Middle East, there is a recent resurgence of distance education. Organizations such as the Arab Open University (AOU) have already more than 22,000 students in seven countries, where more than 50% of students are women.

b) **Open educational resources (OER) centers** are structured banks of online educational resources. Early attempts were around the concept of digital repositories (like Merlot and OER Commons) and allowed content developers to share the educational resources they created (Atkins, Brown, & Hammond, 2007). In 2006, the Khan Academy appeared as a tutoring tool for students and soon became an educational revolution (Kronholz, 2012). The Khan Academy provides structured instructional videos and tests to K–12 students, teachers, and schools systems. The emergence of such approaches has allowed educators and researchers to experiment with different types of delivery methods and test new models such as flipping the class. The flipped classroom approach proposes the use of technology to deliver instruction inside and outside the classroom. Because lectures can be done online, the teachers have more time to engage, interact, and provide feedback to students.

c) **Association of postsecondary institutions** is another interesting model to provide common online services, leveraging their common intellectual capital. Generally based around Clark Kerr's (2001) concept of "multiversity," these new online institutions offer a joint online marketing and delivery to institutions they represent. Many of these offer free access to their course material, but may require fees when students need some type of recognized accreditation (Faviero, 2012). Here are three examples of this model:

   I. **Coursera** was created in 2012 by Stanford professors Andrew Ng and Daphne Koller and is probably the best known of these solutions. Coursera is a for-profit organization mostly financed by venture capital, which offers courses from 33 universities, including Stanford, Princeton, and Caltech, but also includes partners in Canada, Scotland, India, and Switzerland (Faviero, 2012). Coursera mainly uses video lectures produced by university professors, interactive exercises, quizzes, and essays to reinforce course content. As of January of 2013, it was offering 213 university-level courses to over 1.9 million students from 196 countries (Coursera, 2013).

   II. **Udacity** was founded in 2011 by Stanford researchers David Stavens, Mike Sokolsky, and Google's Sebastian Thrun. Initially financed by Thrun and other venture capital firms, Udacity primarily offers courses in science and information technology (Faviero,

2012). With less than a year of operation, over 400,000 students have taken courses on this online platform. Reaching out to the information technology community, Udacity also offers computer science course in collaboration with major organizations like Google, Microsoft, Autodesk, Nvidia, and Wolfram Research ("Udacity," n.d., para. 6)

III. **EdX** is a nonprofit venture spearheaded by the Massachusetts Institute of Technology and Harvard University; each committing over $30 million to the project. Since May 2012, EdX offers free online university-level courses to a worldwide audience. The project grew out of the MITx initiative of MIT President Rafael Reif and Professor Anant Agarwal. Rapidly, other universities joined the "X University" consortium, including University of California, Berkeley; University of Texas Systems; Wellesley College; and Georgetown University. As of January of 2013, more than 150,000 students enrolled in EdX's first course, 6.002x: Circuits and Electronics. Learners earn a certificate issued by "X University" providing the course (Faviero, 2012).

d) Another model appearing in the last decade is the **global online accreditation** program. In this model, international organizations become global educational institutions (Patila & Codner, 2007). One such online program is a joint venture between the International Civil Aviation Organization (ICAO) and Airport Council International (ACI). The Airport Management Professional Accreditation Programme (AMPAP) (Behnke, 2012) was created in 2007 to develop a new generation of airport managers in strategic areas of airport business. Upon completion of this six courses blended program, students are awarded the International Airport Professional (IAP) designation accredited by both ICAO and ACI. In the first 5 years, over 800 airport professionals from 86 countries have taken courses in this specialized program, and 225 have already earned this accreditation.

e) **Massive open online course (MOOC)** is a recent incarnation on the use of online education. The term was coined by Dave Cormier of the University of Prince Edward Island, and Bryan Alexander of the National Institute for Technology in Liberal Education in 2008 ("Massive Open Online Course," n.d., para. 7). MOOCs are online courses where the course material is dispersed across the web. Constructed around the concepts of autonomy, connectedness, diversity, and openness in the educational process, MOOCs are mainly based on cognitivist principles. MOOC is an extension on the concept of digital repository, where a massive amount of instructional material is gathered on a specific course subject and offered to potential learners (Daniel, 2012)

It is still unclear which of these solutions will still be here at the end of this decade, but enthusiasm for new digital learning solutions is growing. Our next challenge as researchers and practitioners is to develop frameworks to analyze and possibly predict the impact and challenges these new digital learning solutions will bring.

A Proposed Framework to Analyze and Plan Digital Learning Ventures

In reviewing some of the digital learning ventures over the last two decades, one easily has the impression that there are as many digital learning failures as there are successes. To better understand this phenomenon, we need to investigate the different aspects of implementing digital learning in education and the workplace in order to recognize the factors that influence the success or failure of these ventures. According to Elloumi (2003), there are many reasons why digital learning ventures fail; they often include business, technical, and pedagogical issues.

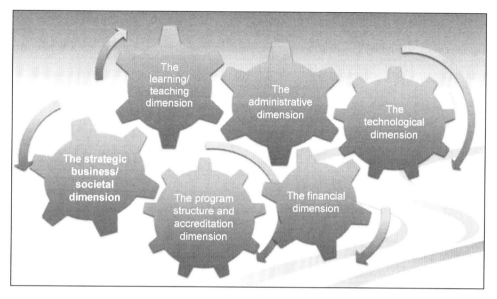

Figure 3.1   The Six (6) Dimensions of the Integrated Digital Learning Model

Initial attempts to analyze the inner workings of digital learning ventures (Woudstra & Powell, 1989) provided a few of the key facets of the organization, but these studies mostly focused on the pedagogical and the business aspects of the organization. Having professionally analyzed and reviewed over 15 digital learning ventures launched over the last two decades, we have refined the existing models and obtained six dimensions that organizations need to consider. We found that these dimensions seem to be intimately interconnected with each other. This is why we decided to use interconnecting cogs to illustrate the model of interdependence between each dimension (see Figure 3.1).

This representation also illustrates well that decisions made in any one of these may affect all the other dimensions. The cog model also represents this as an organic and iterative rather than linear process. In the next section, we will present a summary of each of the six dimensions and explain why these are essential components of a descriptive and prospective digital learning model.

The Strategic Business/Societal Dimension

This first dimension focuses on the needs, goals, and deliverables to be accomplished (Kaufman, Herman, & Watters, 2002). Organizations often consider digital learning solutions to answer some fundamental need, like increasing the access to instruction, developing competencies skills, or providing services for a disperse targeted population. Inspired by Roger Kaufman's "Mega Planning" model, this dimension links the micro or specific digital learning intervention to the larger goal of the organization or society it serves. It proposes that digital learning interventions must be more than surface interventions that are added on top of an existing organization. They need to be intimately aligned with the host organization. It should include requirements for new or updated processes and the impact it will have on organization and the society it serves (Kaufman, 2011). It should map out the main implications and even forecast some of the challenges one might encounter along the way (literacy, access to technology, budget, etc.).

This dimension is strategic as digital learning interventions are often linked to the success or growth of organizational and societal development. According to Global Partnership for Education (2013), training and education are often the keys to unlocking a country's potential for economic growth. They propose that even basic education in developing countries offers tangible results, such as

- each additional year of schooling increases an individual's potential income by up to 10%;
- four years of elementary schooling increases a farmer's productivity by nearly 9%;
- each additional year of education, in the population of a country, increases the annual GDP by 1%.

A good example is India's education and manpower strategy that included massive investment in digital learning solutions over the last two decades (King, 2012). Their strategic use of digital learning helped this country move from a status of underdeveloped to one of international economic leadership. The research on the impact of training and education is steadily growing and provides notable results when the digital learning interventions are aligned with the organizational or societal goals. This dimension is often the first and the last to be accomplished as it allows the project team to determine the needs and goals to be attained at the outset as well as validates whether these needs have been achieved at the end of the process.

The Learning/Teaching Dimension

As with all instructional ventures, there is an intimate relationship between learner characteristics, course content, and instructional strategies. Most instructional designers perform this type of analysis at the course or program level. We propose to extend this type of analysis to the organizational level. Based on the organization's mission statement, this dimension maps out the general characteristics of the different learners targeted and cross matches them to the different types of content to be disseminated. This process connects the characteristics of the learners to the specifications of the content to determine the optimal delivery and instructional strategies. This approach will allow developing general and specific instructional policies and processes to be used as guidelines to develop courses and programs.

This type of mapping is particularly useful when planning a digital learning intervention that targets multiple territories or a loosely specified targeted population. During the development of the AMPAP, this type of mapping identified multiple learners and content characteristics such as language proficiency, technical prerequisites, and collaborative style. It also helped to plan the digital learning environment and the instructional strategies that best fit this diverse and international population.

The Program Structure and Accreditation Dimension

This dimension looks at the way the courses and programs are presented to the population of learners. This dimension investigates how instructional material is packaged and what certificate, diploma, or accreditations are offered once the activities are successfully completed. Closely linked to the strategic business/societal and learning/teaching dimensions, this dimension defines how the program structure and the accreditation offered will bring perceived and tangible value to the targeted learners. In too many online programs, it is difficult to define the actual value of the instruction obtained (Coats, 1999). Many institutions now go out of their way to explain how students will benefit from successfully completing their courses or programs. Institutions like University of Phoenix or the Indira Gandhi National Open University offer a clear rationale on how a course or program may fit in an individual career path and explain their societal mission in this process. Other programs such as the AMPAP have gone further by creating an industry-wide accreditation, the IAP.

This process is often associated with the marketing of a program, but it has become an essential part in the credibility of any digital learning institution. Early digital learning institutions were often associated with online diploma mills (Piña, 2010), where devious online organizations would grant worthless degrees to unsuspecting learners. To prevent the contamination from less credible institutions, many digital learning institutions have now joined national accrediting organizations and offer nationally or internationally recognized diplomas. Another factor is the structure of the program and course catalogue. Many early digital learning projects were an addition to existing offerings, where students needed to go through separated systems, registrations, and catalogues. More recent approaches offer integrated programs or blended competency-based approaches where students are guided through the different types of material. Mapping out the programs, competency, or certification paths greatly helps to see how the students flow through the organization and identifies peaks/bottlenecks for each instructional activity. In this process, the team can identify mandatory and electives activities, prerequisites, and potential challenges in the delivery schedule.

The Administrative Dimension

This fourth dimension looks at administrative activities and how they create a good environment for targeted students. This information might not be essential to attract students, but it is often one of the key aspects to keep them in digital learning programs. Starting with course-centered policies such as grading schema, attendance, and grade reevaluation, these types of administrative processes can make an important difference on how a program is perceived by the student population. Other elements focused on program administration, such as tuition fees, payment methods, drop out/course change policy, equivalencies, and time to completion can also favor or restrict student flow in the instructional activities. For example, in the AMPAP administrative factors were found to have crucial impact in the success of the program, as administrative procedures needed to fit well with the complex schedule and lifestyle of airport professionals registering to the program.

The administration of financial support such as grants and bursaries may also be critical for programs reaching a clientele that has modest financial resources. Administrative processes in a blended or hybrid environment are particularly challenging, as they need to adapt to multiple modes of instructional delivery. Unless they are handled by one generic process, they may create student confusion and frustration. Defining and mapping out the flow of administrative processes helps to understand how these processes need to be performed or integrated in the existing administrative structure. In many digital learning projects, some of the administrative tasks are duplicated or added on top of the existing process giving administrators, teachers, and students additional work.

The Financial Dimension

One dimension that is often partially overlooked in the implementation of digital learning projects is the operational financial aspect. Let's here distinguish between implementation cost and long-term sustainability expenditures. Most digital learning projects require substantial initial investment to offer services. These include the financing of the initial technical infrastructure, the development of courses, and administrative organization. Developing a financial framework for a digital learning organization is a challenge in itself, but the initial investment alone will not ensure the survival of the project. After the initial implementation, long-term sustainability requires a different financing model. It should allow the project to minimally cover the operating cost and, in some cases, growth. Many corporations using digital learning are now requiring projects to become cost neutral or self-sustaining. This means that all sources of funding must be identified and mapped out for both the implementation and the long-term operation of the project. These may include the following:

- The financial support from the parent organization
- Tuition and fee model
- Funding from benefactors, governments, and foundations
- Funding from advertising, sponsorships, or other commercial sources
- Funding from loans and investors

One of the key challenges in this dimension is to distinguish between projection and valid estimates. Tuition fees are an example to illustrate this difference. One can easily make a projection of the tuition revenues by arbitrarily setting tuition-fee levels. A more valid estimation would analyze the tuition cost that the students or parent organizations are willing to pay for that service. Too many times, tuition fees are inflated, thus reducing enrollment levels and overall funding. Once credible sources of funding are identified, they need to be integrated in the project timeline. The incoming funds and expenditures are mapped out to forecast the financial health at different stages of development and operation.

The financial dimension is often a reality check between the needs, the organization to best address it, and the financial means available. Far from being an obstacle to the development of such ventures, it is usually an eye-opener for the parent organization that may then start looking at alternative models of financing and operation. For an organization strapped for funds, the review of the financial dimension often opens the possibility to other sources of funding or partnering with complementary organizations that were rejected initially. In the last decade, we have seen an increased variety of funding for digital learning ventures. This trend will more than likely continue and grow.

The Technological Dimension

The technological dimension is often felt as one of the most challenging aspects of integrating new digital learning solutions. Yet, many digital learning implementations start with the assumption that we need to first look at the technical possibilities that are available, and then evaluate how these can answer the needs of the organization and targeted population. In that context, numerous digital learning implementations use technological solutions that only achieve a portion of the needs and requirements. The balance between what technologies can offer at any given time and the real needs of an organization raises the question on whether we should risk implementing technological solutions that partially respond to the need of the organization (Van Den Ende & Dolfsma, 2005). Too often, technological solutions do not fulfill key administrative, educational, or financial needs. This is often amplified by the fact that few organizations have IT professionals that have strong digital learning technology experience among their ranks.

In this model, we propose that the technical dimension should be the last to be investigated as it may limit or contaminate the needs defined in other dimensions. Only then should we identify the gap between the technical possibilities available and the defined needs. This will greatly help determine the overall impact of the functionalities that are missing or partially addressed. The process itself remains fairly straightforward, where requirements and processes are compared to software functionalities, each being weighted on their compliance and importance to the project. Once the technological dimension is analyzed, we need to go back to all six dimensions and determine what are the remaining challenges and acceptable compromises. Revisiting afterwards all of the dimensions ensures that no one dimension is left to operate in a vacuum, but rather all dimensions work together in a global model.

Minimally, the technological dimension should answer all key requirements for course development and delivery while streamlining administrative processes to reduce their negative impact on students, teachers, and administrators.

Using This Modeling Approach

First, let us say that this chapter only represents a summary of the modeling approach proposed and that each dimension could be described in much more detail. The basic idea behind this model is to develop a system perspective to analyze, plan, and implement digital learning projects. We propose that the six dimensions should be considered as an iterative process that requires analytical thinking and synthesis.

In a *first phase*, a general overview of all six dimensions should be performed to gather the key needs and challenges. It is usually recommended to start with the business/societal and learning/teaching dimensions as they offer a more global perspective and will greatly help for the development of other dimensions. In particular cases, where the goal of the organization is not clear, the other dimensions may offer guidelines to help plan the goal and target of the project.

In a *second phase*, each dimension is revised to consider all the information gathered. Once all requirements and needs from all the different dimensions are assembled, then the team determines how they could influence each other. During this phase, the project team produces a list of conflicting issues and potential solutions/compromises as the global digital learning model is assembled.

In *the third and last official phase*, the organization refers back to the business/societal dimension to ensure that the proposed model answers the goals and needs previously defined and decides whether the project should still go forward. It is not abnormal that organizations withdraw from these ventures once all information has been gathered and they better understand the required resources (financial, human, and technical) to sustain such a venture. Another interesting result occurring at this stage is that organizations may reassess their initial assumptions and accept new out-of-scope possibilities. This is what happens in many global or international organizations when they start with the assumption that they would do this venture completely internally. Once they realize all the implications, many of them understand the need to integrate partners or other financial sources to ensure the sustainability of their digital learning ventures.

Conclusion

As we witness an explosion of new digital learning models appearing in the educational and training landscape, it becomes crucial to develop better investigative tools to analyze, plan, and implement these types of projects. Organizations that want to leverage digital learning solutions need to gather all the necessary information in these six dimensions to obtain sustainable results from these solutions.

The framework presented in this chapter is the first version of a model that has already been applied in over a dozen organizations. The main advantage of this approach is that it offers a more global system perspective that should help guide both theorists and practitioners in their use of digital learning. It will also help envision the different challenges that need to be addressed and the key interrelations that need to be mapped out. We are convinced that this type of modeling will evolve, and we hope it can be used as a starting point to ensure more productive and successful digital learning implementations.

References

Adkins, S. S. (2013). *The worldwide market for self-paced eLearning products and services: 2011–2016 forecast and analysis.* Monroe, WA: Ambient Insight.

Allen I. E., & Seaman, J. (2011). *Going the distance: Online education in the United States.* Babson Park, MA: Babson Survey Research Group, Babson College.

Apollo Group. (2013). *2012 Apollo group annual report.* Phoenix, AZ: Author.

ASTD. (2012). *2012 State of the industry report.* Alexandria, VA: Author.

Atkins, D. E., Brown, J. S., & Hammond, A. L. (2007). *A review of the open educational resources (OER) movement: Achievements, challenges, and new opportunities.* Menlo Park, CA: The William and Flora Hewlett Foundation.

Behnke, P. (2012). Accredited training for airport management: The ACI/ICAO global AMPAP programme. *Journal of Airport Management, 6*(2), 191–194.

Bernard, R. M., Abrami, P. C., Borokhovski, E., Wade, A., Wozney, L., Wallet, P. A., . . . Huang, B. (2004). How does distance education compare with classroom instruction? A meta-analysis of the empirical literature. *Review of Educational Research, 74*(3), 379–439. doi.10.3102/00346543074003379

Bernard, R. M., Abrami, P. C., Borokhovski, E., Wade, C. A., Tamim, R. M., Surkes, M. A., & Bethel, E. C. (2009). A meta-analysis of three types of interaction treatments in distance education. *Review of Educational Research, 79*(3), 1243–1289.

Clark, R. C., & Mayer, R. E. (2008). *E-learning & the science of instruction.* San Francisco, CA: Pfeiffer.

Coats, M. (1999). *Lifelong learning policy and practice: The impact of accreditation on education and training provision for adult women in the UK.* (ERIC Document Reproduction Service No. ED 470495)

Coursera (2013). About Coursera. *Coursera.org.* Retrieved January 6, 2013 from https://www.coursera.org/about

Daniel, J. (2012) *Making sense of MOOCs: Musings in a maze of myth, paradox and possibility.* Research paper presented as a fellow of the Korea National Open University. Retrieved from http://sirjohn.ca/wordpress/wpcontent/uploads/2012/08/120925MOOCspaper2.pdf

Elloumi, F. (2003) Value chain analysis: A strategic approach to online learning in theory and practice of online learning. In T. Anderson & F. Elloumi (Eds.), *Theory and practice of online learning* (pp. 61–92). Athabasca, Alberta, Canada: Athabasca University.

Fallis, G. (2007) *Multiversities, ideas, and democracy.* Toronto, Ontario, Canada: University of Toronto Press.

Faviero, B. F. (2012) Comparing Khan academy, Coursera, Udacity, & edX missions, offerings. *Distance Education Report, 16*(19), 8.

Global Partnership for Education. (2013). *The global partnership for education report 2011–2014.* Retrieved from http://www.globalpartnership.org/our-work/areas-of-focus/aid-effectiveness/

ICEF. (2012). *8 countries leading the way in online education.* ICEF monitor. Retrieved from http://monitor.icef.com/2012/06/8-countries-leading-the-way-in-online-education/

Kaufman, R. (2011). *The manager's pocket guide to mega thinking and planning.* Amherst, MA: HRD Press.

Kaufman, R., Herman, J. J., & Watters, K. (2002). *Educational planning: strategic, tactical, operational.* Lanham, MD, Scarecrow Press.

Kerr, C. (2001). *The uses of the university.* Cambridge, MA: Harvard University Press.

King, K. (2012). The geopolitics and meanings of India's massive skills development ambitions. *International Journal of Educational Development, 32*(5), 665–673.

Kronholz, J. (2012). Can Khan move the bell curve to the right? *Education Digest, 78*(2), 23–30.

Massive Open Online Course. (n.d.). Wikipedia. Retrieved from http://en.wikipedia.org/wiki/Massive_open_online_course

Oncu, S., & Cakir, H. (2011). Research in online learning environments: Priorities and methodologies. *Computers & Education, 57*(1), 1098–1108.

Patila, A., & Codner, G. (2007). Accreditation of engineering education: Review observations and proposal for global accreditation. *European Journal of Engineering Education, 32*(6), 639–651.

Piña, A. A. (2010). Online diploma mills: Implications for legitimate distance education. *Distance Education, 31*(1), 121–126.

Semiral, O., & Hasan, C. (2011) Research in online learning environments: Priorities and methodologies. *Computers & Education, 57*(1), 1098–1108.

Tamim, R. M., Bernard, R. M., Borokhovski, E., Abrami, P. C., & Schmid, R. F. (2011). What forty years of research says about the impact of technology on learning: A second-order meta-analysis and validation study. *Review of Educational Research, 81*(1), 4–28.

Udacity. (n.d.) Wikipedia. Retrieved from http://en.wikipedia.org/wiki/Udacity

UNESCO Institute for Statistics. (2012). *Global education digest 2012.* Montreal, Canada: Author.

Van Den Ende, J., & Dolfsma, W. (2005). Technology push, demand pull and the shaping of technological paradigms—Patterns in the development of computing technology. *Journal of Evolutionary Economics, 15*(1), 83–99.

Woudstra, A., & Powell, R. (1989). Value chain analysis: A framework for management of distance education. *The American Journal of Distance Education, 3*(3), 7–21.

4

Mobile Learning in Higher Education
Current Status and Future Possibilities

Yasemin Gülbahar, Carolyne Jacobs, and Andreas König

What Is Mobile Learning?

Education paradigms are shifting. In many instances, online and blended learning solutions are part of the learning environment. Mobile technologies are beginning to feature in this mix. The use of personal, wireless, mobile, portable and handheld devices has increased dramatically from small-scale, short-term trials to larger, more sustained and blended deployment (Traxler, 2009). The growth in use of mobile devices is followed by widespread usage of apps, changing the way people communicate and access information:

> Smartphones including the iPhone and Android have redefined what we mean by mobile computing, and in the past three to four years, the small, often simple, low cost software extensions to these devices—apps—have become a hotbed of development.
>
> *(Johnson, Adams, & Cummins, 2012, p. 10)*

This use of mobile devices and applications in the learning environment has lead to the concept of mobile learning or *m-learning*.

Mobile technology allows students to become nomads, "carrying on conversations and thinking across campus spaces, as always, but now with the ability to Google a professor's term, upload a comment to a class board, and check for updates to today's third assignment—all while striding across the quad" (Alexander, 2004, p. 31). Similarly, Geddes (2004) defines m-learning as " the acquisition of any knowledge and skill through using mobile technology, anywhere, anytime, that results in an alteration in behaviour" (p. 1). El-Hussein and Cronje (2010) conceptualize m-learning from three different perspectives: mobility of technology, mobility of learner and mobility of learning especially in the higher education landscape.

Mobile learning facilitates individual and collaborative learning, as well as offering opportunities for increased freedom and independence; it engenders with the concept of learning anytime and everywhere. El-Hussein and Cronje describe m-learning as "any type of learning that takes place in learning environments and spaces that take account of the mobility of technology, mobility of learners and mobility of learning" (El-Hussein & Cronje, 2010, p. 20).

Mobile learning is redefining the processes and roles in education, technology and society. From an educational context, one could question whether existing theories for learning and instructional design practice recognize and offer sufficient opportunities to utilize m-learning effectively, and if pedagogical frameworks should now incorporate more collaborative and independent learning activities made possible by mobile technology.

The above discussion highlights current thinking surrounding the notion of m-learning; the next section considers developments which have lead to the important role mobile technologies play in many peoples' lives and why educationalists cannot ignore these developments.

Growth of Mobile Technologies

The past 15 years have seen a growth in the speed and sophistication of networks, an increase in the number of people accessing the Internet and the development of a wide range of different mobile devices. In the last 10 years the emergence of wireless networks, broadband access, increasing bandwidth, quicker transmission speeds and the multiple use of devices, including smartphones, tablets and readers, has a major effect on when and how users access the Internet and how they communicate with each other.

By 2012, over a third (34.3%) of the world's population were online, and in Europe, 63.5% of the population were connected to the Internet (Internet World Stats, 2012). In the United Kingdom, Switzerland and Turkey, the percentage of the population online in 2011 was 85%, 84% and 40%, respectively (Worldwide Independent Network of Market Research [WIN], 2012). In the late 1990s, communication technologies reached new levels of sophistication, and in the early 2000s, broadband access started to replace many dial-up services in Europe, allowing speedier download of data and quicker communications. Wireless networks were introduced in the 1990's; initially adoption was slow, but after 2005 there was an exponential increase in the number of wireless networks and wireless data traffic as many private households, commercial organizations and public institutions in Europe started to implement wireless networks.

Europe has experienced the highest growth in mobile data traffic. The overall growth rate between 2010 and 2015 is predicted to be 193% (Portio, 2012, p. 16). Mobile phones have become increasingly sophisticated in recent years. 3G phones, incorporating services over a wider area and better data transfer rates, became increasingly popular after 2005. Data transmission speeds increased further and the stability of services improved with the introduction of 4G networks, although at the time of writing these have yet to become available in some areas of Europe.

Corresponding developments have taken place regarding the availability of mobile devices. Mobile subscriptions increased globally from 4.5 billion in 2009 to 6 billion at the start of 2012. This growth is likely to continue, with numbers predicted to reach 8 billion by the end of 2016 (Portio, 2012, p. 7). At the beginning of 2012, 86.1% of the world's population had a mobile subscription; in Europe, the percentage stood at 131.4%, with many individuals having more than one subscription (Portio, 2012).

The ownership of tablets is relatively low in comparison to that of traditional mobile phones and smartphones, but tablet ownership is starting to grow. Companies are now launching a wider range of tablets and readers, offering users more choice. This expansion has resulted in increased traffic and data downloads via mobile devices. Research suggests that ownership of traditional mobile phones, computers and laptops is decreasing, whereas that of smartphones and tablets is increasing (WIN, 2012).

The growth in smartphone usage, data traffic and applications (apps) downloads is underpinned by an increase in bandwidth. Worldwide broadband uptake grew exponentially between 2006 and 2011. Adoption was particularly noticeable in Europe where bandwidth per Internet user was the highest in the world in 2011 (ITU, 2012). The cost of data transmission has fallen, making it cheaper for users to download data and communicate with others via smartphone or tablet. Abraham and Schuster (2012, p. 13) noted that the cost per MB worldwide fell by 86% between 2008 and 2011. It is clear from this discussion that users are able to download more data, using more devices, quicker and easier today than they could do previously. But what type of data are they downloading and what are they using their mobile devices for?

Individuals have traditionally used mobile phones for communication. This is still the most popular activity, although text messaging has overtaken voice calls in the top spot. The advent of smartphones with computer-like operating systems, and the growth in associated data services, has seen a rapid growth in users accessing emails and downloading mobile media (ComScore, 2012). After text messaging, the four most popular activities are taking photos, accessing news and information, accessing the web using the browser and accessing the web via apps (ComScore, 2012). The third and fourth of these activities are not mutually exclusive. Many users use both and tailor their activity according to their location. There has been a noticeable escalation in app downloads, which increased by a factor of nine between 2009 and 2011 (Portio, 2012). In 2011, the percentage of the total mobile audience who used apps to access the web was similar to the percentage that used a browser to access the Internet (ComScore, 2012).

What are the implications of these changes for practitioners in the higher education sector? Has the growth in Internet technologies and mobile devices had an impact on how students want to learn and the learning environment? These questions are explored next.

Mobile Device Platforms and Technologies

The significant rise and spread of mobile operating systems started in the 1990s with the Palm and later Windows CE and Symbian systems closely followed by Bada, Blackberry OS and iOS.

Gartner (2012) reported that at the end of Q3 in 2012, the share in the worldwide sales of mobile devices, analyzed by deliverer, showed Samsung (22.9% of global sales to end users or nearly 98 million devices) and Nokia (19.2% or more than 82 million devices) were the top sellers. This is followed by Apple (5.5%), ZTE (3.9%) and LG Electronics (with 3.3%). These figures indicate a noticeable gap. At the same time (Q3), Gartner (2012) showed that the Android was the top mobile operating system worldwide. According to the analyst, more than 122 million Android-based devices had been sold in 2012, representing a market share of 72.4%. iOS made it to 23.5 million devices, or 13.9% of market share. With numbers of devices rising, users demanded additional functionality. Developers tried to deliver a consistent user experience on different platforms and operating systems by employing HTML5, CSS3 and JavaScript (Hartmann, Stead, & DeGani, 2011, p. 2).

The same authors (Hartmann et al., 2011, p. 3) suggested that similar results producing native apps with high performance and integrated technical features can be achieved by cross-compiling, based on developing frameworks that provide application programming interfaces (API) independent of operating systems used (e.g., JavaScript, Ruby or Java). However, this functionality is complex to build and needs to be usable over a number of different platforms. An alternative method is to deploy a virtual machine around the mobile app that simulates the target operating system and thus makes the app work in a number of different environments and delivers high portability and flexibility. A further method is to create a web app that runs in the user's mobile browser using HTML5 and CSS3 with rendering engines like WebKit. In this case, the app runs either in a standalone browser or in another app that integrates a browser view called "hybrid web" (Hartmann et al., 2011, p. 4). In the hybrid case, a native app bridges the desired functions that run in the browser instance to the hardware of the mobile device. Both interfaces, native app and browser instance, communicate via JavaScript or dedicated APIs. This solution is quite popular because it combines the flexibility of the app with the performance of the native device hardware.

Another method that can be used to deploy software on mobile devices is the widget approach. A widget is a small and specialized tool delivering one specific function to the user. Many mobile operating platforms and browsers offer such widgets. However, standardization has not been achieved in the widget approach and may result in developers having to create a range of different apps or widgets to suit different devices. JavaScript, together with a wrapper API, can be used as a general mediating language between most widgets and the respective platforms (Hartmann et al., 2011, p. 5).

Several development frameworks exist. Hartmann et al. (2011, p. 5) classified them into four types—namely, library, framework, platform and product/service. Typical and widespread open source platforms include Rhodes, Phonegap, Appcelerator, MoSync, JQueryMobile and QT.

Based on their technological approach to software development and deployment, Hartmann et al. (2011, 14f) categorized nine different types of m-learning:

1. mVLE-based: mobile extension to a common LMS;
2. content delivery: traditional linear relationship;
3. record of achievement: m-devices record achievements in a portfolio;
4. just-in-time-training;
5. social learning: the m-devices support peer interaction;
6. enhanced reality: augmented reality functions enhance the learning process;
7. learning support: the m-device facilitates learning from other sources (e.g., dictionaries for reading/speaking);
8. experience-based learning: the m-device enhances the user's experience (e.g., offering orientation functions, a camera, etc.); and
9. game-based learning.

These categories represent theoretical constructs and do not necessarily exist as such. They are not mutually exclusive, and some of them may not relate to m-learning and refer to specific situations of use that can intermingle. For example, a concrete learning situation may show aspects of these different types. However, the typology is useful to differentiate between various aspects of usage scenarios as well as approaches that can be used to develop and deploy the software on mobile devices.

Adding this understanding to the development of mobile technology assists in framing a perspective for the existing and potential research in m-learning. The next section of this discussion provides an overview of research and the evolution of m-learning to date.

Mobile Learning Research

For many students in higher education, mobile phones, smartphones and tablets are an integral part of their daily lives. Anecdotal information suggests they use these devices mainly for social interaction and entertainment. Educators and researchers are conscious that students' engagement with mobile devices offers learning and teaching opportunities; Ng'ambi and Lombe (2012, p. 181) stated that "converge social and entertainment uses of mobile devices to scaffold student learning and foster deep engagement with content." In a move to better understand the role that mobile technologies has on students' learning, and could have in the future, a number of researchers are focusing on this area.

Alzaza and Yaakub (2011) explored students' awareness and expectations of m-learning services by investigating higher education students' experiences in Malaysia. They suggest that students in higher education today have adequate technical skills, awareness and self-motivation to use mobile technologies to support their learning. In addition, they conclude that many higher institutions have the necessary technological infrastructure to implement m-learning activities within the curriculum. Alzaza and Yaakub's study identifies that students used mobile devices to access (in order of popularity) assessment results, course registrations, their calendar and schedule services. The study also highlighted a number of barriers. They found that the cost of transaction, slow data exchange due to inefficient networks and concerns over confidentiality of personal information could present obstacles and prevent the widespread implementation of m-learning activities within institutions (Alzaza & Yaakub, 2011).

Uzunboylu, Cavus and Ercag (2009) investigated the increased use of mobile technologies, data services and multimedia messaging systems and students' increasing awareness of the potential use of mobile technology in the learning environment. Their findings indicated that students used mobile phones to capture images of specified environmental issues and then forwarded the images via phone, and exchanged relevant information via SMS messages with other students in their group. The study reveals that many students are aware that mobile technologies can be used to support their academic development and learning, and in many cases are already using them unofficially. Furthermore, the study suggests that the use of mobile technologies could improve engagement and help develop positive attitudes toward learning.

A number of studies have focused on the impact of m-learning on student outcomes or performance. McConatha, Praul and Lynch (2008) conducted a research study in the US to investigate the impact of introducing mobile access to help students access and review study materials. Findings show that implementing this flexible type of approach had a positive effect on performance. In a similar study, Wong, Chin, Tan and Liu (2010) investigated the role of m-learning in a language-learning context. They examine how mobile devices could be used to create artefacts to support mobile assisted language learning (MALL), a methodology which emphasizes learner-created content and contextualized meaning. In this study, students used smartphones to capture photographs of the real-life contexts that related to the language areas being studied. They subsequently used these images as the basis for written or spoken work. Wong et al. concluded that using mobile technologies in a blended learning environment leads to authentic learning experiences for many students.

Jeng, Wu, Huang, Tan and Yang (2010) proposed an m-learning design framework that focuses on mobile users, learning strategies, and situated environments and they stress the importance of underpinning m-learning activities with sound pedagogical strategies. They argue that mobile technology supports the development of "situated classrooms" by allowing students to communicate with each other in class, access relevant data or use built-in functionality, such as a camera or GPS receiver on their mobile device, to create an augmented knowledge-context environment. In contrast, Boyinbode, Bagula and Ngambi (2011) maintained that non-situated, flexible access to learning materials (e.g., podcasts, videos) via mobile devices can support student learning from any location.

Mobile collaborative learning (MCL) environments build on the social, student-to-student or student-to-lecturer communications within the education environment. Lee (2011) introduced the theoretical and technical foundations for designing and developing an MCL application to support student learning. Lee developed and tested a prototype app, based on students' pedagogical requirements, which could be used to facilitate collaborative working and sharing of learning materials. Lee concluded that mobile technologies could provide a useful tool to facilitate interactions which lead to shared understanding.

Järvelä, Näykki, Laru and Luokkanen (2007) explored the use of wireless networks and mobile tools to scaffold collaborative learning. They conducted three design experiments, based on the notion of collaborative learning as an activity with socially shared origins of cognition and self-regulated learning. All experiments investigated innovative ways to structure and regulate individual and collaborative learning using smartphones. The first study explores facilitating students' self-regulated learning processes, the second study encouraged scaffolded collaboration and the third focused on how blended collaborative learning can be used to facilitate socially shared collaboration and community building. Järvelä et al. concluded that mobile devices can contribute to student learning by providing students with additional opportunities that may not otherwise be available, and that they help students engage in meaningful interactions to support shared understanding.

Gupta and Manjrekar (2012) investigated the potential of mobile technologies to bridge the gap between students' expectations and experiences of higher education. Improvements in the quality of higher education were found in collaboration between other institutions and research facilities, bridging the gap between classroom teaching and real-life implementations, teaching strategies and employability of graduates. Mobile technologies have the potential to help bridge the gaps experienced between expectations and experiences and between university learning and the world of work, consequently bringing about improvements in the quality of some aspects of higher education.

Osang, Tsuma and Ngole (2013) delivered empirical data on the implementation of m-learning in the context of Nigerian Open University. Given the high percentage of the availability of mobile devices (with 63.9%), they regard m-learning as "a means to face the endemic crisis in Sub Saharan Africa's teaching and learning development systems" (Osang et al., 2013, p. 3). They discuss the challenges of implementation and conclude that m-learning might be a new trend to revolutionize education in Africa (p. 13), the success of which depends on the insight of users into efficiency and necessity of the respective services and features.

The discussion in this section focuses on the current practice in higher education and theories relating to m-learning in higher education. What conclusions can be drawn? And how can these ideas be taken forward to support students' learning in the near future?

Conclusion

Mobile technologies are now part of everyday life for many people, including students at university. This chapter suggests that students are using mobile devices for learning and that institutions are starting to provide services to support m-learning, and it highlights some of the current research in the area.

It is clear that there are some noticeable gaps in practice and in the literature. First, there is a limited amount of available information about sustainable institution-wide m-learning developments and few recommendations about how to embed m-learning into the curricula. Second, there appears to be a lack of understanding about the pedagogical value of m-learning.

Wishart and Green (2011) pointed to several possible reasons for the lack of institute-wide developments. These include, the lack of skills to facilitate development, the need of appropriate advice and support usage, limited procurement and accounting policies around computer usage, legal issues surrounding data ownership, and concerns about privacy. In addition, the current pressures on staff time lead to lack of resources or enthusiasm to reformat the curricula to accommodate mobile technology.

The focus of many research activities to date is on implementation and student feedback, perhaps indicative of early stage technical developments. Mobile technology has moved beyond the early adopter stage and there are high levels of saturation in many societies. Mobile device ownership is growing rapidly and an increasing number of students use smartphones and tablets, officially or unofficially, as part of their learning. Although technology facilitates learning, it cannot do so without sound underpinning pedagogy.

The current lack of understanding about pedagogical integrity of m-learning is illustrated by a comment made by Koszalka and Ntloedibe-Kuswani (2010, p. 153): "The potential benefits of m-learning are not yet understood from the perspective of either safe or disruptive uses." This viewpoint suggests that further research about m-learning is required to provide a greater understanding about the following key areas:

- How mobile technologies can be used to enhance effectiveness of teaching;
- the role of mobile technologies in supporting individual differences of students, both in terms of preferred learning approaches and subject disciplines;
- using mobile technologies to enhance collaboration and sharing, either for student-to-student or student-to-teacher activities.

Koszalka and Ntloedibe-Kuswani (2010) argued that research is needed to ensure that mobile technology is used to support good curricula design and positive learning experiences. Similarly, Jeng et al. (2010) concluded that "to create new innovative learning opportunities, one needs to take into account the usability and the rationality" (p. 8) of m-learning as an embedded element within the curriculum.

Further studies are required to identify sound pedagogical frameworks to guide colleagues about how best to integrate m-learning into the curricula, create activities which support student learning and offer engaging and satisfying learning experiences. More medium-term or large-scale studies need to be conducted to provide a sound evidence-base. Koszalka and Ntloedibe-Kuswani (2010) suggested that studies to establish the pedagogic integrity of mobile technology would benefit from using the following:

- Experimental or quasiexperimental design;
- follow-up studies for looking at remediation;
- random and clustered sampling (mostly convenience samples);
- really reliable and valid measurement instruments;
- control mechanisms for possible threats to validity and biases;
- mention or address technology problems;
- grounded theory; and
- instructional design strategies.

An additional concern for practitioners in higher education, and elsewhere, is the longevity of any strategies or activities that they implement. Technology has changed rapidly over the last few years and is likely to continue to do so. Future technical developments will inevitably have an impact on individuals' lives and are likely to present new teaching and learning opportunities. The 2012 *Horizon Report* identifies a number of technologies likely to impact teaching and learning over the next few years. They suggest that developments over the next 2 to 3 years could include game-based learning and learning analytics resulting in data-gathering tools to provide better understanding about student engagement and learning. Over the next 4 or 5 years, relevant developments will include gesture-based computing and the Internet of things connecting the physical and digital worlds in order to provide real-time information (Johnson et al., 2012).

Other areas of development are augmented reality (AR), pervasive learning (learning anywhere, anytime, any data and from any device), open educational resources (OER) and massive open online courses (MOOCs).

There is clearly an exciting future ahead for practitioners and students in higher education. The latest developments in technology including mobile technologies have the potential to become an important element in the learning and teaching environment. However, there is also much work still to do in understanding that potential and how it relates to better learning experiences for students and teaching experiences for staff in higher education.

References

Abraham, L. & Schuster, R. (2012, January 23). *Connected Europe: How smartphones and tablets are shifting media consumption*. Presentation at Digital Life Design Conference, Munich, Germany. Retrieved from www.comscore.com/Press_Events/Presentations_Whitepapers/2012/Connected_Europe

Alexander, B. (2004). Going nomadic: Mobile learning in higher education. *EDUCAUSE Review, 39*(5), 28–35.

Alzaza, N. S., & Yaakub, A. R. (2011). Students' awareness and requirements of mobile learning services in the higher education environment. *American Journal of Economics and Business Administration, 3*(1), 95–100.

Boyinbode, O., Bagula, A., & Ngambi, D. (2011). An opencast mobile learning framework for enhancing learning in higher education. *International Journal of u- and e- Service, Science and Technology, 4*(3), 11–18.

ComScore. (2012). *2012 Mobile future in focus*. Retrieved from http://www.comscore.com/Insights/Presentations_and_Whitepapers/2012/2012_Mobile_Future_in_Focus

El-Hussein, M.O.M., & Cronje, J. C. (2010). Defining mobile learning in the higher education landscape. *Educational Technology & Society, 13*(3), 12–21.

Gartner Inc. (2012). *Press release: Gartner says worldwide sales of mobile phones declined 3 percent in third quarter of 2012; smartphone sales increased 47 percent*. Retrieved from http://www.gartner.com/newsroom/id/2237315

Geddes, S. (2004) Mobile learning in the 21st century: Benefit for learners. *The Knowledge Tree: An e-Journal of Learning Innovation*. Retrieved from http://knowledgetree.flexiblelearning.net.au/edition06/download/geddes.pdf

Gupta, M., & Manjrekar, P. (2012). Using mobile learning to enhance quality in higher education. *SIES Journal of Management, 8*(1), 23–30.

Hartmann, G., Stead, G., & DeGani, A. (2011). *Cross-platform mobile app development*. Cambridge, UK: Tribal Labs Group. Retrieved from http://www.mole-project.net/images/documents/deliverables/WP4_crossplatform_mobile_development_March2011.pdf

Internet World Stats. (2012). *Usage and population statistics: Internet users in Europe, June 30, 2012*. Retrieved from http://www.internetworldstats.com/stats4.htm

ITU. (2012). *ICT facts and figures*. Retrieved from http://www.itu.int/ict

Järvelä, S., Näykki, P., Laru, J., & Luokkanen, T. (2007). Structuring and regulating collaborative learning in higher education with wireless networks and mobile tools. *Educational Technology & Society, 10*(4), 71–79.

Jeng, Y. L., Wu, T. T., Huang, Y. M., Tan, Q. & Yang, S. J.H. (2010). The add-on impact of mobile applications in learning strategies: A review study. *Educational Technology & Society, 13*(3), 3–11.

Johnson, L., Adams, S., & Cummins, M. (2012). *The NMC Horizon Report: 2012 higher education edition*. Austin, TX: The New Media Consortium. Retrieved from http://www.nmc.org/pdf/2012-horizon-report-HE.pdf

Koszalka, T. A., & Ntloedibe-Kuswani, G. S. (2010). Literature on the safe and disruptive learning potential of mobile technologies. *Distance Education, 31*(2), 139–157.

Lee, K. B. (2011). Developing mobile collaborative learning applications for mobile users. *International Journal of Interactive Mobile Technologies (iJIM), 5*(4), 42–48.

McConatha, D., Praul, M., & Lynch, M. J. (2008). Mobile learning in higher education: An empirical assessment of a new educational tool. *The Turkish Online Journal of Educational Technology (TOJET), 7*(3), Article 2, 15–21.

Ng'ambi, D., & Lombe, A. (2012). Using podcasting to facilitate student learning: A constructivist perspective. *Educational Technology & Society, 15*(4), 181–192.

Osang, F. B., Tsuma, C., & Ngole, J. (2013, February 20–23). *Prospects and challenges of mobile learning in implementation: Nigeria: Case study National Open University of Nigeria (NOUN)*. International Conference on ICT for Africa 2013, Harare, Zimbabwe. Retrieved from http://ictforafrica.org/attachments/section/4/ict4africa2013_submission_50.pdf

Portio. (2012). *Portio research mobile factbook 2012*. Retrieved from http://www.portioresearch.com/media/1797/Mobile%20Factbook%202012.pdf

Traxler, J. (2009). Current state of mobile learning. In M. Ally (Ed.), *Mobile learning: Transforming the delivery of education and training* (pp. 9–24). Athabasca, Alberta, Canada: AU Press, Athabasca University.

Uzunboylu, H., Cavus, N., & Ercag, E. (2009). Using mobile learning to increase environmental awareness. *Computers & Education, 52*, 381–389.

Wishart, J., & Green, D. (2011). *Identifying emerging issues in mobile learning in higher and further education: A report to JISC.* Bristol, UK: University of Bristol. Retrieved from http://www.bristol.ac.uk/education/research/networks/mobile/publications/emergereport.pdf

Wong, L. H., Chin, C. K., Tan, C. L., & Liu, M. (2010). Students' personal and social meaning making in a Chinese idiom mobile learning environment. *Educational Technology & Society, 13*(4), 15–26.

Worldwide Independent Network of Market Research. (2012). *Connecting the world: Mobile and social media trends.* Retrieved from http://redcresearch.ie/wp-content/uploads/2012/03/Connecting-the-World-MEDIA-REPORT-IT-Tel-Syndicated-Study-Winter-2012-RED-C-WIN.pdf

5

Media-Based Learning Methodology

Stories, Games, and Emotions

Hans W. Giessen

Introduction

In a lot of countries, 'authoritarian' teaching models are still dominant—in 'real school life' as well as in media-based education (Abdazi, 2003). A possible reason for this could be the predominant status of Claude Shannon and Warren Weaver's (1949) communication model among pedagogues, even though current media and social realities seem to point at the superior effectiveness and adequacy of other models. The communication theories of Shannon and Weaver were developed with the aim to standardize the flow of communication in order to find an answer for various (technical) problems in mass communication with the specific character of *point to multipoint*—which of course contains numerous analogies to traditional teaching. Consequently, all too often, unintended transferences of the theories of Shannon and Weaver take place, without verification of their validity for this specific context.

At first view, of course, the direct application of the communication model of Shannon and Weaver in teaching processes can be seen as logical. It describes a person that initiates communication ('encoder/producer') and a person, or several persons, as the target ('decoder/receiver'). Sometimes, the process of communication between the encoder and the decoder requires an intervening *medium* (from Latin: *medium* = middle or midst). The inclusion of the *medium* enables a valid understanding of the encoding–decoding model as a metaphorical concept of communication. Of course, the traditional scientific theories have continuously analysed the function of the medium, and the conditions that have facilitated or influenced negatively the communication flow.

Media-based learning has usually been considered an element that might help to promote and to enable communication in several situations. In a learning process, this could apply in a situation where a teacher is confronted with perceptual, emotional, or cognitive difficulties, either difficulties that arise when working with students or the teacher's own difficulties. In such situations, media support as a complement of teaching seems to probably deliver a certain ease in the learning process, or sometimes even make it possible. In order to ensure the communication flow between 'the encoder' and 'the decoder' in an environment of technical constraints and factors of disturbance, the 'encoder' is frequently forced to standardize the information flow, expecting that a big number of participating 'decoders' will be integrated.

Standardization was a necessary element in Shannon and Weaver's communication model so as to exclude factors of disturbance in the communication process. Here, it seems to enable an adequate reception of learning contents. Furthermore, it creates an 'internal correlation' between the (assumed) validity of the information provided by the 'encoder–decoder metaphor' and the idea of an effective teaching process.

However, even in the times when mass communication media (still) was predominant, it became evident that the 'decoder' showed a differentiated response to media messages. Since the second half of the last century, constructivist learning theories have tried to consider this factor (e.g., Schank, 1995). Recent brain research is now able to explain this phenomenon (Langner, 2012). Meanwhile, new technical (and, consequently, medial) developments offer alternatives to 'authoritarian' approaches in communication strategies.

In the following, further aspects of this development shall be explained in more detail. Digital media is evidently not characterized any more by a *point-to-multipoint* quality. This fact exposes signifying implications of the communication model of Shannon and Weaver and its problematic applications, because of its specific connection to a limited *point-to-multipoint* situation. Giving up the rather authoritarian 'encoder–decoder' communication model opens new perspectives for alternative scenarios that differ from traditional forms of teaching, especially in their attempt to involve narrative, emotional, and action-oriented representations of knowledge. Since these developments were initiated by, or were reactions particularly to the use of new (digital) media, this chapter refers to media-based teaching situations.

Background: Media Theories, Media Impact Research, Theoretical Aspects of Media-Based Learning

Generally, a multimedia object is perceived as a time-lapsed individual expression, or a time-lapsed speech. Regarding its function, it seems to be experienced as a valid equivalent to authentic or spontaneous personal communication, if only limited by technical effects. In fact, the prevailing opinion persists that authentic communication can be technically emulated and be used in diverse applications. In this view, media is an illustration or representation of experiences and personal contacts with people.

Teaching is obviously a communication system, too. Furthermore, teaching has traditionally been defined within a correlation between the teacher and the learning contents, where the relevance and connotations of contents are transmitted to learners. In this context, the teacher provides not only the presentation of contents, but its interpretation as well. The interpretation's aim is to provide the intellectual accessibility of contents. With regard to this understanding of teaching, the teacher is the expert and guardian over values and significance of learning contents, and has an interpretation sovereignty that the learner has to accept.

When a teacher uses didactic aids like books, images, or films in order to promote a better comprehension of learning contents, it is intended to provide the teacher's specialized knowledge to the learner, which in consequence reinforces a clear teacher–learner (encoder–decoder) relation. The interpretations transmitted in the teacher–learner interaction are basically forced acts imposed by means of a system of sanctions. Refusal of interpretations results in poor evaluations for the learner, which provokes a low self-esteem and poses an obstacle in professional prospects. Most importantly, the use of a system of sanctions (for the teacher and the learner) often ignores the integration of a different perspective of learning as a voluntary and agreeable act of identification with the learning contents. Thus, in analogy to a much quoted line in communication science, it seems to be necessary to shift from 'what teaching does for the learner, to what the learner can do with teaching' (in analogy to Sturm, 1978, p. 167). In this alternative view, the learner is not solely a passive element reduced to a receptor role but an active participant.

The changes brought by the new digital media have in the main enforced the insight that the specific character of *point to multipoint* is only technically conditioned in various types of media (and in consequence, in its contents), and does not possess general validity. Certainly, the current prevalent forms of media are not limited to it. The use of digital media applications has lately been intensified in teaching situations (partly actively, as an improving complement to illustrate teaching contents, and to some extent passively, as a result of social or political decisions; cf. Giessen, 2012). Their major properties (possibility of media change, interactivity, openness, participation) offer new perspectives for other forms of communication. The modality and effectiveness of information transfer in media invariably depends on the medium to be used and its specific characteristics (Giessen, 2004; Tamim, Bernard, Borokhovski, Abrami, & Schmid, 2011; Thissen, 2003).

Thus, the use of digital media brings inevitably more open (i.e., increasingly networked) as well as more intense interactive communication, and also more active reception. Furthermore, when compared to the situation in the 1980s, current media users are now much more accustomed to a wider diversity of media, networks, and a stronger consideration of their personal needs and interests. The attributes and features of computers have a steadily growing influence on other media, sometimes of a mere aesthetic quality (e.g., from the use of *roll down menus* to graphic user interfaces in program announcements from television networks: so, computer aesthetics are being taken up and used by the television media, the until-now dominant medium). Frequently, however, dominant media also influences contents. For example, literary scholars have pointed in this context at new tendencies in literature—for instance, since the second half of the last century, apparently caused by the dominance of other media, in this case the cinema, a form of writing to some extent visual and an emphasis on modular took place (see, e.g., Poppe, 2007). Often, such tendencies can be a temporary trend because the respective new media with its characteristics and aesthetic qualities is presumed to be more 'fashionable.' However, due to its multimedia properties, the digital media is not only more 'up to date' but certainly makes specific forms of information transfer more significant, while other specifics, rather typical for more traditional media, are losing some of their importance.

This development becomes apparent in situations that some might perhaps regard as minor aspects. So, the openness of the digital media (choice between different sorts of media as well as the use of feedback channel options) brings an increase of *feedback* communication with the user (readers or learners) by means of questionnaires, or simply an e-mail address. This is now not only possible, but almost expected, and it can be considered a standard.

Likewise, the phenomenon of interactivity, made possible or at least intensified by the digital media, results in a stronger consideration of the user's needs and interests. This is apparent, for example, in the process of navigation, where a user can play a more active role, such as following or ignoring hyperlinks, according to his or her personal interests. Such an active form of reception has an effect not only on the receptive behavior but also on the user's production of meanings.

The characteristic user's situation, as well as the properties of multimedia, have further increased the importance of visual conditions. As described by Giessen (2004), it is, for example, important to be able to understand audio or video properties, which are used for metadata management, segmenting the document into semantically meaningful units, classifying each unit into a predefined scene type, indexing, summarizing the document for efficient retrieval and browsing. Data can be used to automatically search for a specific person in a sequence or for special video sequences. Audio as well as video properties are presented by descriptors and description schemes. There are many features that can be used to characterize multimedia signals. We can analyse audio and video sequences jointly or consider them separately. We consider the following three information channels or modalities within a video document: 1) visual modality: contains everything, either naturally or artificially created, that can be seen in the video document; 2) auditory modality: contains the speech, music, and environmental sounds, which can be heard in the video document, 3) textual modality: contains textual resources that describe the content of the video document.

At this point, properties on a more basic level play an important role. A computer monitor hinders the complete overview of longer texts, allowing only a view of the current screen page. When a text is longer, *scrolling* has to be done; that is, bringing the nonvisible part of the text onto the screen using the scroll bar that usually is located on the right edge of the screen. This might be considered similar to turning pages in books or magazines. However, turning back pages or reading back and forth between a table of contents and the text is much more complicated when using a monitor. Experiments and surveys have shown that almost all computer users concentrate their attention on the current page when reading longer texts, trying to keep in mind preceding pages and an overview of the text that has been read (Giessen, 2004). When reading electronically, locating specific parts of a text is too strenuous a task for many. All too often, it is nearly impossible to find the exact position of a desired text passage; and this problem grows as the size of a text increases. Furthermore, page numbers do not exist in HTML documents, as the representation of pages depends on the user's settings (the numbering of paragraphs, often used in legal texts, has not been accepted as a standard). When the overview of a text is not feasible—a probability that increases with longer texts—few users restart the reading of a text from the beginning, because it is usually perceived as a frustrating experience.

Another decisive fact is that, compared to printed material, digital media creates physiological difficulties and constraints. Unlike printed material, an image flickers on a monitor. Although this problem does not occur on LCD displays, the character resolution on both LCD and CRT displays is relatively low. Moreover, physiological studies have shown that when watching a computer screen, a lower eye-blink frequency occurs, which causes the eyes to be moisturized less frequently and, as a consequence, the eyes tend to fatigue more rapidly (Thissen, 2003). This aggravates the previously mentioned disadvantages of image flickering, low character resolution, and also the effects of screen reflection. Finally, the body posture is almost unchangeable because the computer monitor cannot be easily relocated when the sitting position becomes uncomfortable. Especially when reading, the body posture tenses up strongly, which intensifies fatigue (Giessen, 2004). Users have to sit relatively close to the monitor to work with a keyboard, a mouse, and icons or hyperlinks that need to be clicked.

For the authors, the consequences of these specific receptive situations are a cause of concern. The reading rate is between one-fourth and one-third slower than with printed material, and memory retention is lower than with the same text in a printed version (Thissen, 2003). There is even the impression that many computer users tend to avoid longer texts, and often it has been argued that the traditional concept of 'reading' should not be used when referring to computer-aided media. This is emphasized, for example, by Jakob Nielsen, who wrote already at an early stage that longer texts on a computer monitor usually are avoided, at best 'overflown' or, as he called it, 'scanned' (Nielsen, 2000; Nielsen & Pernice, 2009). Thus, it is clearly asserted that texts in the context of computer-aided media are read differently than print media from a book or magazine. Hence, they should be written and displayed in a different manner. Of course, this refers as well to texts with learning contents. By the way, all these observations lead to the assumption that computer-based learning might not necessarily be more effective than other ways of learning, or other learning media, such as books (Wolf, 2007).

At least authors should keep their texts brief. A text should only need a single screen *scroll* or, even better, it should be viewable without scrolling. According to this, the length of a text should not exceed the size of a single screen page. This creates the necessity of *fragmenting a text in single sense-steps* or *modules.* Some, like Nielsen (2000), consider this process of *modularization* of multimedia texts an indispensable step. Here in turn, the representation of strands of argument are much harder to achieve than in a written text. Argumentative progressions are not easy to represent; in this way, books or *time-based media,* such as films or cartoons, are the better alternative.

However, when previous knowledge about visualized objects exists (this would be a premise, since the images cannot be at first described or explained, but have to be recognized and integrated at once; Arwood & Kaulitz, 2007; Oliva & Torralba, 2007), visual representations allow a much faster transfer of information (because different forms of information are simultaneously present and can be handled without a decoding phase; see Sowa, 1983). Additionally, using specific information allows for connections between the objects shown, as well as temporal progressions, which are easier to understand. For this reason, an instruction manual for a machine in graphical representation is usually more effective than a written manual (see Grob & Breger, 2002).

The digital media continues a development that was already observed when films or television began to be used to transfer information. Studies then took place on how a more emotional transfer of information influences an observer.

Issues, Controversies, Problems

In the 1970s, it was discovered that emotional impressions depend on the type of media; for example, emotional responses of television viewers differ from those of radio listeners (Sturm, 1978). Other early research (e.g., Sturm, von Haebler, & Helmreich, 1972) suggests that emotional responses clearly last longer and are more detailed than knowledge acquired through cognitive means, which usually gets lost in temporal progression, but can be more easily remembered or reactivated when associated with emotional connotations. Recent studies in neuroscience have confirmed these findings (Bar-On, 2007; Gardner, 2009; Goleman, 2009; Johnson, 1997).

Moreover, neuroscience research has shown that information and knowledge are assimilated with different degrees of effectiveness, depending on mood and tendency of emotions (Cohen & Magen, 2004; Cozolino, 2006; Erk et al., 2003). With regard to this, information associated with positive emotions is assimilated through the hippocampus and further processed in the cerebral cortex, while information associated with negative emotions is incorporated through the amygdala (Latin, *corpus amygdaloideum*), an almond-shape set of neurons located deep in the brain's medial temporal lobe. Shown to play a key role in the processing of emotions, the amygdala forms part of the limbic system. In humans and other animals, this subcortical brain structure is linked to both fear responses and pleasure. Its size is positively correlated with aggressive behavior across species. In humans, it is the most sexually dimorphic brain structure, and shrinks by more than 30% in males upon castration. Conditions such as anxiety, autism, depression, posttraumatic stress disorder, and phobias are suspected of being linked to abnormal functioning of the amygdala, owing to damage, developmental problems, or neurotransmitter imbalance.

The amygdala alerts the organism when quick reactions are needed, for instance, in situations that involve conflicts or fleeing. When activated, it produces an increase of blood pressure and acceleration of the pulse rate. Likewise, an entire muscular tension can be determined. This condition enables quick reactions, since the activation of the amygdala occurs simultaneously with a number of other physiological processes. In the history of evolution, being able to flee rapidly or defend oneself in hazardous situations always has been an advantage. In these cases, long periods of reflection would not be useful (and even counterproductive). Here, the amygdala is not invoked when recalling experiences and factual knowledge, or when knowledge is processed (Aggleton, 1992, 2000; Aggleton & Young, 2002; Phelps, 2006; Stone, Baron–Cohen, & Knight, 1998).

The amygdala should not be considered in this context an evolutional relict of no present-life importance—in fact, it still protects us in 'modern' hazardous situations, for example, in road traffic. In diverse types of decisions, it is even indispensable as it contributes to assess potential dangers and promotes critical faculties. In this field, a number of impressive case histories have been compiled by the Portuguese American neurologist Antonio Damasio. They refer to patients whose amygdala were calcified and (apparently because of that) had problems managing a 'reasonable' behaviour (Damasio, 1999, 2002). Scientists researching simulation of intelligence also confirm the theory that critical faculties, including fear, are elementary aspects of *intelligent* conduct (Minsky, 2006; Ogata & Sugano, 2001).

During a learning process, the mode of functioning and the tasks fulfilled by the amygdala are very often problematic. Thus, in a complex society, where interrelations and other mechanisms are to be presupposed and understood, fear and aggression, or authoritarian models of communication, are the wrong advisors. Activation of the amygdala can even be counterproductive, because the amygdala is not able to handle information in a creative manner. It is a known fact that stress can not promote good analytical achievements. Neuroscience has now determined the causes for it (Cahill, Prins, Weber, & McGaugh, 1994). Considering this, learning is a less effective process when boredom, lack of motivation, and hostility prevail. In this context, explicit positive emotions should be evoked.

Therefore, it makes sense to adapt every form of information transfer to the neurological needs of information receivers. This happens ideally when connecting information to positive emotions. These positive emotions can be achieved passively (e.g., with music; Koelsch, Fritz, v. Cramon, Müller, & Friederici, 2006) or, what is important in our context, actively, through participation and integration of the information receiver (user, reader, or learner), giving persons the feeling that they are taken seriously in order to promote their personal engagement (Barab, Evans, & Baek, 2004; Cross, 2006). Thus, the individual reactions that the digital media allows are an ideal frame to achieve this.

In a pleasant emotional context, not the amygdala but the hippocampus will be activated (Andersen, Morris, Amaral, Bliss, & O'Keefe, 2006; Seifert, 1983; Storm-Mathisen, 1990; Traub & Miles, 1991); however, this cerebral region is apparently not involved in quick responses (neither physical nor mental). Though, in the context of successful transfer of information and knowledge, this is an advantage. The hippocampus passes on the recorded information to the cerebral cortex, where it is stored on a long-term basis (this is the case, e.g., with dreams that people experience while they are sleeping). Consequently, 'learning' functions effectively only with the hippocampus, in spite of, or because of its 'slowness' (Thiel, Eurich, & Schwegler, 2002). Creativity as well can only be generated in this form. Therefore, there are neurological reasons why learning contents should not be presented neutrally but in an emotional, interesting, and exciting manner.

Creativity relates less to facts that are supposed to be learned by heart (like historical facts) or must be followed (like mechanical sequences). It rather connects to relations and associations. Meanwhile, there is a prevalent opinion that our networked and complex modern times demand aptitudes that are not basically related to fixed processes or factual knowledge that becomes increasingly faster obsolete. It rather demands flexible answers to permanently changing situations.

Apparently, the media presence is a decisive reason for this broad transformation process, from a static to a more dynamic society (Innis, 1950), because they are able to transfer information rapidly and so alter social, economical, and even technical realities in constant *feedback* processes.

Specifically, the digital media and its relevant forms of knowledge integration, transfer, and representation facilitate such a creative approach in a changing environment.

Consequently, this concept can be summarized as follows: Digital media is less suited for the presentation of facts and rational analysis than for the representation of connections and relations. But, the more the digital media influences our environment, the whole society, economic life, and so on, the less influential some traditional (perhaps only socially) relevant facts will be (the classical 'education'), allowing a more flexible and task-appropriate acquisition and application of relevant information.

Thus, the growing use of media in our society, and as a consequence in our daily lives, has almost inevitably focused attention to forms of information and knowledge acquisition connected to emotions in the human psyche, and has even helped some psychologists to develop their models (McLaren, 2007). With it, there is a growing public awareness about new and more effective forms of learning and teaching.

One media-adequate form of presentation is the integration of information in stories, games, and communicative situations. Users participate in the narration of a story that they consider subjectively interesting, or a game in a context where information is transferred and knowledge acquired. For this reason, the emotional forms of *gaming* and *storytelling* have been found to be adequate alternatives.

Solutions and Recommendations: A Brief Look at the Constructivist Learning Theory

Constructivist learning theory rises to the demand for alternatives. This theory became influential during the second half of the last century. It endorses the idea that the human perception of the environment is not a process of reproducing knowledge. Thus, it does not represent a projection but an active constructive process. Indeed, constructivism does not dismiss the role of the teacher or the value of expert knowledge. Constructivism modifies that role, so that teachers help students to construct knowledge rather than to reproduce a series of facts. The constructivist teacher provides tools such as problem-solving and inquiry-based learning activities with which students formulate and test their ideas, draw conclusions and inferences, and pool and convey their knowledge in a collaborative learning environment. Constructivism tries to transform the student from a passive recipient of information to an active participant in the learning process. Always guided by the teacher, students construct their knowledge actively rather than just mechanically ingesting knowledge from the teacher or the textbook (Harms & Voermanek, 1994).

Ultimately, constructivist learning theories are rooted in neurological findings, too. Biologist and psychologist Humberto Maturana formulated theoretical statements that attempted to explain how living organisms gather and process external sensations (Maturana, 1981). Apparently, this process is not always identical, or at least we do not know yet how other organisms gather, process, interpret, or understand reality. So, there is a possibility that every living organism experiences its existence differently. The assumption that living systems must be understood as autonomous and dynamic entities goes back to Maturana and Varela (Fine, 2006; LeDoux, 2002; Maturana & Varela, 1972).

These entities are not static but rather develop themselves continuously. That means that on one hand they are open, so they can gather and process information about the world. On the other hand, the gathering and processing of information occurs against the background of individual capabilities and specific experiences. This means that an objective image of the real world does not exist, but only subjective constructions that relate information to present experiences and processing capabilities (Vygotsky, 1962). Since an objective and comprehensive image of the world is not feasible—if all present sensations were processed simultaneously our brain would be overstrained—this also contributes to achieving a certain efficiency, or rather allows the creation of a manageable image of the surrounding reality, in order to enable a reasonable processing of the incidental sense data. Furthermore, this concept implies that information is not processed passively. In fact, the brain processes and modifies it actively (comparing, and sometimes 'adapting' it to previous information).

In the 'radical' interpretations of the constructivist theory, expressed particularly by von Glaserfeld (1995), it is even postulated that the brain does not enable perception but (simply) organizes the own realm of experience. This would imply that the brain (also) 'constructs' meaning in a 'real world,' where meaning actually does not exist (or maybe only other meanings, beyond its subjective abilities and possibilities of perception), an old 'topos' of *Gestalttheorie* (Wertheimer, 1925).

So, the subjective and contextual character of information is underlined, and the binding objective reality replaced with the learner's cognitive reality. This theory corresponds with the previously exposed neurological findings, whereby information is always processed in a different way, depending on the emotional connotations they are related to. In some cases they might be easily kept in mind and actively used; in other cases, probably not.

Another concept related to this theory refers to the fact that the brain constantly strives to keep its 'sensory construction' consistent. In this context, Niklas Luhmann has introduced in Germany the term *Selbstreferenz*, that he incidentally also uses in an analogical mode in other systems—the media system, and the educational sector (Luhmann, 2006). 'Self-referential' means that a system seeks to preserve its sensory construction. This is given up only when it absolutely does not apply to reality, and even in that case, with a certain resistance. Incidentally, this also would explain why educational establishments adhere so strongly to their prerogative of interpretation. On the other hand, it would also explain why learners are nearly not reachable when teaching does not fulfill their needs and expectations.

Unlike a widespread misunderstanding within constructivism, the individual construction of reality is of course not arbitrary, but also determined by social consensus that develops through interactive communication (Harms & Voermanek, 1994). Applied to the educational sector, it means that the relevance of learning contents is determined jointly between the teacher and the learner. Here, it is important to integrate the learners' interests, knowledge, and previous experience, because they affect the learning behaviour and the willingness to assimilate new information. It must also be considered that previous experience and knowledge can be drastically heterogeneous. Nevertheless, they pose the decisive points of connection for the transfer of learning contents, since learners basically tend to look for familiar items of information. The implication for the constructivist learning theory is the concentration to the frame of reference in which the learning contents are shown and interpreted. A learning experience occurs when a learner can relate the new information to previous experience and knowledge, and order the learning contents in a personal structure of knowledge.

Future Trends: Emotion-Based, Action-Oriented, and Narrative Information and Knowledge Transfer

Up to now, empirical evidence from research on computer-based learning methods gives diverse results on whether and in how far they are superior to traditional learning methods (Giessen, 2003). There are major advantages in certain contexts, such as providing independence from time and place, which is important for language learners (Bufe & Giessen, 2005). All in all, however, it is still not yet clear what teaching methods are adequate to media-based learning (Giessen, 2004).

Hints from communication science, neuroscience, and cognitive science suggest the effectiveness of methods connected with emotions, like games and storytelling. These are widespread and well-established forms of knowledge transfer (Huizinga, 1939). This has been confirmed by the recent findings in neurological research (Cohen & Magen, 2004; Cozolino, 2006; Erk et al., 2003). These are deeply human-rooted forms of knowledge transfer, present in every culture and in every medium throughout history (Gredler, 2004).

In every culture, narrated stories have had the function of transferring knowledge between individuals, groups, and generations (Hillocks, 2006). Narrated stories appear in all sorts of media that have been developed in our society. The knowledge transmitted is not limited to facts, but also implicitly includes cultural values, opinions, emotions, and problem-solving. A story provides a structure for a narrative representation of content, almost like an ordered list—in sequences—as well as a timeline represented with a linear language. Furthermore, successful stories are in essence transmitted structures of dramaturgical contents rooted in ancient myths, and related to emotional needs based on depth psychology. Thus, a coexistence of traditional forms of oral storytelling, multimedia narration in mass media, and digital storytelling in the Internet might occur—but this does not diminish the attraction of traditional storytelling for the narrator and the listener.

The attraction of a story is based on its subjective perspective that enables the construction of an interesting thematic frame that interacts on a vivid and captivating level. Audiences feel attracted to, are able to feel with, the story. The same categories can also be applied to games and other forms of action-oriented group learning.

Narrative and emotional forms of information and knowledge transfer have always been confronted with the objection of relativism. This criticism can be addressed with the constructivist concept of history, which stresses the constructive character of history as well as its resulting controversies. Narrative structures might be able to offer a closer access to the 'truth' because they contribute to achieving stronger empathy and participation, and thereby an 'inner insight.'

Narrative, and consequently emotional, media-based forms of representation also allow interaction, and thus not only lead to emotional participation, but also (via specific action oriented and networked forms of information and knowledge transfer) to an exchange with other learners.

The participation of the recipient (learner) as the co-author is at the same time an essential element of the hypertext-theory (Dillon, 1994). Emotional, narrative, and action-oriented forms of information and knowledge transfer are thus a media-adequate answer (initiated by the digital media) to current challenges using high standards of production and representation.

Conclusion

The current state of knowledge in the areas of pedagogies, neuroscience, and research on the effects of media proposes the use of action-oriented, narrative, and emotional approaches for the information and knowledge transfer. Cognitive learning achievements appear stronger and are more enduring when combined with emotional connotations and personal involvement. Furthermore, cognitive learning methods include the learner in the process of knowledge development, consciously and as much as possible. This, in turn, has implications in the modalities of conveyance. When excitement and interest are aroused, learners will be willing to include their own experiences and to construct their own interpretations. Emotional, narrative, and action-oriented forms of involvement for learners as co–authors—for instance, using *gaming* or *storytelling*—are essential elements in the hypertext-theory that can be transferred to media-based learning scenarios.

References

Abdazi, H. (2003). *Improving adult literacy outcomes: Lessons from cognitive research for developing countries.* Washington, DC: World Bank Publications.

Aggleton, J. P. (1992), *The amygdala: Neurobiological aspects of emotion, memory and mental dysfunction.* London, UK: Wiley.

Aggleton, J. P. (2000), *The amygdala: A functional analysis.* Oxford, UK: Oxford University Press.

Aggleton, J. P., & Young, A. W. (2002). The enygma of the amygdala: On its contribution to human emotion. In R. D. Lane & L. Nadel (Eds.), *Cognitive neuroscience of emotion* (pp. 12–23). Oxford, UK: Oxford University Press.

Andersen, P., Morris, R., Amaral, D., Bliss, T., & O'Keefe, J. (Eds.). (2006). *The hippocampus.* Oxford, UK: Oxford University Press.

Arwood, E. L., & Kaulitz, C. (2007). *Learning with a visual brain in an auditory world.* Shawnee Mission, KS: Asperger.

Barab, S. A., Evans, M. A., & Baek, E-O. (2004). Activity theory as a lens for characterizing the participatory unit. In D. H. Jonassen (Ed.), *Handbook of research on educational communications and technology* (pp. 199–214). Mahwah, NJ: Erlbaum.

Bar-On, R. (2007). How important is it to educate people to be emotionally intelligent, and can it be done? In R. Bar-on, J. G. Maree, & M. J. Elias (Eds.), *Educating people to be emotionally intelligent* (pp. 1–14). Westport, CT: Praeger.

Bufe, W., & Giessen, H. W. (2005). La visoconférence transfrontalière. In W. Bufe & H. W. Giessen (Eds.), *La visioconférence transfrontalière* (pp. 9–12). Paris, France: Harmattan.

Cahill, L., Prins, B., Weber, M., & McGaugh, J. L. (1994). B-adrenergic activation and memory for emotional events. *Nature, 371,* 702–704.

Cohen, A., & Magen, H. (2004). Hierarchical systems of attention and action. In G. W. Humphreys & M. J. Riddoch (Eds.), *Attention in action: Advances from cognitive neuroscience* (pp. 27–68). New York, NY: Taylor & Francis.

Cozolino, L. (2006). *The neuroscience of human relationships: Attachment and the developing social brain.* New York, NY: Norton.

Cross, J. (2006). *Informal learning: rediscovering the natural pathways that inspire innovation and performance.* San Francisco, CA: Wiley.

Damasio, A. R. (1999). *The feeling of what happens: Body and emotion in the making of consciousness.* New York, NY: Harcourt/Harvest.

Damasio, A. R. (2002). A second chance for emotion. In R. D. Lane & L. Nadel (Eds.), *Cognitive neuroscience of emotion* (pp. 12–23). Oxford, UK: Oxford University Press.

Dillon, A. (1994). *Designing usable electronic text: Ergonomic aspects of human information usage.* London, UK: Taylor & Francis.

Erk, S., Kiefer, M., Grothe, J., Wunderlich, A. P., Spitzer, M., & Walter, H. (2003). Emotional context modulates subsequent memory effect. *Neuroimage, 18,* 439–447.

Fine, C. (2006). *A mind of its own: How your brain distorts and deceives.* New York, NY: Norton.

Gardner, H. (2009). Ausblick: Fünf Kompetenzen für die Zukunft. In H. W. Giessen (Ed.), *Emotionale intelligenz in der schule* (pp. 136–148). Weinheim, Germany: Beltz.

Giessen, H. W. (2003). Conditions requises pour l'emploi des « nouvelles technologies » dans l'instruction (en tenant compte particulièrement de l'enseignement des langues étrangères). In W. Bufe & H. W. Giessen (Eds.), *Des langues et des médias* (pp. 133–148). Grenoble, France: Presses Universitaires de Grenoble.

Giessen, H. W. (2004). *Medienadäquates publizieren. Von der inhaltlichen konzeption zur publikation und präsentation.* Heidelberg, Germany: Spektrum Akademischer Verlag.

Giessen, H. W. (2012). Mediengestütztes Lernen—bei welchen Medien, bei welchen Inhalten, mit welchen Lernern? In T. Tinnefeld, unter Mitarbeit von I. A. Busch-Lauer, H. Giessen, M. Langner, & A. Schumann (Eds.), *Hochschulischer Fremdsprachenunterricht—Anforderungen, Ausrichtung, Spezifik* (pp. 203–214). Saarbrücken, Germany: HTW.

Goleman, D. (2009). Über Emotionale Intelligenz. In H. W. Giessen (Ed.), *Emotionale Intelligenz in der Schule* (pp. 14–26). Weinheim, Germany: Beltz.

Gredler, M. E. (2004). Games and simulations and their relationships to learning. In D. H. Jonassen (Ed.), *Handbook of research on educational communications and technology* (pp. 571–582). Mahwah, NJ: Erlbaum.

Grob, H. L., & Breger, W. (2002). *Präsentieren und Visualisieren.* München, Germany: Deutscher Taschenbuch Verlag.

Harms, I., & Voermanek, A. (1994). Interaktiv heißt die Zukunft. *Medienpsychologie, 4,* 241–251.

Hillocks, G. Jr. (2006). *Narrative writing: Learning a new model for teaching.* Portsmouth, NH: Heinemann.

Huizinga, J. (1939). *Homo ludens. Proeve eener bepaling van het spel-element der cultuur.* Amsterdam, The Netherlands: Pantheon.

Innis, Ha. A. (1950). *Empire and communications.* Oxford, UK: Clarendon Press.

Johnson, M. A. (1997). *Developmental cognitive neuroscience.* Malden, MA: Blackwell.

Koelsch, S., Fritz, T., v. Cramon, D. Y., Müller, K., & Friederici, A. D. (2006). Investigating emotion with music: An fMRI study. *Human Brain Mapping, 27*(3), 239–250.

Langner, M. (2012). Digitale medien, e-learning—und was "sagt" unser Gehirn dazu? In T. Tinnefeld, unter Mitarbeit von I. A. Busch-Lauer, H. Giessen, M. Langner, & A. Schumann (Eds.), *Hochschulischer Fremd- sprachenunterricht—Anforderungen, Ausrichtung, Spezifik* (pp. 191–202). Saarbrücken, Germany: HTW.

LeDoux, Jo. (2002). *Synaptic self: How our brains become who we are.* New York, NY: Viking.

Luhmann, N. (2006). *Soziale systeme: Grundriss einer allgemeinen theorie.* Frankfurt am Main, Germany: Suhrkamp.

Maturana, H. R. (1981). Autopoiesis: Reproduction, heredity and evolution. In M. Zeleny (Ed.), *Autopoiesis, dissipative structures and spontaneous social order* (pp. 48–80). Boulder, CO: Westview Press.

Maturana, H. R., & Varela, F. J. (1972). *De máquinas y seres vivos.* Santiago, Chile: Editorial Universitaria.

McLaren, N. (2007). *Humanizing madness: Psychiatry and the cognitive neurosciences.* Ann Arbor, MI: Future Psychiatry Press.

Minsky, M. (2006). *The emotion machine.* New York, NY: Simon & Schuster.

Nielsen, J. (2000). *Designing web usability.* Indianapolis, IN: New Riders.

Nielsen, J., & Pernice, K. (2009). *Eyetracking web usability.* Indianapolis, IN: New Riders.

Ogata, T., & Sugano, S. (2001). Consideration of emotion model and primitive language of robots. In T. Kitamura (Ed.), *What should be computed to understand and model brain function? From robotics, soft comput- ing, biology and neuroscience to cognitive philosophy* (pp. 1–22). Mountain View, CA: World Scientific.

Oliva, A., & Torralba, A. (2007). Building the gist of a scene: The role of global image features in recognition. In S. Martinez-Conde, M. Stephen, L. M. Martinez, & J-M Alonso (Eds.), *Visual perception part 2, volume 155: fundamentals of awareness, multi-sensory integration and high-order perception* (pp. 23–36). Amsterdam, The Netherlands: Elsevier.

Phelps, E. A. (2006). Emotion and cognition: Insights from studies of the human amygdala. *Annual Review of Psychology, 57,* 27–53.

Poppe, S. (2007). *Visualität in Literatur und Film. Eine medienkomparatistische Untersuchung moderner Erzähltexte und ihrer Verfilmungen.* Göttingen, Germany: Vandenhoeck & Ruprecht.

Schank, R. C. (1995). *Tell me a story: Narrative and intelligence.* Evanston, IL: Northwestern University Press.

Seifert, W. (1983). *Neurobiology of the hippocampus.* London, UK: Academic Press.

Shannon, C. E., & Weaver, W. (1949). *The mathematical theory of communication.* Urbana: University of Illinois Press.

Sowa, J. F. (1983). *Conceptual structures: Information processes in mind and machine.* Reading, MA: Addison-Wesley.

Stone, V. E., Baron-Cohen, S., & Knight, R. T. (1998). Frontal lobe contributions to theory of mind. *Journal of Cognitive Neuroscience, 10*(5), 640–656.

Storm-Mathisen, J. (1990). *Understanding the brain through the hippocampus: Hippocampal region as a model for studying brain structure and function.* London, UK: Elsevier.

Sturm, H. (1978). Emotionale wirkungen—das medienspezifische von hörfunk und fernsehen: Ergebnisse zweier untersuchungen und weiterführungen. *Fernsehen und Bildung, 12*(3), 158–167.

Sturm, H, von Haebler, R., & Helmreich, R. (1972). *Medienspezifische lerneffekte.* München, Germany: T. R. Verlagsunion.

Tamim, R. M., Bernard, R. M., Borokhovski, E., Abrami, P. C., & Schmid, R. F. (2011). What forty years of research says about the impact of technology on learning: A second-order meta-analysis and validation study. *Review of Educational Research, 81*(1), 4–28.

Thiel, A., Eurich, C. W., & Schwegler, H. (2002). Stabilized dynamics in physiological and neural systems despite strongly delayed feedback. In J. R. Dorronsoro (Ed.), *Artificial Neural Networks, Proceedings of the International Conference on Artificial Neural Networks, ICANN 2002* (pp. 15–20). Berlin, Germany: Springer.

Thissen, F. (2003). *Screen design handbook.* New York, NY: Springer.

Traub, R. D., & Miles, R. (1991). *Neuronal networks of the hippocampus.* Cambridge, UK: Cambridge University Press.

von Glasersfeld, E. (1995). Radical constructivism: A way of knowing and learning. London, UK: Falmer.

Vygotsky, L. (1962). *Thought and language.* Cambridge, MA: MIT Press.

Wertheimer, M. (1925). *Über Gestalttheorie.* Erlangen, Germany: Verlag der Philosophischen Akademie.

Wolf, M. (2007). *Proust and the squid: The story and science of the reading brain.* New York, NY: HarperCollins.

6

A Case of Distance Education Through Social Network Sites

Giovanni Farias

Distance Education Through Social Network Sites

Social network sites (SNS) such as Facebook, Google+, and Twitter have changed the way in which many people around the world use the Internet. Billions of SNS users share hundreds of millions of pictures and send billions of messages every day. This information exchange generates trillions of page views every month through smartphones, tablets, notebooks, and desktops. Regardless of precise statistics generated by the ever-increasing use of SNS, we can doubtlessly conclude that a large portion of our society frequently uses these web-based services. This conclusion has motivated some scholars to research how to use social network sites in order to foster face-to-face and/or distance education, as well as the impact of the use of SNSs on the learning process.

The first research findings were published some time before the SNSs and have occupied an outstanding position in the Internet scenario. Actually, the first researchers focused on the use of computing-mediated communication (CMC) in general as an educational tool, not specifically the use of SNSs. This means that the use of a simple teacher website, or a blog, can be considered a tool that supports CMC. Tidwell and Walther (2002) stated that students who use CMC may find it easier to develop personal relationships than face-to-face ones. They also found that students who communicate via CMC with other students use more intimate questions and self-disclosures than students in face-to-face conversations. Additionally, students who viewed an instructor's website [developed] high levels of mediated immediacy, including forms of self-disclosure, and reported high levels of motivation and affective learning, indicating positive attitudes toward the course and the teacher (O'Sullivan, Hunt, & Lippert, 2004).

After the introduction of SNS, scholars noticed that the experience they offered to the user as a CMC tool was quite different from simply accessing the teacher's website (Mazer, Murphy, & Simonds, 2007). SNS allow students and teachers to connect with one another based on their social and/or educational network. Furthermore, these connections could count on attractive resources, such as blogs, image and video postings, and sharing features, among other resources technologically integrated or connected to the SNS. In short, the scholars concluded that there were many other aspects to be considered in the study of CMC in education when SNSs were used rather than a simple social media tool, such as a teacher website or blog.

Definition of Social Network Sites

Various definitions of social network sites can be found in scholastic papers, each one with a different connotation. Two of them can be joined to reach a more complete definition about social network sites. First, Boyd and Ellison (2007) defined SNS as follows:

> We define social network sites as web-based services that allow individuals to (1) construct a public or semipublic profile within a bounded system, (2) articulate a list of other users with whom they share a connection, and (3) view and traverse their list of connections and those made by others within the system.
>
> *(p. 211)*

Hoffman (2009) expanded this definition, stating, "Social network sites commonly also allow users to leave persistent comments on a friend's profiles and send private messages" (p. 93). Furthermore, SNSs offer resources for file sharing (text, images, audio, and video), blog discussions, content cocreation, and external resources linking and tagging. The integrated use of these social media and collaborative tools makes SNSs very interesting for educational purposes.

When SNS are used for educational purposes they can include other kinds of social media, such as publishing media (e.g., Blogger, Wikipedia, Wikia) and sharing media (e.g., YouTube, Flickr, Slideshare). This integrated use of different social media is illustrated in Figure 6.1, which presents a set of social media tools categorized as for publishing- and sharing-purpose tools. The SNS specifically focuses on social engagement, but SNS also have limited capacity for sharing files. They can use other social media resources in order to support more specialized tasks.

Types of Social Network Sites

There are different technological options that lead to different types of social network sites. Basically, SNSs can be divided into three different types: public SNS, SNS management systems, and software as a service. Listed below are the characteristics, advantages, disadvantages, and examples for each type of SNS in the educational scenario.

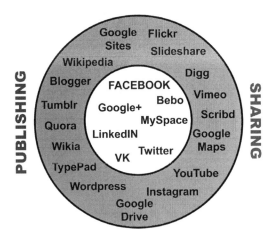

Figure 6.1 Set of samples of social media that can be integrated to different SNSs to share or publish content through social networking

Credit: Fundação Roberto Marinho.

Public SNS

A public SNS is generally hosted by a private service provider and supported directly or indirectly by an advertisement business model. Thus, any Internet user can create an account and build his or her own virtual social network. It generally does not involve any expense on the part of the user. Its set up process is simple and can be done immediately. Depending on the chosen site, the teacher counts on a large number of students that already use, or know how to use, the service. This saves a lot of cognitive effort. Generally, the SNS already offers integration facilities with a wide range of social media, which makes for the easier publishing of external content. In addition, the teacher has total freedom to perform the tasks and the interactivity processes that he or she plans, sometimes without depending on following strict rules established by the educational institution that he or she works for.

Facebook, Twitter, and Google+ are the best examples of this kind of SNS. In addition, there are SNSs that are very popular in specific parts of the world, such as Orkut (South America and Asia/Pacific areas), Bebo (Europe and Australia), and QQ (China) (Hoffman, 2009).

Since the system is maintained by a company that offers this free service, the user must strictly follow the terms of use determined by the service provider. These terms include what kind of interactivity can be performed, what external technology integrations are available, what privacy policy must be accepted by the user, what kind of resources are available for the user, among other aspects of the user policy. Thus, there are not a lot of options for customizing the resources or the appearance of the site. Furthermore, there are privacy issues involved, as the network is not the property of the users or of the educational institution.

SNS Management Tools

There is software that schools and universities can use to deploy their own social network sites, hosted by their own structure or by a web-hosting service provider. This is a good option for those institutions that need or want to keep control over what happens in the learning process in the SNS. The open software tools offer the advantage of being totally customizable in terms of user interface and functionalities. In addition, software tools allow the use of private solutions for SNSs, which give control over the related data and its policy of usage.

The most important examples of this case are Mahara and Elgg. Both are widely used across the world by several educational institutions because they are open software and have good quality technology. The SNS Landing (https://landing.athabascau.ca/), of the Athabasca University, is an example of the use of Elgg software.

The fact of the SNS being hosted and controlled by the educational institution limits its use by the teacher. The number of students accustomed to the SNS user interface is likely limited and the technology available is not the most sophisticated. Besides, there are not as many options for integrating the SNS to other social media sites as for public SNSs.

Software as a Service

The concept of software as a service implies the deployment of private social network sites using proprietary software, hosted by its technology owner. An example of this type of SNS is the website Ning. In this way, several private SNSs can be built using the same software and hosted by the same service. However, each SNS is independent, and the network owner can establish its own usage policy in accordance with the software provider policy. This means there is a blend of the first two types of SNS. On one hand, the SNS works in a hosting service-provider structure, which also provides the SNS technology. On the other hand, the SNS can be considered private, since its owner specifies the usage policy.

Case: Using Google+ for Educational Purposes

At the beginning of 2012, the Roberto Marinho Foundation,[1] a very important nonprofit Brazilian institution, needed to implement a course program named the Tutoring Formation Program (TFP). This program aimed to train twenty-two secondary schools teachers in online tutoring methods using social media and social network tools. Actually, it was a pilot course to check the feasibility of the method. At this time, all the participants were high school teachers from the public education system of the State of Espírito Santo, Brazil. Depending on the results obtained in this pilot project, the TFP could be expanded to include teachers on a larger scale in the future.

The main idea was to provide knowledge and practice in order to enable them to use distance education resources and methods. Thus, they could improve the face-to-face educational activities in the public education system in Brazil. When I was contacted by them to provide technical and consulting services to implement the program, all the pedagogical strategy had been established already. They intended to use Elgg software to deploy a private SNS and to use it to support a blended course, with face-to-face classes and online activities as well. However, the online activities represented most of the planned program.

As their consultant on distance education, I strongly suggested a change from Elgg to a public social network site, because it would be very important to use a technological solution that could be used by teachers in their own teaching processes. Elgg, as an SNS management system, requires a paid infrastructure to be used, and most of the public schools would not have the budget, structure, human resources, and/or managerial support for the idea. Thus, most of the teachers would not have the opportunity to replicate some of the teaching methods learned during the TFP. Furthermore, using a Google solution, as I had suggested, the teachers could use the entire ecosystem provided by that company, ready for using and for free. This ecosystem includes an online site builder service, blog, online document storage and editing service, web-conferencing tools, an online calendar, among other social media. As all the Google social media have an integrated authentication, they allow the user to access the different services with the same login and password. In other words, once the user logs in to one social media, he or she can access other social media in the same browser without needing to authenticate again, at least until leaving the browser or logging out. It would be very interesting for those teachers who do not have strong digital inclusion, since this single authentication makes the navigation and the use, among different social media, much easier.

Ning, another SNS, was also considered, but as it would not offer the same quantity of free resources provided by Google, its use was dismissed. My suggestion was accepted and the TFP used Google+ to support its online teaching activities. Thus, I could move on to the next step: the instructional design of the program using Google tools.

The Tutoring Formation Program

The program was composed by four modules, each one focusing on a different aspect of online tutoring, including:

1. Education—concept and methodology. It regards the basic concepts and methods to teach online. Its content was structured on Google Sites.
2. Technology—content and resources. It concerns the technology used to publish content and provide interaction among the participants of an online course. Its content was structured in a blog hosted by Blogger, a Google blog service.

3. Management—general competencies and roles. It focused on the roles and competencies involved in a distance education process. Its content was structured on Google Drive.
4. Assessment—models applied to the project. Finally, it presents the assessment models applied to the learning outcomes and distance education resources. Its content was hosted by You-Tube and Google Drive, but published through the stream postings in a Google+ site.

The content access was strictly controlled, since Google accounts allowed the user to choose who would access the content hosted by its different social media resources, and when this access should have happened. The Google+ site stream was viewed only for those that were allowed to participate of the TFP. The Google social media offered a complete set of resources to strictly control the access to content and interaction activities.

For each module, the students should access the content, discuss it in the Google+ stream, and experiment with the resources and methods mentioned in the content and in the discussions. At this point, Google+ presented strong advantages. Because public social media were used to support the course, the participants could use them to teach as well, with autonomy and without any cost or fear of making mistakes.

Social Media Resources

Figure 6.2 shows that the main publishing and communication resource was Google+. A Google account was created for the instructor, and a Google+ site was set up to unify all the discussions during the course. Using its publishing stream, the course instructor could release the links to the contents as long as they allowed access to the participants. In addition, the content itself could be inserted directly into the Google+ stream, such as YouTube videos and pictures. By using a Google+ site, which is impersonal, the instructor could share the site management with other instructors by including their personal Google accounts as site managers.

For each module, a different social media was chosen to share its respective content from among a set of options of publishing tools, as presented in Figure 6.2. In this way, the course participants

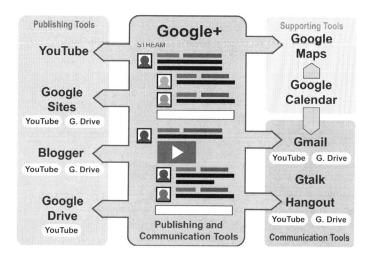

Figure 6.2 The scheme used for social media content publishing and communication. The YouTube content could be embedded in different social media. It is being indicated by the small YouTube icon.

Credit: Fundação Roberto Marinho.

could experience the facilities and difficulties in using different social media to deliver content. At the same time, they could explore the module content by watching videos hosted by YouTube, reading Portable Document Format (PDF) and PowerPoint files hosted by Google Drive, as well as HTML content, generated by the use of Blogger and Google Sites.

The communication process was optimized since all the tools used were integrated. Thus, when someone posted a message on the Google+ stream, all the group participants could be automatically notified by an e-mail sent by the system. The content itself could be sent to participants by e-mail or directly from the social media (e.g., YouTube or Google Drive). Basically, the participants could authenticate to access their Gmail account to access the e-mail messages. From Gmail, with single authentication, they could access Google+ or any social media directly from the top menu in the Gmail interface, using the same browser.

The instructor counted on Google Calendar to structure the course agenda and notify participants about new events or updates directly from this social media. Once the instructor added or edited an event in the calendar, all the participants could immediately be notified by e-mail. In addition, the respective calendars of the participants presented the updated event. Occasionally, the instructor could add a street address where some face-to-face event would take place. The link to Google Maps would be generated automatically, indicating the precise place of the event on the map, and this information could be sent to all participants by e-mail or through Google Calendar, attached to an event.

The communication among the participants was done asynchronously, mainly by posting on Google+, as presented in Figure 6.3. The instructor used Google+ stream to deliver messages to the whole group (see thick arrow in Figure 6.3) and to lead to the content hosted by other social

Figure 6.3   Google+ main stream with the main elements highlighted

Credit: Fundação Roberto Marinho.

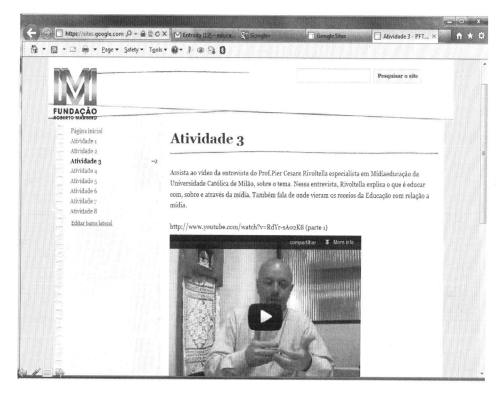

Figure 6.4 Course content structured on Google Sites with a YouTube video embedded

Credit: Fundação Roberto Marinho.

media (see fine arrow), such as Google Sites (illustrated in Figure 6.4). The participants could count on the privacy established by the circles of the social network. Thus, only the participants either could access the TFP Google+ stream and discuss topics published there (see rectangle in Figure 6.3) or could publish a new message there (see dashed rectangle in Figure 6.3).

During a virtual meeting on Hangout, all the participants could view and hear each other, manipulate Google Drive files collaboratively, present a YouTube video synchronously with the others, and share their screen, besides chatting by text.

Synchronous communication was also possible by using Gtalk and Hangout (see oval in Figure 6.3).

It is important to notice that all the publishing, supporting, and communicating resources were available for the use of mobile devices. It was a great advantage for fostering social presence since all participants could use their respective smartphones or tablets to interact more frequently. It allowed substantial interaction improvement because the participants could have more immediate response from instructors and peers.

The Course Dynamics

For each of the four modules, the class had a face-to-face meeting. As the participants were from different public schools, a different school was chosen to host the meeting for each on-site activity. These face-to-face meetings were used to present the modules, the basis of the main theory related to them, and the instructions to carry out the online activities during the following two months.

The participants could explore the content as long as it was published in different social media (e.g., Google Sites, Google Drive, and Blogger) according to the module. The publishing content in each session was always preceded by an instigating post in Google+ stream in order to make the participants reflect on what they should study and practice. As long as the participants explored the content, they could insert comments in that initial post or create new posts in Google+ stream to share questions and ideas. The circle feature of Google+ was used to guarantee that only the invited Google users would have access to the discussion stream. Private individual communication could be established by e-mail (Gmail) or synchronous text chatting (Gtalk). Gmail and Gtalk were useful for the exchange of experiences and discussion among the participants in a private way. If some significant topic or questioning justified more attention from the instructor, a Hangout session could be booked via Google Calendar for a group of participants to debate any concerns.

During the course, the participants were encouraged to put into practice what they learned. At this point, the choice for Google social media ecosystem showed its value. The participants could use the same tools to prototype their secondary courses (mathematics, physics, chemistry, Portuguese). Actually, they went beyond what was planned; they used unexpected social media resources, extrapolating the Google ecosystem borders. They used other resources than those provided by Google, such as Facebook, Slideshare, Flickr, and Skype. At the same time, they could apply the methods and theories discussed during the course in their day-by-day teaching practice. They had the opportunity to implement online structure to support their virtual tutoring, while still under the supervision of experienced instructors who could guide them to the best practices. Furthermore, each participant was expected to share his or her experience with peers for discussion, feedback, and social interaction.

Program Outcomes

Research on the outcomes perceived by the program participants was done to identify its strengths and weaknesses. The 22 program participants were invited to answer a 12-question online survey. Fifteen participants, eight women and seven men, responded to the survey, providing valuable information about the program learning outcomes. The average age of the respondents was 39.7 years old ($SD = 6.6$), while their average teaching experience was 15.7 years ($SD = 7$).

Digital Inclusion

One of the most important outcomes obtained from the program was the improvement of the respondents' digital inclusion. The respondents were asked to answer about what level of digital inclusion each one considered for himself or herself. The question was based on the following criteria: (a) nonexistent: no computing skills; (b) basic: using text editor, sending/receiving e-mails, and basic Internet browsing; (c) intermediate: using e-mails with attachments, buying online, using social networks and slide presentation software; (d) advanced: storing files online, downloading and installing programs, editing pictures, setting up blogs and websites; and (e) specialist: having no difficulty dealing with technology.

Figure 6.5 indicates this improvement by showing the level of digital inclusion evaluated by each of the respondents. Notice that there was an improvement in the digital inclusion of the participants after they participated in the program that used social media in its training strategy. It demonstrates the importance of using social media concomitantly to the theory of TFP resulting in an important tool for fostering the digital inclusion among the respondents.

The respondents of the survey indicated that the device most used for accessing the Internet for the program purposes was desktop, followed closely by notebook. Four of the 15 respondents

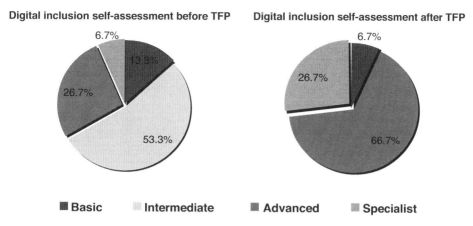

Digital inclusion self-assessment before TFP

Digital inclusion self-assessment after TFP

■ Basic   Intermediate   ■ Advanced   Specialist

Figure 6.5   Self-assessment of the program participants' digital inclusion
Credit: Fundação Roberto Marinho.

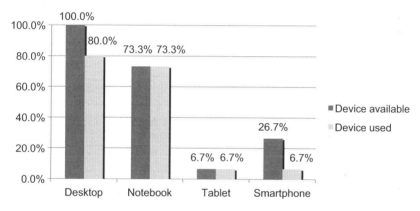

Figure 6.6   Device availability versus device use for accessing the program activities
Credit: Fundação Roberto Marinho.

could have accessed the Google+ and related social media using a smartphone. However, only one of them effectively used a mobile device to access the Internet, encouraged by the program. The low level of use of mobile devices, such as tablets and smartphones, during the program activities indicated the lack of habitual use of this kind of equipment for educational purposes. Furthermore, the TFP instructors did not foster the use of mobile devices during the program activities.

The respondents were asked to indicate what social media (a) they had already used before the program, (b) they went on to use during the TFP, (c) they intended to use in the future, or (d) they did not have any intention of using at all. Figure 6.7 demonstrates that the respondents had already used some of the social media, especially YouTube, with 14 out of the 15 teachers using before the TFP.

The main social media used during TFP for interaction and content delivery (Google+, Google Sites, Google Drive, and Blogger) had low levels of previous use, but the program activities sparked interest from the respondents to use these resources for educational purposes.

Another question focused on the perceived importance for each social media for educational use. The respondents were asked to rank the ten social media presented according to their order

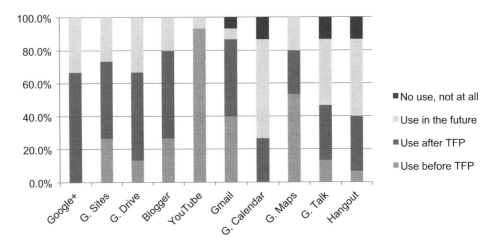

Figure 6.7   Use of social media before and after the TFP
Credit: Fundação Roberto Marinho.

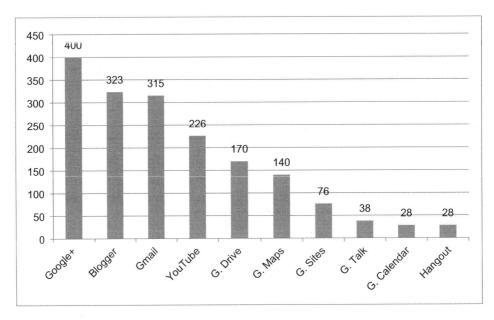

Figure 6.8   Order of importance of the social media according to the respondents
Credit: Fundação Roberto Marinho.

of importance for the TFP. A different score was attributed for each position in the respondent list: 10 points for the first place, 9 points for the second place, 8 points for the third place, and so forth, until the last place, which received 1 point. Finally, the total score of each social media was summed based on respondents' rank. The final result is shown in Figure 6.8, which presents the 10 social media according to their importance perceived by the respondents during the TFP.

The most important social media was Google+, which was expected, since it was used as the main interaction element of TFP. Blogger comes in second place, since it can be used in a very similar way to Google+. Gmail was considered essential because of its integration with social media within the whole communication process.

The way in which social media was used for educational purposes was also approved by the participants. They demonstrated clearly that either they intended to use, or already had gone on to use, most of the same social media used in the TFP in their own educational routine. The perceived importance of social media among the respondents was approximately the same as my perception while designing the interactive process of TFP. This reinforces the adoption of the same social media chosen for the TFP, according to the grade of importance planned for this scenario.

Different aspects of the TFP outcomes were questioned by using a 5-point Likert scale: (a) *totally agree*; (b) *partially agree*; (c) *neutral*; (d) *partially disagree*; and (e) *totally disagree*. The scale was used to evaluate the methodology, the content, the social media used, the learning outcomes as a whole, and the applicability of the method in the respondents' work context. Figure 6.9 presents results from the five aspects that indicate an overall positive response. The content used in TFP was the only aspect that received a neutral vote in the responses.

The respondents who chose *partially agree* in the analysis expanded their reasons through open-ended questions. The partial satisfaction with learning outcomes was mainly due to the lack of training in the use of the social media used in TFP. In fact, the responsibility of learning how to use the social media was delegated exclusively to the TFP participants, with no previous training offered. Thus, some of them felt that it was a difficult task to be faced with a previously designated technical support. A common concern was the need of on-site training in the use of social media and educational technologies, which should be done on a regular basis and provided by the school within a predefined human resource policy.

Some respondents criticized the low tutoring activity. They expected more interaction with the tutor through Google+ or other social media. This was the main reason why they were partially satisfied with the methodology. It is important to highlight that tutor mediation is an important feature for online courses in Brazil, due to a common expectation of high perception of virtual presence from the tutor.

As mentioned, the respondents had the opportunity to express their opinions and concerns through open-ended questions. When asked what other social media or technological resources

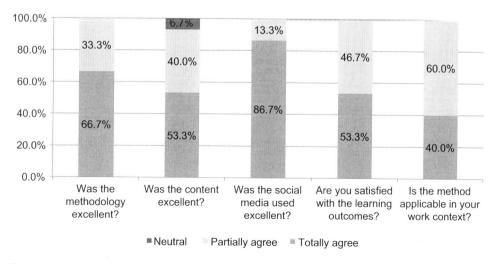

Figure 6.9 Likert scale that demonstrates the respondent satisfaction with different aspects of TFP
Credit: Fundação Roberto Marinho.

they had been using beyond the social media used in TFP, the responses included: Facebook, Orkut (another Google social network, popular in Brazil), Google Groups, Yahoo Groups, Slideshare, Wiki, Skype, Jing, and Podomatic. Three of the respondents did not mention any previous experience with other social media than those used in TFP. Another common perception was that they were going to use what they had learned in their work, and expected to enrich the pedagogical activity with the use of social media resources they had used in TFP.

Conclusion

At the end of the program, no participant had abandoned the course. The level of participation satisfied both the instructors and the program managers, while learning outcomes exceeded everyone's expectations. The program was expected to be expanded in the future, to include hundreds of secondary school teachers from dozens of institutions, with many more instructors tutoring the course.

The results showed the importance of presenting the theory of online tutoring but with the practical use of technology to perform the presented concepts. The testimony of the participants and the absence of previous use of Google+ demonstrate the importance of training the teacher to optimize the use of social networks for educational purposes. The fact that social media was used in the delivery of content, and social network was used for organizing the interaction process among participants, allowed the instructors to improve the digital inclusion of teachers effectively. Furthermore, it helped to improve the student retention because the participants noticed that the presented theory could be put into practice during the TFP. The perception of value of the learning process was very high because of the practice aligned with the theory.

Last, this study shows the efficacy of the use of SNSs in education, as other researchers have previously shown over the last few years, such as Cohen (2012) and Griffith and Liyanage (2008), who studied the use of SNS in education. The results obtained make me confident that SNS will be widely and successfully used as an educational tool in the future. As the technology keeps evolving, new resources will bring new ways to use SNS for educational purposes. This makes important the continuous research on the use of SNS for educational purposes.

Note

1 The Roberto Marinho Foundation was created in 1977 by Roberto Marinho, journalist and founder of Globo Organizations—the largest communication group in South America—and has already trained millions of Brazilians through Telecurso, a TV program that offers classes for those who need or want to complete elementary education and that carries out several other projects in the environmental, educational, and cultural fields.

References

Boyd, D. M., & Ellison, N. B. (2007). Social network sites: Definition, history, and scholarship. *Journal of Computer-Mediated Communication, 13*, 210–230.

Cohen, J. N. (2012). Professional resource: The potential of Google+ as a media literacy tool. *Journal of Media Literacy Education, 4*(1), 93–96.

Griffith, S., & Liyanage, L. (2008). An introduction to the potential of social networking sites in education. In I. Olney, G. Lefoe, J. Mantei, & J. Herrington (Eds.), *Proceedings of the Second Emerging Technologies Conference 2008* (pp. 76–81). Wollongong: University of Wollongong.

Hoffman, E. (2009). Evaluating social networking tools for distance learning. *Proceedings of Technology, Colleges & Community Worldwide Online Conference* (Vol. 1, pp. 92–100). Retrieved from http://etec.hawaii.edu/proceedings/2009/hoffman.pdf

Mazer, J. P., Murphy, R. E., & Simonds, C. J. (2007). I'll see you on "Facebook": The effects of computer-mediated teacher self-disclosure on student motivation, affective learning, and classroom climate. *Communication Education, 56*(1), 1–17.

O'Sullivan, P. B., Hunt, S. K., & Lippert, L. R. (2004). Mediated immediacy: A language of affiliation in a technological age. *Journal of Language and Social Psychology, 23*, 464–490.

Tidwell, L. C., & Walther, J. B. (2002). Computer-mediated communication effects on disclosure, impressions, and interpersonal evaluations. *Human Communication Research, 28*, 317–348.

7

Multimedia Production Projects

Relevant Issues and Possible Models for Mobile Learning

Izabel de Moraes Sarmento Rego, Joni de Almeida Amorim, Per M. Gustavsson, and Sten F. Andler

Introduction

New technologies can be used to promote educational practices. This statement fits into the contemporary context and demands that academic research focusing on education also seeks to accompany technological developments and potential use of such technologies by society.

Considering this scenario, in this chapter we present reflections on learning with mobility, emphasizing the use of mobile devices (particularly, tablets and smartphones) in the educational field, also called mobile learning, or m-learning. Researchers in various parts of the world are conducting experiments with the intention of exploring the limits and possibilities of mobile learning. In many situations, these experiences are limited to a restricted scope, and there are few cases where mobile learning experience is designed for larger groups of participants. In order to cope with this situation, in this text we offer reflections on project management for the development of multimedia to mobile learning courses.

We will present technical and pedagogical issues related to the development of learning objects (LOs), highlighting their possibilities for large-scale use to access open educational resources (OERs) that may be used on initiatives like massive open online courses (MOOCs). We take the definition of LOs as digital or nondigital entities that can be used or referenced during learning or teaching processes. We will follow with considerations regarding the management of educational projects. Finally, we will present an experience of production of LOs for mobile learning in a vocational education course held in Brazil, as a matter to illustrate this aspect of management of educational projects.

Additionally, we believe that the understanding of the specificities of this project held in Brazil will be useful to reflect on how the use of mobile devices can transform learning experiences. This approach will endorse the reflections on useful methods and practices when a large scale project is demanded. After presenting the experience, we detail an analysis from the perspective of the Educational Project Management Office, or EduPMO (Amorim, 2010), useful for the management of educational projects. Proposals for future work are presented together with the conclusion of this study.

Background Information

LOs enhance the use of technology at different levels and types of education. With the Internet and the increasing use of mobile devices, it becomes possible to make use of LOs with texts and hypertexts, animated images, games, simulations, audios, and videos. Numerous technological issues affect the design, production, and sharing of LOs.

In some cases, the technological complexity may require a support team to assist in the production of LOs following international standards like the Multimodal Interaction Framework (W3C, 2012) to better share and reuse via the web. In other cases, when intending only to produce a single media, such as video or audio, mobile phones, or other similar equipment can be used to capture, edit, and share images and videos in websites such as YouTube (2013) or TeacherTube (2007).

According to the Learning Technology Standards Committee from the Institute of Electrical and Electronics Engineers (IEEE, 2002), currently, the LOs are most often developed for computer use and, in many cases, they are not totally compatible with mobile devices. This aspect impacts on technical issues related to mobile learning.

From the theoretical point of view, there is no consensus on the definition of m-learning. Translating this term into other languages can give rise to different interpretations of the terminology. In Portuguese, for example, m-learning can be translated either as "learning mobile" or "learning with mobility." In an attempt to broaden the discussion and bring light to different theoretical conceptions of m-learning, we pointed out some considerations and definitions proposed by researchers.

First, we assume that mobile learning involves two aspects: mobility and learning. Hayes and Kuchinskas (2003), referenced by Moura (2010), consider that mobility can be related to the technologies as well as to the learner or even to the LOs. According to Traxler (2009), some theorists argue that m-learning is defined on account of technologies and devices involved. Others argue that the term refers to the situation of mobility of students, in this case, individuals going from one place to another while learning. Still other researchers point out that the term is appropriately related to the situation of mobility of the learning experience, where teacher, students, and so forth are not in a fixed location.

Among the advantages of this modality, Ally (2009) stated that by the use of mobile wireless technologies, mobile learning allows anyone to have access to learning materials and information anytime and anywhere. The author argues that this access empowers learners and gives them autonomy and control of their own learning.

This change in behavior is part of the processes of digital literacy, where different mechanical and cognitive skills are constantly demanded. The access to the information technology tools causes changes in how people access information and in how they create meaning in texts constructed quickly and integrating various resources.

We believe these advantages will be better utilized in educational settings where teachers and designers go beyond the previously established limits in traditional classrooms and implement innovative educational strategies that exploit the resources of mobile devices. We argue that the use of mobile devices by themselves does not automatically promote educational innovation.

According to Saccol, Reinhard, Schlemmer, and Barbosa (2010), as a way to have the innovation, the use of new technologies necessary have to be linked to methodologies, practices, and processes of pedagogical mediation developed with the understanding of the nature and specific potential of these technologies. Overcoming the uses of these technologies to reproduce traditional learning strategies demands thinking in new ways of teaching, considering the individual learning styles of students and the possibility of making meaning while exploring different semiotic modalities (Cope & Kalantzis, 2009).

Besides the educational aspects, if one thinks of m–learning it becomes necessary to consider technological aspects. We emphasize the need of more studies on technical standards, posing features and technical requirements of mobile devices for the development of virtual learning environments for m–learning. In this way, virtual environments dedicated to m–learning must meet needs related to different perspectives that may include technical, educational, economical, and socio–cultural. As an example, the shift to mobile technologies could leave behind users that cannot access the learning material due to a lack of the appropriate hardware infrastructure, in this way increasing the digital divide instead of benefiting learners from developing regions with a possible leapfrog effect (Napoli & Obar, 2013).

Research Methodology

Considering the educational, social, and technological aspects previously mentioned, we pointed out the need for experiencing mobile learning in different situations so the development of LOs can take into account different contexts and needs. As specified below, these experiments will be most successful if they come from detailed plans that consider the context from where students, teachers, and developers emerge.

The research methodology involved (a) defining a strategy for project evaluation, (b) documenting a project, (c) analyzing the selected project, and (d) identifying opportunities for the improvement of management. To evaluate the project we selected the strategy based on the application of Kerzner's (2009) four critical issues for each of the nine prospects of the EduPMO framework.

Kerzner (2009) suggested four critical issues to be considered at the end of each project: 1) What was done right? 2) What was done incorrectly? 3) What future recommendations can be made? 4) How, when, and to whom should such information be disseminated? In general, the application of such issues involves both identifying the most relevant processes in order to improve the management of future initiatives as well as documenting and disseminating lessons learned for such access by authorized users.

In this research, the application of the four critical issues of Kerzner (2009) occurs for each of the nine dimensions of the EduPMO framework, developed by Amorim (2010) after an extensive review of the literature on multimedia production and based on the analysis of numerous projects for approximately 5 years. We present below the nine dimensions of the EduPMO framework.

We consider a framework to be any set of assumptions, concepts, values, methods, and practices that constitutes a way of perceiving reality. The dimensions of EduPMO constitute a reference that enables an organization interested in project management of production and/or use of digital content in education to ensure that all relevant factors were considered.

In the EduPMO model, the dimensions are separated into two types: explicit and implicit. The explicit dimensions are those effectively presented and explained, either partially or totally, to the members of the different teams involved in the project. The implicit dimensions are not directly presented even considering that they affect the work of the different teams of the project; they are part of the repertoire of strategies used by the project management office (PMO) as well as by managers of each project during their work. Although there is a clear interrelationship between the different dimensions, whether explicit or implied, these dimensions were divided into a group of four in the first case and into a group of five in the second, as shown below.

In the scope of the four explicit dimensions, we have Content Dimension (CD), which refers to the correct understanding of the fundamental requirements of design, particularly with regard to the content involved. The Pedagogical Dimension (PD) refers to the considerations on aspects of teaching and learning involved. The Technological Dimension (TD) refers to the process of detailing the technical requirements for products to be produced and/or used. The Management Dimension (MD) refers to many aspects, including specific knowledge areas such as project integration management, scope management, time management, cost management, quality management, human resources management, communication management, risk management, and project procurement management.

There are five implicit dimensions. The Strategic Management Implicit Dimension (SMID) refers to achieving specific strategic objectives through centralized management of multiple programs and/or portfolios, which includes identifying, prioritizing, authorizing, managing, and controlling projects of these portfolios. The Implicit Knowledge Management Dimension (IKMD) refers to essential aspects to producing effective management of knowledge, such as harvesting, filtering, configuring, implementing, and disseminating. The Change Management Implicit Dimension (CMID) refers to the management of several transitions in the context of the design or shape in work teams given the unique context of a specific project. The Maturity Model Implicit Dimension (MMID) refers to the quest for process improvement. The Intellectual Property Implicit Dimension (IPID) refers to aspects of innovation management and property rights.

For each dimension of the EduPMO framework (Amorim, 2010), macroprocesses are defined. Each macroprocess may be presented through a description and/or a diagram highlighting the activities and/or tasks to perform, with indications of inputs and outputs of the macroprocess as well as the useful tools and techniques for the implementation of the macroprocess under consideration. In this way, for each dimension we have different artifacts for macroprocesses: description, diagram, inputs, outputs, tools and techniques useful for the implementation of macroprocesses together with standardized document templates provided by the PMO. All nine dimensions comprehend 199 macroprocesses. In order to illustrate this approach in a practical situation, the next section will present a project focused in the development of LOs for mobile learning.

Experiment

More than 42 million students have enrolled in schools of the National Service of Industrial Learning (SENAI) since its creation. SENAI is a Brazilian institution focused in vocational education for industry workers. In 2012, this organization comprised 250 Professional Education Centers, 39 Technology Centers, 118 Training Centers/Agencies, 306 Mobile Units, and 310 Mobile Action program kits (SENAI, 2013). Since new technologies may be relevant for vocational education, the SENAI's regional department of São Paulo (Brazil) in partnership with the national department carried out the project Development of Learning Objects for Mobile Media in Vocational Courses at SENAI between the years 2011 and 2012, with a total duration of 12 months.

This project aimed to systematize data related to the use of mobile devices in vocational education, as well as to identify results of the experience of learning with LOs in mobile devices. We applied project management methods and practices to a research project with the purpose of a future implementation of a comprehensive structure to the production of LOs for mobile devices. We organized the project into the following steps: planning, development, implementation, and evaluation. The following paragraphs discuss the steps.

During the planning stage, we raised the need for technical and theoretical subsidies to design the LOs. Therefore, theoretical and practical examples were considered to serve as a starting point to understand m-learning. We analyzed scientific papers, books, and news related to the subject, composing a catalog in order to provide theoretical and technical support for the project. In addition, we looked for a classroom teaching situation where there was great difficulty in achieving learning satisfactorily. To meet this need, we identified a group for the pilot application of LOs for mobile devices at the school Suiço-Brasileira Paulo Ernesto Tolle (SENAI-SP, 2013), in São Paulo, Brazil.

In the development stage, we purchased various mobile devices and software. We selected a specific topic within the technical course in precision mechanics, in the assignment called Quality Planning and Control of Mechanical Instruments. In this course, students learn in a laboratory to manipulate and to maintain measurement tools such as hygrometers, manometers, dial indicators, and others.

The implementation stage involved the testing of LOs in class and collecting data for future analysis. The expectation was that experience induces the development of skills and abilities related to the technical area as well as in the manipulation of digital tools, fostering the digital literacy of students. The experiment took place over two days at the school.

From this context, and based on the information previously presented, it was possible to evaluate the development of content for mobile devices in the fourth step. The aim was to analyze technical and pedagogical parameters previously specified in relation to the following: operating systems, mobile devices, and tools used to develop LOs.

Analysis of the Experiment

In order to analyze the experiment reported here, we applied the set of four critical issues of Kerzner (2009). These issues were presented briefly in the research methodology section of this paper. In this section, the issues are considered for each one of the nine dimensions of the EduPMO framework (Amorim, 2010). The analysis of the experiment is presented in summary form in Table 7.1, which includes the macroprocesses that were considered more relevant for this specific study. Detailed information about these macroprocesses may be found in Amorim (2010).

Table 7.1 Summary of Questions and Answers Using EduPMO Macroprocesses Selected for the Analysis of the Experiment

1—Content Dimension (CD)
1.1—What was done right?
Answer: CD 01.03—Plan business analysis activities.
1.2—What was done incorrectly?
Answer: CD 03.03—Keep requirements for reuse.
1.3—What future recommendations can be made?
Answer: CD 01.02—Conduct stakeholder analysis.
1.4—How, when, and to whom should such information be disseminated?
Answer: Professional staff planning and content development.
2—Pedagogical Dimension (PD)
2.1—What was done right?
Answer: PD 02—Analyze profile of learners.
2.2—What was done incorrectly?
Answer: PD 06—Rate instructional results.
2.3—What future recommendations can be made?
Answer: PD.01—Evaluate instructional needs.

(Continued)

Table 7.1 (Continued)

2.4—How, when, and to whom should such information be disseminated?

Answer: Professional team who deals with the curriculum development and educational assessments.

3—Technological Dimension (TD)

3.1—What was done right?

Answer: TD.01—Assessing technology needs.

3.2—What was done incorrectly?

Answer: TD.06—Planning manufacturing.

3.3—What future recommendations can be made?

Answer: TD.02—Define parts of products.

3.4—How, when, and to whom should such information be disseminated?

Answer: Professional team who deals with planning and implementation of technological resources.

4—Management Dimension (MD)

4.1—What was done right?

Answer: MD.01.05—Control of changes in an integrated manner.

4.2—What was done incorrectly?

Answer: MD.08.05—Plan response to risk.

4.3—What future recommendations can be made?

Answer: MD.02.02—Define scope.

4.4—How, when, and to whom should such information be disseminated?

Answer: Professional staff who deal with the functions of project management.

5—Strategic Management Implicit Dimension (SMID)

5.1—What was done right?

Answer: SMID.01.01.06—Monitor and control the performance of the program.

5.2—What was done incorrectly?

Answer: SMID.01.02.04—Developing the architecture of the program.

5.3—What future recommendations can be made?

Answer: SMID.01.11.03—Engaging stakeholders of the program.

5.4—How, when, and to whom should such information be disseminated?

Answer: Professionals who deal with the strategic management may be warned.

6—Implicit Knowledge Management Dimension (IKMD)

6.1—What was done right?

Answer: IKMD.04—Implement the solution.

6.2—What was done incorrectly?

Answer: IKMD.02—Analyze initial state.

6.3—What future recommendations can be made?

Answer: IKMD.05—Evaluate results.

6.4—How, when, and to whom should such information be disseminated?

Answer: Professional team who deals with the functions of knowledge management.

7—Change Management Implicit Dimension (CMID)

7.1—What was done right?

Answer: CMID.05—Analyze final state.

7.2—What was done incorrectly?

Answer: CMID.02—Identify changing needs.

7.3—What future recommendations can be made?

Answer: CMID.01—Plan the management of change.

7.4—How, when, and to whom should such information be disseminated?

Answer: Professional team with the functions of coordination of actions of innovation.

8—Maturity Model Implicit Dimension (MMID)

8.1—What was done right?

Answer: MMID.03.10—Support services and products.

8.2—What was done incorrectly?

Answer: MMID.01.01—Planning improvements.

8.3—What future recommendations can be made?

Answer: MMID.05.05—Innovative organizational improvement.

8.4—How, when, and to whom should such information be disseminated?

Answer: Professional team with the functions of innovation management.

9—Intellectual Property Implicit Dimension (IPID)

9.1—What was done right?

Answer: IPID.05—Collect terms of sale.

9.2—What was done incorrectly?

Answer: IPID.02—Set intellectual property policy.

9.3—What future recommendations can be made?

Answer: IPID.01—Plan management of intellectual property.

9.4—How, when, and to whom should such information be disseminated?

Answer: Professional team dealing with the functions of intellectual property management.

Adapted from Amorim, 2010.

Conclusion and Future Work

Nowadays, the possibility of reaching a bigger audience with the increased access to educational resources using the Internet through mobile devices allied with the simplification and cheapening of tools for production of multimedia brings about a scenario in which it is feasible to think of producing LOs on a large scale. Accordingly, we believe that systematizing the management of the production of these LOs becomes a crucial aspect to ensure success and optimization of the usage of organizational resources.

The experience presented here showed the many different aspects involved in the management of educational projects. In this way, it can be highlighted that various aspects need to be considered for the success of a project that may involve multimedia production and/or reutilization. As future work, we aim to develop and/or improve models for the management of projects for multimedia production considering the new challenges related to m-learning. MOOCs for higher education are especially relevant nowadays and suggest new perspectives for research considering the Brazilian context. We point out, also, the need to bring about strategies and teaching methodologies that specifically exploit the features of mobile devices such as tablets and smartphones. Additionally, future work may involve the planning of courses on cyber security for the training of different stakeholders at SENAI.

References

Ally, M. (Ed.). (2009). *Mobile learning: transforming the delivery of education and training.* Athabasca, Canada: AU Press.

Amorim, J. A. (2010). *Multimedia engineering* (Doctoral dissertation, Campinas, Universidade Estadual de Campinas). Retrieved from http://www.bibliotecadigital.unicamp.br/

Cope, B., & Kalantzis, M. (2009). A grammar of multimodality. *International Journal of Learning, 16*(2), 361–425.

Hayes, K., & Kuchinskas, S. (2003). *Going mobile: Building the real-time enterprise with mobile applications that work.* San Francisco, CA: CMP Books.

IEEE. (2002, July 15). *Learning object metadata standard* (IEEE LTSC 1484.12.1. Draft Standard for Learning Object Metadata. Learning Technology Standards Committee). Retrieved from http://www.ieeeltsc.org

Kerzner, H. (2009). *Project management: A systems approach to planning, scheduling, and controlling.* New York, NY: Wiley.

Moura, A.M.C. (2010). *Apropriação do Telemóvel como Ferramenta de Mediação em Mobile Learning: Estudos de Caso em Contexto Educativo* (Doctoral dissertation, Braga, Universidade do Minho). Retrieved from http://repositorium.sdum.uminho.pt/bitstream/1822/13183/1/Tese%20Integral.pdf

Napoli, P., & Obar, J. (2013). *Mobile leapfrogging and digital divide policy—Assessing the limitations of mobile internet access.* New America Foundation. Retrieved from http://newamerica.net/publications/policy/mobile_leapfrogging_and_digital_divide_policy

Saccol, A. Z., Reinhard, N., Schlemmer, E., & Barbosa, J.L.V. (2010). M-learning (mobile learning) in practice: a training experience with it professionals. *JISTEM* [Online], 7(2), 261–280.

SENAI. (2013). *Escola Senai "Suíço-Brasileira Paulo Ernesto Tolle."* Serviço Nacional de Aprendizagem Industrial (SENAI). Retrieved January 30, 2013 from http://suicobrasileira.sp.senai.br/

SENAI-SP. (2013). *Serviço Nacional de Aprendizagem Industrial—São Paulo (SENAI-SP).* Retrieved from http://www.sp.senai.br/

TeacherTube, LLC. (2007). *TeacherTube.* Retrieved January 30, 2013 from http://www.teachertube.com/

Traxler, J. (2009). Learning in a mobile age. *International Journal of Mobile and Blended Learning, 1*(1), 1–12.

W3C. (2012, October 25). MMI architecture. In J. Barnett (Ed.), *World Wide Web Consortium (W3C) Recommendation.* Retrieved from http://www.w3.org/TR/mmi-arch/

YouTube, LLC. (2013). *YouTube.* Retrieved from http://www.youtube.com/

8

Learners of Digital Era (LoDE)

What's True, and What's Just Hype About the So-Called Digital Natives

Emanuele Rapetti and Lorenzo Cantoni

Introduction

Looking at young people using digital technologies, it would seem they are naturally adept—or have developed a special skill—when it comes to new media. Many observers and scholars adopted this understanding and claimed that if information and communication technologies (ICTs) are so important in everyday life experiences, it is reasonable to consider young people as a generation of digitalized learners. This approach to learners and new media sprouted during the 1990s (Strauss & Howe, 1991; Papert, 1993; Tapscott, 1998), grew during the following decade (Oblinger & Oblinger, 2005; Prensky, 2001b; Tapscott, 2009), and is still a mainstream reading (Jones & Shao, 2011; Prensky, 2011).

Since 2008, however, critical voices arose from all over the world. In particular, Bennett, Maton, and Kervin (2008), from Australia, criticized the anthropological level supporters of the digital natives approach, talking about an educational "give up"; Bullen, Morgan, Belfer, and Qayyum (2009), from Canada, reframed the technological expectations in learning; Schulmeister (2010), from Germany, compared all research made on this topic and scaled down the concept of "media skill" to the ability of information gathering. As we will see in this chapter, a massive use is not by itself a competent usage, and familiarity does not automatically imply proficiency. In order to conclude such, we will move from the analysis of the literature, stressing how controversial the debate is; then, we will suggest a cautious and well-rooted perspective; finally, quantitative data from research called "Learners' Voices @USI-SUPSI" (from Switzerland) will be presented in order to support our conclusions.

Gen Y, Net Generation, and Digital Natives: The Beginning and Diffusion of Three Lucky Labels

"Generation Y," "Digital Natives," and "Net Generation" are three widespread expressions in the public debate; they are used almost worldwide to identify and typify people born after 1980 who have experienced, since early childhood, the massive presence of media devices in their everyday life. Many other labels have been coined, but those three have gained a peculiar fame due to their intrinsic metaphorical power: Actually, they put in evidence three key aspects of the abovementioned group of people. The first one focuses on the generational aspect: Never before in the history of humanity have children had the chance to handle so many media. The second one stresses the novelty of such a situation, namely, the fact that the tools are digital. The third one puts in evidence the pivotal role played by the Internet.

As we will see later in the chapter, from some important intuitions, a huge corpus of reflections appeared to describe in detail this "generation" and its traits. In addition, many scholars enlarged the consideration of the problem—from a historic-sociological reading to a psychological and/or pedagogical interpretation. The question then became "how do we teach the digital learners?" and a number of voices arose to provide educational recipes to deal with this "generation of digital learners."

It is possible to approach this complexity through many paths of analysis; a historical analysis of the evolution of the debate around "learners and new media" seems to be particularly convenient here in order to better present the topic. The main voices orienting the reflections and animating the discussion worldwide have been appearing for more than 20 years. Analyzing this period, an evolution in approaches emerges.

During the first decade (1991–2000), authors from different fields contributed to the establishment and the diffusion of the theory about a generation of digital learners. Then, after the end of the millennium, the theme gained greater attention and became more relevant and urgent to different stakeholders' agendas; probably because of this larger popularity, one can register a plurality of voices. This second decade (2001–2010) saw the emergence of contrasting and opposite opinions. The certainty of the 1990s—a generation of digital learners does exist—became a doubt. And the debate went hot. The work of Strauss and Howe can be considered the starting point for the establishment of a theory about a generation of digital learners because it captured attention around the theme and also because of the persistence of their intuitions during the past two decades.

In their famous book, *Generations: The History of America's Future, 1584 to 2069* (Strauss & Howe, 1991), they provided a very interesting and appealing reading of the American history, based on the idea of an endless circle of four archetypes of generations (heroes, artists, prophets, and nomads) following one after another throughout centuries, bearing certain recurring universal traits. Then, because of the historical climate, each generation developed peculiar characteristics; at the time of publication, it was the turn of Generation Y (referring to the fact that they came after the so-called Generation X), or Millennials (see their subsequent text: *Millennials Rising: The Next Great Generation*, published in 2000)—born from 1982 until 2005—said to be "heroes."

"Heroes" means:

> Increasingly protected as children, they become increasingly indulgent as parents. Their principal endowment activities are in the domain of community, affluence, and technology. . . . They have been vigorous and rational institution builders. All have been aggressive advocates of economic prosperity and public optimism in midlife; and all have maintained a reputation for civic energy and competence even deep into old age.
>
> *(Strauss & Howe, 1991, p. 84. To deepen the "millennials" characteristics, see also Strauss & Howe, 1991, pp. 335–343)*

The cohort of Generation Y, as described in Strauss and Howe (1991) and Howe and Strauss (2000), has seven distinguishing traits, drawn by crossing the historical characteristics attributed to "heroes" and the specific sociological and contextual data related to them:

• Special—They feel this way because they were the first in history to receive such enormous amounts of economic and educative attention from their parents.

- Sheltered—Never before have children received so much protection in medicine as well as in social experiences.
- Confident—They trust authority because parents and educators gave them a lot.
- Conventional—In opposition to Generation X, they prefer to respect rules of conduct, proper dress, and social authority and not to take risks (their revolution is not about "changing the world" but in doing their best in order to score better).
- Team oriented—Due to their experience in school and to the many opportunities offered by the Internet, they want to participate on a team.
- Achieving—Generally speaking, they score better academically than any other generation before them.
- Pressured—They have been spoiled and coddled to reach the top, and now they feel it's time to give something back (often young Millennials suffer because of anxiety, stress, and similar pains).

After Strauss and Howe, there were a growing number of publications aiming to better describe and define people belonging to the digital generation. The following timeline explores the evolution of this idea, mentioning those authors who gained more popularity in academic/scientific papers. While the huge amount of related publications cannot be reported here, a sample of them—among the most influential—is included in Table 8.1.

Table 8.1 shows how the hypothesis of Strauss and Howe continuously grew in reputation, achieving the level of a theory, being applied and verified, and, finally, transforming into a scientific perspective, as reported and well discussed in "Deconstructing the Media Use of the Net Generation" (Schulmeister, 2010).

Table 8.1 Timeline of the Theory of Digital Learners During the First Decade

Year	Evolution of the theory
1991	Strauss and Howe open the way. People born (on average) after 1982 are different. This difference is based on generational traits, and the digital *milieu* plays a major role. They invented the "Generation Y" label, which is still in use.
1991	Soloway coins the "Nintendo Generation" expression, putting the attention on the never-seen-before trait of young people: they are video gaming.
1993	According to Papert, it is more than a historical or sociological difference. The theme involves pedagogy and psychology. People grown up with a remote controller at hand are used to change and switch: they have a "grasshopper mind."
1995	Controversies implied by Internet usage start to come to the surface. It is the time of "Life on the Screen: Identity in the Age of the Internet" by Turkle, exploring an unknown issue, such as the *multiusers* identity.
1998 (2009)	Tapscott inaugurates a strand of research about the habits of the "Net Generation"— namely, the ones who are "growing up digital" (and who, in 2009, are "grown up digital"). He leads research projects meant to observe how they are different in learning because of ICTs and the growing importance of the Internet. In his opinion, they have the chance to be the greatest generation ever because of the infinite chances to access knowledge.
2000	Howe and Strauss double their success, exploring—at the millennium turn—the expected traits attributed to the "Millennials." Young people are described like the "next great generation." After 10 years, their generational theory has percolated the public debate—from academia to newspapers.
2000	Frand discusses how to deal with the implications for higher education due to the "changes" in students' mindset.

The hypothesis of a generation of digitalized learners has been pivotal for many innovation processes at any level, from class experiences to educational policies; nonetheless, incontrovertible empirical proof of its existence is still missing. It probably gained prestige because it explained cogently and briefly a complex reality, which was worrying both parents and educators. The concept offered a commonsense-based interpretation, easy to understand, based on the everlasting contraposition between the younger and the older. It arrived to fill a void of knowledge and understanding in the theory of education, business, and community life (OECD-CERI, 2012, pp. 93–112).

Ten years later, the idea transformed into a socio–pedagogical matter of fact. Video–game consultant Marc Prensky, inventor of the notorious "digital natives" label, became a promoter of the burning debate.

Voices of Concerns and the Debate About Them

The second decade can be synthetically expressed with the following question: Does a generation of digitalized learners exist? At the beginning of the millennium the debate became more articulated, and from a main root of reflection developed multiple, and even contrasting, trends.

The first and more decisive contribution came from Prensky. In two articles, "Digital Natives and Digital Immigrants" (Prensky, 2001a) and "Do They Really Think Differently?" (Prensky, 2001b), Prensky pointed out the existence of a generation of people socialized to learning through ICTs since early childhood. Because of this, they are likely to be adept with computers, creative with technology, and, above all, highly skilled at multitasking in a world where ubiquitous connections are taken for granted. Following this line of thought, young people's continuous use of ICTs is assumed to have important implications for the development of their intellectual competences and cognitive skills to the extent that they are supposed to think differently. In light of a review of the literature, it is correct to state that this position represents a merging of the various concepts that emerged during the previous decade. To synthesize his view, Prensky invented the famous label "digital natives" and claimed that

> it is now clear that, as a result of this ubiquitous environment and the sheer volume of their interaction with it, today's students think and process information fundamentally differently from their predecessors. These differences go far further and deeper than most educators suspect or realize. "Different kinds of experiences lead to different brain structures" says Dr Bruce D. Berry of Baylor College of Medicine . . ., it is very likely that our students' brains have physically changed—and are different from ours—as a result of how they grew up. But whether or not this is literally true, we can say with certainty that their thinking patterns have changed.
>
> *(Prensky, 2001a, p. 1)*

This difference has structural implications in socializing, behaving, and learning processes, as remarked on and extended in his subsequent text, *Don't Bother Me Mom, I'm Learning!* (Prensky, 2006). Prensky colored and led, for better or worse, all the subsequent debate. Actually, what especially warmed the status of reflection is the hypothesis that not only the environment but people can be digital (Prensky, 2001a).

As said, during this second decade, many trends developed. Three are clearly recognizable. The first aggregated around the followers of the theory of a generation of digital learners. The second came out in clear opposition to a positive attitude toward this generation, expressing a preoccupied position because of the risks provoked by the widespread diffusion of digital devices and facilities. Then, around the second half of the decade, a third trend appeared: Scholars belonging to this last group started to critically investigate the idea of a generation of digital learners, aiming to demonstrate its fallacies.

The negative feelings started because of the growing number of risks and problems implied in new media use, reported during the previous years. The American association, MAVAV—Mothers Against Videogame Addiction and Violence—constitutes the first impactful and well-documented (2002) actor of this trend. The "dark side" of the *digital* generation seems to cover a lot of facets; younger children are said to be violent, online bullies, net addicted to pointless activities (MAVAV, 2002–2006), and their media diet is connected with emerging deviant behaviors (Sieberg, 2011; for a documented and well-organized panorama about the effects of connectedness, see OECD, 2012).

To understand such a position, an excerpt from the provocative *The Dumbest Generation: How the Digital Age Stupefies Young Americans and Jeopardizes Our Future* (Bauerlein, 2008) can be useful:

> Hyper-networked kids who can track each others' every move with ease, but are largely ignorant of history, economics, culture, and other subjects. And the fault comes exactly from ICTs usages for digital immigrants, people who are 40 years old who spent their college time in the library acquiring information, the Internet is really a miraculous source of knowledge. Digital natives, however, go to the Internet not to store knowledge in their minds, but to retrieve material and pass it along. The Internet is just a delivery system.
>
> *(Bauerlein, 2008)*

Since roughly the middle of the decade, scholars have developed new reflections, expressing perplexity not about the positive effects of ICTs, but rather on the idea itself of a generation of digitalized learners.

Both theoretical assumptions and empirical research began to be criticized. On one side, the theory of a generation of digital learners is questioned for its linguistic inconsistency or risk (Bennett et al., 2008; Bullen et al., 2009); on the other side, results from empirical research reveal the complexity of the relationship between learners and new media, which does not match with the universal traits attributed to digital learners (Kvavik, 2005). Recently, Schulmeister (2010) remarked that anthropological assumptions about the idea of a monolithic generation, simply based on familiarity with ICTs, are hazardous in pedagogy, while it must be remembered that media use is just a part of leisure time, together with sports, arts, time with parents, and time with peers.

Thinkers following this third trend tend to consider the idea of a digital generation of learners as an inspiring starting point rather than as an established theory.

> A review of literature on the millennial learner and implications for education reveals that most of the claims are supported by reference to a relatively small number of publications. The works most often cited are Oblinger & Oblinger (2005), Tapscott (1998), Prensky (2001a, b), and Howe & Strauss (2000). Other works that are often mentioned, although less frequently, include Seely Brown (2002), Frand (2000) and Turkle (1995). What all of these works have in common is that they make grand claims about the difference between the millennial generation and all previous generations and they argue that this difference has huge implications for education. But most significantly, these claims are made with reference to almost no empirical data. For the most part, they rely

on anecdotal observations or speculation. In the rare cases, where there is hard data, it is usually not representative.

(Bullen et al., 2009)

Table 8.2 shows how the debate evolved during this second decade. The rationale behind the table is the same expressed for the previous one: It is not meant to be an exhaustive list of contributions; rather, it tries to show how many contrasting voices arose around this debate during the second decade.

Table 8.2 Timeline of the Debate During the Second Decade

Year	Evolution of the theory and development of contrasting trends
2001	Prensky coins the famous label "digital natives," meant to describe the young learners growing up in a digital environment; he suggests that, because of the everyday practice with ICTs, people developed a different brain. Such condition creates a dramatic gap of skills between the natives and the immigrants.
2001	Lenhart and colleagues offer a new definition: "Instant Messaging Generation." Such a label consolidates an approach launched by "Nintendo Generation" to define young learners with their digital behaviors. It will be a transversal attitude during this second decade.
2002–2006	The association Mothers Against Videogame Addiction and Violence expresses many concerns about the digital development. Problems such as online violence, web bullying, and net addiction are highlighted and pushed onto educators' and policy makers' agendas.
2002	Reflecting about how the Internet is changing the way to access information, Brabazon classifies the youngest as "the ones who click, instead of thinking, when looking for knowledge."
2002	Similarly, Seely Brown and Duguid discuss many controversies of digital living and learning in their book about the social life of information.
2004	Carstens and Beck argue that children and adolescents are developing new cognitive and relational skills due to their prolonged condition of being video gamers; the fact of being "gamers" will help them with adult life's tasks.
2005	Oblinger and Oblinger explain how to educate the net generation, adopting the label popularized by Tapscott. Their starting point is the empirical observation of their children. Thanks to their paper, EDUCAUSE adopts the idea that there is a net generation, and starts to provide many documents on how to deal with this generation.
2006	The New Millennium Learners project is launched by OECD, under the supervision by Pedrò.
2006	Rivoltella writes "Screen Generation," pointing on a common trait of all the digital devices: the screen.
2006	Veen invents the label "homo zapiens," enlarging to all users of digital tools the intuition proposed in 1993 by Papert.
2006	Twenge tries to offer a complex and integrated view of positive and negative traits in "Generation Me: Why Today's Young Americans Are More Confident, Assertive, Entitled—and More Miserable Than Ever Before."
2007	Keen synthesizes the educators' concerns about the abuse of search engines and web encyclopedias, defining digital learners "the ones who take Google as Gospel."

Year	Evolution of the theory and development of contrasting trends
2008	2008 is a hard year for younger people who are great users of ICTs; indeed, they are defined as narcissist (Twenge, Konrath, Foster, Keith Campbell, & Bushman, 2008); dumb and ignorant (Bauerlein, 2008); coddled, adrift, and slackers (Damon, 2008); shameless (Durham, 2008).
	2008 is also important because of thinkers expressing criticisms worldwide. In Australia, Bennett and colleagues enter into debate with Prensky's work, unveiling the risk of an "educational give up" if the gap between natives and immigrants is described in terms of generational difference. They suggest starting deeper and contextualized research and avoiding hypergeneralizations.
	In Germany, Schulmeister (2010) defines a mystification about the dominating concept of the net generation, providing evidence that a difference in the use of ICTs between younger and older is observable only for what concerns the information-seeking ability.
	The fame of the "digital natives" approach, however, is at the top.
	Also, Switzerland enters in the worldwide arena about the theme. Palfrey and Gasser publish "Born Digital," depicting the digital generation with a quasi-ethnographic approach.
	Ferri and Mantovani write the book *Digital Kids*, meant to establish a pedagogy for the natives.
2008–present	The research consortium led by Bullen and composed by researchers from the British Columbia Institute of Technology, the University of Regina, and the Universitat Oberta de Catalunya launches the Digital Learners in Higher Education research project. Outputs are a number of papers demonstrating weaknesses and errors of the generational theory. Moreover, they start the blog netgenskeptic.org, which collects all the papers related to the topic, offering a systematic critical review.
2009	The number of positions is, by this time, almost uncountable.
	So, at Oxford University, researchers of the TALL group elaborate a new label, to express concepts very close to digital natives and immigrants but making them milder. Suggested labels are "digital residents" and "digital visitors."
2010	The Pew Research Center publishes the report *The Millennials: Confident. Connected. Open to Change.*
2010	Despite 20 years of debate, the second decade ends with Margaryan, Littlejohn, and Vojt asking critically whether digital natives are a "myth or a reality."

Needless to say, the debate is still ongoing: The third decade of debate started with the book *Deconstructing Digital Natives* (Thomas, 2011), containing contributions written by authors following different trends, and Prensky himself provided a more balanced view; indeed, he writes that ICTs can make people "truly wiser," and in order to go beyond the counterposition of natives/immigrants he suggests the new label *Homo Sapiens Digital*, meaning the concept of digital wise (Prensky, 2011).

As seen among the main criticisms against the hypothesis of the existence of a generation of digital natives is the lack of quantitative supporting evidence and the tendency to overgeneralization. In the following paragraphs, a quantitative research about a specific localized case is presented, to test, at least in that context, what is science and what is the hype about the so-called digital learners.

Listening to the Voice of Students to Understand Their Learning With New Media: A Research

In this section, the research "Learners' Voices @ USI-SUPSI" is presented and discussed. The research as a whole has been designed to combine a quantitative phase with a qualitative one (Rapetti, Ciannamea, Cantoni, & Tardini, 2010); the research architecture was, consequently, a combination of hypotheses to be statistically checked and open questions to be qualitatively addressed. Hereafter, we will present data related to the following three hypotheses:

1. The presence of ICT use with Learners of the Digital Era (hereinafter LoDE) is extensive.
2. ICT predilection in learning contexts is explainable/predictable, thanks to the age variable.
3. LoDE express a learning preference that is digitally oriented.

Please note that in order to avoid any adoption of the above-presented labels, contemporary learners are named LoDE: Learners of the Digital Era. The final dataset was composed by 562 students from USI (Università della Svizzera italiana) and SUPSI (University of Applied Sciences and Arts of Southern Switzerland). Even if the sample was self-selected, statistical data treatment is solid and reliable, since the population was 4,449 and the margin of error is therefore under the critical threshold (i.e. ±5%). Data were collected in October 2009 via an online questionnaire structured in 25 questions, and based on the protocol developed in a JISC (Joint Information Systems Committee; see www.jisc.ac.uk) consortium research project (JISC Consortium, 2009), meant to explore students' experience with technologies.

LoDE: Who Are They?

Personal Details of Participants

Average *age* is 24.5 years, while the median, which divides the sample into two equal portions, is 23 years. The age ranges from a minimum of 17 years to a maximum of 75 years ($SD = 5.85$). Though, even not considering the three extreme cases/outliers (i.e., 17, 50, and 75 years), the mean does not change significantly (24.3); therefore, in order to boost the variance within the sample, the three cases have been kept.

Despite half of students in the sample being between 21 and 26 years, age was divided into three age groups:

- 17 to 23 years (58.5% of the sample),
- 24 to 29 (28.1%), and
- and 30+ (13.3%).

This is primarily aimed to highlight any possible differences between LoDE, who are said to belong to Gen Y—namely, the ones born after 1980—and the others, who in 2009 were over 30 years. Second, it was valuable to make a further comparison within the Gen Y itself, between those who are at the beginning of this generation and the younger ones, who are presumably more "digitized."

Concerning other socio-demographic data, the sample was distributed as follows.

Gender: Respondents were 318 (56.5%) female and 244 (43.4%) male.

Countries of origin: Both USI and SUPSI have an international public, mainly due to the multilingualism of Switzerland, the proximity to Italy, and the fact that most master's programs are taught in English. Consequently, most people come from Switzerland (316 individuals, 56.2% of total), but there is a significant presence of Italians (24.9%), and a considerable number of people coming from the rest of Europe, namely 12.5%; finally, students from Africa, the Americas, and Asia altogether number 6.4%.

Study: Among the respondents, 56.6% of students come from SUPSI and 45.4% from USI. Observing the distribution in departments, the two bigger groups were students attending the Faculty of Communication Sciences at USI (25.6%) and the Department of Business and Social Sciences at SUPSI (24.6%), composing about half of the sample.

First Hypothesis: Massive Presence of ICTs

Data related to the first hypothesis show a reality that is substantially coherent with the expectations. Nine students out of 10 own a camera and a laptop; it must be observed that the relatively low ranking of desktop computers (58.8%) and, in particular, that "new generation" tools (handheld, notebook, tablet) occupy the last places; in "others," people reported a significant number of iPod or mp3 readers (17, or 2.0%; see Figure 8.1).

Daily Internet access takes place mainly in two forms: at the university for short slots of time, where 48.1% of respondents use the Internet for less than 30 minutes, and at home, for longer (36.8% access for 1–3 hours, and 27.9% for more than 3 hours; see Figure 8.2.).

Finally, observing the so-called media diet, the following uses are enacted every day: using search engine (79.3%); e-mailing (78.1%); watching movies/listening to music (38.5%); reading newsletters (36.6%); reading online newspapers (34.8%); social networking (30.9%).

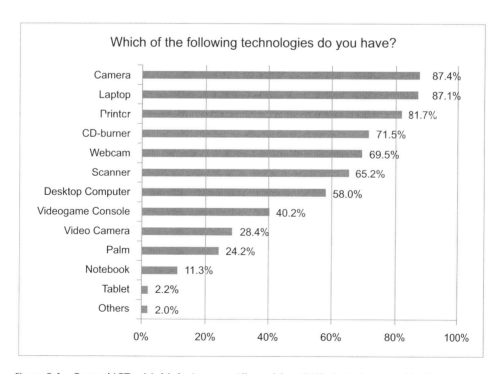

Figure 8.1   Owned ICTs—Multiple Answers Allowed (*n* = 562); Data Expressed in %

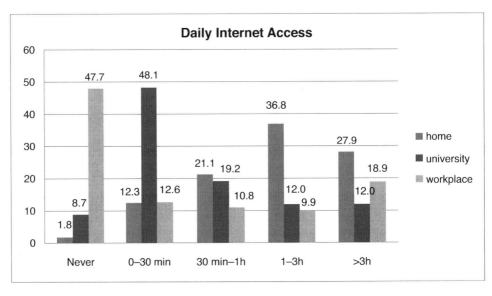

Figure 8.2 Daily Internet Access (*n* = 557); Data Expressed in %

Data allowed an interesting deepening of the relationship between "old" and "new" media, specifically, uses of printed and online newspapers and books. With newspapers, data are not so astounding: just a little preference for printed (everyday: 48.7%) versus online (everyday: 34.8%). On the contrary, printed books are clearly preferred (35.0%) against e-books (6.8%); all in all, it may sound quite astonishing that some tertiary education learners never read books (6.8%) or e-books (63.8%).

In sum, the hypothesis "The presence of ICTs in the LoDE experience is massive" is verified—only 1.8% of respondents never accessed Internet, while those who own ICTs are the vast majority and use them often.

LoDE: How Do They Learn?

Second Hypothesis: Age Is a Predictor Variable

Questions used to test this hypothesis proposed a list of statements concerning the importance of ICTs in the educational experience, and respondents had to express their agreement/disagreement.

A crosstabs procedure was run for all the possible crossings with "age groups." The relationship between two variables is inspected via chi-square tests; if the case occurs, the analysis of symmetric measures reveals the strength and the direction of relationships. We kept under control the Pearson's chi-square results to check the assumed relationship (i.e., $p > .05$), as literature in the field suggests, while to determine its nature we considered the Cramér's V value (converted in %).

Out of 81 crossings, Pearson's values resulted significant in eight cases, meaning the "age groups" (see Personal Details of Participants section for details) variable has a statistical influence. Observing the Cramér's V, we can say what follows in Tables 8.3, 8.4, and 8.5.

In other words, in Tables 8.3, 8.4, and 8.5, "the fact of being older" means literally "the fact of being part of an older cohort," namely, an example from Table 8.3: If one is in the age range 24/29 years, he or she has a 4.0% more likelihood of answering "It would be good if there were more e-learning in my courses"; 8.0% more if part of the "30 and older" age group.

Table 8.3 Crosstabs' Synthetic Results "Age Groups"

The fact of being older . . .	. . . increases of . . .	. . . the likelihood to answer that . . .
	4.0%	"It would be good if there were more e-learning in my courses"

Table 8.4 Crosstabs' Synthetic Results "Age Groups"

The fact of being older . . .	. . . increases of . . .	. . . the likelihood to consider that ICTs improved significantly . . .
	0.8%	"the way you practice your hobbies or interests"
	0.5%	"the way you do your students' tasks"
	0.1%	"the way you learn"
	3.9%	"the way you collaborate with your peers"

Table 8.5 Crosstabs' Synthetic Results "Age Groups"

The fact of being older . . .	. . . increases of . . .	. . . the likelihood to be more in favor of . . .
	0.2%	"lectures in classroom"
	0.6%	"printed dictionary/encyclopedia"
	0.3%	"online platforms (e-learning)"

As the tables show, percentages are very low; furthermore, as age increases, contrasting results are found. Overall, it emerges that older learners are 4.0% more likely to ask for more e-learning, and 3.9% more likely to declare ICTs impacted the way they collaborate with their peers. Therefore, we can affirm that the hypothesis "ICTs' predilection in learning contexts can be explained/predicted thanks to age variables" is false.

Third Hypothesis: LoDE Prefer to Learn Digitally

An overall observation of results shows a picture of LoDE that seems to be somehow contradictory: They declare to be massive ICT users, but, on average, they master elementary or medium levels of ability with media; furthermore, they want to have ICTs at hand, but new technologies do not play a major role in their learning. In fact, we see that

- for 76.6% of respondents, ICTs changed the way they share and collaborate; but only 22.1% consider a strategic process to choose a partner skilled in media use to collaborate with in a project assignment;
- they prefer to learn in places digitally equipped, though the favorite strategy to learning for 94.1% is the lecture in the classroom; and
- they extensively use communication tools that allow for mobile learning, but the fact that they can have mobile learning is relevant to only 15.5% of respondents.

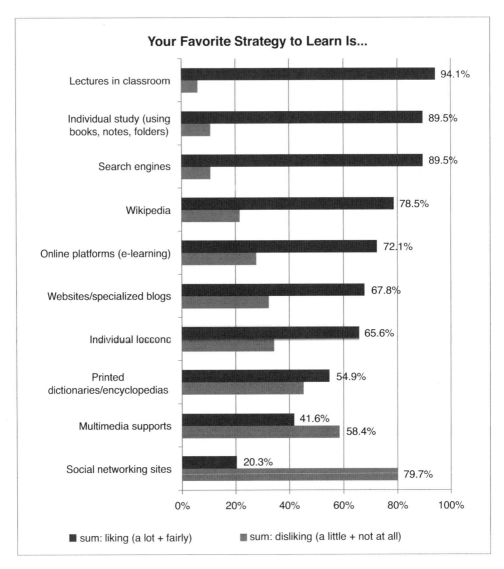

Figure 8.3   Favorite Strategies to Learn (*n* = 512)

In sum, the concept of people smartly dealing with media convergence seems to be more explanatory than the idea of digital learners. The picture emerging from data depicts learners who know how ICTs can be useful in learning; nevertheless, the focus and the preference remain on "analog" experiences. Figure 8.3 shows, beyond any rhetoric, that LoDE do not express a pattern of learning preferences that are digitally oriented.

The most important piece of information outstanding from such results is that LoDE do express a clear preference toward a "classical" way to learn, despite living in a digitalized context. Nine out of the 10 surveyed prefer "lectures in classroom," "individual study," and "search engines" to learn.

If looking only at "a lot" of answers, the picture does not dramatically change: In first place are "search engines" (57.2%), followed by "lectures in classroom" (52.3%), and "individual study"

(50.8%); all the other choices are substantially preferred by less than half of the sample. LoDE, according to such data, are likely to be more analog-styled than digital-styled in learning behaviors, and only information seeking has been dramatically shaped by the Internet.

Likewise, at the bottom of the list, 48.0% of respondents picked "multimedia supports" and "social networking sites." Such a rejection of social networks weakens the expectation of a learning transfer from informal to formal learning experiences. An important reflection must be done about the rankings of search engines versus printed dictionaries and encyclopedias: it seems that search engines and Wikipedia have taken the place of the latter, most likely because of convenience in terms of speed and cheapness.

The hypothesis "LoDE express a learning preference that is digitally oriented" is false by our results. Learners in the sample seem to be great appreciators over constant users of ICTs. They want to have at hand all the possibilities/tools/facilities to learn, then compose their learning paths, which are surely digitally enhanced but rarely digitally centered. Such results substantially give an evidence-base to what Buckingham stated in *Deconstructing Digital Natives*: "The history of technology suggests that change, however rapid, is generally incremental, rather than revolutionary. . . . Technologies have possibilities and limitations (or 'affordances'), but they do not produce social change in themselves" (Buckingham, 2011, pp. ix–x).

Conclusion and Outlook

The chapter has presented the debate about Gen Y, net generation, and digital natives (and so many other similar labels), analyzing the main roots and authors, and providing a comprehensive timeframe to better interpret it. While enthusiastic voices do present the vast majority of contributions, negative as well as critical voices have also been introduced and discussed.

Because critical voices stress mainly the lack of empirical evidence on contemporary learners and suggest that they may have been just the result of overgeneralization from anecdotal cases, an empirical research has been proposed in the second part of the chapter. Its results portray university learners who extensively use ICTs but prefer to learn in classes and with books and notes; only information seeking, thanks to Google and Wikipedia, appears to be clearly digitally oriented.

For sure these results are specific to the studied Swiss case (even if the sample was highly international). The authors do not want to overgeneralize them—hence, doing something they criticized in other researches—but believe that they can be relevant, at least when it comes to similar situations—technologically advanced, affluent contexts—and should be considered when thinking of Learners of the Digital Era.

References

Bauerlein, M. (2008). *The dumbest generation: How the digital age stupefies young Americans and jeopardizes our future (or, don't trust anyone under 30)*. London, UK: Penguin Books.

Bennett, S., Maton, K., & Kervin, L. (2008). The 'digital natives' debate: A critical review of the evidence. *British Journal of Educational Technology, 39*(5), 775–786.

Brabazon, T. (2002). *Digital hemlock: Internet education and the poisoning of teaching*. Sidney: University of New South Wales Press.

Buckingham, D. (2011). Foreword. In M. Thomas (Ed.), *Deconstructing digital natives: Young people, technology and the new literacies* (pp. v–xi). New York, NY: Routledge.

Bullen, M., Morgan, T., Belfer, K., & Qayyum, A. (2009). The net generation in higher education: Rhetoric and reality. *International Journal of Excellence in E-Learning, 2*(1). Retrieved from http://www.box.net/shared/fc5i4qfu53

Carstens, A., & Beck, J. (2004). Get ready for the gamer generation. *TechTrends, 49*(3), 22–25.

Damon, W. (2008). *The path to purpose. Helping our children find their calling in life.* New York, NY: Free Press.

Durham, M. G. (2008). *The Lolita effect: The media sexualization of young girls and what we can do about it.* Woodstock, NY: Overlook Press.

Ferri, P. (2008). Come costruiscono il mondo e il sapere i nativi digitali. In S. Mantovani, & P. Ferri (Eds.), *Digital kids: Come i bambini usano il computer e come potrebbero usarlo genitori e insegnanti* (pp. 1–38). Milano, Italy: ETAS.

Frand, J. (2000, September/October). The information age mindset: Changes in students and implications for higher education. *EDUCAUSE Review, 35*(5), 15–24.

Howe, N., & Strauss, W. (2000). *Millennials rising: The next great generation.* New York, NY: Vintage Books.

JISC Consortium. (2009). *The learners' voices project outcomes.* Retrieved from www.jisc.ac.uk/whatwedo/programmes/elearningpedagogy/learneroutcomes/learnervoices

Jones, C., & Shao, B. (2011). *The net generation and digital natives: Implications for higher education.* New York, NY: Higher Education Academy.

Keen, A. (2007). *The cult of the amateur: How today's Internet is killing our culture.* New York, NY: Currency.

Kvavik, R. M. (2005). Convenience, communications, and control: How students use technology. In D. Oblinger & J. Oblinger (Eds.), *Educating the net generation* (pp. 7.1–7.20). Retrieved from www.educause.edu/educatingthenetgen/

Lenhart, A., Rainie, L., & Lewis, O. (2001). *Teenage life online: The rise of the instant-message generation and the Internet's impact on friendships and family relations.* Retrieved from http://www.immagic.com/eLibrary/ARCHIVES/GENERAL/PEW/P010620L.pdf

Margaryan, A., Littlejohn, A., & Vojt, G. (2010). Are digital natives a myth or reality? University students' use of digital technologies. *Computers & Education, 56*(2), 429–440.

Mothers Against Videogame Addiction and Violence. (2002–2006). *Video game addiction and violence in underground video game cultures.* Retrieved from www.mavav.org.

Oblinger, D., & Oblinger, J. (Eds.). (2005). *Educating the net generation.* EDUCAUSE. Retrieved from www.educause.edu/educatingthenetgen/

OECD-CERI. (2012). *Connected minds.* Paris: OECD-CERI (Centre for Educational Research and Innovation) Education: Educational Research and Innovation.

Palfrey, J., & Gasser, U. (2008). *Born digital: Understanding the first generation of digital natives.* New York: Basic Book.

Papert, S. (1993). *The children's machine: Rethinking school in the age of the computer.* New York: Basic Books.

Pedró, F. (2009). *The new millennium learners: Main findings.* New Millennium Learners Conference, Bruxelles. Retrieved from http://www.oecd.org/dataoecd/39/51/40554230.pdf

Pew Research Center. (2010). *The millennials: Confident. connected. open to change.* Retrieved from http://pewresearch.org/pubs/1501/millennials-new-survey-generational-personality-upbeat-open-new-ideas-technology-bound

Prensky, M. (2001a). Digital natives, digital immigrants, part 1. *On the Horizon, 9*(5), 1–6.

Prensky, M. (2001b). Digital natives, digital immigrants, part II: Do they really think differently? *On the Horizon, 9*(6), 1–9.

Prensky, M. (2006). *"Don't bother me mom, I'm learning!" How computer and video games are preparing your kids for twenty-first century success and how you can help!* St. Paul, MN: Paragon House.

Prensky, M. (2011). Digital wisdom and homo sapiens digital. In M. Thomas (Ed.), *Deconstructing digital natives: Young people, technology and the new literacies* (pp. 15–29). New York, NY: Routledge.

Rapetti, E., Ciannamea, S., Cantoni, L., & Tardini, S. (2010). The voice of learners to understand ICTs usages in learning experiences: A quanti-qualitative research project in Ticino (Switzerland). *Proceedings of World Conference on Educational Multimedia, Hypermedia and Telecommunications 2010, Toronto* (pp. 2527–2536).

Rivoltella, P. C. (2006). *Screen generation, gli adolescenti e le prospettive dell'educazione nell'età dei media digitali.* Milano, Italy: Vita & Pensiero.

Schulmeister, R. (2010). Deconstructing the media use of the net generation. *QWERTY Journal of Technology, Culture, and Education* [Special Issue on Generation Y, Digital Learners and Other Dangerous Things], *5*(2). Retrieved from http://www.ckbg.org/qwerty/index.php/qwerty/article/view/98/69

Seely Brown, J., & Duguid, P. (2000). *The social life of information.* Boston, MA: Harvard Business School Press.

Sieberg, D. (2011). *The digital diet: The 4-step plan to break your tech addiction and regain balance in your life.* New York, NY: Crown.

Strauss, W., & Howe, N. (1991). *Generations: The history of America's future, 1584 to 2069* (1 Quill ed.). New York: Quill.

TALL Group (Oxford University). (2009). *Digital residents and visitors.* Retrieved from http://tallblog.conted. ox.ac.uk/index.php/2009/10/14/visitors-residents-the-video

Tapscott, D. (1998). *Growing up digital: The rise of the net generation.* New York, NY: McGraw-Hill.

Tapscott, D. (2009). *Grown up digital: How the net generation is changing the world.* New York, NY: McGraw-Hill.

Thomas, M. (Ed.). (2011). *Deconstructing digital natives: Young people, technology, and the new literacies.* New York, NY: Routledge.

Turkle, S. (1995). *Life on the screen: Identity in the age of the Internet.* New York, NY: Simon & Schuster.

Twenge, J. (2006). *Generation me.* New York, NY: Free Press.

Twenge, J. M., Konrath, S., Foster, J. D., Keith Campbell, W., & Bushman, B. J. (2008). Egos inflating over time. A cross-temporal meta-analysis of the narcissistic personality inventory. *Journal of Personality, 76*(4), 875–902.

Veen, W. & Vrakking B. (Eds.). (2006). *Homo zapiens: Growing up in a digital age.* London, UK: Network Continuum Education.

9

Blended Learning in Higher Education

Fayiz M. Aldhafeeri

Introduction

The chapter examines blended learning in the context of higher education. It attempts to investigate the origins of blended learning, the relationship to e-learning, and the implications, limitations, and future trends of blended learning. It is also aimed at targeting higher education decision makers who are actively considering the deployment of e-learning solutions for their institutions. The chapter additionally serves as a useful instrument to academic and training institutions having an interest in pursuing alternatives methods of learning in the face of fully online or traditional instruction-led learning.

The emergence of online technologies attracted the attention of educators worldwide to search for new methods of delivery for efficient learning material. This learning approach of making available the best practices and ideas to the right learners through both face-to-face and electronically monitored interactions at the right time and place has commonly been termed 'blended learning' (Oliver & Trigwell, 2005). In the context of teaching, blended learning is concerned with delivering the required knowledge, skills, and attitudes to improve the learner's performance. Blended learning can be a strategic tool that assists learners to obtain multiple perspectives related to their professional development. Shukla and Koh (2004) contend that blended learning is a viable alternative for attending on-campus courses on a regular, hardline basis. According to Hentea, Shea, and Pennington (2003), the term 'blended learning' covers a wide set of applications and processes which include distance education. They encourage the investment of quality in their educational programs by carefully considering blended learning programs, which, in return, offer the basis for achieving great promise of quality and expectations of any educational programs.

The need for constant and cost-effective training and learning have made blended learning an interactive proposition to many learning organizations, as well as evidenced empirically as an effective delivery method of instruction (Smart & Cappel, 2006). This has appealed to educational institutions, especially at higher education levels, even in the Arab world, as is the case in the Arab Open University in Kuwait. According to Bersin (2004), some of the economic benefits of implementing blended learning over traditional methods of delivery are obvious. Derntl and Motschnig-Pitrik (2004) stated that educational institutions and organizations have the desire to utilize the advantages of blended learning; however, success requires more than moving education and training to the web. A viable and sustainable blended learning solution requires the formulation of an appropriate blended learning strategy involving the appraisal of training needs, successful implementation of blended learning solutions, and continuous evaluation and revision.

Many research studies have focused on describing the basic elements and structure of blended learning programs and related it to the learning process for adult learners. Other studies introduced the fundamental terms, concepts, and methods for designing and developing a successful blended learning course. Considerations toward the technical requirements as well as instructional requirements are also discussed alongside the benefits of blended learning over e-learning, such as social and cultural factors.

Blended learning is a relatively new and evolving method, which has only a few established models, frameworks, and standards. Therefore, an extensive literature review was conducted to highlight the state of blended learning trends. The current chapter attempts to cover many aspects of the blended learning approach. A wide range of research studies have been carried out in this context to identify the basic elements of the blended learning approach, including its related terminologies, technicalities, and characteristics. This chapter provides thoughtful ideas to conceptualize a model for blended learning. The review of relevant literature, furthermore, reveals several findings related to the pace of blended learning, interaction barriers, course structuring, and instructional strategies and tools.

Blended Learning Approach

Quemada et al. (2004) viewed blended learning as an approach that combines e-learning with other learning strategies, including face-to-face instructor-led learning. Since blended learning is a subset of e-learning, it utilizes both e-learning characteristics and classroom environment characteristics, therefore, making blended learning continuous. It increases learning opportunity by enhancing flexibility through e-learning and other methods of delivery. University-level students learn to both get good grades (current goals) and also to have a good career (future goals). They learn in order to be ready for the future jobs, thus, work becomes learning and learning becomes work. In addition, blended learning is personalized. It is tailored to the existing knowledge base of the learner and the learner's personal preferences and learning styles. Not all learners share the same interest when they join a course. Furthermore, blended learning is dynamic; it is adjustable to the current demands of an organization or educational institution.

Consequently, many universities tend to extend or enhance but not replace classrooms with web-based instructions (Bade et al., 2004). The success of blended learning in organizations is primarily due to the implementation of an effective feedback mechanism (Thorne, 2003).

The blended learning approach extends to different areas and is not solely restricted to being an instructional strategy. Bade, Nussel, and Wilts (2004) discussed the integration of blended learning in the training development and human resources development plans. For example, in large organizations, to qualify its employees or partners, a process of testing can be followed in two sequent forms. This process of qualification consists of two exams, one is the theoretical part, which can be taken online, and the other is the practical exam which can be taken in the classroom.

On the other hand, Sharpe, Benfield, Roberts, and Francis (2006) outlined several characteristics of blended learning. They stress that blended learning allows individuals, pairs, or groups to do the following:

- Focus on the current entry levels of the learners, not the levels specified by the instructor or course.

- Take advantage of the Internet: Work concurrently at a learning site, anywhere, anytime and relate that to classroom meetings.
- Enrich classroom meetings through shared experiences made possible by online collaborations.
- Learn systematically through questions and activities, and by incorporating more than one learning method (e.g., classroom meetings, simulation, and individual instruction; self-paced).
- Incorporate administrative functions such as testing, monitoring, progressing, registering, and many more.
- Improve learner's performance through obtaining feedback and coaching.

The use of a blended learning approach extends the implications of e-learning. However, one of the problems of entirely adopting online learning is the lack of sufficient attention to the social and personal needs of online communities (Henning & Westhuizen, 2004). Therefore, the blended learning approach, in fact, the whole of e-learning itself, fulfills the needs of the learners to trust technology through supportive face-to-face interactions. Although online learning proved to be an appropriate method of learning as evidenced by Magenheim and Scheel (2004), fully online learners are less likely to achieve most of the learning objectives compared to those who follow traditional courses of instruction. Online learning, however, is not a substitute for instructor-led teaching. Thus, blended learning is a solution to complement classroom instruction, as fully online alone does not guarantee effective learning. Learning takes place in and out of the regular classroom and should be available to any learner, at anytime and anywhere.

Encouraging Learning Engagement

Learning is an ongoing process that takes place as knowledge is consumed, regardless of the place and time. Accessing daily information at home to help individuals perform their tasks is an example of learning. Thus, learning does not have to be a formal instructional course in which learners are introduced to experiences in order to learn. Consequently, many can learn without attending courses. Adult learners would prefer to not constantly sit in a classroom, they would rather share experiences. Winston Churchill once said, "I am always ready to learn, although I do not always like being taught" (Waller, 2005, p. 73). In light of this argument, Knowles (1996) described adult learning in relation to the term *andragogy*, or 'adult education.' He perceived that learning can take place if learners become self-directed. In this context, learners are responsible for their own learning progress in order to help them meet the required skills and knowledge for their job. The learner's consciousness regarding the lack of knowledge and skills required to survive in the workplace is important.

However, Oliver and Trigwell (2005) warn institutions from moving rapidly to online learning. They perceive a lack of social interaction between the instructors and the learners and among the learners themselves. According to their study, this is the pitfall of online learning—that the learning environment is no fun. They also found that most organizations turn away from online training because their employees prefer face-to-face instructions. In such situations, blended learning is a solution—learners can acquire the basic knowledge and skills online and then, have face-to-face interaction for problem solving (Sharpe et al., 2006). Thus, this approach incorporates the best of both—face-to-face instruction and online learning.

Customized to Individuals

Blended learning supports individual needs to receive customized learning with adequate instructional methods. Like online learners, blended learners are responsible for their own learning; individual accountability is a major characteristic of the e-learners, as they are able to manage and implement their own learning and development plans. Unfortunately, many educational designers impose fixed, inflexible instructional plans for students who enroll for courses. There is no analysis of the specific needs of these students despite the fact that blended learning programs can provide the designers with flexible systems to ensure that learners receive legitimate teaching and instruction. Hopson et al. (2002) advocated the use of a blended learning approach to make learning more creative and fun while still being manageable. They however warn institutions to conduct extensive research before using this method to judge its effectiveness.

Research shows that blended learners can learn faster compared with solely instructor-led instruction; it enhances the retention of materials (Thorne, 2003). E-learning technologies can augment live classroom instruction with the use of 3D visualization and animation. In this context, the mouse becomes an extension of the fingertips. Learners can complete exercises by dragging, inserting, and by clicking.

In addition to raising the quality of individualized distance instruction, content via the e-learning medium can be updated concurrently, making information more accurate and up to date. Furthermore, students are encouraged toward paced-based learning because it is more convenient. They can receive instructions at a time that is most suitable to them (in the case of asynchronous delivery). This feature can be easily adapted to the blended learning approach, which makes the learning process relevant to the needs of the learners.

One of the main obstacles that online instructional delivery faces is the relevance of the course. Blended learning adds power to traditional classroom learning. One of the reasons why learners move away from face-to-face classroom learning and turn to e-learning is because classroom learning does not take into account the individual needs and expectations of the learners. Since a blended learning course allows for self-development plans and classroom interactions, learners are encouraged to set up the order and the topics to be carried in courses to enhance their skills and knowledge. Furthermore, blended learning courses assist learners to gain *competitive* skills and knowledge.

Effective blended learning solutions allow educational institutions to improve performance and productivity by responding to the demands of the learners and by making learning available 24 hours a day, 7 days a week, and all year long. This approach will surely generate a high return on the investment; in addition, attitudes toward learning will increase.

Blended learning responds to learners' just-in-time needs for knowledge and skills. Free access to the learning system encourages learners to participate in academic discussions with other classmates. Even coaching techniques, such as one-to-one instruction, can be utilized in an e-learning environment. Hopson et al. (2002) conclude that blended learning can promote learning in many ways, as it

- enables lifelong learning;
- enables independent learning;
- delivers updated and widely distributed information;
- generates new ideas and practical experiences;
- fosters individualized learning;
- helps learners better interact with subject matter experts; and
- helps learners control their own learning experiences.

Lanham and Zhou (2003) suggested that the blended learning approach should be used as a solution to accommodate different learning styles and to create a flexible learning environment for all learners from different cultural backgrounds. According to Henning and Westhuizen (2004) two factors might affect the adaptation of e-learning: acceptance of the technology and readiness for it.

Several studies have shown that culture plays an important role in embracing the online environment. The nature of individuals in receiving instruction varies from one place to another in this world; some parts of the world would rather try new things while others would not. For example, the presentation of TV satellite technology had been discussed a lot and for long time (approximately five years) in Saudi Arabia before it entered people's houses. Likewise, the use of online learning has been widely used in both educational and corporate sectors in America, Europe, and parts of Asia while other regions are still debating. The acceptance of mixed methods of instructions requires smart design of flexible courses that allow for several levels of learning style (Sharpe et al., 2006). Lanham and Zhou (2003) contended that blended learning accommodates cross-cultural values and ensures that the learners are not offended but are responsible for their own learning. The use of blended learning is becoming the solution for some of the weakness associated with 'complete' online learning; for instance, the lack of social presence. Christner (2003) indicated that social interaction is usually associated with physical classrooms. Henning and Westhuizen (2004) stressed the importance of social and cultural experiences for the success of e-learning and criticized the ready-made e-learning modules, which adopt the Western way of instruction in the light of global learning.

Accommodating Different Learning Styles

Learners should be able to choose the most comfortable learning method to enable them to achieve the objectives of the given course. Blended learning enables the instructors to monitor the learners' progress continuously, with higher consideration toward learning styles (Dagada & Jakovljevic, 2004). In their study of blended learning and online learning experiences and learning styles, Dodero et al. (2003) compared two learning experiences developed with different styles during an academic semester at two universities. The objective of the study was to test the advantages of the blended style of learning in terms of students' participation and initiative in the learning process. The study revealed that information technology improved the students' participation during traditional classroom-located teaching, but did not help them increase their participation when the learning process is completely online and not complemented by regular classes.

Structuring Flexible Instruction

One of the main characteristics of blended learning is that it has a flexible approach. It provides high-quality skills that take into account individual learning styles and increase their learning outcomes; it also leads to a nationally recognized training. Making learning flexible for today's learners encourages the competitiveness of enterprises and their contributions toward the national economical position. The structure of blended learning allows for the integration of new technologies to improve communications and skills development through accessible learning, and real-life practices.

In its simplest form, a blended learning course merges e-learning with the traditional methods of delivery. The main characteristic of a blended learning course structure uses responsive learning strategies to mix between totally online and face-to-face instruction. This process involves planning, developing, and facilitating a range of learning strategies that meets the needs of individual learners. According to Lanham and Zhou (2003), considering international cultural differences during the course design and layout prevent reluctance among the learners. For example, color type is interpreted differently from one culture to another.

Content and technology (infrastructure) are the two major components that comprise blended learning. Content varies from basic HTML pages, fully interactive simulations, to classroom meetings. Technology, on the other hand, is responsible for enabling this content through creation, distribution, tracking, and administering the learning content. E-learning technology infrastructure consists of three main elements, which are learning management systems (LMS), collaboration, and services.

- The LMS delivers and supports the content by providing the ability to track, manage, and report the learning activities.
- Collaboration allows for peers and instructors to communicate. It can be self-paced (asynchronous) or real time (synchronous). Most importantly, collaboration must provide departure from traditional distance learning such as books and CD-ROMs.
- There are different types of services, which are available to help the designer implement adequate e-learning solutions. For example, content development services, some of the apps that are available in the market today enhance authoring and presentation of content such as iBook Author app, that help the designer choose optimal strategies for delivering content. There are also consulting services, such as Andrada Ariones, Bersin and Associates, Global Learning Consulting, and many others, that provide guidelines and instructions for using and preparing learning strategies and implementations. Hosting services is required for deploying e-learning systems.

Choosing Between Different Instructional Strategies

There are no specific, constant strategies to build a successful and effective blended learning course. However, there are general guidelines and models that blended learning designers can follow to obtain optimal learning. Blended learning enables a collaborative learning environment and enables learners to realize strategies of self-directed learning to support learning online (Magenheim & Scheel, 2004).

Online learning encourages cooperative and collaborative learning. With the availability of an online facilitator, the effect of online learning can greatly influence the learning process; for example, virtual community engages learners to be involved in shared experiences and practices. Online learning supports interactive learning among not only the learners but also between the learners and the facilitator, and between the learners and the tutorial. One of the best online learning strategies that support individual understanding and needs is individualization, which makes instruction more interesting, relevant, and effective. It accommodates certain elements of personalization (Dagada & Jakovljevic, 2004). The philosophy of the active nature of learning that has implications for online learning is constructive learning, it also encourages growing the learners' knowledge through experiences. In this type of learning, the construction of knowledge is the responsibility of the learner.

The blended learning facilitator utilizes the advantages of different learning strategies that are supported by both traditional and online methods of instruction and allows access to the instructor's notes. It is a flexible learning approach that allows the use of various learning strategies—from online instruction to instructor-led, which further depends on both the content and the given concept. There is the option of using tutorials, simulations, and drill. For example, the facilitators use the drill and practice strategy when they want the learners to acquaint themselves with the speed and accuracy of performing certain tasks.

Using Existing Tools Including E-learning

A mixture of different types of learning tools is a systematic approach in the blended learning approach. Christner (2003) stated that the availability of different channels of learning increases the interactions among the learners themselves, with the instructor, and with the content. The tools include communication, assessment tools, class management tools, content management tools, and several others. Shukla and Koh (2004) concluded that online learning has a unique ability for allowing learners to assist their current knowledge and skills through attempting to repeatedly practice online quizzes. In this case, the blended learning instructor should utilize the existing tools available in e-learning packages to support the learning process. Shukla and Koh (2004) found that learners prefer online course material to traditional course materials; they reported that 77% of the surveyed subjects found online course materials useful for their learning. They additionally suggested that four elements make online course materials more useful and these are as follows: adding components that are more practical; making learning more interactive; adding more graphics; and increasing bandwidth to reduce access time. When there is a possibility of having a slow access to online material, then a choice of classroom material is more useful.

Summary of the Review of the Literature

Clearly, most studies so far have advocated that the blended learning approach enhances learning and engages learners. Most of the findings of the previous research studies show high consideration toward the elements of the blended learning approach in order for it to be successful. The blended learning approach enhances learning when it has been carefully considered and is used for creating harmony among course structure, learning activities, instructional strategies, materials, and special needs of the learners. Several studies encourage the use of online learning meetings for collaborations and elaborations among the learners and between the learners and the instructors, while other studies, such as Oliver and Trigwell (2005), warn educators from adopting defective blended learning solutions. Consequently, the current study attempts to experimentally examine the effect of the blended learning approach on student engagement, interaction, and participation in comparison with a face-to-face instruction.

Blended Learning in Kuwait

In 2003, a steering committee was announced by the minister of education in Kuwait to come up with a plan for use of blended learning in the Kuwait curriculum. The committee attempted to achieve the following objectives:

1. Examine the literature for determining essential blended learning models and components.
2. Develop a model for educational technology leaders to test in an integrated environment of e-learning and face-to-face instruction-led learning.
3. Examine the effectiveness of the blended learning approach on students' engagement, interaction, and satisfaction.

In addition, Kuwait University and many other academic institutions have moved rapidly to integrate e-learning into their courses of instructions. Committees have been established to study and plan for this adoption and they have given considerable importance to regulations, accreditations, and technical solutions. However, little attention was given to the effect of these newly adopted methods of delivery on students' participation levels, interaction, or even satisfaction with the course itself. Consequently, many of the instructors at Kuwait University, when deciding between traditional courses and e-learning courses, chose to shift several courses across subjects to online learning without proper attention to the instructional strategies. This rapid change appeared to cause harmful learning outcomes and seemed to defect the students' learning instead. Therefore, presenting a new approach of teaching with the use of online technologies would make learning more engaging, which the current study attempts to outline.

Researchers in Kuwait and the GCC region (Gulf States) are attempting to investigate the effectiveness of blended learning in their educational systems. Kuwait and the GCC countries generously fund unique research on blended learning and how it can be integrated into the curriculum. These countries have taken initiatives to guide educators and policy makers in both public and higher education institutions to identify the effectiveness of the blended learning approach on all elements of the learning process. However, there still exists a lack of presentable models for structuring blended learning courses and materials.

- *Blended learning materials.* Units of content that can be stored and transferred in digital or non-digital format. They include books, tapes, multimedia CD-ROMs, and other supportive content learning management systems used by learners, but also by educators to support their instructional activities.
- *Blended learning activities.* Services that are provided in order to support the accomplishment of a specific educational objective. This is achieved through the creation of a learning environment consisting of educators, educational materials, communication infrastructure, meeting places, and other situational environments. The aim of blended learning activities is to work on the enhancement of knowledge or skills that can be acquired.
- *Blended learning facilitator.* The blended learning facilitator is responsible for assisting the learner to acquire the basic skills required for accessing the course materials online, which enable them to gain the required knowledge and skills. The blended learning facilitator is then responsible for relating online courses with classroom meetings.
- *Learning management system (LMS).* Learning resources include e-learning packages such as Moodle, Blackboard, Edmodo, and so forth. These are systems aimed at supporting both the learners through their learning process and the instructors in the learning activities that are under their control. LMS supports both the exchange of reusable educational materials (based on open standards) and the collaboration of instructors over the network for educational activities.

In terms of pedagogical thinking of blended learning, this chapter presents a suggested model for integrating e-learning with face-to-face instruction. See the illustration in Figure 9.1.

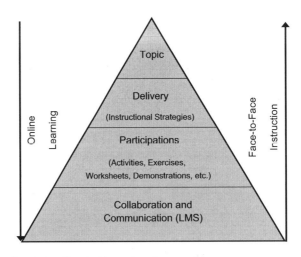

Figure 9.1 Hierarchy of the Blended Learning Approach

The blended learning approach starts with topic introduction, the least important element for online delivery, and ends with collaboration and communication, the most important element to be facilitated online. During both online and face-to-face meetings, the course leader plays the role of the facilitator and monitor. The instructor encourages students to participate in discussions more during face-to-face meetings than during online interactions. Much time in instructional delivery is more suitable for face-to-face instruction than for online instruction. To encourage students' participation, there are more learning activities, exercises, demonstrations, and so on conducted in the online mode than in the face-to-face mode. During the online meetings, the students play roles that are more active by collaborating and communicating through the learning management system (LMS). When moving to a new topic, a face-to-face meeting is called again. During the online meetings, a lab assistant is always present to mark students' attendance and provide technical assistance. Regular course exams and assignments are conducted in the traditional manner.

Aldhafeeri (2007) found that students' engagement, interaction, and satisfaction are higher when exposed to the blended learning approach. His findings coincide with the findings of Irons et al. (2002) and Hopson et al. (2002). Perhaps web access and the ability to easily communicate with instructors and other students made the blended learning approach more convenient. Other factors that might have affected this finding were probably the countless features of the current learning management systems that allow learners to instantly access their grades, course materials, and instructor feedback. Therefore, the blended learning approach engages the students and provides them with opportunities for clarification and organization.

The blended learning approach was found to be engaging for students since it complements classroom instruction with more flexible learning tools and multimedia. It also encourages students to pose questions and elaborate on the discussions. Another reason for students' engagement with the learning process in the blended learning approach is probably, as mentioned by Lanham and Zhou (2003), the blended structure of the course. Hence, the proposed model of the learning approach presented in this study could be a success factor for increasing students' engagement. Indeed, one of the findings revealed that students in the blended learning approach preferred discussing the course topics during the face-to-face instruction. This finding strongly supports the blended learning approach proposed in this study, where the author suggests that topic introduction should be discussed more in the face to face meetings than in the online meetings.

Unlike the 'complete' e-learning model, the blended learning approach structurally combines two ways of interacting, first among the learners and second between the learners and the instructor. This combination increases the overall level of interaction. Students, by utilizing features of the communication technology, are able to overcome the social barriers of e-learning by having frequent face-to-face meetings. In addition, they have greater access to classroom discussion and even more access to the course instructor. While on the one hand, they are able to benefit from face-to-face interactions; on the other hand, the students are also able to both communicate with the instructor and classmates, and access course materials at a time that is convenient to them. This finding is supported by several previous research studies, such as Christner (2003), Sharpe et al. (2006), and Henning and Westhuizen (2004).

Furthermore, other findings revealed that students are more satisfied with their learning when the blended learning approach is implemented. Irons et al (2002) and Salmon (2000) advocated such a finding and anticipate its effect. Oliver and Trigwell (2005) support the use of a carefully designed blended learning approach in order to satisfy the learning needs of the students. Consequently, this research coincides with the literature and presents a well-designed and structured model of teaching for blended learning. The approach provides learners with a more flexible method of gaining clarification on difficult points than relying solely on the traditional method of instructor-led or completely online e-learning. Similar to Thorne (2003), the study found that the blended learning approach enables the students to return to previously discussed topics and have a more customized learning, while still being able to diagnose and resolve their learning difficulties during traditional classroom meetings.

Conclusion

The use of the blended learning approach is considered a key element of the higher education of the future. Throughout many studies, the chapter in this handbook notes the significant educational and training opportunities for blended learning, while recognizing the immaturity of the field in terms of strategy, pedagogy, and therefore the weakness of delivery in terms of technology infrastructures and services. The implications are then that technology-enabled learning should take the form of a blended learning, at least until learners are advanced enough to trust technology and avoid isolation modes.

For educators and academic institutions considering raising standards in regard to blended learning, this chapter presents careful considerations that must be made:

1. *Strategy.* Adopting the blended learning approach should focus strongly on instructional strategies and interchanging among different learning strategies, including e-learning, but not reinforcing the traditional methods of instruction and devaluing innovation.
2. *Implementation.* Giving more areas of collaboration and interaction is the key element in the blended learning approach. All systems of education and training institutions should utilize the proposed course structure suggested in this chapter in order to make the blended learning approach a success; however, research studies should be carried out to refine or refute the model presented in this chapter.

References

Aldhafeeri, F. (2007). Effectiveness of blended learning approach on student's engagement, interaction, and satisfaction. *Studies in Curriculum and Instruction, 125,* 1–22.

Bade, D., Nussel, G., & Wilts, G. (2004). Online feedback by test and reporting for e-learning and certification programs with TCmanger. In S. Feldman (Chair), *Proceedings of the 13th International World Wide Web Conference on Alternate Track Papers* (pp. 432–433).

Bersin, J. (2004). *The blended learning book: best practices, proven methodologies, and lessons learned.* New York, NY: Jossey-Bass/Pfeiffer.

Christner, T. (2003). A classroom of one (book). *Library Journal, 128*(1), 130.

Dagada, R., & Jakovljevic, M. (2004). Where have all the trainers gone? E-learning strategies and tools in the corporate training environment. *Proceedings of the 2004 Annual Research Conference of the South African Institute of Computer Information Technologies on IT Research in Developing Countries* (pp. 194–203).

Derntl, M., & Motsching-Pitrik, R. (2004). Pattern for blended, person-centered learning: Strategy, concept, experiences, and evolution. *Proceedings of the 2004 ACM Symposium on Applied Computing* (pp. 916–923).

Dodero, J. M., Fernandez, C., & Sanz, D. (2003). An experience on students' participation in blended vs. online styles of learning. *ACM SIGCSE Bulletin, 35*(4), 39–42.

Henning, E., & Westhuizen, D. (2004). Crossing the digital divide safely and trustingly: How ecologies of learning scaffold the journey. *Computer and Education, 42*(4), 333–352.

Hentea, M., Shea, M. & Pennington, L. (2003). A perspective on fulfilling the expectations of distance education. *Proceeding of the 4th Conference on Information Technology Curriculum* (pp. 160–167).

Hopson, M. H., Simms, R. L., & Knezek G. A. (2002). Using a technology-enriched environment to improve higher-order thinking skills. *Journal of Research on Technology in Education, 34*(2), 109–119.

Irons, L., Keel, R., & Bielema, C. (2002). Blended learning and learner satisfaction: Keys to user acceptance? *USDLA Journal, 16*(12), 31–43.

Knowles, M. (1996). Adult learning. In R. L. Craig (Ed.), *ASTD training and development handbook: A guide to human resource development* (pp. 253–265). New York, NY: McGraw-Hill.

Lanham, E., & Zhou, W. (2003). Cultural issues on online learning: Is blended learning a possible solution? *International Journal of Computer Processing for Oriental Languages, 16*(4), 275–292.

Magenheim, J., & Scheel, O. (2004). Integrating learning objects into an open learning environment: Evaluation of learning processes in an informatics learning lab. *Proceedings of the 13th International World Wide Web Conference on Alternate Track Papers* (pp. 450–451).

Oliver, M., & Trigwell, K. (2005). Can blended learning be redeemed. *E-learning, 2*(1), 17–26.

Quemada, J., Huecas, G., De-miguel, T., Salvachua, J., Fernandez, B., Simon, B., Maillet, K., & Lai-cong, E. (2004). Educanext: A framework for sharing live educational resources with Isabel. *Proceedings of the 13th International World Wide Web Conference on Alternate Track Papers* (pp. 11–18).

Salmon, G. (2000). *E-moderating: the key to teaching and learning online.* London, UK: Kogan Page.

Sharpe, R. Benfield, G., Roberts, G., & Francis, R. (2006). *The undergraduate experience of blended e-learning: A review of UK literature and practice.* Helsington, UK: The Higher Education Academy.

Shukla, R., & Koh, D. (2004). Transition from online support to online course: Blended with ICT. *Proceedings of the Winter International Symposium on Information and Communication Technology* (pp. 1–7).

Smart, K., & Cappel, J. (2006). Students' perceptions of online learning: A comparative study. *Journal of Information Technology Education, 5*(1): 199–219.

Thorne, K. (2003). *Blended learning: How to integrate online and traditional learning.* London, UK: Kogan Page.

Waller, V. (2005). *Is learning for everyone achievable?* Retrieved from http://www.learningtechnologies.co.uk/magazine

10

ePortfolio Development and the Potential Relationship to Learning Theories

Anthony Ralston

Introduction

This chapter includes an introduction of ePortfolios and their uses in relation to Web 2.0 technology in higher education, as well as a perspective on learning theories related to ePortfolio development. Based on the literature reviewed, definitions of an ePortfolio are presented so as to provide a framework for this approach to learning design. In addition, the developmental processes related to ePortfolios and their relationship to online learning is examined, as well as perspectives from the literature of the claims in education that ePortfolios have offered.

In academic literature related to ePortfolio development, aspects of learning with respect to combining both transformational learning and self-motivational learning, there are opportunities to further examine the potential that this combining of learning approaches can have. The structure of this chapter is based on providing evidence of ePortfolio use and development in a higher educational setting, as well as concepts and practical application of learning theories that are not normally associated with portfolio development as a whole. First, this chapter outlines the origins of portfolio use and defines what an electronic portfolio is. Second, there are learning theories that are absent from the mainstream literature that show a direct connection between portfolio development (and teaching approaches) and these theories. Finally, a framework that can be adapted for ePortfolio development is presented as a way of providing a practical solution to portfolio learning.

ePortfolio Development

The origins of a portfolio stem back to its use in more traditional art and media design–oriented skills and competencies. The paper-based portfolio has long been the standard for representing one's work in the media field (Smith, 2007; Van Wesel & Prop, 2008). A portfolio can be defined in the following manner: either a more traditional paper-based format that contains representation of artefacts created by the student or a digital (online) portfolio that would also include artefacts that can demonstrate achievement and record progress, reflections on learning, and an overall picture of one's abilities (Abrami & Barrett; 2005; Barrett, 2004; Dubinsky, 2003).

In the current technology available within Web 2.0, there are a variety of online tools that students can utilize in order to design and develop electronic portfolios. The choice of ePortfolio development tool can often be influenced by the needs of the individual student and his or her goals. Development software tools can be categorized as open source (Mahara, Sakai), commercial (Desire 2 Learn, Blackboard), generic (Adobe Dreamweaver), or internally developed tools, where students would need to assess their needs and select the right tool that serves their purposes.

Housego and Parker (2009) pointed out that over the past 20 years the development of the communication technologies inclusive of the Internet has provided new opportunities for the portfolio to be included in teaching and learning. The portfolio in its modern form is now being recognized in the educational community as something that can provide value and opportunities related to lifelong learning, planning, reflection, and career development. Studies by Baume and Yorke (2002), Brandes and Boskic (2008), and Chatham-Carpenter, Seawel, and Raschig (2010) defined an ePortfolio as a medium for collecting artefacts or a structure for capturing ideas and learning. The ePortfolio can provide a repository for resources and digital artefacts that illustrate competency or skills (see Figure 10.1). The collection of materials in an ePortfolio can comprise graphics, multimedia, or text-based artefacts. The literature (Cheryl, 2007; Crichton & Kopp, 2008; Hallam & Creagh, 2010) suggests that students become engaged in a reflective process with a portfolio whereby they link ideas or concepts, thus developing a scaffolding process connected to deeper learning. A study by Brandes and Boskic presented the concept of reflection and its benefits by concluding that "students were 'forced' to look back on their learning and life not only as a collection of various artefacts, but as evidence of their constant growth, a mirror of their beliefs, cultural values and, oftentimes, teaching perspectives" (Brandes & Boskic, 2008, p. 8).

Bolliger and Shepherd (2010) looked at how graduate students integrated an online portfolio into their studies. They focused on the aspects of connectedness, communication, and how ePortfolios can contribute to learning. Based on the authors' study, does the aspect of age and gender factor into ePortfolio experiences, and can the ePortfolio assist students to reflect and share with other students? The authors claimed that there has been little research in how ePortfolios influence student perceptions of communication and connectedness. They therefore investigated student perceptions of ePortfolios in online graduate courses. The authors concluded that the overall effect of communication with respect to ePortfolios is inconclusive and requires more study. They concluded that the ePortfolio did not have a positive effect on communication but had value in distance learning. The aspect of communication online has been shown to present challenges that are associated with the technology itself. The study noted conclusions from related literature that points to the fact that a portfolio can be utilized to facilitate reflective learning and collaboration as well as a structure for lifelong learning. The study noted that the

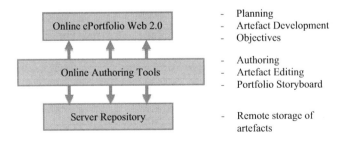

Figure 10.1 ePortfolio Process

Adapted from Brandes & Boskic, 2008, p. 8.

use of an online portfolio was viewed positively by students, as its feedback and peer interaction contributed a deeper learning and increased reflection. The subjects in this study used the online portfolio as a sharing opportunity: "ePortfolio entries among 16 online doctoral students resulted in additional revisions and higher quality documents" (Bolliger & Shepherd, 2010, p. 298). This study and others concluded that an ePortfolio could influence perceptions related to communication, but they (the students) did not necessarily feel more connected. The aspect of connectedness and communication in an online environment as noted by the authors requires a long-term investment (Driessen, Van Tartwijk, Van Der Vleuten, & Wass 2007).

Definitions of ePortfolios

Educational Portfolios

The use of educational portfolios (EPs) as an educational and learning tool is quite widespread. The literature suggests (Cimer, n.d.; Fitch, Reed, Peet, & Tolman, 2008; Hallam & Creagh, 2010) that there is a growing number of schools recognizing the educational potential of EPs. Typical content included in educational EPs includes personal information; education, including institutions and applicable courses; academic course work, such as research papers; skills and capabilities; educational work experience, such as internships and practicums; and awards and recognition.

Abrami and Barrett (2005), Irby and Brown (2000), and Johnson, Mims-Cox, and Doyle-Nichols (2006) have noted a number of unique advantages that EPs have over their paper-based counterparts. Learners can easily integrate multimedia materials, allowing them to use a variety of tools to demonstrate and develop understanding. Digital portfolios are superior for cataloguing and organizing learning materials, better illustrating the process of learner development. Digital portfolios have communication advantages. The portfolio is easy to share with peers, teachers, parents, and others, and lets them provide feedback through a single electronic container (Rugg & Pearle, 2006).

Used appropriately, EPs

> give students new avenues for integrating learning from their courses and extracurricular activities; they help students see ways that courses such as the ones we teach fit into the larger picture. With the embedded features of the software . . . students gain practice in presentation skills by creating a variety of views on their work, tailored for different audiences . . . they have the opportunity to reflect on the learning they've experienced, and the products they've created.
>
> *(Dubinsky, 2003, p. 97)*

As learners experience critical moments in their learning, they can express their responses, collect and organize information, and plan their next steps, potentially within one integrated digital environment. Figure 10.2, based on the Kolb experiential learning cycle, illustrates this process of continuous learning based around dialogue and collaborative activity with others. With hindsight, many learners identify the sense of control that such ePortfolio building yields as instrumental to their eventual success.

Such narratives about the self are updated easily online, developing over time to provide a record of the learning journey that each learner is engaged in. In addition, ePortfolio use can generate many of the skills that learners need to effectively navigate their way through the various options that the current Web 2.0 technology offers (Owen, 2010; Zhang, Olfman, & Ractham, 2007). Through ePortfolio development, skills of collaboration and selection, even a sense of

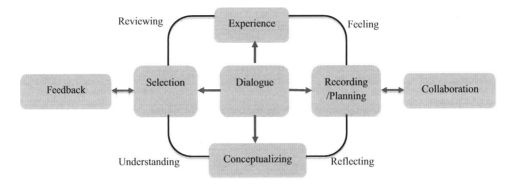

Figure 10.2   ePortfolio Learning Concept, Based on Kolb (1984)

audience, can be acquired. The case studies in this guide explore in more depth the circumstances in which ePortfolio development can

- improve understanding of the self and the curriculum;
- engage and motivate learners, both individually and as part of a community of practice;
- personalize learning;
- support models of learning appropriate to Web 2.0 technology tools (Mahara); and
- promote reflective practice.

Development Framework

Framework Model

To assist in the portfolio learning processes, the Portfolio Development and Learning Theories model should be used (PDLT; see Figure 10.3). The framework model for ePortfolio development as it relates to coinciding learning theories (transformational and self-motivational) is built upon the premise of integrating these theories in practice into the ePortfolio development process.

The PDLT model focuses on an approach whereby students are engaged in a dual learning process that combines ePortfolio development and self-motivational and transformational learning theories under the guidance of experienced educators.

I would argue that the process of planning a portfolio inclusive of self-assessment, project planning, and engaging in a critical review process are the real strengths of the portfolio development process—Web 2.0 technology serves as the delivery mechanism and should not constitute the focal point of the experience but should fit the requirements of the portfolio approach to learning. The literature is not prone to skepticism toward technology when talking about portfolios, but rather technology becomes the focus of the portfolio process itself (Zhang et al., 2007).

The model is composed of two main learning theories (transformational and self-motivational) that are overlaid throughout the ePortfolio design and development process. Learning activities that promote the two theories are interwoven into the curriculum, thus providing the students with avenues that enhance their portfolio processes. There are six elements to the model that can be broken down as follows:

- ePortfolio development cycle
- Baseline

- Project management
- Outcomes
- Self–motivational and transformational baseline
- Self–motivational and transformational learning application
- Self–motivational and transformational outcomes

The ePortfolio development cycle is composed of nine components that involve the student and guide the student through the ePortfolio design and development stages. A baseline stage allows the student (under the mentorship of a teacher) to self–assess his or her skills and competencies that reflect the beginning of the portfolio process. The project management phase introduces the student to concepts that will link to self–motivation and transformational outcomes in that they are required to think strategically and plan their goals and the processes by which they can achieve them through a portfolio process.

The outcomes stage is the final stage in the process related to portfolio development, and relates to both learning theories in practice and requires students to review, reflect, and compare their own growth in competencies and skills to their personal baseline.

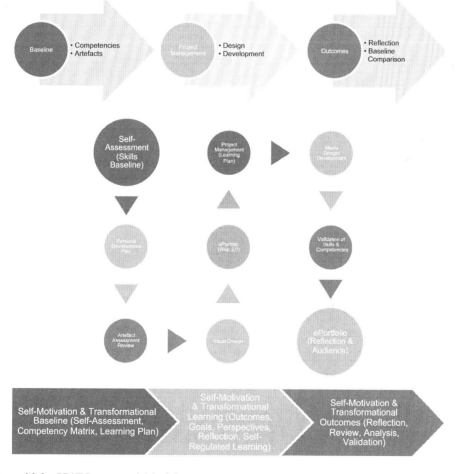

Figure 10.3 PDLT Framework Model

The self-motivational and transformational learning theory phases are interwoven into the design and delivery of the curriculum, thus allowing for the combining of both of these theories to be applied to the portfolio process itself. This integration of these theories is represented by three levels of utilization: baseline, learning application, and outcomes. Each phase contains activities and related learning resources that allow the student to reflect and apply these concepts while at the same time moving through the ePortfolio development phases. This combining of both processes provides a robust framework in which learning theory and portfolio development co-exist and which can effect a positive impact on the student and teacher. I draw from the knowledge and application of this model in developing and teaching an ePortfolio methodology course for bachelor-degree-level communication students. The learners are given a set of guidelines in terms of the number of artefacts they need to create or select to be used in both the paper-based and the electronic portfolio. They are encouraged to use artefacts from previous academic experience and professional work. They must show comprehension in all the aspects of portfolio development based on the introductory course they received, which is inclusive of established electronic portfolio types.

Knowledge and Motivation

Issues related to learner motivation, institutional goals, role of the portfolio, and objectives are common among academic institutions (Peacock, Gordon, Murray, Morss, & Dunlop, 2010; Tosh, Penny Light, Fleming, & Haywood, 2005). Any amalgamation of a portfolio learning approach can test the limits of learners who ideally would be more prone to new experiences as noted by Van Zwanenberg (2000), with respect to the Honey and Mumford's Learning Styles Questionnaire (LSQ; n.d.): "Activists are people who, for example, enjoy new experiences, are active, tend to make decisions intuitively, but who dislike structured procedures" (Van Zwanenberg, Wilkinson, & Anderson, 2000, p. 4). The integration of the portfolio concept into the curriculum initially required strategic planning involving faculty and senior administration in order to determine the realization of this approach, which is invariably time-consuming and requires dedication on the part of faculty and learners alike. However, it is clear that faculty members involved in portfolios need to devote more time to developing learning outcomes and rubrics for student learning to be effective (Fitch, Reed, Peet, & Tolman, 2008).

The philosophical study of epistemology according to Jacobson (2006) is one's own epistemological knowledge which is a staged developmental process. In particular, he cites the works of Schommer and Walker (1997) with respect to the five potential factors that contribute to epistemology (Jacobson, So, Teo, Lee, Pathak, & Lossman, 2006, p. 2):

1. *Simple knowledge*: Knowledge consists of discrete facts; whether people perceive knowledge as separate and unrelated facts or as interrelated elements.
2. *Certain knowledge*: Absolute knowledge exists and will eventually be known; the extent to which people believe that knowledge is certain and absolute or tentative and constantly changing.
3. *Omniscient Authority*: Authorities have access to other inaccessible knowledge.
4. *Innate Ability*: The ability to learn knowledge is primarily genetically determined and is not the product of achievement.
5. *Quick learning*: Learning occurs quickly or not at all.

The common belief that constructivism and portfolio learning are closely connected reaffirms the belief that the learner has the balance of responsibility for the construction of knowledge. The acts of discussion and feedback combined with a scaffolding of knowledge lead to the opportunity for "certain knowledge" to be attained by the learner and community (Stefani, Mason, & Pegler, 2007). The formation of a community is not an easily attained environment and requires support from the teacher (Scardamalia & Bereiter, 2010). As an exemplar, Athabasca University, Canada, recognizes "reflective learning activities" (Conrad, 2008, p. 142) in the experiential learning process, by which the student is owner of the portfolio and thereby the knowledge. The university also uses a PLAR (Prior Learning Assessment) process in which the portfolio is used to assess previous work or experience. As a result, they recognize formal and informal learning in the process of assessment of skills and knowledge.

(Maton, n.d.) suggested that cumulative learning is representative of the knowledge that is required, what is known as the "knowledge economy," which is in contrast to the approaches in current education that is based on "segmented learning—where students learn a series of ideas or skills that are strongly tied to their contexts of acquisition" (p. 43). This concept of building new ideas based on previous knowledge is of a primary importance in portfolio learning, rather than a segmented thinking that does not allow for integration or a connecting of knowledge over time. Zhang, Olfman, and Ractham (2007) put forth the concept that a learning portfolio needs to have three main components: "documentation, reflection, and collaboration" (p. 203). They maintain that recent developments in web-based portfolio systems have a capacity to accommodate such activities and provide assessment and collaboration.

Self-Motivational Learning

With respect to self-motivation and learning, I propose that there is greater potential when ePortfolio development is partnered with motivational learning. Professional experiences dealing with teaching ePortfolio and traditional portfolio has influenced my opinion on motivation and its importance in learning. The authors who define motivation as that which brings about greater awareness on the part of the learner is noted in studies, but not necessarily within the context of portfolios (Boekaerts, Pintrich, & Zeidner, 2000; Keller & Burkman, 1993).

A study by Roeser and Peck (2009) based its inquiry on the question "what is self and what relation does self have with motivation and self-regulated learning?" (Roeser & Peck, 2009, p. 120). They used the Basic Levels of Self (BLoS model), as it is a more comprehensive theoretical framework that looks at persons, contexts, and their dynamic interactions. They put forward the point that they see a narrower difference now between motives and goals in terms of defining these concepts that are related to motivation as somehow different from other cognitive or emotional states.

The authors also pointed to other literature that often frames self-regulated learning as an active participation on one's own learning through the organization of "emotional, cognitive, attentional, and environmental resources" (Roeser & Peck, 2009, p. 121). The concept of the self is integral to research in the areas of motivation and self-regulated learning, in which the authors state that there are still questions as to the meaning of self. The concept of "self" can be acquainted with motivation, but intrinsic and extrinsic motivation are often present in the learning context. The professional experience that I draw upon often shows evidence of extrinsic tendencies and, in fact, that students are only motivated by the grade or outcome. To a lesser extent, intrinsic motivation arises in students, and the inherent desire to learn contributes to self-motivation.

Self-assessment, as it relates to self-motivation (Donham, 2010), entails being able to review one's own performance and use internal criteria to determine what we need to know or what we don't need to know. This aspect of metacognition and awareness is necessary to attain self-assessment. The role of the teacher is integral to shaping the abilities of students to become self-reliant, and for them to become aware of what they know and how to make adjustments for themselves. When applying this approach of greater teacher involvement to ePortfolio, I would add that I see a dramatic increase in motivation and the willingness for self-assessment, so long as the infrastructure is integrated into the curriculum. The attributes that Donham (2010) pointed out, with self-assessment and its connection to self-motivation, show merit on their own, but it is only when these theories are overlaid with an ePortfolio model that the opportunities for elevated performance could be greater—as is the basis for my argument and research.

It is quite often that once an assignment is completed that a student will move on to the next assignment without the necessary review or reflection. Missing this opportunity to engage the student in self-assessment or self-motivational activities is a lost learning opportunity. The act of looking back at previous work, looking at finished work, and looking toward the future is integral to self-motivational learning and can contribute to a better experience.

With respect to ePortfolio and the online learning environment, there can be challenges (Keller & Suzuki, 2010) associated with motivation in the virtual environment. As part of recognized best practices in online engagement, there are three elements that can aid in motivation. The first element is gaining and sustaining the students' attention, followed by showing relevance, and finally confidence, whereby they associate their successes with their abilities.

Transformative Learning

I am of the opinion that transformational learning is on its own a valued process whereby the learner can come to realizations and perspectives, especially when combined with self-motivational learning approaches.

The concept of transformative learning as seen by Brock (2010) involves a person's own realization of a new concept, and then connecting that to make a change in a person's life. I would argue that this process of transformation is lacking in ePortfolio development based on a review of the literature, and if integrated into curriculums could provide avenues for higher thinking on the part of the student. The concept of transformative learning began with Mezirow in 1978 and was offered as a 10-step process whereby cognitive aspects such as exploration, assessment, self-examination, and planning are part of the experience. Whether this act of transformation occurs over time or in a single moment is debatable, according to the literature, but it is safe to conclude that transformative processes can yield positive results from engaging in group discussions or self-reflection through autobiography (or journaling).

The literature, and in particular Brock (2010), claims that there has been little done to fully replicate the 10 steps of transformation, although I note that reflection is a key element in the transformative process—one that lends itself well to the portfolio learning approach. Mezirow has strongly defended that self-reflection is one of the key steps in education. To achieve self-reflection and change, the aspect of challenge from the instructor plays an important role in providing the framework for helping one perceive a greater awareness of the world. How one interprets the world and experiences can be also seen as part of the reflection process, necessary in portfolio development (Cranton, 1994).

Another study by Christopher, Dunnagan, Duncan, and Paul (2001) links their research to Mezirow as an author of authority on transformational learning approaches. Again, we see this theme of self-reflection being brought forward as the cornerstone in any transformational learning dichotomy. The premise in this learning approach is based in helping students to assess their perspectives on life through educational pursuits.

The report's positive elements of transformative learning include fundamental changes on one's view of the world through self-reflection. This change in perception leads to the potential to make changes in one's life, increased self-awareness, and awareness of how one's previous assumptions have constrained his or her worldview. The reported outcomes of transformative learning include a new sense of empowerment, increased self-confidence, compassion, and greater connections to others.

Boyer, Maher, and Kirkman (2006) reported that when teaching in an online environment (which can occur with ePortfolio development), using self-directed techniques associated with transformative learning showed an increase in students' ability to delve deeper into the subjects at hand. The transformative environment, when supported by an instructor in the online environment, can have positive effects on students' beliefs, preconceived ideas, and acting on new ideas.

I see great potential for the use of transformative learning (based on the review of articles) in combination with the ePortfolio learning process. These two approaches would provide the learner with the potential for greater empowerment, which connects to the self-discipline that is required in ePortfolio development.

Summary

This intent of this chapter was to introduce ePortfolios and identify learning theories that can be associated with the design and development processes in ePortfolios. In addition, the chapter looked at drawing some parallels that are not normally shown in the literature regarding the integration of theories dealing with transformational and self-motivational learning methods.

As we can see from the literature, ePortfolio development can be linked closely with self-motivational learning (Keller & Suzuki, 2010; Roeser & Peck, 2009; Song & Keller, 2001) and provides opportunity for greater involvement in the learning process and benefits with respect to ePortfolio development. This aspect of combining self-motivational learning and transformative learning approaches can provide a more substantive learning environment.

It is clear that more study is required in exploring the potential to create a greater link between combining both collaborative learning and self-motivational process for ePortfolios, as these approaches contain aspects that would integrate well into lifelong learning and planning. There are also challenges (technical and institutional) that are associated with electronic portfolio development that emerge in the literature and speak to issues related to the time requirement for ePortfolio approaches, security, and privacy, and acceptance of portfolios in general. As is the case with many institutions, there are common challenges that can be summarized as follows (Prammancee & Moussa, 2010, p. 5):

- Inadequate technological skills for both students and staff
- Lack of support when problems exist
- Software and hardware issues
- Privacy and security of data
- Trustworthiness and reliability of equipment
- Lack of standardization across a variety of electronic portfolio systems

Razavi and Iverson (2006) reported that in terms of privacy, they found that there was some unwillingness on the part of students to post some types of artefacts online due to a lack of privacy security systems. Bemis (2002) reported that role(s) of the faculty have to be clearly identified so that the students understand the true value of the exercise to produce a portfolio.

In some cases there is interest on the part of faculty: "Although individual instructors may have embraced the use of portfolios, most institutional structures, climates, and processes are poor hosts for portfolio development" (Johnson, Mims-Cox, & Doyle-Nichols, 2006, p. 10). The degree of time and commitment on the part of faculty and learners is an issue that spans many institutions. Johnson, Mims-Cox, and Doyle-Nichols (2006) reported that

> there is no doubt that portfolios are time-consuming both to prepare and to evaluate because they require clarity in goals, outcomes, criteria, and expectations and assurance that all stakeholders understand. Spelling out careful guidelines and benchmarks that are understood and agreed upon by all the stakeholders, along with building in support for meeting the standards and criteria.
>
> *(p. 26)*

Razavi and Iverson (2006) reported that "our results show that many of the participants already employ certain strategies to achieve their desired level of privacy when the tool does not provide it" (p. 463).

Another challenge identified by Chatham-Carpenter, Seawel, and Raschig (2010) involved the aspect of a change in philosophy in education and faculty perspective as being that "many faculty don't see the point or see it as too much work. Some of this has to do with a larger resistance to assessment and to new teaching approaches" (p. 445). Closely associated with faculty acceptance of a portfolio learning approach is the needed change in learning culture in a higher education environment. The issue of learning the associated technology itself presents a number of challenges that border technological infrastructure and the time necessary to learn the technology on the part of faculty and learners alike. Chatham-Carpenter, Seawel, and Raschig (2010) reported that they found that their adult learners viewed the electronic portfolio as a very time-consuming venture and also viewed the entire process as being too large to comprehend. They found it necessary to help their students by "helping people to see that it is manageable, if taken in small chunks" (p. 445).

These challenges represent a set of common themes faced by institutions who are engaged in this approach to learning. However, these challenges speak to a greater need for developing a stronger base from which ePortfolio learning and learning theories (Transformational and Self-Motivational) can coexist, thereby creating a more substantive learning program.

References

Abrami, P., & Barrett, H. (2005). Directions for research and development on electronic portfolios. *Canadian Journal for Learning and Technology, 31*(3). Retrieved from http://www.cjlt.ca/index.php/cjlt/article/view/92/86

Barrett, H. (2004). *Competing paradigms in portfolio approaches.* Retrieved from http://electronicportfolios.com/systems/paradigms.html

Baume, D., & Yorke, M. (2002). The reliability of assessment by portfolio on a course to develop and accredited teachers in higher education. *Studies in Higher Education, 27*(1), 7–25.

Bemis, S. (2009). *The Impact of Faculty and Staff Perceptions on Integrating ePortfolios in Higher Education Institutions.* (Doctoral dissertation) Retrieved November 22, 2010, from http://proquest.umi.com.ezproxy.royalroads.ca/pqdweb?index=11&sid=1&srchmode=1&vinst=PROD&fmt=6&startpage=-1&clientid=4565&vname=PQD&RQT=309&did=1978959561&scaling=FULL&ts=1290433290&vtype=PQD&rqt=309&TS=1290433384&clientId=4565\

Boekaerts, M., Pintrich, P., & Zeidner, M. (Eds.). (2000). *Handbook of self-regulation.* San Diego, CA: Academic Press

Bolliger, D. U., & Shepherd, C. E. (2010). Student perceptions of ePortfolio integration in online courses. *Distance Education, 31*(3). Retrieved from http://www.tandfonline.com/doi/abs/10.1080/01587919.2010.513955#.VGoMtzTF-IA

Boyer, N., Kirkman, S., & Maher, P. (2006). Transformative Learning in Online Settings. *Journal of Transformative Education, 4*(4), 335–339. Retrieved from http://jtd.sagepub.com.ezproxy.royalroads.ca/content/4/4/335.full.pdf+html

Brandes, G. M., & Boskic, N. (2008). Eportfolios: From description to analysis. *The International Review of Research in Open and Distance Learning, 9*(2). Retrieved from http://www.irrodl.org/index.php/irrodl/article/view/502/1041

Brock, S. E. (2010). Measuring the importance of precursor steps to transformative learning. *Adult Education Quarterly, 60*(2), 123–125.

Chatham–Carpenter, A., Seawel, L., & Raschig, J. (2010). Avoiding the pitfalls: Current practices and recommendations for ePortfolios in higher education. *Journal of Educational Technology Systems, 38*(4). Retrieved from http://baywood.metapress.com/media/c28459nn4p6kpj4b7g7t/contributions/0/9/j/3/09j3k52531781608_html/fulltext.html

Cheryl, C. (2007). Taylor & Francis online: illuminating qualities of knowledge communities in a portfolio making context. *Teachers and Teaching, 13*(6), 620–625.

Christopher, S., Dunnagan, T., Duncan, S., & Paul, L. (2001, April). *Family relations, 50*(2), 134–142.

Cimer, O. (n.d.). The effect of portfolios on students' learning: Student teachers' views. *European Journal of Teacher Education, 34*(2), 161–192.

Conrad, D. (2008). Building knowledge through portfolio learning in prior learning assessment and recognition. *The Quarterly Review of Distance Education, 9*(2), 139–150.

Cranton, P. (1994, November–December). Self-directed and transformative instructional development. *The Journal of Higher Education, 65*(6), 726–744. Retrieved from http://www.jstor.org.ezproxy.royalroads.ca/stable/2943826?seq=1

Crichton, S., & Kopp, G. (2008). The value of eJournals to support eportfolio development for assessment in teacher education. *Canadian Journal of Learning and Technology, 34*(3). Retrieved from http://www.cjlt.ca/index.php/cjlt/article/view/502/233

Donham, J. (2010). Creating personal learning through self-assessment. *Teacher Librarian, 37*(3), 14–21.

Driessen, E., Van Tartwijk, J., Van Der Vleuten, C., & Wass, V. (2007). Portfolios in medical education: Why do they meet with mixed success? A systematic review. *Medical Education, 41*(12), 1224–1228.

Dubinsky, J. (2003). Creating new views on learning: ePortfolios. *Business Communication Quarterly, 66*(4), 97.

Fitch, D., Reed, B. G., Peet, M., & Tolman, R. (2008). The use of portfolios in evaluating the curriculum and student learning. *Journal of Social Work Education, 44*(3), 37–42.

Hallam, G., & Creagh, T. (2010). ePortfolio use by university students in Australia: A review of the Australian ePortfolio project. *Higher Education Research & Development, 29*(2), 179–181.

Honey and Mumford Learning Styles Questionnaire. (n.d.). Retrieved from http://www.nwlink.com/~donclark/hrd/styles/honey_mumford.html

Housego, S., & Parker, N. (2009). Positioning ePortfolios in an integrated curriculum. *Education and Training, 51*(5/6), 409–412.

Irby, B., & Brown, G. (2000). *The career advancement portfolio.* Google books. Retrieved from http://books.google.ca/books?id=YDZ9XOrMl50C&printsec=frontcover&dq=the+career+advancement+portfolio&hl=en&ei=qmLJHTcmdEIP1sgaL1M32DQ8&sa=X&oi=book_result&ct=result&resnum=1&ved=0CC8Q6AEwAA#v=onepage&q&f=false

Jacobson, M., So, H.-J., Teo, T., Lee, J., Pathak, S., & Lossman, H. (2006). Epistemology and learning: Impact on pedagogical practices and technology use in Singapore schools. *Computers & Education, 55*(4), 1694–1706.

Johnson, R. S., Mims-Cox, J. S., & Doyle-Nichols, A. (2006). *Developing portfolios in education: A guide to reflection, inquiry, and assessment.* SAGE Publications. Retrieved from http://books.google.hu/books?id=N74JDYut3XwC

Keller, J., & Suzuki, K. (2010). Learner motivation and e-learning design: A multinationally validated process. *Journal of Educational Media, 29*(3) 229–232.

Keller, J. M., & Burkman, E. (1993) Motivation principles. In M. Flemming & W. H. Levie (Eds.), *Instructional message in design: principles from behavioral and cognitive sciences* (pp. 3–49). Englewood Cliffs, NJ: Educational Technology Press.

Kolb, D. A. (1984). *Experiential learning: Experience as the source of learning and development* (Vol. 1, pp. 31–34). Englewood Cliffs, NJ: Prentice-Hall.

Maton, K. (n.d.). Cumulative and segmented learning: exploring the role of curriculum structures in knowledge building. *British Journal of Sociology of Education, 30*(1) 43–45. Retrieved from http://www.legitimationcodetheory.com/pdf/2009Cumulative.pdf

Owen, H. (2010). Why use ePortfolios and Web 2.0 tools and what do Web 2.0 tools have to offer? *Learning Communities: International Journal of Learning in Social Contexts: ePortfolio Edition, 2,* 74–103. Retrieved from http://www.scribd.com/doc/19750766/Why-Use-ePortfolios-and-Web-20-Tools

Peacock, S., Gordon, L., Murray, S., Morss, K., & Dunlop, G. (2010). Tutor response to implementing an ePortfolio to support learning and personal development in further and higher education institutions in Scotland. *British Journal of Educational Technology, 41*(5), 849–864.

Prammancee, N., & Moussa, M. (2010). Electronic portfolio use in Thailand. *First Monday, 15*(2). Retrieved from http://firstmonday.org/htbin/cgiwrap/bin/ojs/index.php/fm/article/view/2835/2453

Razavi, M., & Iverson, L. (2006). A grounded theory of information sharing behavior in a personal learning space. Retrieved from http://pdf.aminer.org/000/122/100/a_grounded_theory_of_information_sharing_behavior_in_a_personal.pdf

Roeser, R., & Peck, S. (2009). An education in awareness: Self, motivation, and self-regulated learning in contemplative perspective. *Educational Psychologist.* Retrieved from http://www.ncbi.nlm.nih.gov/pmc/articles/PMC2858411/

Rugg, B., & Pearle, W. (2006). *ePortfolio: Expanding the educational vision (our educational saga).* In Proceedings of the 34th Annual ACM SIGUCCS Fall Conference (pp. 321–324). ACM SIGUCCS

Scardamalia, M., & Bereiter, C. (2010). A brief history of knowledge building. Retrieved from http://www.cjlt.ca/index.php/cjlt/article/view/574

Schommer, M., & Walker, K. (1997). Epistemological beliefs and valuing school: Considerations for college admissions and retention. *Research in Higher Education, 38*(2), 173–186.

Smith, S. (2007). Transitioning from paper-based to electronic teaching portfolios: Student perceptions and recommendations. In R. Carlsen et al. (Eds.), *Proceedings of Society for Information Technology & Teacher Education International Conference* (pp. 180–182). Chesapeake, VA: AACE. Retrieved from http://editlib.org/p/24527/

Song, S., & Keller, J. (2001). Effectiveness of motivationally adaptive computer-assisted instruction on the dynamic aspects of motivation. *Educational Technology Research and Development, 49*(2), 5–22. doi:10.1007/BF02504925

Stefani, L., Mason, R., & Pegler, C. (2007). *The educational potential of e-portfolios—Supporting personal development and reflective learning.* London, UK: Routledge.

Tosh, D., Penny Light, T., Fleming, K., & Haywood, J. (2005). Engagement with electronic portfolios: Challenges from the student perspective. *Canadian Journal of Learning and Technology, 31*(3). Retrieved from http://cjlt.csj.ualberta.ca/index.php/cjlt/article/view/97/91

Van Wesel, M., & Prop, A. (2008). Comparing students' perceptions of paper-based and electronic portfolios. *Canadian Journal of Learning and Technology, 34*(3). Retrieved from http://cjlt.csj.ualberta.ca/index.php/cjlt/article/view/505/236

Van Zwanenberg, N., Wilkinson, L., & Anderson, A. (2000). Felder and Silverman's index of learning styles and Honey and Mumford learning styles questionnaire: How do they compare and do they predict academic performance? *Educational Psychology, 20*(3), 365–367.

Zhang, S. X., Olfman, L., & Ractham, P. (2007). Designing ePortfolio 2.0: Integrating and coordinating Web 2.0 services with ePortfolio systems for enhancing users' learning. *Journal of Information Systems Education, 18*(2), 203–214.

11

Development of a Context-Appropriate E-learning Site

Tanim Ashraf, Shekh Mohammad Mahbubul Kadir, and Sanjib Saha

Introduction

The world was home to seven billion people in 2011, and 35 per cent of this population was connected to the Internet (International Telecommunication Union, 2011). Five years earlier, the world's population was 6.5 billion, and only 18 per cent of this population was connected to the Internet. In 2006, 34 per cent of Internet users were from developing countries whereas in 2011, the majority of Internet users, 62 per cent, were from developing countries (International Telecommunication Union, 2011). Even excluding Internet users from India and China, still more than 30 per cent of the world's Internet users belonged to developing countries (International Telecommunication Union, 2011). A few factors have contributed to this rapid growth in the developing world's share of Internet connectivity, such as a reduction of cost of Internet connection and data, and easy accessibility to mobile broadband.

Between 2008 and 2010, fixed broadband prices in developing countries were reduced by up to 50 per cent. At the same time, mobile/cellular prices dropped by 22 per cent (International Telecommunication Union, 2011). Developing countries successfully used the mobility of mobile broadband to overcome infrastructure and price barriers in areas that were not previously connected to the Internet.

But there is a big gap between the Internet user experience in developed and developing countries. For example, in developed countries, Internet penetration and Internet speed is high, quality assurance mechanisms are in place, and the price is low. Whereas in developing countries, Internet penetration and Internet speed is low, quality assurance mechanisms are yet to develop, and Internet connections are less affordable, both in terms of availability and price (International Telecommunication Union, 2011).

Despite these barriers, developing countries have seen a rapid increase in Internet use, creating a platform that can be used to deliver a multitude of web-based services such as e-learning, e-health, and e-governance. These services can have significant impact on people's lives. E-learning can benefit both the formal and informal education sectors. But the context of learning differs from country to country in terms of accessibility to the Internet; speed of the Internet connection; education level of people, both in terms of language and information and communication technology (ICT); cultural aspects and priorities of individuals; socio-economic and demographic make-up of the population; responsiveness to change; and more. All these factors pose a challenge while developing an e-learning website.

This chapter focuses on e-learning services, describing how BBC Media Action—the BBC's international development charity—developed an e-learning site for a developing country, Bangladesh, by addressing both technological and cultural aspects of its area of work and target audience, respectively.

Background

Internet Landscape in the Home of BBC Janala: Bangladesh

From the introduction it can be seen that the Internet scenario in the world has changed in the last 6 to 7 years. And, like other developing countries in the world, Bangladesh saw a rise in Internet penetration. In 2005, Internet penetration in Bangladesh was 0.2 per cent. In 2012, this figure grew to 5 per cent (World Bank 2012; see Figure 11.1).

The latest Bangladesh Telecommunication Regulatory Commission (BTRC) data show (October, 2012) that 95 per cent of total Internet users in Bangladesh access the Internet using a mobile operator's data connection (BTRC, 2012). Figures (October, 2012) from BTRC also show that there are 97.475 million active mobile subscribers in Bangladesh (BTRC, 2012). In July 2012, Bangladesh had more than 29 million active Internet connections (BTRC, 2012).

The online scenario in Bangladesh is changing fast and, whilst social networking has been the forerunner in this digital movement, educational sites are also popular. According to the National Media Survey 2011 (The Nielsen Company Bangladesh Limited, 2011), most Internet users in Bangladesh belong to the age group 15–34, are from SEC A–B, and frequently use the Internet from home (at least twice a week). This growth is attributable to

- availability of Internet through mobile phone;
- increase in the number of Internet service providers (ISPs);
- increase in speed and reduction in tariff;
- cyber cafés and print/copy shops;
- emergence of social media; and
- easy availability of hardware (modems).

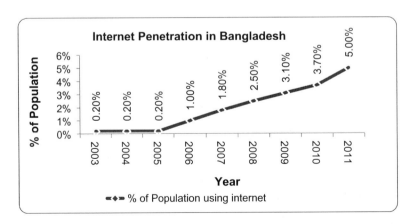

Figure 11.1   Internet Penetration in Bangladesh from 2003 to 2011

The World Bank: Bangladesh

Boston Consulting Group (BCG), on behalf of the Telenor Group, also undertook research in 2010 that showed that Bangladesh web access is likely to reach 18.3 million by the year 2020—translating to a 32 per cent household Internet penetration (Grameenphone, 2010). These numbers have the potential to grow much bigger with the government-sponsored vision of Digital Bangladesh 2021, although the success of this vision depends on continuing the sponsorship across government terms.

English in Action and BBC Janala

English in Action (EiA) is a 9-year (2008–2017) language education project aiming to develop communicative English language skills for 25 million people in Bangladesh. It is funded by the UK government and is working closely with the Ministry of Primary and Mass Education (MoPME) and the Ministry of Education (MoE), government of Bangladesh. Implementation of the project is done through a consortium of partners: BMB Mott MacDonald, BBC Media Action (formerly the BBC World Service Trust), Open University (OU), UK, and two national NGOs—Underprivileged Children's Educational Programme (UCEP) and Friends in Village Development Bangladesh (FIVDB). EiA has initiated ways of delivering communicative English to different sectors of the society, including primary and secondary students, teachers, and adult learners. To enhance the quality of learning in schools, EiA is using a combination of existing and new methods, including interactive audio technology, mobile technology, print, and ICT-based materials. EiA is also providing training and materials to teachers and teacher trainers to put these innovative methods in use in the classroom.

BBC Janala is a part of EiA, working towards the same goal but with the adult population (age range: 15–45). BBC Janala was developed and is operated by BBC Media Action and includes delivery of media outputs to facilitate adult learning as well as associated research, monitoring, and evaluation activities. After its inception, BBC Janala received multiple awards (Global mobile awards for Best Product, Initiative or Service for Underserved Segments, WISE award, Manthan, Microsoft, eAsia, mBillionth, etc.).

Why BBC Janala?

With the goal of enabling millions of Bangladeshis to learn English through TV, mobile, Internet, print media (books and newspapers), community radio, language clubs, and CDs, BBC Media Action launched BBC Janala ('window') in November 2009. BBC Janala's main target audience is people between 15 and 45 years old from socio-economic classes[1] (SEC) A to D, with a focus on C and D. To have a better understanding of the intervention concept and technology usage landscape of Bangladesh, a nationally representative baseline survey with a sample size of 6,300 was commissioned in 2008. This baseline study also contributed in finding out the need of learning English among the mass population. The research found that

- 84 per cent wanted to learn English.
- 64 per cent felt embarrassed to speak English.
- 47 per cent considered English to be too expensive to learn.
- 44 per cent felt that English was difficult to learn.
- 38 per cent felt that learning English was only available to those able to afford it.
- 28 per cent felt unable to learn English. (BBC Media Action, 2011)

Looking at the media consumption behavior of Bangladeshi people and their access to TV and mobile, BBC Media Action found that media was potentially a convenient, affordable, and accessible way to learn English. Hence, BBC Janala developed a multiplatform approach, aiming to ensure adequate access points to English learning materials; change perceptions of learning English amongst the adult population; reduce barriers to learning; and support the development of an innovative educational media sector.

Brief Overview of Current BBC Janala Website

The exponential growth in Bangladesh's Internet use in preceding years created a robust platform and user base, providing enough justification to launch an e-learning website to complement the overarching objectives of BBC Janala. Moreover, a web platform had the potential to provide a space where learning materials from other platforms could be accessed: since the web is capable of accommodating many types of rich media content that can enhance a learner's writing, speaking, listening, and reading skills. An Internet presence was also important to facilitate the sustainability of the project.

From 2009 to January 2012, the BBC Janala website went through a major change. Initially, the website contained categorised lessons with learners free to read any lesson they wanted, in any order. But evaluative research indicated that learners wanted a clear progression path and more structured learning content. They wanted to have a start point and an end point to their learning.

The focus then shifted from a website based on categorised, independent lessons to a progressive English learning course. There are now three levels of courses planned for this website—Course 1, Course 2, and Course 3. Course 1 was live and Course 2 was available in the first quarter of 2013, followed by Course 3 in 2014. Course 1 is for beginner-level learners, and the language proficiency level increases with the levels. The lessons are highly relevant to real-life scenarios so that learners can relate these lessons to themselves. Whereas the beginners' course focuses on day-to-day life, the preintermediate and intermediate courses will concentrate more on workplace scenarios.

The main characteristics of this website are:

- Lightweight, with only text and small-sized images so that learners can access the website even through lower speed connections.
- Use of Bangla as the main language of the website, so that learners feel comfortable and can easily navigate through the site. Even the error messages of the site are in Bangla.
- Emphasis on mouse-click motions rather that typing, to adjust to the level of web and language literacy of learners.
- Integration with Facebook, for sharing the result of the course so that learners can tell their friends that they have taken and completed the course.
- Use of lightweight audio files.
- A course report: a token of appreciation, after completing the total course to enhance learner motivation.
- The site remembers the progress of learners.
- Flash-based (graphic software) games to bring in fun and aid learning.

More on the features of the site can be found in later parts of this chapter.

The current website has been able to generate a significant response since its launch in March 2012. It has more than 130,000 registered learners, with more than 10 million page views. The average time spent on the website is 15 minutes, just below Facebook, and in each visit an average learner goes through around 15 pages.

Developing a Context-Appropriate E-learning Site

Developing a context-appropriate website is like solving a jigsaw puzzle. It has different parts that need to be put together correctly to get a complete picture. The different factors that need to be considered for building a context-appropriate website are

- the Internet landscape of the country;
- the target audience and their needs;
- users' Internet literacy and specific behaviors;
- language, culture, and social norms;
- feedback collection from users and web analytics after launch, and continuous improvement;
- marketing and promotion; and
- internal factors, such as organization's policy.

Now let's explore each of the parts from the perspective of BBC Janala.

Internet Landscape of the Country

The Internet landscape of the country provides vital input for starting the journey of developing a context-appropriate website. The Internet landscape of a country can include the following data:

- number of Internet users in a country,
- their demographic breakdown (age, gender, socio-economic class),
- mode of access to the Internet (mobile, computer, tablets),
- speed of Internet connection,
- preferable time slot of using the Internet,
- types of websites and Internet-based services preferred by Internet users, and
- frequency of usage.

At the time of the National Media Survey 2009, Internet penetration in Bangladesh was 3.1 per cent (World Bank, 2012). At that time, most Bangladeshi Internet users

- used the Internet at least twice a week;
- used the Internet from home, workplace, and cyber cafés;
- lived in metro cities;
- were male;
- used the Internet for e-mails, downloading files and software, playing games, listening to music, job-related browsing, and for getting news updates; and
- mostly used Yahoo and Google.

Looking at all this data, the original BBC Janala website was built in such a way that it could be easily browsed from a 150 kbps connection, with the resolution optimized for the CRT monitors usually found in cyber cafés. Download features were also included in the site, reflecting user behavior. Initially, Facebook integration was not particularly prominent because only 9 per cent of Internet users used Facebook in 2009 (Nielsen Company Bangladesh Limited, 2009). Though there was no data available on how many people browsed the Internet using a mobile, looking at the BTRC data, BBC Media Action also developed a mobile version of the BBC Janala website.

In 2011, it was found that Internet penetration in Bangladesh had reached up to 5 per cent (World Bank, 2012). Little had changed in terms of user make-up and behavior since 2009, except for a significant increase in the use of Facebook, so some social media integration was introduced in the new version of the website. Recent research from BBC Media Action shows that this figure has gone up to 8.1 per cent (BBC Media Action, 2012). This equates to a figure of around 9 million. Currently, an average regular Internet user accesses the Internet three times a day, and browses four websites in each session. The time spent and usage is higher in the morning. Most Internet users use e-mail services, browse social media sites such as Facebook, download or stream songs, and search for the latest news (Milion, 2012). According to Socialbakers.com, Bangladesh currently has 3,349,020 Facebook users, which translates to around 2 per cent penetration in the country. But in terms of numbers, Bangladesh ranks 49th in the world (Socialbakers.com, 2013). But, at the same time, in terms of download speed, Bangladesh ranks 170th among 189 countries (Ookla, 2013).

Identifying the Target Audience and Their Needs

BBC Media Action spent time and resources identifying the target audience, mapping them by demography and behavior, and finding out what they needed. Their needs were assessed from both an implicit and explicit perspective: recording what respondents actually 'say' about their needs as well as identifying needs by examining empirical data on their behavioral patterns, physical gestures, and demography. These data were then fed in, to develop the syllabus and to identify the right difficulty level for the content.

BBC Media Action worked with Ericsson, Attic Media, AC Nielsen, and SIRIUS Marketing to define the audiences and the BBC EiA brand:

- a nationally representative baseline survey with 6,300 Bangladeshis
- a nation-wide survey of 3,000+ mobile/Internet users in Bangladesh
- cross analysis of results with Ericsson's 3,000 person survey of mobile users' consumer habits, lifestyles, and attitudes in Bangladesh

And all this research resulted in adoption of the following target audience segments:

- mainstream youth: trendy, conformist value-seekers
- modern housewives: middle-class, knowledgeable urbanites
- educated materialists: socializing attention-seekers
- busy midlevel merchants: late tech-adopters

Initially, BBC Janala had categorised content but had no clear line of progression. A user could go to the website and see any lesson he or she wanted to. BBC Janala went for subsequent user experience research and also gathered user feedback through a variety of channels, such as one-to-one interviews, e-mail feedback, Facebook user feedback, and cohort panel research. Users gave the following suggestions:

- to categorise content according to difficulty level;
- to use nonnative (specifically Bangladeshi) speakers for English inserts in the audio version of lessons, to enable learners to understand the content more easily;
- to provide a clear progression path of learning, with a learner joining at a defined starting point and undertaking step-by-step, progressive learning, with the aim of having increased their level of English by the end of their learning journey; and
- to develop lessons that learners can relate to themselves.

Users also suggested that Bangla should continue to be the main language of the website, to cater for easy understanding and navigation of the website.

Following this feedback, BBC Media Action (2010) started developing a course curriculum under the pilot name of Adult Learning Course from September 2010. The course was to be available through mobile, web, mobile web, and newspaper. After a year of rigorous research and development work, the course website was finally launched on 17 January 2012, and was publicly promoted on 1 March 2012. As the development of the new course and website was to take more than a year, BBC Media Action took the following steps to cater for users' demand until the launch of the course:

- Categorised all the content under two difficulty levels: Step 1 (beginner-level content) and Step 2 (intermediate and advanced-level content), enabling users to be guided to lessons according to their level.
- Added three new lessons series:

  o English for Work—targeted towards people who need to speak English in the workplace.
  o Practical Vocabulary—lessons for learning sets of useful words needed in day-to-day life.
  o Beginner-Level Pronunciation—lessons for learning the correct pronunciation of English words used in day-to-day life.

  These lesson series were a product of suggestions from users. The essence of these lessons has been carried forward to the lessons available in the course.

- Kept Bangla (the mother tongue of the target audience) as the main language of the website.

Users' Internet Literacy and Specific Behaviors

BBC Media Action rolled out a series of user tests to learn more about the Internet literacy and behavioral pattern of the target audience. A user test is a qualitative research activity where a representative sample from the population gives in-depth feedback on specific issues by experiencing a prototype. Also, a user's interaction is observed to identify usability issues that are difficult to discover through verbal question and answer sessions. For the website, BBC Media Action conducted more than eight rounds of user tests from 2008 to date, involving more than 100 people. In most cases, BBC Media Action took a prototype of the website or a print out of sample web pages so that respondents could provide clear feedback, based on their experience with the prototypes. In later tests, the users were provided with laptops to browse through the site and software was used to track mouse movements and gather navigational insights. Insights from user testing that influenced the design and functionality of BBC Janala's current website (the course) are:

- The desire for a progressive course structure, with clear start and ending points.
- Use of mouse rather than keyboard. Most people in the target group are more comfortable with clicking than typing, so, with the exception of the registration module of the website, most functions are click based, including the quizzes where a user has to click on a radio button[2] to give answers.
- People have no issues scrolling a long page. At the same time, they also find it comfortable browsing multiple pages to complete a lesson as long as they have clear instructions to do so. Therefore, the website has a mix of scrolling and page-to-page browsing motions. In fact, presenting a single lesson in multiple pages enabled the introduction of an easily understandable structure.

- Users tend to click on objects rather than text. The object can be a box with text on it, a radio button, check box, or image. For example, on the home page, there are images of three people representing the teachers of the three courses. When respondents were asked to go to a course, they tended to click on images rather than the text label of the image. Also for this reason, all the clickable instruction labels such as 'go to next page' and 'click here to see your answers' are written on colored boxes.
- For registration of the course, a unique identifier was needed. From the user tests, it was found that most of the people in the target audience have e-mail because to have a Facebook account, an e-mail address is needed. Also, in Bangladesh, people are not familiar with the term 'user name.' So, for registering in the course, e-mail address was chosen as the unique identifier.
- People also want to 'save' the lessons. For this, audio versions of the lesson and PDF practice sheets were included on the website. This enabled a user to refer back to lessons even when remote from an Internet connection.
- Visual aids enable a user to understand lessons and instructions properly. It was found that visual aids such as a dynamic progress bar, images, and signs enabled users to understand their progress in the course and also motivated them to go forward. Particularly successful was the dynamic progress bar, which filled up with completion of each lesson and acted as a driving force for lots of users. Inclusion of relevant images in the lessons was also found helpful by the users, as it broke up lesson text and gave a feeling of the practical context of the lesson.
- The idea of flash-based games, where users have to go through a drag-and-drop[3] motion to play the game, was thought to be difficult for users. But during user tests, almost all respondents successfully played the game. Even respondents with very limited experience using a mouse ended up playing the game successfully without any prompts. Seeing the amount of time taken to play the quizzes, an instructional animation and text was given on the page so that users could understand how to play the game.

Language and Culture

Language and culture issues have been addressed, in part, earlier, but this specific factor deserves separate attention. Research has found that, while replicating a concept beyond borders, language and cultural adaptation of the concept turns out to be the most important factor behind acceptance among people, and in Bangladesh, where people have fought and died for the survival of their language, this is particularly important. A website cannot be context appropriate as long as it does not fit in with the culture of the targeted community. While developing the BBC Janala website (both old and new), language and culture were therefore considered high-priority issues. To maintain the language and cultural contexts, BBC Media Action did the following:

- used Bangla as the main language of the website;
- used conversational and easy Bangla so that most of the people can understand;
  - for example, the 'formal' Bangla translation of 'mobile phone' is 'মুঠো ফোন' (literally, handheld phone), whereas the popular term is 'মোবাইল' (mobile). So the term 'mobile' is used in BBC Janala lessons;
- avoided regional Bangla dialects, to prevent perceptions of bias;
- avoided mentioning controversial political issues and issues that can raise controversy or be perceived in a negative way;

- avoided words that can be perceived as racist or chauvinist;
- avoided images or colors on the website that can be interpreted as promoting nationalism or promoting a specific group of people;
- used culturally appropriate photographs (including the color and style of people's dress and the locations used to illustrate the lessons); and
- developed content with social inclusion in mind (lessons containing female and male characters, characters from all religions and from different sections of society).

The quality of the learning contents of the website was maintained by engaging both local and international ELT experts throughout the content development and life cycle of the project. Appropriateness of the content was assured by having cultural and linguistic context as the main focus of content development. For example, in the conversation lessons, there is one segment on household products and the English dialogue content was prepared as 'Can I have (number) **bar/bars** of soap?' But, in Bangla, the word 'bar' (which has no meaningful translation in Bangla) is omitted from the sentence, and instead, 'Can I have (number) soap/soaps?' was used to maintain contextual integrity.

Feedback Collection From Users and Web Analytics After Launch and Continuous Improvement

Although prototype testing provided a thorough understanding of user interaction, it did not give a holistic picture of users' opinions and behaviors. In a dynamic environment such as e-learning and web, it is important to be aware of the way that learners are making use of material, in order to cater for their developing needs. BBC Media Action regularly analyses data from web analytics as well as undertaking in-depth interviews with users to identify the good/bad, like/dislike, and 'could be better' aspects of the website and how they can be improved. Users who have had an in-depth experience with the website can also come up with completely fresh ideas. Learning from postlaunch user feedback has proved to be vital for the BBC Janala website and has allowed a number of bugs and technical issues to be corrected. Some of the important postlaunch feedback and suggestions from BBC Janala new website users have included

- more social media presence (e.g., a function to allow sharing of lessons on Facebook);
- having a Facebook page;
- increasing the scope of the website to include information about the organisation and project as a whole as well as the course itself; and
- development of a test (proficiency level test) to enable users to gauge which of the three courses is suitable for them.

Web analytics can give an overview of users' behavior and of the website's performance. They also help to set the standard figure for a number of benchmark indicators (e.g., when the average dwell time drops below 12 minutes, BBC Media Action is alerted to the potential of a new technical issue that is impacting users' experience). Web analytics data can also help to define the optimum technical specifications of the website (e.g., optimisation for different operating systems, browsers, and screen resolutions) and can feed into choosing right audiences, channels, and times for online marketing (e.g., sending newsletters, marketing e-mails, and informative e-mails during daytime). From web analytics, BBC Media Action found the following:

- In the new website, people tend to view more pages in one visit than the old website. The average time spent per visit is also higher than on the old website. The course, which was introduced to increase users' involvement level, turned out to be a success.

- The website is mostly visited during office hours, although there is also significant traffic during evening and night.
- The website is visited more during weekdays and less visited during weekends and holidays.
- Users tend to view most pages on their first visit.
- During promotions, traffic to the website increases.
- Most visitors come from referral sites, such as ads on daily newspaper websites and Facebook.
- Most users who arrive through a search engine come via Google.
- Most users use Mozilla Firefox for browsing the website. Chrome, Internet Explorer, and Opera follow.
- Most visits have been made from a Windows computer, with Windows XP and Windows 7 topping the list.
- Most of the screens from which visits were made had a resolution of 1,366 x 768 (resolution of 17-in CRT monitor and most of the LCD monitors). Twenty-seven per cent of the visits are being made from 14-in CRT monitor resolution (800 x 600 and 1,024 x 768).
- The website is also browsed from mobile (5.41 per cent of total visits).
- Web analytics also allow an analysis of the keywords used in search engine visits that direct users to the site.

Marketing, Promotions, and Multiplier Effect of Multiplatform Approach

BBC Janala is a multiplatform project and has the advantage of being able to cross-promote its platforms. BBC Janala used TV commercials, pop-up promotions, referrals from TV programs, mobile platform promotions, and newspaper advertisements to build awareness amongst the population. The fact that all of BBC Janala's platforms share a common English learning syllabus means that cross-promotion is particularly effective, since a learner accessing content on one platform can easily reinforce their learning on another.

The website is placed within the project as the common hub for content aggregation. The course reports, which users receive after completing the course on any of the project's platforms, are distributed through the website. Without the limitations of space or time that are inherently a feature of the project's newspaper and audio-based mobile lessons, the website is also the most resource-rich teaching platform, offering additional materials to users who initially access learning in other ways.

Internal Factors Such as Organization's Policy and Guidelines

While developing this specific instance of a context-appropriate website, it was very important to align the content according to BBC guidelines for content, color, and brand. BBC Media Action adheres to strict editorial guidelines for any product with a view to maintaining quality of output, gender equality, social inclusion, and appropriateness of content.

Conclusion

Throughout the development of BBC Janala, the primary guiding source of information has been user feedback and insights. The project has tried to facilitate and open as many avenues as possible to gather user inputs and combined these with user feedback and analytics data to shape and refine BBC Janala products. This simple but powerful approach is the key to BBC Janala's success. The future holds significant challenges for BBC Janala in terms of maintaining the high demand and production value of its English learning services. BBC Janala intends to build a sustainable learning hub for learners, academics, and researchers. BBCjanala.com will evolve as a common repository for material from all project platforms, rather than a course-only site. Social media will also flourish, and BBC Janala will take advantage of the rapidly growing social media uptake in Bangladesh to build and engage with its users. Social collaborative learning is also an active consideration for BBC Janala.

Notes

1 Socio-economic class is defined by the profession/occupation and education of the chief wage earner of a household. SEC A (at the top end) through to SEC E.
2 According to dictionary.com, radio buttons are found in a graphical user interface, any of a set of options from which only one may be selected at a given time.
3 According to dictionary.com, drag and drop is a common method for manipulating files (and sometimes text) under a graphical user interface. The user moves the pointer over an icon representing a file or objects and presses a mouse button. He or she holds the button down while moving the pointer (dragging the file) to another place, usually a directory viewer or an icon for some application program, and then releases the button (dropping the file).

References

Bangladesh Telecommunication Regulatory Commission (BTRC). (2012). *Mobile phone subscribers in Bangladesh*. Retrieved from http://www.btrc.gov.bd/index.php?option=com_content&view=article&id=619: mobile-phone-subscribers-in-bangladesh-january-2012&catid=49:telco-news&Itemid=502

BBC Media Action (formerly World Service Trust). (2010). *BBC Janala web usability and functionality user testing report*. Dhaka, Bangladesh: BBC Media Action.

BBC Media Action (formerly World Service Trust). (2011). *BBC Janala web usability and functionality user testing report*. Dhaka, Bangladesh: BBC Media Action.

BBC Media Action (formerly World Service Trust). (2012). *BBC Janala web usability and functionality user testing report*. Dhaka, Bangladesh: BBC Media Action.

Grameenphone. (2010, January 21). *Study reveals 20 million internet subscribers by 2020*. Retrieved from http://www.grameenphone.com/about-us/media-center/press-release/2010/150/study-reveals-20-million-internet-subscribers-2020

International Telecommunication Union. (2011). The world in 2011—ICT facts and figures. Retrieved from http://www.itu.int/ITU-D/ict/facts/2011/material/ICTFactsFigures2011.pdf

Milion, N. (2012, July 13). Internet trends in Bangladesh. *The Daily Star*. Retrieved from http://www.thedailystar.net/newDesign/news-details.php?nid=241836

Nielsen Company Bangladesh Limited. (2009). *National media survey, 2009*. Retrieved from http://www.nielsen.com/ca/en.html

Nielsen Company Bangladesh Limited. (2011). *National media survey, 2011*. Retrieved from http://www.nielsen.com/ca/en.html

Ookla (2013). *Household download index*. Retrieved from http://www.netindex.com/download/allcountries/

Socialbakers.com. (2013). *Facebook statistics by country*. Retrieved from http://www.socialbakers.com/facebook-statistics/?interval=last-week&orderBy=users&orderDir=desc#chart-intervals

World Bank. (2012), *Internet users (per 100 people)*. Retrieved from http://data.worldbank.org/indicator/IT.NET.USER.P2

12

Education's Second Life

Virtual Learning in Higher Education

Shelagh A. McGrath and Carlo M. Trentadue

Introduction

Since their inception, social media technologies have been reinventing the communal and cultural traditions of our society. They have repeatedly shown their ability to uproot deeply seeded customs and replace them with new methods of interaction. Businesses and corporate institutions are quickly turning to virtual learning in order to train new staff and educate corporate elites. Individuals adopted 'digital personas' which serve as an online representation of their physical being. Accordingly, educational methodologies are drastically affected by the rapid growth of social media technologies. Leading this andragogical revolution is Second Life, "an online, three dimensional virtual environment in which users take on the form of avatars, a representation of themselves, and then interact with other users in the synthetic environment" (Inman, Wright, & Hartman, 2010, p. 45). Within this simulated environment, users are able to actively collaborate and interact with surrounding objects, people, and the environment. If harnessed correctly, Second Life has the potential to house complex virtual educational institutions whereby users are able to dynamically engage with academic material, interact with peers, and ultimately complete university credits, all over an online virtual platform. Thus, the realm of Second Life is an extraordinary example of how andragogical strategies can be shifted to develop new educational practices in terms of an immersive online world. This approach to social media in education is one that will change the face of pedagogy and andragogy in the future.

Defining Social Networking Sites, Forums, and Virtual World Forums

Ellison and Boyd define Social Networking Sites (SNS) as "web-based services that allow individuals to (1) construct a public or semi-public profile within a bounded system, (2) articulate a list of other users with whom they share a connection, and (3) view and traverse their list of connections and those made by others" (Boyd & Ellison, 2007, p. 2). In today's technological age, where a majority of the population possesses some type of social media, this definition seems too banal to utilize in terms of online education systems. This is a classification primarily employed to emphasize SNS's ability to view alternative networks and make other profiles visible. In doing so, a user is able to grow a social network on a personal level; sites like Facebook, LinkedIn, and Myspace are classified as SNS. In a sense, these systems function as personal directories. For example, Google, the world's most-utilized online search engine, essentially made the Yellow Pages obsolete by eliminating any need to physically search information pertaining to businesses. Google has fundamentally evolved from the physical directory to an online variation that encompasses virtually every avenue available in terms of searching for business information. Similarly, Facebook is quickly transforming into the 'Google for people', because a user can quickly and easily find an acquaintance by searching through other user's friend lists. LinkedIn operates in the same manner, allowing business professionals to connect and grow their network through colleagues' connections. Thus, SNS is significant because it provides an efficient yet informal way to connect with people, but it lacks the structure to support a wider range of capabilities specifically pertaining to educational strategies.

Subsequently, there exists a definition more suitable for social networking technologies in an educational setting: a Social Networking Forum (SNF). Grimes and Fields suggest "a new classification system for examining SNF and their features, related to the forms of communication they enable, the personal profiles they allow users to create, the networking residues they encourage, and the hierarchies of access they afford" (Grimes & Fields, 2012, p. 3). This classification system broadens the scope of social media technologies to incorporate sites that feature more than just network lists and personal profiles. There are two features of SNF that are pertinent in understanding the effectiveness of Second Life in a andragogy setting, specifically, personal profiles and hierarchies of access. A personal profile is the most basic form of an individual's digital persona. It contains general information about the individual, typically displaying a photo, and divulges data pertaining to the user's interests, hobbies, and connections, thereby allowing for a type of cohesion between users. Alternatively, hierarchies of access are typically depicted as a system of limitations or restrictions that prompt the user to purchase or exchange valuable information in return for exclusive in-world materials.

In Second Life, personal profiles come in the form of avatars, a virtual representation of the user. Avatars are able to "move though virtual space, talk, and often gesture to others" (Grimes & Fields, 2012, p. 42), thus providing the user with a type of customized characterization of themselves. This is certainly a significant notion in terms of the success of virtual learning as it provides an element of realism and personal attachment to the avatar. The user essentially becomes emotionally invested in the recreation of a virtual self. Moreover, the hierarchies of access in SNF most commonly manifest themselves in the form of extra privileges to users who subscribe or commit themselves to that online community. This 'velvet rope' approach is generally employed as a marketing strategy that rewards the "purchase of a particular accessory or membership subscription" by granting "enhanced privileges that might include broader access to friends, items, and activities" (Grimes & Fields, 2012, 45). This is a promotional strategy that is widespread in a plethora of online communities and forms the basis of financial profit in social media businesses. In regard to Second Life, in order to further the customization of a user's avatar, the purchase of 'virtual funds' is required, which can be spent on digital clothing and accessories. In parallel to the physical world, digital representations of the user must continually spend money to keep their appearances updated and portray themselves in a certain way. An individual can choose to create a human avatar or a fantasy avatar. This representation of themselves also comes with entrance to particular groups. For example, a 'tiny' (an avatar resembling a small teddy bear) associates and socializes with other 'tinies' and the virtual world at large. Therefore, within the virtual world, cultures, norms, and dynamics evolve. These are concepts that are discussed further in terms of social and cultural capital. Similarly, the enrollment into a virtual learning academy may also embody the 'velvet rope' approach and is an interesting interpretation of how hierarchies of access manifest themselves in other ways.

Nevertheless, there exists a third definition that we propose should be united with these two features of SNF, specifically when dealing with platforms like Second Life. Second Life is unique in that it is an immersive technology that creates an inimitable virtual world. A virtual world is defined as an environment that "exists whether a user is logged in or not, it is populated by many users [sic], it provides the illusion of 3D space, avatars represent user's in-world, and an interactive chat function is available" (Inman, Wright, & Hartman, 2010, p. 44). Thus, it is clear that Second Life can be classified as both a SNF and a virtual world, subsequently allowing for an amalgamation of the two classifications to create a new one: a Virtual World Forum (VWF). A VWF consists of (1) a three-dimensional and interactive space that exists regardless of online or offline users, (2) an avatar that serves as the basic medium for users to participate within the environment, and (3) communicative methods that allow interaction between other users and materials within the environment, ultimately allowing for collaboration to occur.

Increasing Social and Cultural Capital

In a world where digitalization is becoming the norm, it is no surprise that educators and businesses are turning to online solutions. VWF is a platform rapidly drawing attention, primarily due to its ability to effectively increase a user's social and cultural capital. Furthermore, the realistic approach by VWF mimics the external world and encourages, in every sense of the word, a second life. This is a concept that is quickly becoming a reality; individuals are effectively capable of living both a physical and digital life. In doing so, the credibility of this virtual world is increasing, which ultimately translates into the legitimization of acquiring university accredited courses through an online system. Alternatively, part of the reason so many people are enthralled with Second Life is because of its ability to further social networking between people. David Gauntlett suggests that social capital revolves around the specific social relationships or networks an individual possesses whether online or in the real world. He asserts that "just as a supply of money can enable you to do things that you otherwise could not do, a stock of social relationships will also make it easier to do things that otherwise you could not" (Gauntlett, 2011, p. 129). Second Life is an application that fosters an individual's relationship with other users through the use of virtual characters, and thus translates into the heightening of social capital in an online capacity. Virtual worlds enable users to expand their personal networks beyond the constraints of geography, ethnicities, and even time, in some cases. Through Second Life, users are able to extend past the physical boundaries of the real world, permitting interaction with various people they otherwise would not be able to. In an andragogical setting, a user is able to network with esteemed professors from foreign countries and collaborate on academic materials. More importantly, users are able to interact with students on an international scale, thereby creating multinational social connections. In that sense, Second Life is a unique and valuable tool in that it provides a medium for the extension of an individual's social capitalism. Subsequently, a second form of capital manifests itself in Second Life—one that is evident in real society as well.

Cultural capital typically encompasses intangible traits that allow for social mobility, particularly beyond economic means. This is inclusive of everything from ethnicity, style, and appearance, but most importantly education. One could argue that in paralleling humanity's real society, Second Life has inherently developed its own virtual capitalist economy. For example, through the purchase of 'Linden Dollars,' users are able to creatively express themselves through their avatar by spending their Linden on virtual clothes. These expressions ultimately lend to notions of social stature and status despite existing in a simulated environment. In fact the most common manifestation of cultural capital in Second Life "concerns newcomers ('newbies' or 'noobs'), but also spots forms of 'appearance status' and 'skills inequality' as expressions of something like a Second Life class structure" (Bell, 2009, p. 521). The initial experience that comes with using Second Life can be equated to immigrating to a foreign land. Avatars begin their initiation at a welcome point providing basic information on navigation, dressing, and places to find free items, such as clothing. They are informed of the 'destination guide' and encouraged to visit these simulators (Sims). As one explores

Second Life, it becomes evident there is a culture. As in 'real life' there are social norms for a variety of different groups, etiquette, colloquialisms, and choices in groups one can be part of. Second Life is global and affords the opportunity to interact with organizations, groups, and individuals from all over the world. Second Life's mimesis of real-world concepts and social structures is exactly what makes its virtual space so appealing. Furthermore, avatars can create businesses within Second Life and further the economy while practicing their entrepreneurship. Many avatars find employment through other avatars' businesses, and therefore the economy and culture evolve independently from Linden Labs (Second Life developer). Linden Dollars can be converted to real US dollars, which allows for the digital world to actually become a viable, 'real life' business.

Pierre Bordieu's work on the forms of capital particularly emphasizes how the tools of acquiring capital are constantly changing. Second Life is yet another technological innovation that functions as a vehicle to obtain further capital. Moreover, Bourdieu suggests that with "academic qualification, a certificate of cultural competence which confers on its holder a conventional, constant, legally guaranteed value with respect to culture, social alchemy produces a form of cultural capital which has a relative autonomy" (Bourdieu, 1986, p. 9). Thus education and higher learning are the cornerstones in capturing the highest degree of cultural capital in today's society. Moreover, becoming educated about foreign cultures is a valuable trait in regard to the business world as employment worldwide relies heavily on aspects of cultural intelligence. Since large corporations are interacting with clients from all over the world "business people can benefit more than ever from demonstrating cultural intelligence in today's global economy" (Siegal, 2010, p. 45). Therefore, not only does Second Life permit users the ability to increase cultural intelligence but it also provides a virtual platform for foreign corporations to interact and share material. Second Life enables a user to increase their social capital and cultural intelligence; what benefits does this application have in terms of andragogical usage?

The world of Second Life is an expansive realm of dozens of different interests, passions, and uses. Communities of artists, actors, singer songwriters, sports enthusiasts, real-world businesses, universities, and colleges coexist with the ability to explore and participate in one another's space at any time. Add to this the global appeal and one can see the power and potential of increasing cultural capital. Specific to education is the growing attention to Second Life as a viable means of providing learning experiences. The Virtual World Best Practices in Education conference focuses on a multitude of successes in using virtual worlds. It affords the opportunity for professors, educators, learning and development professionals, and people with a general interest in this area to network and learn from one another. Activities allow individuals to increase cultural capital through learning and networking without boundaries. There is no 'prerequisite' to hold a position in an educational field, so an individual with a passion for the area can participate, learn, and gain insight into a personal passion. In fact the participation in such activities can motivate an individual to further their education in an environment such as a VWE. The credibility of the presenters, topics, and the event itself lends viability to future work in this area. Much like the evolution of MOOCs (Massive Open Online Courses) the ability to further one's knowledge and skill through formal and informal interaction in a virtual world is an attractive option.

Skepticism, Criticism, and New Developments

With any innovation comes a certain degree of skepticism and criticism. A study done in 2008 measured the pedagogical potential of virtual worlds like Second Life and ultimately concluded that "due to the slow graphics and high demand of computer software, Second Life should be viewed mainly as a learning tool that compliments rather than substitutes other teaching forms" (Wang &

Braman, 2009, p. 236). This criticism, however, underestimates the collaborative potential of virtual student work groups and faults the mechanical aspects of the application. Since that time Second Life has continued to adapt, expand, and advance the technology, making it easier and more stable for users to utilize. Barring the technical requirements, researchers found a multitude of potential advantages for introducing Second Life into the classroom. Primarily, Second Life could be implemented as an invaluable "tool for distance education, since it allows for synchronous virtual experiences and information seeking as well as meeting opportunities" (Inman et al., 2010, p. 54). Universities and colleges internationally employ Second Life to create rich, immersive educational experiences. For example, Loyalist College is the first Canadian college to offer online classes in the Second Life community. This is particularly successful for students interested in the animation and gaming industries. Students who helped Loyalist College develop their online environment asserted that Second Life afforded the student body a free atmosphere which makes it easy to overcome inhibition and can learn without barriers. Essentially, reserved or introverted students are able to express themselves more openly in a virtual world. Furthermore, this lack of inhibition allows for collaborative work between students to become easier and more comfortable. In fact, this was a characteristic of virtual worlds that instructors acknowledged aided in didactic group work. Researchers found that "engaging in group work and group projects is another potential use of Second Life recognized by educators, as students successfully worked together and in some instances preferred to be together rather than alone" (Inman et al., 2010, p. 54). Yet another example manifests itself in the Open University (OU), a higher educational institution based in the United Kingdom that offers degree programs through distance education. The OU innovative approach to educational delivery includes six virtual locations that range from teaching and learning spaces, socialization lounges, virtual campuses, and an 'auditorium'. This advance in educational methods provides a replication of the teaching experience received in a classroom except on a simulated platform. Despite Second Life's rapid growth and functionality within the pedagogical and andragogical realm, there is still much work to be done to make Second Life a staple within the classroom environment. Many institutions lack the knowledge, time, and resources to fully exploit the advantages that Second Life offers.

Theoretically speaking, educators must recognize the evolution and continuing need for encouraging self directed learning. With the advent of free open university course providers, such as Coursera, individuals are moving into an educational space affording them the opportunity to experience knowledge acquisition completely designed by them and for them. We see Second Life as a potential tool to foster self-directedness. Coined by Stewart Hase, *heutagogy* places specific emphasis on learning how to learn, double-loop learning, universal learning opportunities, a nonlinear process, and true learner self-direction. Whereas andragogy focuses on the best ways for people to learn, heutagogy also requires that educational initiatives include the improvement of people's actual learning skills themselves, learning how to learn as well as just learning a given subject itself. Similarly, whereas andragogy focuses on structured education, in heutagogy all learning contexts, both formal and informal, are considered. (Chapnick & Meloy, 2005)

As education opportunities continue to evolve in an open source medium, educators need to facilitate the improvement of 'ways to learn'. Appealing to a variety of learning styles is more effective in VWF because it allows the learner freedom to explore concepts in an innovative and creative way. Each unique learning style has the opportunity to flourish through the use of the many aspects of Second Life: collaborative group work, the experience of orienting oneself to the culture and environment, disseminating norms and socially acceptable behaviour, and incorporating these skills into their learning experiences. As augmented reality continues to evolve we see the potential for further advancement in VWF. Many faculties can benefit from virtual world learning, such as medical fields, where practicing suturing or complex surgeries can greatly improve a learner's experience and confidence. The gaming industry can also benefit as a majority of its work takes place over a virtual platform. Regardless, any field requiring practical application can utilize the concepts of augmented reality. Second Life can provide a platform for practical application and the furthering of skill and aptitude.

Conclusion

The potential exists for more universities and institutions of higher learning to become 'virtual', and offer accredited online courses through a virtual world platform. Although Second Life is initially perceived as a game, innovative pioneers in the didactic realm act upon the potential to create a certain degree of success in introducing the virtual world to the academic world. As these successes are communicated and evolve, the benefit of virtual education is advancing. From a social media perspective, Second Life affords these groups an increase in cultural intelligence by associating with other institutions from across the globe. Moreover, universities and colleges also possess the ability to increase their own social circles because they are able to interact and work in partnership with other learning institutions. Thus, Second Life provides a stable environment where students can collaborate together or with staff, access indispensable academic material, and interact with foreign cultures through a simulated representation. Institutions can continue to advance their programs, learn from others, and support the innovation that social media affords.

As development continues both technologically and academically, more and more learners will look for alternatives to traditional bricks and mortar. The opportunity exists for higher learning institutions to begin the climb to innovative and student-centric perspectives that result in highly attractive programs. The future of higher education is contingent on the ability of these institutions to recognize and act on the possibilities. More research and development is required to effectively predict and act upon the potential of VWE. Specifically, universities and colleges can no longer ignore the power of mainstream social networking in the development of programs.

References

Bell, D. (2009). Learning from second life. *British Journal of Educational Technology, 40*(3), 515–525.

Bordieu, P. (1986). Forms of capital. In J. Richardson (Ed.), *Handbook of theory and research for the sociology of education* (pp. 241–258). New York, NY: Greenwood.

Boyd, D. M., & Ellison, N. B. (2007). Social network sites: Definition, history, and scholarship. *Journal of Computer-Mediated Communication, 13*(1), 1–19. Retrieved from http://jcmc.indiana.edu/vol13/issue1/boyd.ellison.html

Chapnick, S., & Meloy, J. (2005). From andragogy to heutagogy. *Renaissance elearning: Creating dramatic and unconventional learning experiences. Essential resources for training and HR professionals* (pp. 36–37). New York, NY: John Wiley and Sons.

Gauntlett, D. (2011). *Making is connecting: The social meaning of creativity, from DIY and knitting to YouTube and Web 2.0.* Cambridge, MA: Polity.

Grimes, S. M., & Fields, D. A. (2012). Kids online: A new research agenda for understanding social networking forums. *The Joan Ganz Cooney Centre at Sesame Workshop*, 1–69.

Inman, C., Wright, V. H., & Hartman, J. A. (2010). Use of Second Life in k-12 and higher education: A review of research. *Journal of Interactive Online Learning, 9*(1), 44–63.

Siegal, S. E. (2010). Gaining cultural intelligence through Second Life learning interventions. *International Journal of Advanced Corporate Learning, 3*(3), 45–51.

Wang, Y., & Braman, J. (2009). Extending the classroom through Second Life. *Journal of Information Systems Education, 20*(2), 235–247.

13

Lifelong Learners and Teachers' Time-Management Competency in E-learning

Margarida Romero and Elena Barberà

1. Introduction

Time is a critical factor in e-learning (Barberà, Gros, & Kirschner, 2012; Romero, 2010), both for the teachers and for lifelong learners engaged in e-learning courses. In this chapter we analyse the time factor in e-learning, focusing on the time-management competencies of online learners and teachers in relation to the temporal model of online education and the temporal constraints of the online learners and teachers. The chapter begins by introducing the time-management competence and then moves on to discuss methods for evaluating distance learners' and teachers' time-management competencies. We then ask whether the traditional task-independent questionnaires for assessing time management are adequate in the context of online learning, and we introduce guidelines for assessing time-management competencies in lifelong learners and teachers in e-learning. The chapter ends with a discussion of the best strategies for assessing and developing the learners' and teachers' time-management competencies.

2. Time for Lifelong Learning

In the knowledge society, there is a need for continuous Lifelong Learning (LLL), especially in knowledge-based sectors (Watkins, Marsick, & Kim, 2012). The quantity and quality of usable time for learning, or LLL time, must be balanced with professional and family responsibilities to ensure the person's overall well-being and personal development. However, finding an appropriate balance between different life domains is neither easy nor instantaneous (Metzger & Cléach, 2004). The need for a Work Life Balance (WLB) must include Lifelong Learning requirements in the 21st century, moving us toward a new challenge—the Work Life Learning Balance (WLLB). To address this challenge we analyse two ways of balancing the equation: (1) increasing the flexibility of the learning time through blended learning and online education and (2) promoting online learners' and teachers' time competencies to manage their learning times. In the following sections we explore both of these aspects.

As shown in Figure 13.1, we consider the strategies of online education time flexibility (1) and the time management developed (2) by online learners and online teachers. In order to develop time-management competencies, we should start by assessing the current level of these

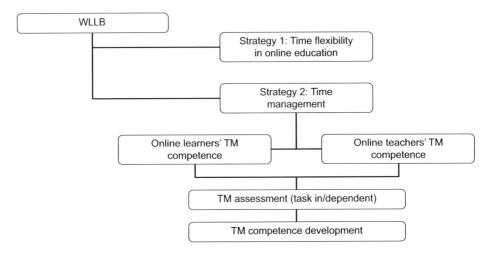

Figure 13.1 Online Education Time Flexibility and Learners' and Teachers' Time Management

competencies using the different tools we will review in the sixth section of the chapter and later decide on the best strategies for promoting the development of these competencies.

3. Time Flexibility in Online Education

Because the virtual campus may be 'spaceless', it is not timeless. All learning processes require time, and we should not confuse the flexibility of time in online education with a reduction of the time required to achieve the learning objectives. In the context of online education, students' time flexibility is defined as their ability to regulate their time-on-task according to the learning time they have available, the instructional time requirements, and the adaptability of the learning tasks (Romero & Barberà, 2011). According to Chung (2005), time flexibility is increasing in higher education and is enhanced by asynchronous learning activities. Time flexibility has been analysed and determined to be one of the key advantages of distance education in comparison with face-to-face learning. Time flexibility allows lifelong adult learners, showing a temporal pattern of professional, family, and social time constraints, to overcome their lack of time for higher education by enrolling in virtual campuses. According to Fadel and Dyson (2007) "flexibility of time is an important characteristic to all full time workers who still have to study. Twenty-four hour courses enable participants to study during the night or at weekends" (p. 335). Nevertheless, while temporal flexibility is an advantage, it also creates a challenge for some online learners in the virtual campus: academic time-regulation responsibility. In distance learning situations, the students are in charge of their time-on-task allocation, which could be a challenge when this is in conflict with the student's WLLB equation, and also in cases in which the online learner is not mature enough to regulate their time-on-task. Temporal flexibility imposes a greater requirement for time regulation competencies, including both the planning and regulation of the academic time-on-task and the ability to maintain the activity focus in a context of increasing temporal permeability between work, family/social life, academic activities, and multitasking. Time-management competencies, including time regulation, could be a challenge for two types of online learner profiles: the younger students and the procrastinators. First, for younger students enrolling in online courses after a traditional face-to-face education (where the synchronous times were strictly regulated), the transition could be risky if the learner fails to self-impose the necessary time-on-task allocation. The second profile at risk in the context of highly flexible time is that of learners with temporal regulation difficulties such as procrastinators. Steel (2007) defined procrastination as "to voluntarily delay an intended course of action despite expecting to be worse off for the delay" (p. 66). In academic contexts, procrastination is a frequently observed behaviour in traditional face-to-face contexts. Ellis and Knaus (1977) observed that approximately 95% of college students experience different degrees of procrastination. A study by Gallagher, Golin, and Kelleher (1992) showed that "52% of surveyed students indicated having a moderate to high need for help concerning procrastination". Procrastination is related to the level of self-regulation. According to Tuckman (2002), the more that learners are able to self-regulate themselves, the less procrastination they show. We should then consider that the context of online education has a higher requirement for internal or self-regulation than highly externally regulated face-to-face onsite education (Romero & Lambropoulos, 2011). Procrastination behaviour, in a context of face-to-face onsite universities, could be reduced and contained by highly externally regulated learning times. In on-site higher education, the faculty, tutors, and even peers exercise external regulation of learning times that could help the moderate to high-level procrastinators to better regulate their academic time-on-task. In the online education context, the flexibility of times carries a lower external regulation of times and a higher internal regulation of times. While online learners with high levels of time management and regulation could take advantage of the internal regulation responsibilities, the procrastinators have a larger margin of procrastination, which increases their risk of not completing continuous assignments and preparing for the assessment activities. Having a larger margin of allocated time without having established a good habit of regulating time-on-tasks increases the risk of failure and even contributes to an increase of dropouts related to poor time-management competencies.

4. Online Learners' and Teachers' Profiles in Time-Management Competence

Previous studies in the field of online learning have pointed the learners' time constraints as a very important instigator for choosing to study online (Moka & Refanidis, 2010). With the aim of being more specific, we will identify the characteristics of learners and teachers in terms of time-management competencies in e-learning.

4.1. Learners and Their Time-Management Competence

Online students are typically adults who have limited time for learning because of their professional and family activities. The time constraints of these students require their time-management competencies to be highly developed in order to balance their different professional, social, and learning activities (Romero, 2010). Researchers define temporal patterns among the various activities in which the learning times are often inhibited by professional and family responsibilities (Carreras & Valax, 2010; Demeure, Romero, & Lambropoulos, 2010). To balance their different activities, distance learners should develop their time-management competence and apply different types of time-management strategies in individual and collaborative activities. Consequently, online learners should develop a high capacity for self-regulated learning, in general, and a high capacity for self-regulation of the learning time, specifically.

The literature summarises the academic temporal management competence, including a range of specific subcompetencies that would mainly include planning learning objectives connected with expected results, concentrating efforts on priorities, not leaving tasks unattended and unfinished, completing and delivering tasks on time, using time effectively, using tools for better management (study schedule, etc.), handling multitasking, and considering short, medium, and long-term goals while attending to a broad range of activities (Kaya, Delen, & Ritter, 2012).

Nevertheless, online learners are not free from time difficulties that frequently drive them to drop out. Researchers have observed that many dropouts are due to a lack of time which mainly comes from an excessive load of duties—mainly family and work related. Thus, being an efficient learner is one of the requisites for success as a lifelong learner. Furthermore, the time factor is one of the challenges mentioned most often in distance education, especially in the context of online collaborative learning (Roberts & McInnerney, 2007). According to recent research (Romero & Barberà, 2013), low time budgets, a lack of a balanced learning plan, a limited sense of time control, poor time quality, and procrastination are other notable difficulties that lifelong learners suffer and need to overcome constantly.

4.2. Teachers and Their Time-Management Competence

From the perspective of online teachers, time regulation is also a challenge. Online teachers need to regulate the instructional times and the educational rhythms of their online learners, in the context of the time flexibility allowed by their distance education institution. The online teachers should regulate their instructional times according to their temporal constraints in a certain time zone, which could limit their availability for synchronous interactions with the students.

Smith (2005) identified up to 51 competencies for successful online teaching related to pedagogy, administration, and technology, and almost a third are linked with time in some manner. Wheeler (2012), for example, identified a system of online teacher competencies based on

> the ability to: manage one's online presence, creating, organising, repurposing and sharing content, managing online identity and protecting personal data, are all important, but perhaps transliteracy is one of the most important as it represents the ability to be equally adept across a variety of platforms. The benefits of engaging with social media can far outweigh the limitations and dangers, if the appropriate literacies are practiced.
>
> *(p. 24)*

Some proposals have reduced these required competencies to five groups (time competencies are also present in all of five groups, and these are presented in italics):

1. Teaching and learning (state objectives, expectations, and policies; establish communication rules and group decision-making norms; *give effective feedback*);
2. technology attitude (know the e-learning platform utilities; seek technology assistance and be creative and flexible);
3. classroom administration (*check and manage roster*, submit grades according to university policy and *manage drop/adds*);
4. faculty workout management (*define time frames, develop schedule and responsibilities*, communicate expectations); and
5. building community (foster dialogue and interaction and *provide space/time for instructional and social interactions*). (Hill, 2011)

We need to take into account that an online course takes two or three times more time than a face-to-face course (due to the nature of the communication: normally written and asynchronous) and because it involves a bigger workload and more time to balance with other responsibilities (with the consequent probability of unexpected events). Delayed feedback is another of the most common consequences of teachers with low time competencies. Teachers have to manage a large amount of text-based corrections at the same time and often in different places (forums, debates, work groups, assignments) (Hart, 2012).

A lack of temporal investment in online tutoring produces low-quality communities of learners and reduces the students' engagement and motivation. So, the ideal solution for lifelong learning seems to involve not only increasing the time budget for learning while balancing work and personal lives but also ensuring that this time is quality time (Romero & Barberà, 2011).

5. Research Framework and Levels of Analysis of Time-Management Competencies

It is important to frame learners' and teachers' time-management competencies and not to understand them in an isolated way. There are many important reasons for carrying out research into time-management competencies in online learning. Most of these reasons are socially orientated, as the social approach is rather difficult to separate from educational and economic structure (Barberà, 2010a). Surprisingly, and despite these important reasons, in general terms, time competencies attract the attention of researchers but other time factors that are very closely related are ignored, most likely because they are simply taken for granted (Bullen, 2010). In many cases this occurs in educational research, methodologically speaking as well (Reimann, 2009), as we will see in the assessment instruments section later.

Even though time competencies are presented as unconnected and unframed, they will need to be located in an explicit framework, especially in research and innovation processes. This lack of structure is probably due to the time term *volatility*, which needs to be captured and properly defined in a conceptual construct. To do that, more theoretical and empirical studies and reviews need to be done, but, for our part, we are contributing to this preliminary construct based on two actions: identifying the levels of analysis highlighting time competence location and drawing up a very preliminary construct, which only seeks a better and integrated explanation of time competencies intermingling levels and topics that influence competence development.

Although different approaches to time and competencies generally come from diverse perspectives, we do not tackle philosophical, epochal, or even theoretical perspectives at this point. We will briefly tier what we think are the different levels for approaching this omnipresent object of study in the online educational field (from more psychological and pedagogical perspectives). While waiting for evidence from further needed research, we have a preliminary framework to test reliable relationships amongst variables (see Figure 13.2). What is important is not to consider time competencies as an individual and preexisting ability that learners and teachers already have, but to think that the design and the implementation of online education can offer opportunities to increase and refine these competencies through the lifelong learning process. The following is an introductory classification of levels of analysis and some preliminary interwoven elements to facilitate this systemic view for time competencies online.

a. *Macro level*: Covers the institutional plane of the educational time and includes permanent aspects that constitute the contextual approach. Labeled as 'institutional time', it would involve all contextual elements which establish an indirect influence on the teaching and learning process. Infrastructure, including technological material, is the container holding the process of time, but institutional time refers to how time is used and managed by the educational institution: general online schedules (starts and closings, openness); e-class time organisation (semesters, courses, credits, etc.); sequence patterns (series of online habits and cycle of routines), etc.

b. *Meso level*: Covers the teaching plane of the educational time and includes methodology and pedagogical aspects that constitute the mediating approach. Labeled as 'instructional time', it entails

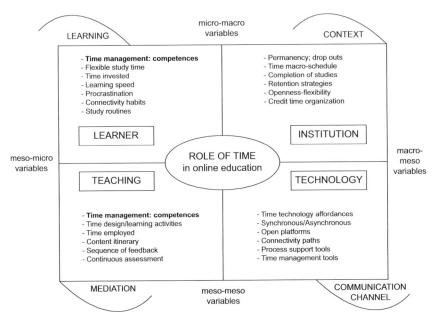

Figure 13.2 Framework for Time Competencies in E-learning

Adapted from Barberà, 2010b.

all the elements that constitute the teaching process which directly influence learning and the cobuilt knowledge process. Didactic modules, methodological use of technology, and instructional design are the main constitutive elements of this time level. Some examples are didactical online sequences, immediacy of e-feedback, pace, collaboration in teamwork, and teaching availability.

c.   *Micro level*: Covers the learner plane of the educational time and includes individual constraints and affordances regarding time for study in this learning approach. Labeled as 'learning time', it engages all elements connected to learner characteristics and perspectives such as expectations, perceptions, sensitivity, and persistence, viewed from the time aspect. Specifically, as examples: student time patterns, study sequence preferences, connectivity habits, cooperation flexibility, answer latency, technology readiness. Here we identify learners' time competencies.

Correspondingly, students' time competencies are influenced by learning design at meso, macro, and micro level. At the meso level, teachers of a specific institution will help students to master time competencies when reflecting on teaching design (including activities, itineraries, or feedback that develops these competencies deliberately). Moreover, at the same time, institutional decisions that are represented at the macro level point out to the global selection of technology for the particular center and also openness of resources, retention strategies, and so forth. Finally, at micro level, students bring time–management tools themselves, also an interpretation of asynchronicity–flexibility, also freedom to use online platform support, and so forth.

Similarly, this influence occurs with teachers' time competencies, which, of course, depend to a great extent on individual capabilities, but which can also be the objective of the institution (agendas, scholar schedules, teaching competence, etc.) and be helped by the technology (time-teaching tools, automatic feedback, tutorials, digital summaries, etc.).

To close, we offer an illustration combining the levels and elements named up to this point. A preliminary schematic integration of these levels will lead to the role of time in online education, and we can only show a first draft to be completed by a whole community of researchers (Barberà, 2010b).

6. Assessment of the Time-Management Competence

Having already framed and analysed the importance of online learners' and teachers' competencies in the previous sections, we should consider the way to develop these competencies. We start by diagnosing the current level of development of online learners' and teachers' competence through the different time-management assessment methods. This section explores the assessment methods for evaluating the academic temporal management competence in online learners and teachers, separating task-dependent (specifically related to the learning task developed by the students) and task-independent (generic assessment tools that could be used in different contexts) methods of the time competence.

6.1. Task-Independent Measures

Most studies use task-independent measures, which are characterised as validated instruments that have been developed to be used generically, independently of the context of the tasks. We consider five task-independent methods that could be useful for online learning contexts in order to diagnose online learners' and teachers' time-management competencies (TMBS, TMQ, TMS) and the main time factor variables influencing online education (PASS, ZTPI).

   The task-independent measures related to the time-management methods include the Time Management Behaviour Scale (TMBS; Macan, Shahani, Dipboye, & Phillips, 1990), the Time Management Questionnaire (TMQ; Trueman & Hartley, 1996), and the Time Management Scale (TMS), created by Zampetakis and colleagues (Zampetakis, Bouranta, & Moustakis, 2010). The TMBS is one of the most commonly used time-management assessment instruments in professional and academic contexts. The TMBS is composed of a 5-point Likert-type scale including 4 factors: setting goals and priorities, mechanics of time management, preference for organization, and perceived control of time. Marchena and colleagues (2009) highlight the relevance of the use of the TMBS scale for diagnosing the time-management competence of the students in self-regulated learning activities, and the use of the results to better support the college students showing the greatest difficulties. The TMQ is another validated instrument used to assess the time-management competence, including three main factors: daily planning, confidence in long-term planning, and perceived control of time. The TMS is a third alternative for assessing the time-management competence, which combines questions from Trueman and Hartley's (1996) TMQ with items from the scale proposed by Claessens, Van Eerde, Rutte, and Roe (2004).

   The task-independent measures related to the time factor variables are the procrastination and the time perspective. In the third section of this chapter we discussed how procrastination is a time-delay behaviour that could hinder students' achievement in the context of the temporal flexibility of online education. In order to diagnose online learners' and teachers' levels of procrastination, one of the validated instruments that could be used is the Procrastination Assessment Scale for Students (PASS), developed by Solomon and Rothblum (1994) for measuring the frequency of cognitive and behavioural aspects of procrastination. In the context of online education, Rakes and Dunn (2010) use the PASS to observe the procrastination increase in those students with lower levels of intrinsic motivation to learn and showing less effort to self-regulate their learning. Another important factor related to the subjective experience of time is the way that individuals experience the different categories of past, present, and future. The construct defined to analyse this has been called the Time Perspective (TP) and could be diagnosed with the Zimbardo Time Perspective Inventory (ZTPI), developed by Zimbardo and Boyd (1999). The ZTPI includes five main factors: the past-negative, past-positive, present-hedonistic, present-fatalistic, and future orientation. The students' temporal perspectives (particularly future orientation) influence their academic performance and the way they manage their time. Past and present-orientated students could show more difficulties regulating their learning times than future-orientated students. In online learning, Usart, Romero, and Barberà (2012) have analysed learners' TP in relation to their learning process in the context of Game Based Learning (GBL).

6.2. Task-Dependent Measures

One of the challenges for analysing the participant's time use and time competence is the methodologies chosen to study these situations (Carreras & Valax, 2010). Most previous studies have used task-independent measures, such as questionnaires or interviews, in which participants declare their time use and time management at a specific moment, without an event-centred approach (Reimann, 2009) and an authentic task-orientation approach. The task-dependent measures aim to analyse the time use and time management based on the actual activities carried out by the participants. In the context of online learning, Computer Learning Environment (CLE) logs could support temporal data collection and help to describe online learners' and teachers' temporal use and time-management behaviours: their times of connection, the frequency of their interactions, and other structural measures related to the time factor. Most of the studies using task-dependent measures analyse students' time-on-task. The engaged time, or Time-on-Task (ToT) in the context of the Academic Learning Time (ALT) model (Caldwell, Huitt, & Graeber, 1982), refers to the time spent by the online learners to develop a certain learning activity. The flexibility of the engaged time is very high in online learning because of the flexibility offered in the allocated time defined by the online teachers to complete a certain assignment. To measure online learners' Time-on-Task we can use self-declared measures or time logs and CLE cues.

- The self-declared measures of the time-on-task are based on the online learners' declarations of prospective or retrospective times spent on the online learning activities. These measures have been shown to be affected by the bias in time estimates. The bias are errors in judgment of the time duration, which are specially pronounced in the case of prospective time estimates, affected by the optimistic underestimation of completion times related to the 'planning fallacy' bias (Buehler, Griffin, & Ross, 2002), which was also found in the context of a French-speaking virtual campus (Romero, 2010).
- The use of CLE in the context of online education allows the time logs registered by the CLE to be exploited. The analysis of the time logs and CLE temporal cues in online learning environments provides an objective measure, allowing one to create an inference of the learners' time-on-task. The time logs and CLE temporal cues could overcome the subjectivity and bias of self-declared time-on-task measures.

In the previous sections we have observed the existence of different instruments to diagnose the time-management competence of online learners and teachers, their procrastination level, temporal perspectives, and time-on-task. The use of these measures constitutes an important advance in helping to diagnose online learners' time-related factors; however, these measures and instruments show two main limitations from our point of view. First, they do not explicitly consider the concept of time quality (Romero & Barberà, 2011) and focus on quantitative approaches to time. Second, most of these measures and instruments address the competence in individual settings, despite a higher number of learning activities in online learning being based on Computer Supported Collaborative Learning (CSCL) activities.

7. Developing the Time-Management Competence in Online Learners and Teachers

Once online learners' and teachers' time factors have been diagnosed, it is highly recommended to follow a twofold strategy, including adapting the online learning experience according to the learners' profile and helping them to develop the time-management competencies necessary to succeed in online education. Some online higher education institutions such as the Open University of Catalonia (UOC) have developed guidelines for managing the load of online learners' course hours according to the online learners' temporal profile. In the context of the UOC, this profile takes into account the learners' working hours in order to suggest an optimal number of courses to enrol in each semester. If the learner is new to distance education programmes, the number of simultaneous courses considered as optimum is one or two, depending on the number of years since the learner's last degree. These course restrictions should allow the incoming online learner to adapt to this new learning context and confirm the real temporal availability for studying online. In a North American context, Lu, Yu, and Liu (2003) also observed that first-time online students have low levels of time-management skills. The current diagnosis and personalisation made in the context of the UOC does not consider the other time-related factors that we have reviewed in this chapter, such as time-management development, procrastination level, and temporal perspectives. However, this effort to consider the UOC learners' time availability in order to calculate the number of courses to enrol on is already one of a few examples of personalisation being carried out by distance-learning institutions.

Based on the recommendations developed in previous sections of this chapter, we suggest enriching the personalisation of online education programmes by considering the level of time-management development, the procrastination level, and the time perspectives of the online learners. We summarise below the main strategies for adapting online education for each of these elements described:

- In the case of *low levels of time-management development*, the strategies for adapting the online education experience include reducing the number of courses enrolled on, in terms of course hours or European Credit Transfer and Accumulation System (ETCS) units. Also reducing the quantity of collaborative learning activities is recommended. Managing time in collaborative settings is harder than managing time individually because of time-zone differences and the diversity of time uses and time-management levels within the different members of a distance-learning virtual team (Romero, 2010; Rutkowski, Saunders, Vogel, & Van Genuchten, 2007). Moreover, students showing difficulties in TM can negatively affect their teammates during a virtual learning task. Specific seminars for developing this competence could help these learners to develop their TM. In the context of the UOC, this recommendation could be implemented through the tutoring actions received by the freshman online students.

- In the case of a *high procrastination level*, online learners could benefit from a higher level of externally regulated time and an increased intermediate deadline, instead of proposing longer times for achieving the assignments that could invite the learners to procrastinate. In order to help the students having a moderate to high need for help concerning procrastination there is a need to proceed to diagnose their level of procrastination through a validated instrument such the PASS (Solomon & Rothblum, 1994).

- In the case of students showing *present-orientated perspectives*, particularly the present hedonist profiles oriented to enjoy the now moment and be less worried for the past and future, it is recommended to decrease the delay of feedback from the instructors or peers to potentiate the instant gratification mechanism of present-orientated students (Davies & Omer, 1996). Delayed feedback is adapted for future-orientated students but should be avoided or reduced for present-orientated students. *Future-orientated learners* are more prone to succeed in their learning activities both in onsite and online situations because of their tendency to think forward and delay gratification. *Past-orientated students* should be aware of the present and future nature of online learning and the benefits of their online education in order to avoid living in their (positive or negative) past while trying to learn online. The diagnosis of the learners' temporal perspective requires them to pass the ZTPI (Zimbardo & Boyd, 1999) and train the online tutors to adapt their external regulation strategies according to the different time perspectives profiles of the online learners.

This chapter has introduced the implications of online learners' and teachers' time-management and time-based competencies. We have described the implications of distance-learning time flexibility in terms of the opportunities offered to adult lifelong learners with limited time, and also its requirements in terms of the higher level of time regulation by learners. Time flexibility in distance education could be increased by better adapting the time constraints of the online courses and tasks to the online learners' temporal constraints, which implies a better characterisation of the temporal profiles of online learners who decide to enrol in online programs. Online learners' time-management competencies, including their procrastination level, temporal perspectives, and time-on-task, should be measured in order to adapt their online learning experience to suit their profiles and offer them the development opportunities for improving their temporal profiles and competencies for a successful online learning experience.

References

Barberà, E. (2010a). Time factor in e-learning. *eLC Research Paper Series, 0,* 12–15. Retrieved from http://elcrps.uoc.edu/ojs/index.php/elcrps/

Barberà, E. (2010b). *Time in online education: Nature and approaches.* Saarbrücken, Germany: LAP-Lambert Academic Publishing.

Barberà, E., Gros, B., & Kirshner, P. (2012). Temporal issues in e-learning research: A literature review. *British Journal of Educational Technology, 43*(2), 53–55.

Buehler, R., Griffin, D., & Ross, M. (2002). Inside the planning fallacy: The causes and consequences of optimistic time predictions. In T. Gilovich, D. Griffin, & D. Kahneman (Eds.), *Heuristics and biases: The psychology of intuitive judgment* (pp. 250–270). Cambridge, UK: Cambridge University Press.

Bullen, M. (2010). Relevant voices around the world. *eLC Research Paper Series, 0,* 5–11. Retrieved from http://elcrps.uoc.edu/ojs/index.php/elcrps/

Caldwell, J. H., Huitt, W. G., & Graeber, A. O. (1982). Time spent in learning: Implications from research. *Elementary School Journal, 82,* 471–480.

Carreras, O., & Valax, M. (2010). Temporal structure and flexibility in distance work and learning. *eLC Research Paper Series, 1,* 61–70.

Chung, F. K. (2005, August 8). Challenge for teaching training in Africa with special reference to distance education. Paper presented at DETA conference, Pretoria.

Claessens, B. J., Van Eerde, W., Rutte, C. G., & Roe, R. A. (2004). Planning behavior and perceived control of time at work. *Journal of Organizational Behavior, 25*(8), 937–950.

Davies, G., & Omer, O. (1996). Time allocation and marketing. *Time & Society, 5*(2), 253–268.

Demeure, V., Romero, M., & Lambropoulos, N. (2010). Assessment of e-learners' temporal patterns in an online collaborative writing task. *eLC Research Paper Series, 1,* 5–17.

Ellis, A., & Knaus, W. J. (1977). *Overcoming procrastination.* New York, NY: Institute for Rational Living.

Fadel, L. M., & Dyson, M. C. (2007) Enhancing interactivity in an online learning environment. *Lecture Notes in Computer Science, 4663,* 332–344.

Gallagher, R. P., Golin, A., & Kelleher, K. (1992). The personal, career, and learning skills needs of college students. *Journal of College Student Development, 33*(4), 301–310.

Hart, C. (2012). Factors associated with student persistence in an online program of study: A review of literature. *Journal of Interactive Online Learning, 11*(1), 19–42.

Hill, C. (2011). Five critical competencies for teaching online. Retrieved from http://www.cvc.edu/2011/02/five-critical-competencies-for-teaching-online/

Kaya, F., Delen, E., & Ritter, N. L. (2012) Test review: Children's Organizational Skill Scales. *Journal of Psychoeducational Assessment, 30*(2), 205–208.

Lu, J., Yu, C. S., & Liu, C. (2003). Learning style, learning patterns, and learning performance in a WebCT-based course. *Information & Management, 40*(6), 497–507.

Macan, T. H., Shahani, C., Dipboye, R. L., & Phillips, A. P. (1990). College students' time management: Correlations with academic performance and stress. *Journal of Educational Psychology, 82*(4), 760–768.

Marchena, E., Navarro, J. I., et al., (2009, November 16–18). *Self regulated time schedule strategy for better learning.* Conference of Education, Research and Innovation, Madrid, Spain.

Metzger, J.-L., & Cléach, O. (2004). White-collar telework: Between an overload and learning a new organization of time. *Sociologie du travail, 46,* 433–450.

Moka, E., & Refanidis, I. (2010). Towards intelligent management of a student's time. *Lecture Notes in Computer Science, 6040,* 383–388.

Rakes, G. C., & Dunn, K. E. (2010). The impact of online graduate students' motivation and self-regulation on academic procrastination. *Journal of Interactive Online Learning, 9*(1), 78–93.

Reimann, P. (2009). Time is precious: Variable- and event-centred approaches to process analysis in CSCL research. *Computer-Supported Collaborative Learning, 4,* 239–257. Retrieved from http://www.springerlink.com/content/h568v8226342p556/fulltext.pdf

Roberts, T. S., & McInnerney, J. M. (2007). Seven problems of online group learning (and their solutions). *Educational Technology & Society, 10*(4), 257–268.

Romero, M. (2010). *Gestion du temps dans les APMD.* Sarrebrück, Germany: Editions Européenes Universitaires.

Romero, M., & Barberà, E. (2011). Quality of e-learners' time and learning performance beyond quantitative time-on-task. *The International Review of Research in Open and Distance Learning IRRODL, 12*(5), 122–135.

Romero, M., & Barberà, E. (2013). Las dificultades temporales de los estudiantes universitarios en formación a distancia. *RED, Revista de Educación a Distancia, 38*(1), 1–17.

Romero, M., & Lambropoulos, N. (2011). Internal and external regulation to support knowledge construction and convergence in CSCL. *Electronic Journal of Research in Educational Psychology, 9*(1), 309–330.

Rutkowski, A. F., Saunders, C., Vogel, D., & Van Genuchten, M. (2007). "Is it already 4 am in your time zone?" Focus immersion and temporal dissociation in virtual teams. *Small Group Research, 38*(1), 98–129.

Smith, T. C. (2005). Fifty-one competencies for online instruction. *The Journal of Educators Online, 2*(2), 1–18.

Solomon, L. J., & Rothblum, E. D. (1994). Procrastination Assessment Scale–Students (PASS). In J. Fischer & K. Corcoran (Eds.), *Measure for clinical practice* (Vol. 2, pp. 446–452). New York, NY: The Free Press.

Steel, P. (2007). The nature of procrastination: A meta-analytic and theoretical review of quintessential self-regulatory failure. *Psychological Bulletin, 133*(1), 65–94.

Trueman, M., & Hartley, J. (1996). A comparison between the time management skills and academic performance of mature and traditional-entry university students. *Higher Education, 32,* 199–215.

Tuckman, B. (2002, August). *Academic procrastinators: Their rationalizations and web-course performance.* Paper presented at the 110th Annual Meeting of the American Psychological Association, Chicago, Illinois.

Usart, M., Romero, M., & Barberà, E. (2012, August 22–24). *The role of students' time perspective in game based learning.* 34th IATUR Conference on Time Use Research, Matsue, Japan.

Watkins, K. E., Marsick, V., & Kim, S. (2012). The impact of lifelong learning on organizations. *Springer International Handbooks of Education, 26*(4), 859–873.

Wheeler, S. (2012). Digital literacies for engagement in emerging online cultures. *eLC Research Paper Series, 5,* 14–25.

Zampetakis, L. A., Bouranta, N., & Moustakis, V. S. (2010). On the relationship between individual creativity and time. *Thinking Skills and Creativity, 5*(1), 23–32.

Zimbardo, P. G., & Boyd, J. N. (1999). Putting time in perspective: A valid, reliable individual-differences metric. *Journal of Personality and Social Psychology, 77*(6), 1271–1288.

14

Library Support for Online Learners

Katherine M. Tyler

The academic library, once the province of book stacks, is now the gateway for digital content and a common area for students to congregate, collaborate, or study. Students see the university library in terms of a resource for e-books, databases, course reserves, and research assistance as well as a physical space to create, expand, and—find a printer. Online learners require an academic library, which provides a comprehensive host of resources and services around the clock (Gardner & Eng, 2005), regardless of whether they have access to an on-site campus. Johnson, Trabelsi, and Fabbro (2008) opined that librarians must continually reevaluate the ways in which they deliver services to students who are not visiting the physical library while also retaining the human factor during communications and interactions in the context of e-services. Currently, many resources necessary for learners are still available only in a print format; therefore, a balance in terms of funding and access is needed to provide a wide spectrum of digital content.

The proliferation of digital content, services, and resources provided by academic libraries, combined with those available through open resources and Internet search engines, are having an impact on students' use of information sources. Meanwhile, many new electronic tools are available to online learners. Google Scholar allows learners to browse scholarly items through a popular and user-friendly interface, and the accompanying Library Links program uses an authentication process to link an institution's catalogue holdings through the same popular searching tool. The Online Computer Library Center offers the Open WorldCat project, enabling a search of library holdings through its member collections. As apps and tablet computing become more mainstream, libraries are adapting with a variety of reference, e-reading, and e-reference services. For example, Ohio State University's app ties library resources with a student's ID (Adolphus, 2009; Ahmad & Brogan, 2012; Johnson, Adams, & Cummins, 2012). Library e-book collections are growing as the cost per use for digital books is reduced (Chrzastowski, 2011). Subsequently, online learners who are able to access digital content easily and efficiently are then supported by their institution, resulting in a better learning experience. In the context of designing and providing quality online education, one of the Sloan Consortium's five pillars of effective online learning is student satisfaction—support services such as access to online library resources and services help promote successful academic outcomes (Moore, 2008). An examination of online library services begins with a review of the progress of online academic content.

Evolution of the Academic Library

In the early 1990s, as networked systems, communication technologies, and cable television changed the way consumers and students searched for information, librarians called for an exploration of information literacy. Evidence of the reinvention of the academic library is found through several areas of focus and include (a) the library as place, (b) the role of librarians, (c) integration with information technology, (d) awareness of online library services, and (e) the navigation of library websites.

Moyo (2004) described virtual patrons as persons "whose accesses/use of library services and resources is unbounded by space or time" (p. 188). She describes those virtual patrons in terms of three types: (a) on-campus, (b) off-campus, and (c) students learning from a distance. On-campus users include students with access to an on-the-ground campus and access the library either in person or online. Off-campus patrons access the library from a location away from the campus (but with access to both). Distance learners are those virtual patrons whose only access to the academic library is online.

Regardless of where learners are accessing their online academic library, all users expect 24/7 connectivity to resources and services, and libraries are continually evolving to meet those anytime, anywhere student demands. McKiel (2008) found that the holistic transformation of libraries from a print-based resource, to one that is primarily electronic, changes the nature of library operations. As libraries build their digital content, the academic community embraces pedagogy with technology and information in ways previously untested. Librarians are asked to push content to students, and physical library buildings are transformed for new purposes.

Library as Place

The library at Goucher College in Baltimore, Maryland, received *Library Journal's* 2012 top award as a Landmark Library based on several factors, including its community engagement, design, functionality, and, not surprisingly, its 47% increase in use since it opened in 2009 (Goucher College, n.d). With its Leadership in Energy Environmental Design (LEED) gold certified and innovative buildings, students have 24/7 access to study space, a spacious commons area, study carrels, lounge chairs, and group presentation rooms. The idea of the college library turned student forum is leading the way for academic librarians to rethink the way they deliver services and resources, integrate instructional technology, and create an intellectual community and social crossroads. In Europe's largest library in Amsterdam, described as an epicenter of culture, a 250-seat theatre is found within a seven-story atrium and contains lounge beds for music, movies, art, and study booths (Munzenmayer, 2008).

Roles of the Librarian

Librarian roles are evolving along with the expanding numbers of online learners. Library professionals must change their approach to traditional services and embrace new functions. The services of librarians were once required based on the complexity of large volumes of manuscripts and other products of the printing press. Their specialized roles in the acquisition, distribution, and cataloging of materials are even more important as the sheer numbers of electronic documents, resources, and communication devices necessitate change (Gilman & Irons, 2011; Hall-Ellis, 2006; McKiel, 2008).

In recent years, degree requirements in library information science programs changed to include a theoretical basis for cataloging electronic resources, information technology competencies, information literacy instruction, and mastery in a variety of communication formats (Hall-Ellis, 2006; Kirk, 2008; McKiel, 2008). Librarians need Web 2.0 fluency for content creation and sharing, using social software tools such as blogs and wikis to market library resources (Anyakou, Ezejiofor, & Orakpor, 2012). At the University of Huddersfield in the north of England, roving librarians use tablet computers to provide personalized assistance to students in various locations across the campus (Sharman & Walsh, 2012).

On campuses where the function of the computer services or instructional technology teams are merged with the academic library, the lines are blurred between the competencies required of the chief information officer and the dean of libraries to positions of library technology director or similar. In the Athenaeum at Goucher College, the information commons includes an information technology help desk and, nearby, a librarian service desk (Shaper, 2012). Responding to students' needs for technical assistance and around-the-clock librarian services, the staff at Xavier University in Cincinnati, Ohio, created a learning commons. The Conaton Learning Commons—open 24 hours—houses study, lounge, instruction, and group collaboration spaces in addition to providing circulation, reference, and traditional reserves services (Xavier University, n.d.).

Many college campus libraries have also lifted the ban on eating in the library and have installed cafes offering sandwiches and soups, which can be consumed among the books and computers. Embracing the concept of late-night study groups and creating a more inviting place to gather, library administrators find it helps to include food in the mix which also encourages interaction among diverse groups of students (Foster, 2008).

The role of the librarian also is shifting in universities which support online learning with embedded librarian programs. The librarian now plays a unique role in some cases as a team teacher in the virtual environment, and in others as an additional component to course-specific resources linked within the learning management system (Adolphus, 2009). Librarians create links, post course-specific documents, provide literacy instruction, and generally support student learning as the subject specialist. The integration of library resources and services with the online learning environment allows learners to become aware of the library at the same time the embedded librarian offers course specific information literacy instruction. Adolphus (2009) discusses the results of a United Kingdom study on library integration in the online learning environment and describes how the Open University adopted Moodle as its learning content management system and then linked RSS (Really Simple Syndication) feeds for the delivery of course-specific resources to students and developed an application to embed their federated search tool. The main premise was to provide almost seamless resourcing within the course with easy-to-use navigation and a single sign-on. While universities may have roving and embedded librarians to support online learners, many students remain unaware of online library resources and services.

Awareness of the Library

Islam and Ahmed (2011) conducted a study of students' perceptions regarding ease of use and satisfaction with a university library in Dhaka, Bangladesh and found that many students—30% of those surveyed—were not aware of the resources and services of the campus library. Results also indicated that students who knew of the library did not make use of it frequently. The investigators did not determine if lack of use was due to awareness or from students' perception of the library's limited usefulness, although 63% of students who completed the survey reported finding what they needed only some of the time, and 15% rarely found their search items.

Statement of the Problem

The growth of e-learning has contributed to changes in the way librarians deliver services to patrons. Meeting the needs of virtual patrons accessing an academic library is highly complex, with the advancement of information sources available through the Internet utilizing a variety of computer technologies, social software tools, and devices. A review of recent research, however, does not include a study of online learner satisfaction as it relates to the use of academic libraries. Therefore, it is unknown whether librarians are meeting the needs of virtual patrons. Library administrators may use this information to implement necessary improvements to the resources and services of academic libraries, specifically those available through the online library. It is suggested that improvements may support demand for 24/7 access and lead to a higher level of perceived student satisfaction.

Definitions and Research Questions

In this study, student satisfaction is operationally defined as meeting the needs (Sahin & Shelley, 2008) of the student accessing an online academic library. Relevant demographic factors that may influence student satisfaction are also discussed. Based on a review of the relevant literature the following research questions were generated:

1. How do online library resources satisfy virtual patrons?
2. How do online library services satisfy virtual patrons?
3. How do demographic factors influence virtual patron satisfaction with the resources provided by the online library?
4. How do demographic factors influence virtual patron satisfaction with the services provided by the online library?

Definition of Terms

Database. A database is "a collection of information organized in such a way that a computer program can quickly select desired pieces of data" (Webopedia, 2003, para. 1).
Learning management system. Also called a virtual learning environment or content management system, a learning management system is a software tool, which supports planning, designing, developing, implementing, and administering online learning (Davidson-Shivers & Rasmussen, 2006).
Satisfaction. Satisfaction is operationally defined as meeting the needs of virtual patrons.
Student status. Student status refers to the academic status of a college student (i.e., freshman, graduate student, doctoral student, etc.)
Virtual patron. "A virtual patron is one whose accesses/use of library services and resources is unbounded by space or time" (Moyo, 2004, p. 188).

Theoretical Framework

The Technology Acceptance Model, or TAM (Davis, 1989) provides the theoretical framework for this research. The TAM permits prediction of the process of user acceptance of information systems (Davis, 1989). The online library is a system with end-users—virtual patrons—who will either accept or reject it as an information system. Davis, Bagozzi, and Warshaw (1989) describe the model through an equation as acceptance = ease of use + usefulness. The TAM (Davis, 1989) establishes a user acceptance of information technology systems resulting from two constructs: (a) perceived ease of use and (b) perceived usefulness. Factors of ease of use and usefulness play an important role in students' perception of library support.

Methodology

Survey research was used to determine students' satisfaction with the resources and services of an online academic library. The survey design is cross-sectional to collect data at one point in time (Babbie, 1990; Creswell, 2008). During the Spring 2010 semester at the University of West Florida in Pensacola, Florida all enrolled undergraduate and graduate students taking at least one online class comprised the study population. A sample size of 1,500 students was considered appropriate for the research population. The researcher used Survey Monkey to conduct the web-based survey and enabled limitations within the instrument to prevent students from completing the survey more than once from a specific Internet protocol address.

Based on enrollment demographics at the University of West Florida during the Spring 2010 semester, undergraduates represented 85% of the student population and graduate students 15% (UWF, 2009). A stratified random list was generated from the 5,454 online students.

Virtual Patron Library Survey

A survey instrument was modified, validated, and tested for reliability, and named the Virtual Patron Library Survey (Tyler, 2010). A pilot test determined reliability and validity. Students participating in the pilot test provided feedback regarding the clarity and readability of the instrument. Students also provided feedback on the web-based survey's navigation and directions. A Cronbach's alpha coefficient of .92 for the scale determined reliability for the survey.

Results

Following the collection of e-mail addresses from 1,275 undergraduate and 225 graduate students taking a minimum of one online class at the University of West Florida during the Spring 2010 semester, completed surveys resulted in a 29% response rate. Descriptive and inferential data inform students' perceptions of satisfaction with the library's online resources and services.

Following data collection and prior to analysis, the online library's resources and services were grouped into subscales to determine statistical significance based on demographic factors. Nine items comprised the resources subscale:

- instant search box (on home page),
- library catalogs,
- online databases,
- Google Scholar,
- magazines and journals,
- newspapers,
- e-books,
- books, and
- e-reserves.

The following eleven items comprised the online library services subscale:

- ask a librarian,
- timeliness of response by reference librarian,
- value of information provided by reference librarian,
- subject specialist,

- interlibrary loan,
- book delivery,
- document delivery,
- article or other material delivery,
- online tutorials,
- about the library (hours, maps, directory), and
- subject research guides.

Several demographic characteristics were collected within the survey instrument. Four main areas indicate significant results, which influence student satisfaction with the University's online library: (a) age, (b) gender, (c) student status, and (d) computer experience.

Age

Traditional college-age students, 17–25 years old, represented the majority (59.5%) of survey participants. Student age groups were aggregated into three categories for data analysis: (a) 17 to 25, (b) 26 to 40, and (c) 41 and older. An analysis of variance (ANOVA) was used to determine if age influenced virtual patron satisfaction with the online library's resources and services. A significant difference in the 17 to 25 age group was indicated for satisfaction with the library's online resources $F(2, 176) = 3.604, p < 05$. No significant difference was found for satisfaction with the online library's services (Tyler, 2010).

Gender

More females (69.9%) than males (30.1%) participated in the web-based survey. An independent samples t test was conducted to determine if gender influenced virtual patron's satisfaction with library's online resources. Results indicate females are significantly more satisfied than males $t(177) = -2.766, p < .05$. No significant difference was found for satisfaction with the online library's services (Tyler, 2010).

Student Status

ANOVAs with seven categories of student status (freshman, sophomore, junior, senior, master's, specialist, and doctoral) indicated no significant difference in satisfaction with the University's online library resources. Student categories were then collapsed into two groups (undergraduate and graduate) and significant differences were found following an independent samples t test. Undergraduates are significantly more satisfied than graduate students with the library's online resources $t(175) = 2.046, p = 042$. No significant difference was found for student satisfaction with the online library's services (Tyler, 2010).

Computer Experience

Several questions were posed to students in the Virtual Patron Library Survey to determine their computer experience. Computer experience questions were related to ownership of laptops and handheld Internet-capable devices, and participation in online learning. Student were also asked five questions about their experience with computer-related tasks: (a) using e-mail, (b) posting to discussion boards, (c) participating in social networking, (d) purchasing goods/services online, and (e) conducting research/homework online. Students chose answers from a Liker-type scale with five levels to describe themselves from *extremely experienced* to having had *no experience.*

Values from the computer experience questions were aggregated to produce an overall computer experience group variable with a mean of 4.64 and a standard deviation of .510, ($N = 425$), indicating students were very experienced with computer related tasks (Tyler, 2010).

Correlational analyses were conducted to analyze student's computer experience and satisfaction with the University's online library resources and services. Items in the computer experience questions were interval data and collapsed into a computer experience group for analysis. A Pearson's r was conducted to determine if any correlations existed between student's computer experience and satisfaction with the library's online resources. Results indicate a significant correlation $r(180) = .252, p < .05$. Students with more computer experience reported greater satisfaction with the University's online library resources. Students with more computer experience were also significantly $r(102) = .269, p < .05$ more satisfied with the University's online library services (Tyler, 2010). Results are in contrast to a study on student perceptions and satisfaction with a university library: researchers Islam and Ahmed (2011) found that computer experience did not affect student opinions regarding ease of use of the library system, although many cited not knowing how to use the system as the reason for not using the online catalog.

Awareness Responses

Students answered four questions regarding their awareness of the University's online library. Only 11.4% of those surveyed reported they had not accessed the UWF library home page. When asked if they had seen a link to the UWF library in an e-learning course, 44.4% of students surveyed reported they had not; however, 79.9% indicated that an instructor had suggested a visit to the library through an e-mail, discussion thread, or course announcement.

Qualitative analyses of the narrative responses also indicate students' awareness of the library resources and services available online. Many comments indicate students' were not aware of the online library or of the variety of resources and services available. Comments included the following:

- I think we need to inform more students about it. Some students are too busy going to work to go to the site. So, I believe if they had a quick tutorial on where to see the online library, they would not miss out on the chance.
- As a result of this survey I will definitely check it out. I am at the end of my master's program and have never utilized it! Most of my research has been done on the Internet through Internet Explorer.
- Increased awareness of UWF online resources.

Open-ended Question Responses

Students provided narrative comments to two open-ended questions in the survey: "How may the UWF library better serve online learners?" and "What additional library resources/services should be available online?" Three major themes emerged following qualitative analyses: (a) awareness of the online library, (b) ease of use of the library website, and (c) greater access to online materials. Comments on students' lack of awareness of the online library are discussed in the previous section. The following comments reveal students' general frustration with navigating the library website and requests for more online resources. Typical (verbatim) comments were as follows:

- Make the database clearer to understand, and expand the articles available online.
- Make the homepage more friendly. Sometimes it takes a while for me to find where I need to go to access the resources I need.

- More e-books and better system for viewing them (ability to read e-book on iPhone for instance).
- Make subject matters easy to search without going into all the different databases.
- I think a more simplistic manner in the online database search technique may help novice users of online research.

When students were asked about which additional resources and services the library should provide, two major items emerged—more journals and more e-books. Students' comments regarding ease of use of the library website and the need for access to more materials is an indication of their satisfaction with the online library. Allen and Dee (2006) wrote, "how easy-to-use and intuitive end-users interfaces are, becomes the developmental keystone of a successful online library presence"(p. 69). The need for a more user-friendly website (ease of use) and for more successful searching (perceived usefulness) is a reflection of satisfaction based on the Technology Acceptance Model, which frames this research. Students may have been unsuccessful in finding items online because of the difficulty in navigating the library website.

Implications

The results of the Virtual Patron Library Survey have direct implications for several stakeholders: students, faculty, administrators, and librarians. Online learners have been, and continue to be, a significant sector of higher education, with 6.7 million students taking at least one online course during the fall 2011 term (Allen & Seaman, 2013).

Students

Females participated in this study at twice the rate of males, which may indicate a higher rate of interest in library-related resources and services. Females were also significantly more satisfied than males with the online library. Findings suggest students should seek out tutorials and participate in library-skills training. Online learners should also seek out classes or workshops on the use of computer applications.

Faculty

Professors should provide direct links to relevant course materials through the learning management system or course site. It is important for faculty to not assume that students who grew up "online" are inherently literate in digital media. Directing students to online tutorials and digital reference services assists in allowing learners to manage their learning environment. Faculty can play a significant role in assisting with their informational needs.

Administrators

University library administrators are called to support online learners in many areas, including access, communication, and resourcing. Changes to technology will impact the breadth of online academic library offerings in dynamic ways, necessitating the need to continually seek out students' informational requirements. Simultaneously, administrators must also consider the digital media literacy of students to successfully find and access online materials.

Librarians

Research on embedded librarian projects indicates student learning outcomes are enhanced with the integration of library services and a university's e-learning platform (Adolphus, 2009; Chesnut et al., 2009). Recognizing their dynamic roles, librarians who remain student-centered and focused on delivering an array of virtual resources and services to online learners must be cognizant of students' preferred technology tools and communication devices. Library staff integrated with the academic technology department must respond to demands for 24/7 technological and reference assistance through a variety of formats.

Conclusion

Academic libraries are partners in the educational process—serving the needs of students' scholarly pursuits, whether they are in the physical building browsing book stacks with a mug of coffee from the café or texting students hundreds of miles away with answers to reference questions. Library administrators who recognize the partner relationships of faculty and university staff work to create a synergistic role as the hub of the university—from creating content to pushing content out to students and instructors. As technologies morph, online library administrators must continue to take the lead in bridging information gaps allowing faculty and students to contribute to the body of knowledge in their respective disciplines. Digital media literacy must become part of the university or library training curriculum. Issues of ease of use, usefulness, and awareness are a prelude to making the online library germane to virtual patrons.

Librarians' roles have shifted from collection providers to curators and creators of digital scholarship. To remain relevant to online learners who have access to a plethora of Internet based content, virtual library administrators must consider the human factor and promote methods that engage students to think critically as a function of scholarly reflection.

References

Adolphus, M. (2009). Making the best use of VLEs. *Library & Information Update, 8*(3), 45–47. Retrieved from http://www.cilip.org.uk/publications/updatemagazine

Ahmad, P., & Brogan, M. (2012). Scholarly use of e-books in a virtual academic environment: A case study. *Australian Academic & Research Libraries, 43*(3), 189+. Retrieved from http://go.galegroup.com/ps/i.do?id=GALE%7CA308293705&v=2.1&u=21667_hbplc&it=r&p=GPS&sw=w

Allen, I. E., & Seaman, J. (2013, January). *Changing course: Ten years of tracking online education in the United States, 2013*. Retrieved from http://www.onlinelearningsurvey.com/reports/changingcourse.pdf

Allen, M., & Dee, C. (2006). A survey of the usability of digital reference services on academic health science library websites. *Journal of Academic Librarianship, 32,* 69–78.

Anyakou, E. N., Ezejiofor, V. O., & Orakpor, A. M. (2012). Knowledge and use of Web 2.0 by librarians in Anambra State, Nigeria. *African Journal of Library, Archives and Information* Science, *22*(1), 31+. Retrieved from http://go.galegroup.com/ps/i.do?id=GALE%7CA297427072&v=2.1&u=21667_hbplc&it=r&p=GPS&sw=w

Babbie, F. (1990). *Survey research methods* (2nd ed.). Belmont, CA: Wadsworth

Chesnut, M. T., Henderson, S. M., Schlipp, J. & Zai, R. III. (2009). Value-added library resources and services through Blackboard. *Kentucky Libraries, 73*(1), 6–12.

Chrzastowski, T. E. (2011). *Assessing the value of ebooks to academic libraries and users*. Preprint from the Proceedings of the 9th Northumbria International Conference on Performance Measurement in Libraries and Information Services. Retrieved from https://www.ideals.illinois.edu/handle/2142/28612

Creswell, J. (2008). *Educational research: Planning, conducting and evaluating quantitative and qualitative research* (3rd ed.). Upper Saddle River, NJ: Pearson Education.

Davidson-Shivers, G. V., & Rasmussen, K. L. (2006). *Web-based learning: Design, implementation and evaluation.* Upper Saddle River, NJ: Pearson Education.

Davis, F. D. (1989). Perceived usefulness, perceived ease of use, and user acceptance of information technology. *MIS Quarterly, 13,* 319–339.

Davis, F. D., Bagozzi, R. P. & Warshaw, P. R. (1989). User acceptance of computer technology: A comparison of two theoretical models. *Management Science, 35,* 982–1003. Retrieved from http://mansci.journal. informs.org/content/35/8/982.full.pdf+html

Foster, A. L. (2008, January). Snacks in the stacks: Libraries welcome food amid the books. *Chronicle of Higher Education.* Retrieved from http://chronicle.com/article/Snacks-in-the-Stacks-/34823

Gardner S., & Eng, S. (2005). What students want: Generation Y and the changing function of the academic library. *Portal: Libraries and the Academy, 5,* 405–420. doi:10.1353/pla.2005.0034

Gilman, I., & Irons, L. (2011). Open access & open lives: The changing role of academic libraries. In J. Barlow (Ed.), *Internet 2.0: After the bubble burst 2000–2010* (pp. 117–139). Forest Grove, OR: Berglund Center for Internet Studies. (Authors' manuscript)

Goucher College. (n.d). *Congratulations! Goucher College awarded #1 new landmark library award.* Retrieved from http://goucher.edu/the-library/new-landmark-library

Hall-Ellis, S. D. (2006). Cataloging electronic resources and metadata: Employers' expectations as reflected in American libraries and AutoCAT, 2000–2005. *Journal of Education for Library and Information Science, 47,* 38–51.

Islam, M. M., & Ahmed, S. M. (2011). Measuring Dhaka University students' perception of ease-of-use and their satisfaction with University library's online public access catalogue. *Performance Measurements and Metrics, 12,* 142–156. doi:10.1108/14678041111196631

Johnson, K., Trabelsi, H. & Fabbro, E. (2008). Library support for e-learners: E-resources, e-services, and the human factors. In T. Anderson (Ed.), *The theory and practice of online learning* (2nd ed., pp. 397–418). Retrieved from http://www.aupress.ca/index.php.books/120146

Johnson, L., Adams, S., & Cummins, M. (2012). *The NMC horizon report: 2012 higher education edition.* Austin, TX: The New Media Consortium.

Kirk, T. (2008). The merged organization: Confronting the service-overlap between libraries and computer centers. *Library Issues, 28,* 1–4. Retrieved from http://www.libraryissues.com

McKiel, A. (2008). Academic libraries after print. *Against the Grain, 20,* 40–46. Retrieved from http:// www.against-the-grain.com

Moore, J. (2008). *A synthesis of Sloan-C effective practices.* Retrieved from http://www.sloan-c.org/effective/ v12n3_moore-2.pdf

Moyo, L. M. (2004). The virtual patron. *Science & Technology Libraries, 25,* 185–209. doi:10.1300/ J122v25n01_12

Munzenmayer, R. (2008). Architecture as advocacy. *NextSpace, 10,* 12–13. Retrieved from http://www. oclc.org/nextspace

Sahin, I., & Shelley, M. (2008). Considering students' perceptions: The distance education student satisfaction model. *Educational Technology & Society, 11,* 216–223. Retrieved from http://www.ifets.info/

Sharman, A., & Walsh, A. (2012). Roving librarian at a mid-sized, UK-based university. *Library Technology Reports, 48*(8), 28+. Retrieved from http://go.galegroup.com/ps/i.do?id=GALE%7CA312618079&v= 2.1&u=21667_hbplc&it=r&p=GPS&sw=w

Shaper, L. (2012, July 28). New landmark libraries 2012: #1 Goucher Athenaeum Goucher College. *Library Journal.* Retrieved from http://lj.libraryjournal.com/2012/06/buildings/national-landmark-academic-library-1-goucher-athenaeum-goucher-college/

Tyler, K. M. (2010). *Factors influencing virtual patron satisfaction with online library resources and services* (Doctoral dissertation, University of West Florida). Retrieved from http://library.uwf.edu

University of West Florida (UWF). (2009). *UWF at a glance: 2008–2009.* Retrieved from http://upic.uwf. edu/OIR/QuickFacts/Files/AtaGlance2008–2009.pdf

Webopedia. (2003, June 27). *Database.* Retrieved from http://www.webopedia.com/TERM/D/database. html

Xavier University. (n.d.) *About the library.* Retrieved from Xavier University website: http://www.xavier. edu/library/about.cfm

15

2D and 3D Virtual Environments

Communication Potentialities for E-learning Education

Tatiana Stofella Sodré Rossini and Edméa Oliveira dos Santos

The dynamics of a globalized society brought by the WWW (World Wide Web) has demanded more changes in the educational processes that meet the cyberculture needs. The increased supply of undergraduate Internet courses has allowed the study and improvement of educational practices with interactive Web 2.0 interfaces (Silva, 2010; Santos, 2006; Okada, 2006) and three-dimensional (3D) online virtual worlds (Mattar, 2008; Morgado, 2009; Schlemmer & Backes, 2008). In this sense, training teachers to act in an articulated and coherent way with digital communication technologies is an essential and urgent challenge. The lack of investments in teacher education has led to the simple transposition of content and face-to-face classroom practices supported by the paradigm of transmission (Silva, 2010) and also the underutilization of Web 2.0 interfaces.

Courses offered in e-learning environments actually end up being conducted like DE (distance education), prevailing instructionism and conservatism. The technologies and services that are remotely available on the web are becoming more advanced and integrated, reflecting social, political, educational, entertainment, and consumption needs. This is possible due to the intense involvement of users as producers and consumers in the development and construction of open-source applications. With this change in behavior, information and codes are no longer restricted, making them available to be reused and remixed. With the advent of Web 2.0, social networking software (i.e., Orkut, Ning, Facebook), open-source software (i.e., Linux, Moodle, OpenSimulator), weblogs (i.e., Blogspot, WordPress), microblogs (i.e., Twitter, Jaiku), podcasts, P2P (i.e., Napster, LimeWire), wikis, and MMORPG (massively multiplayer online game role playing) have emerged.

Web 2.0 applications are no longer products but are becoming services that are remotely available on the Internet. Services are constantly updated (perpetual beta) and are always looking for new users to further their improvement. You can also combine digital content and services from different sites, creating hybrid applications. This type of reuse and remix is called mashup (Yee, 2008). Digital technologies enable the creation of e-learning virtual environments, which provide specific resources. Each of these environments contributes to the broadening of social networks in multiple connections composed by people, institutions, or groups. Thus, virtual environments are hybrid spaces that can gather two-dimensional (2D) and/or three-dimensional (3D) content and communication within synchronous and asynchronous interfaces. The composition of these interfaces is flexible, varying according to the educational purpose. The virtual environments can be found on the Internet through hypertext, e-mail, Google Docs, learning management systems (LMS), social networking, virtual worlds, and others. The LMSs are designed to be used pedagogically in e-learning education. The synchronous and asynchronous modes, coupled with the participation of teachers and students, allow for the authoring, sharing, and knowledge production. Their management structure allows the teacher to monitor the student's participation closely in the environment, through administrative interfaces.

With this, "the new creative processes can be potentialized by the socio-technical streams of the virtual learning environments (VLE) that use the digital as support" (Santos, 2006, p. 225). Moodle (Modular Object-Oriented Dynamic Learning Environment), for example, is a free educational 2D software that is widely and collaboratively used, where everyone can contribute to its improvement. Equipped with collaborative asynchronous (forum, glossary, wiki, diary) and synchronous (chat) interfaces with emphasis on text, it favors the decentralization and information sharing of teaching, learning, and knowledge construction. Its predominance in virtual rooms is due to its consolidation as a stable, safe, and easy handling environment. It is not necessary to know programming techniques to develop a course; it is enough to know its various features and functionalities. This is because Moodle is not a programming language but an online class environment.

Besides Moodle, there is another open-source software that is also being used for educational purposes: the OpenSimulator. The OpenSim, as it is commonly called, is a 3D multiuser server like Second Life (SL). The big difference, besides being free, is its easiness on adding modules (adds-on) of different technologies, which is not possible in SL. The SL is a proprietary program of Linden Labs. The 3D worlds use online resources to build virtual spaces and remote interaction between the participants through special software that uses virtual reality modeling language (VRML). Mattar (2008) stated that this type of virtual environment provides important spatial references for the simulation activities. For him, "there is a sense of place that justifies the idea of immersion, so closely associated with these 3D online virtual worlds, which allows the simulation in a way impossible to achieve with only text" (Mattar, 2008, p. 5). Virtual reality allows the participant to be represented by an avatar (3D character that represents the participant and moves in the virtual world), which gives the feeling of being within the digital landscape. This feeling is due to the immersion process that transforms virtual space into a real extension. In this context, the individual can build a virtual identity (avatar), equal or not in terms of his or her real appearance (Salen & Zimmerman, 2003).

In this 3D space, the students have opportunities to interact synchronously with each other, act and manipulate the objects and contents available, as well as to simulate and build collaboratively (Mattar, 2008, 2009; Mattar & Valente, 2007; Schlemmer & Backes, 2008). Although it is possible to freely access SL, it is restricted to the rules imposed by the owner. To upload multimedia files (animation, image, sound, video, presentation) and enjoy all the features offered by the environment, you must have permissions on your user account. The OpenSim allows the creation of 3D virtual worlds that may be available in a public grid of regions. With this, you can install it in a local or remote server on different operating systems (Windows, Linux). This environment provides an immersive virtual representative through an avatar, that is, a graphical representation in a 3D virtual world (Schlemmer, Trein, & Oliveira, 2008). The avatar can move more freely, using real-world geographic coordinates: latitude, longitude, and altitude. Moreover, it has specific features, such as text chat and voice chat, built of 3D objects, instant messaging, teleportation, notecard, animation, multimedia files, and inventory.

Both Moodle and OpenSim can be integrated via Sloodle. Sloodle is an open mashup initially developed for the integration of Moodle with SL. It maps the structure of the Moodle activities in SL/OpenSim, allowing avatars to play, fly, and walk among them. The Moodle's blocks appear as 3D objects in SL/OpenSim. The chat logs, pictures, and objects in SL can be stored in Moodle. Thus, the SL and OpenSim can make use of asynchronous communication interfaces—the structured activities, the files stored in recorded chats offered by Moodle. And Moodle provides its users to participate in 3D virtual worlds chats and vice versa. Therefore, the cyberspace provides powerful virtual environments that can be articulated and/or integrated as education demands. There are no rules and restrictions regarding the adoption of specific virtual environments, but there are inspiring and creative possibilities.

Education in Cyberspace

The Internet has a major influence on global changes experienced in 21st-century society. Lemos and Lévy (2010, p. 23) stated that "the growth is exponential and has global access." The social and politic communications are being interfered by the technical field where everything is transformed, processed, and distributed on the web. Words once restricted to Internet users (Facebook, Twitter, MSN, Skype, blogs) are incorporated into the vocabulary of the Portuguese language, for example, *tweet* and *blogging*. We also have incorporated technological terms in the English language that became popular because of the Internet. They are *fotolog, bluetooth, e-book, tablets,* and *pop-up.* These are just some examples of how new forms of communication and social relations reshape and transform the planetary societies.

Ubiquitous computing and seamless connection via laptops, tablets, and smartphones provide the continuous body coupled with the virtual space. Thus, new e-learning communicational ambiance implies the emergence of a unique language: the language of networks. This language has hypermedia syntax—that is, the integration of multiple data formats available on the Internet (images, text, video, and sound). Cyberculture creates an intersection with various cultural forms in the world, homogenizing habits and customs with respect to digital artifacts—singular object—that travel in the world of culture.

Therefore, cyberculture is not an exclusive cyberspace phenomenon but the relationship with socio-technical interactive media and the required cognitive capital (Trivinho, 2007). Digital technologies increasingly permeate our lives in several sectors, often subtly, becoming almost ubiquitous. In education, they contribute to the breakdown of traditional paradigms, where the teacher is considered the knowledge holder. Interactive media have great potential for com munication, which allows for participation, intervention, information sharing, and collaborative knowledge construction. To explore them educationally and promote interactivity, teachers need to be in tune with cybercultural time.

E-learning education is a cyberculture phenomenon (Santos, 2010) that provides great communication and pedagogical potentialities when collaborative interfaces are articulated with intense and provocative teacher mediation. Teachers need to know the features of each interface so that they can exploit them according to their needs. In this case, cyberculture continuously demands teachers' educational programs that allow them to be able to act and contribute to pedagogical innovations, always taking into account the interactivity.

One of the greatest educational challenges is how to restructure methodology and pedagogical content in order to approach and involve this new cultural profile— socially disengaged, scattered, fragmented, and disorganized. One aspect lies in the following problem: teachers, "digital immigrants" (Prensky, 2001), "contemplative readers," or "moving readers" (Santaella, 2007), using technology only to support traditional practices, transmitting ordered, rigid, closed-content, text-centered material are reflecting a linear thinking. Specific skills should be developed by teachers so that they can plan creative and dynamic activities, with various contents formats, such as sounds, videos, images, and hypertexts.

While the hypermedia language is used by students, some teachers speak analogically. Consequently, students end up losing interest in school because of outdated procedures adopted in education, both in physical classroom attendance and e-learning styles. The adoption of a hypertext and hypermedia thinking opens up a range of potentialities that can be applied both in design and in teacher mediation, raising the students' engagement.

Teacher Mediation and Interactivity

Another important challenge that needs to be considered is the understanding of teacher mediation and interactivity as the essential educational foundation. Although the society is influenced by the web as a whole, teaching is still at the oral and print stage. Knowledge is still passed on and repeated in a standardized, rigid, one-way mode by many traditional educators. From Vygotsky's (1934/2001) mediation concepts, language is the main social product responsible for characterizing the complex and dynamic relationship between humans and context. Therefore, there is no mediation without sign and language. Mediation occurs in the field of meaning, which includes the creation and use of signs that reflect the language reality.

Signs are already beginning in thought, which includes perception and action. Perception is constituted by the meaning that internalizes generalized concepts of reality, translated into action mode (instruments). Knowledge is not achieved immediately, requiring detours and mediations performed by humans. With this dynamic process, mediation involves the potential of context to mold the action and use by individuals as mediators. All signs can be externalized in various media (speaking, writing, sound, and image) and also in technical/technological supports, establishing communication. The media are the support for the language materialization, promoting socio-cultural impacts. The development of higher cognitive functions happens in social interactions mediated by the signs and the media (Vygotsky, 1934/2007). So, higher thought is socio-culturally constructed and seeks the control of mediation and internalization.

Internalization is the transformation of active internal factors produced by external factors (Frawley, 2000). Thus, social processes are transformed into internal processes coming to consciousness, (re)creating it. The cultural-historical theory of Vygotsky argues that society precedes the individual and thus, internalizes the content from social relationships and developing higher thinking. While human activity is producing and creating objects of knowledge, it transforms humans into a subject of their knowledge. Knowledge is (re)constructed over time through instruments and cultural mediation.

According to Vygotsky (1934/2007, p. 9), "the instruments and their products are flows in development of the internalized language and conceptual thinking, which sometimes walk alongside and sometimes fuse, influencing each other." So, the human being, in its active relations with the world, becomes responsible for the production of his or her knowledge reconstructing and interfering in this world. This learning process is individual, but it is symbolically mediated through social experiences.

Therefore, the experience, built through social relations, allows the subject to make abstractions that go beyond meanings, contributing to learning. This subject-language-medium relation can be also materialized in virtual environments through interfaces that promote collaboration, authoring, building, and knowledge sharing. However, the teacher mediation in virtual environments happens according to the paradigm adopted by the educator and/or educational institution. Epistemological assumptions are inevitably transposed from the physical classroom to the digital media, often contradicting the essence of cyberculture. Mediation in virtual spaces is not replaced by communication and collaboration interfaces.

The environment provides immersion and interactivity but needs an effective teaching practice. Research conducted in an undergraduate course in pedagogical online virtual environments involving hybrid 2D and 3D environments (Rossini & Silva, 2011) revealed that it is useless to provide a range of sophisticated features and interfaces if there is no teacher mediation with interactivity. Without mediation, it is impossible to establish the interactivity and hence the engagement of students in activities. Delegating teacher mediation to the communication and collaboration interfaces reinforces instructionism and self-instruction. The virtual learning environments, in general, need to be flexible and open spaces, where all participants can contribute to its design and its dynamic curriculum (Santos, 2006). To do this, interactivity is an essential element to promote construction and knowledge sharing in the e-learning environment. Without it, the computer becomes a simple machine for reading, writing, and information processing. Interactivity provides the greatest acceptance of communication (Silva, 2010). In other words, it promotes genuine participation, allowing the cocreation of the message among all to all (interactive model). The interactivity, to be established, needs an environment that provides it.

For this, the interfaces are responsible for providing a complex communication context, which allows the connection, participation, and collaboration among all the participants. Likewise, it is important to highlight some issues regarding the structure and dynamics that should include interactivity in virtual environments:

> a) create hypertextual sites that aggregate intertextuality, links to other sites or documents, connections to the same document; multivocality, add multiple points of view, navigability, simple and easy access environments and transparency of information; mixing, integration of multiple languages: sounds, text, dynamic and static images, graphics, maps, multimedia, media integration of various supports; b) enhance interactive synchronous, real-time and asynchronous communication, at any time—sender and receiver need not be at the same time; c) develop research activities that encourage the knowledge construction from problem situations where the individual can contextualize local and global issues of his cultural universe; d) create ambiance for formative assessment, where knowledge is constructed in a communicative process of negotiations, where making decision is a constant practice to a procedural (re)signification of authorships and co-authorships; e) provide and encourage ludic, artistic and fluid navigation connections.
>
> *(Santos, 2006, p. 227)*

From these issues, the educational activities should be structured and operated in the interfaces of virtual environments. Therefore, underutilization of the virtual environments potentially promotes the emergence of poor e-learning education. According to Giolo (2008), there is no social network life, and the structure of the face-to-face classroom and the physical contact are a guide for the teaching–learning process. Demo (2006), in a less radical point of view, advocated the adoption of educational practices that explore the balance between e-learning and physical presence. For him, both the virtual environment and the physical classroom are complementary. It is not possible to replace one with another. If physical contact is eliminated, learning will be precarious because the teacher cannot take care of the students' learning. These assertions are mainly based on linear virtual environments, which implement instructional and behaviorist models of education.

Silva (2010) systematized five suggestions for teachers to overcome the pedagogy of transmission and promote interactivity:

1. Provide opportunities for multiple trials and expressions. The teacher should promote group work to encourage collaboration, participation, dialogue, and exchange between all

participants. The discussions should be conducted in the physical classroom and e-learning environments. Questions and arguments should be exposed for discussions between teacher and students.

2. Provide an intuitive and usable learning design offering easy navigation, collaboration and creative production to the students. The design should be flexible enough to be molded according to the interactions between teachers and students. Several media languages should be used and mixed both in face-to-face and e-learning environments.

3. Raise creative situations. Promote, encourage, and stimulate the participation of students to solve problems independently and cooperatively, sharing attitudes of respect for diversity and solidarity. Problems should enable the development of skills to (re)signify ideas, concepts, and procedures.

4. Collaboratively think up hypertext pathways. Explore the advantages of hypertext. The course must be proposed in different ways, with the contents combined and connected in multiple languages and resources.

5. Raise the experience of knowing. Consider the previous experience of the course's participants. The activities should be developed to encourage free expression, the confrontation of ideas, collaboration, sharpened observation, and interpretation of the attitudes of everyone involved.

In accordance with Silva (2010), teachers can promote participation and engagement between the participants when adopting these five suggestions. The knowledge is proposed in order to provide a complex web of overlapping and potentiating activities. The pedagogical route is open and dynamic and can be restructured according to the interests of the group. Indeed, virtual environments are great ways for achieving these suggestions to promote interactivity. The interfaces and the features can be configured and operated in accordance with the appropriate educational needs. To provide interactivity in virtual environments, teachers must know their capabilities and interfaces, develop routes, connect content, raise participation, and collaborate among all in an intuitive, dynamic, and motivating way.

Silva (2010) suggested adopting the hypertext metaphor, where the educator assumes the role of knowledge challenger. Knowledge is available in a potential state, allowing students to experience and participate in the development of their learning. The exchanges can be performed either with the teacher or with peers. These open connections develop the autonomy of the student and knowledge permutability. Nothing is static and consolidated. The knowledge is (re)constructed and (re)signified in every interaction with the world. In this case, cyberculture demands for teachers to be able to act and contribute to pedagogical innovation in all forms of education, always taking into account the mediation with interactivity.

The Articulation of 2D and 3D Virtual Spaces to Enhance E-learning Education

Due to the increasing technological advances and lowering cost of mobile devices and telecommunications, global society has demanded increasingly sophisticated 3D software resolution. After the explosion of Web 2.0, new ways to interact, create, collaborate, and share in cyberspace are emerging. For example, the 3D online virtual worlds have provided a greater level of immersion compared to 2D interfaces. Santaella (2007) said that representative immersion via avatar allows the perception of the subject to be transported to 3D virtual worlds. Furthermore, the simulation and role playing features of 3D virtual worlds bring new learning possibilities when comparing with the traditional LMS.

According to Kapp and O'Driscoll (2010), a trend that is being observed in courses via the Internet is the convergence between Web 2.0 technologies and those of 3D virtual worlds. This trend shows the need for a coexistence of different technologies to enhance their capabilities and interfaces. For them, the future of the Internet will be immersive as a whole, providing a higher quality of interactions since it requires a higher concentration of users immersed in real-time activity. In this virtual space, the individual has the opportunity to interact beyond the learning content (e.g., text, video, presentation, image, audio), enabling real-world experimentation.

For example, Moodle offers several communication and collaborative powerful asynchronous and synchronous interfaces. The asynchronous interfaces can be used anytime and anywhere, without the need for a simultaneous participation of all involved in the learning process. In the synchronous interface, all participants must be connected at the same time. Moodle, as open-source software, allows for adding multiple applications, providing a greater amount of resources according to the required needs. The SL/OpenSim is a 3D virtual world fully built and inhabited by avatars, which simulates real life.

Although it seems like a game, it cannot be considered one because there is no story to follow. It, in fact, "is a world completely unlimited and the only limitations you will encounter will be established for your time, curiosity and imagination" (Tapley, 2008, p. 5). This world offers voice and text chat interfaces and 3D objects building tools. It also has a variety of features that enable individuals to get closer to the real world, such as a camera, group contact list, search for objects and places, objects' inventory, text messaging, ways to move the avatar (walk, run, jump, dance, and fly), and maps, among others. The avatars, or residents of 3D virtual worlds, can build objects in accordance with their creativity and goal, shaping the software to behave like a game, a learning environment, a social networking site—in other words, in line with their educational, social, or marketing purposes. In the educational model, these objects can be integrated with Moodle by Sloodle. That way, some interfaces of Moodle can be extended and integrated into SL/OpenSim, increasing the resources available for e-learning teaching and learning.

According to Klastrup (2003), 3D virtual worlds are hybrids because they have characteristics gathered from various digital technologies. This allows for "a diversity of forms of interaction, which can be developed through different communication languages: textual, verbal, gestural and graphic" (Schlemmer, Trein, & Oliveira, 2008, p. 2). These structures are fluid and dynamic and can be remixed to create new collective senses.

Therefore, the LMSs and the 3D VLEs are two powerful virtual environments for education via the Internet. Resources and communication interfaces, when articulated, are great tools for teachers to make course participants feel as close as they would be in a face-to-face, collaborative, interactive, dialectical, constructivist, and democratic classroom (Freire, 2002; Silva, 2010; Tardif & Lessard, 2008; Teixeira, 2004; Vygotsky, 1934/2001). The articulation of these two environments contributes to the knowledge construction, the cocreation, sharing information, collaboration, simulation, collaborative construction of 3D objects, and autonomous development. Since each environment has its specificities, each of which aims to develop specific skills, the underutilization of one in favor of the other triggered limitations on learning, especially in courses for the training of teachers. Future e-learning teachers need to know their potential so they can use them in the present and the future in creative and interactive ways.

Conclusion

The e-learning courses are offered most often in the traditional style, that is, the paradigm of trans-mission of sealed packages of knowledge (Silva, 2010), like instructionism and self-instruction. As a consequence, the pedagogical practices and classroom activities focused on the discourse of teachers are just transposed into the virtual environment. Hence, there is underutilization of 2D and 3D environments, to the detriment of education. The interactivity promoted in virtual environments requires that teachers provide communication (Silva, 2010) and promote interaction among all participants. The main actions of teacher mediation are to encourage the student's participation and the co-authoring between all of them. Without teacher mediation, the learning process will be limited (self-study). Teachers need to be present and attentive to all course participants' interactions, both among themselves and with context, to ensure interactivity. Without interactivity, learning becomes mechanical and linear, not allowing for autonomous knowledge construction. The growing demand for e-learning undergraduate courses requires even more attention. How may poorly trained teachers in an e-learning style practice in any kind of teaching?

According to Morgado (2009), the social behavior is not changed only by technology insertion but when new forms of use are associated with it. Schlemmer and Backes (2007) agree with Morgado (2009) by stating that teachers learn as they go, feeling the need of using technological resources to perform some activity. There is no use training teachers with e-learning tutorials if they do not make sense for their actions. Kapp and O'Driscoll (2010) emphasized the importance to think beyond the traditional paradigm of education to empower the creation of new forms of learning using the web potentialities.

The creation of collaborative virtual environments allows new ideas and concepts to be generated by a collective vision. The Web 2.0 interfaces, when combined, can provide new teaching practices and allow for exploring of content in different ways. For this to happen, digital technologies need to be present in teachers' lives in the form of courses or constant updates. The important thing is for teachers to be always up to date regarding their practices and epistemological concepts. This does not mean they will have to be slaves of the technology (Trivinho, 2007), but rather educators tuned in to cybercultural time.

References

Demo, P. (2006). Instrucionismo e nova mídia. In M. Silva (Ed.), *Educação online: teorias, práticas, legislação, formação corporativa* (pp. 77–90). São Paulo, Brazil: Loyola.

Frawley, W. (2000). *Vygotsky e a ciência cognitiva: linguagem e integração das mentes social e computacional*. Porto Alegre, Brazil: Artes Médicas Sul.

Freire, P. (2002). *Pedagogia do oprimido*. Rio de Janeiro, Brazil: Paz e Terra.

Giolo, J. (2008). A educação a distância e a formação de professores. *Revista Educação e sociedade, 105,* 35–48. Retrieved from http://www.scielo.br/pdf/es/v29n105/v29n105a13.pdf

Kapp, K., & O'Driscoll, T. (2010). *Learning in 3D: Adding a new dimension to enterprise learning and collaboration*. San Francisco, CA: Pfeiffer.

Klastrup, L. (2003). *A poetics of virtual worlds*. Melbourne, Australia: DAC.

Lemos, A., & Lévy, P. (2010). *O futuro da internet: em direção a uma ciberdemocracia*. São Paulo, Brazil: Paulus.

Mattar, J. (2008). O uso do Second Life como ambiente de aprendizagem. *Revista Fonte, 8,* 88–95. Retrieved from http://www.prodemge.gov.br/images/revistafonte/revista_8.pdf

Mattar, J. (2009). *Technological minimalism and Second Life: Time for educational technology and content minimalism*. Boise, ID: Boise State University. Retrieved from http://www.pgsimoes.net/Biblioteca/TM&SL_Joao_Mattar.pdf

Mattar, J., & Valente, C. (2007). *Second Life e Web 2.0 na educação: o potencial revolucionário das novas tecnologias*. São Paulo, Brazil: Novatec Editora.

Morgado, L. (2009). Os mundos virtuais e o ensino-aprendizagem de procedimentos. *Revista Educação e cultura contemporânea, 12,* 35–48.

Okada, A. (2006). Desafio para EAD: Como fazer emergir a colaboração e a cooperação em ambientes virtuais de aprendizagem? In M. Silva (Ed.), *Educação online: teorias, práticas, legislação, formação corporativa* (pp. 275–293). São Paulo, Brazil: Loyola.

Prensky, M. (2001). Digital natives, digital immigrants. *On the horizon, 9*(5). Lincoln, NE: MCB University Press. Retrieved from http://www.marcprensky.com/writing/Prensky%20-%20Digital%20Natives,%20Digital%20Immigrants%20-%20Part1.pdf

Rossini, T., & Silva, M. (2011) Mediação docente e interatividade em ambientes virtuais 2D e 3D. In R. Linhares & S. Ferreira (Eds.), *Educação a distância e as tecnologias da Inteligência: novos percursos de formação e aprendizagem* (pp. 169–188). Maceió, Brazil: EDUFAL.

Salen, K., & Zimmerman, E. (2003). *Rules of play: Game design fundamentals.* Cambridge, MA: MIT Press.

Santaella, L. (2007). *Navegar no ciberespaço: o perfil cognitivo do leitor imersivo.* São Paulo, Brazil: Paulus.

Santos, E. (2006). Articulação de saberes na EAD *online*: por uma rede interdisciplinar e interativa de conhecimentos em ambientes virtuais de aprendizagem. In M. Silva (Ed.), *Educação online: práticas, legislação, formação corporativa* (pp. 219–232). São Paulo, Brazil: Loyola.

Santos, E. (2010). Educação *online* para além da EAD: um fenômeno da cibercultura. In M. Silva, L. Pesce, & A. Zuin (Eds.), *Educação online: cenário, formação e questões didático-metodológicas* (pp. 29–48). Rio de Janeiro, Brazil: Wak Ed.

Schlemmer, E., & Backes, L. (2007). O aprender e ensinar na formação do educador em mundos virtuais. *Revista Educere et Educare, 4,* 129–140.

Schlemmer, E., & Backes, L. (2008). Metaversos: novos espaços para construção do conhecimento. *Revista Diálogo Educação, 24,* 519–532.

Schlemmer, E., Trein, D., & Oliveira, C. (2008). Metaverso: a telepresença em mundos digitais virtuais 3D por meio de avatares. *Anais do Simpósio Brasileiro de Informática na Educação.* Retrieved from http://www.br-ie.org/pub/index.php/sbie/article/view/735

Silva, M. (2010). *Sala de aula interativa: educação, comunicação, mídia clássica. . . .* São Paulo, Brazil: Edições Loyola.

Tapley, R. (2008). *Construindo o seu Second Life.* Rio de Janeiro, Brazil: Alta Books.

Tardif, M., & Lessard, C. (2008). *O trabalho docente: elementos para uma teoria da docência como profissão de interações humanas.* Petrópolis, Brazil: Vozes.

Teixeira, A. (2004). Mestres de amanhã. *Revista Brasileira de Estudos Pedagógicos, 209/210/211,* 143–148.

Trivinho, E. (2007). *A dromocracia cibercultural: lógica da vida humana na civilização mediática avançada.* São Paulo, Brazil: Paulus.

Vygotsky, L. (2001). *A con strução do Pensamento e da Linguagem.* (P. Bezerra, Trans.). São Paulo: Martins Fontes. (Original work published 1934)

Vygotsky, L. (2007). *A formação social da mente* (J. Cipolla Neto, Trans). São Paulo, Brazil: Martins Fontes. (Original work published 1934)

Yee, R. (2008). *Pro mashups Web 2.0: Remixando dados e serviço da web.* Rio de Janeiro, Brazil: Alta Books.

16

Open and Virtual Universities Worldwide

Susan Bainbridge and Mohamed Ally[1]

Introduction

Open universities (OUs) were established to grant individuals a 'second chance' to obtain a tertiary education without having to meet the common criteria required for traditional universities. Students are able to register for programs regardless of location, age, gender, or academic history. The fundamental principles of open universities stand firmly on the concepts of flexibility and 'learning' rather than 'teaching' (Dabbagh, 2005; Geith, 2008; Khoja, Sana, Karim, & Rehman, 2008; Lorentsen et al., 2001). The flexibility afforded to open university students translates into a form of democratization of education in the sense that individuals who have not been able to complete secondary school or physically attend a higher education institution (HEI) are able to further their education. The emphasis on learning rather than teaching naturally led open universities to implement learner-centred approaches rather than the common teacher-centred lecture of brick-and-mortar institutions of the 20th century.

Open and distance education (DE) have by their nature developed a historical partnership with emerging technologies. Through the 20th and into the 21st centuries they have embraced print material, radio, television, documentaries, video, compact discs (CDs), digital video discs (DVDs), the Internet, Information and Communication Technology (ICT), the World Wide Web (WWW), asynchronous forums through Learning Management Systems (LMSs), and Social Media, and, more recently, synchronous platforms to enhance course delivery and design.

As learning technologies emerge and become more affordable and user friendly, open universities are moving away from print to electronic resources. As a result, they can provide flexibility in delivering where learners can access learning materials from anywhere at any time. At the same time, ICTs allow learners to access their tutors from anywhere and at any time. Learners also use social media to interact with each other and to work in teams. Open and virtual universities that use emerging technologies are also catering to the new generations of learners who are comfortable using technology for learning and for interacting with each other. The increasing availability of open education resources that can be accessed by computers, tablets, and smartphones will allow education to be reachable and more affordable for learners so that the goal of education for all can be possible.

All open university courses are offered through DE, and today the use of e-learning and mobile learning are increasing due to the availability of affordable technologies and the new generations of learners in education. Consequently, open universities do not have to be concerned with a large, physical campus, as most or all students study off campus and some faculty also work from a distance. As a result, open universities are some of the largest institutions in global higher education. The OU institutions reviewed in this chapter are listed in order of size (student enrollment). Enrollment is based on the numbers obtained from each OU website as of January 2014.

Open Universities

Indira Ghandi National Open University

Headquartered in New Delhi, India, Indira Ghandi National Open University (IGNOU) was founded in 1985. It began as both an on-campus and distance-learning institution. Its growth in open e-learning has been exponential, and it is a leader in initiatives to bring further education to a dispersed and large population throughout India and 36 other countries. Today it serves over 4 million students through 21 schools of studies, 67 regional centres, and a network of over three thousand learner study centres. IGNOU also acts as an accreditor for open university and distance-learning programs throughout India. Perhaps the most significant milestone of IGNOU was the launch of EduSat (a satellite solely dedicated to education) on September 20, 2004. This has provided IGNOU students with network connectivity at all regional and study centres, enabling students to interact with digital content.

The Open University of China

Formerly the China Central Radio and Television University, the Open University of China (OUC) serves over 3.5 million students. One unique practice within their mandate is a "lenient entry, stringent exit" (see http://en.ouchn.edu.cn/) policy, which encourages students to complete courses as they must go through several interviews and counselling sessions in order to withdraw from their studies. Another unique concept is the OUC Credit Bank. Each student has a lifelong learning portfolio which contains credits, diplomas, and certificates for their personal learning achievements. The credit bank can transfer credits for such accomplishments across programs and so "bridges and connects" (see http://en.crtvu.edu.cn/about/structure) various learning achievements. The OUC has 44 provincial radio and TV university campuses, as well as approximately two thousand county campuses and 60 thousand tutorial centres.

Allama Iqbal Open University

Allama Iqbal Open University (AIOU) was established in 1974. Centred in Islamabad, Pakistan, it offers courses throughout Pakistan and the Middle East. It operates over 40 regional campuses, regional centres, and academic centres to assist over one million students (AIOU, 2014). Its particular mandate is to offer quality higher education to Pakistani citizens residing in rural and isolated regions of the country. AIOU works under a mandate similar to all open universities, with a particular emphasis on keeping enrolment costs low to assist marginalized people in obtaining further education. One recent and significant goal outlined by the vice chancellor is the emphasis on female opportunity and education. Since the implementation of this goal, female students now outnumber male students at AIOU.

Ramkhamhaeng University, Thailand

Ramkhamhaeng University (RU) was established in 1971 to enable the many Thai students who could not be accommodated at existing universities. It operates within a completely open philosophy and does not require any form of entrance exam to applicants. It offers programs in Thai, English, and Chinese. Part of its mission is to ensure that higher education opportunities are offered throughout the nation, with total equality for all students. The university emphasizes international knowledge as a fundamental goal of all graduates. RU has established 22 regional campuses and 36 examination centres throughout Thailand, as well as 36 examination centres worldwide and manages an enrolment of over 600 thousand students. Its current mandate is to transform itself into a technologically advanced eUniversity, offering students all courses and materials online.

Dr. B. R. Ambedkar Open University

Dr. B. R. Ambedkar Open University (BRAOU) is located in Hyderabad, India. It was established as Andhra Pradesh Open University in 1982 and revised its name in 1991. With an enrolment of approximately 450 thousand students and more than 200 study centres throughout the region, BRAOU is the second largest university in India. An important mandate of BRAOU is to ensure the socially disadvantaged have access to further education. In its early years, BRAOU spent a great deal of time educating the public with regard to open and distance learning and 'why' it was of value. Today the emphasis has shifted to the 'how' and 'what' of programs and delivery.

Bangladesh Open University

Bangladesh Open University (BOU) is the result of a long history of interest in DE in Bangladesh, beginning in 1956 when the government established radio receivers in over 200 educational institutions. The Audio-Visual Education Centre (AVEC) was established in 1962, the School Broadcasting Pilot Project (SBP) in 1978, the National Institute of Educational Media and Technology (NIEMT) in 1983, then the Bangladesh Institute of Distance Education (BIDE) in 1985, and culminating in the Bangladesh Open University Act, which established BOU in 1992. Today it offers courses to about 400 thousand students. BOU operates 12 regional resource centres, 80 coordinating offices, and over 1,100 study centres. The university is currently embarking on a massive project to greatly expand course/program offerings across all disciplines.

University of South Africa

The University of South Africa's (UNISA) roots stem from traditional university structures, yet early in 1946 UNISA opened the Division of External Studies to offer DE courses to students who were not able to attend the college. It was the first university in the world to teach exclusively through DE. It has, since then, evolved into a large open and distance university. It operates three campuses, seven regional offices (including one in Ethiopia), and 28 learning centres throughout the nation. It has a current enrolment of 350 thousand students. UNISA operated on a foundation based on three pillars: teaching, research, and community engagement. Each pillar aims to strengthen the university's vision "towards *the* African university in the service of humanity."

The Open University, UK

Established in 1969 and opening its doors to students in 1971, the Open University (OU) has worked diligently to improve public awareness and acceptance of the quality of open and distance learning (ODL). The main campus at Milton Keynes is assisted by 13 centres throughout the United Kingdom, as well as study centres based at other higher education institutions. It refers to its delivery of courses and programs as 'supported open learning', which strives to ensure that all students can study when and where they choose, with assistance from tutors and peers through study centres and online facilitation. Unique to its definition of 'open', the OU has also included the concept of 'open to new teaching methods', which has assisted in its innovative approach to new technologies. It was the first in the United Kingdom to offer its material on iTunes U free of charge to its 250 thousand students as well as to a global audience.

Open University of the Netherlands

The Open University of the Netherlands (OUN) offers courses, bachelor and master programs. Studying at the OUN allows professionals to improve their knowledge and skills. Many of its students already have degrees and take one or more courses to acquire additional know-how or to retrain for a different occupation. Students enrolled at the OUN are following one of the university's courses or fully accredited Bachelor or Master degree programs. Most of the students are working full time while studying. The courses are modular which allows students to enroll in either full-length degree programs or they can choose to study one or more courses.

Korea National Open University

Korea National Open University (KNOU) faces challenges particular to its nation's cultural educational paradigms. The educational system of Korea is a stringent process with practices and norms deeply entrenched in the Korean worldview. Students are expected to move upward through the system in a uniform and standardized format. The concept of 'a second chance' or 'open' opportunities is seen as undermining the existing educational system. The current enrolment of 179 thousand students demonstrates the need for ODL in Korea, and the KNOU is working diligently to change attitudes and offer opportunities to students who do not succeed in the national educational system. KNOU is working to focus national attention and awareness towards lifelong learning and the importance of offering continual opportunities for individuals to enhance their knowledge base.

Open University of Japan

Formerly known as the University of the Air (Air-U) the institution changed its name in 2007 to the Open University of Japan (OUJ). Operating 50 study centres throughout Japan to approximately 83 thousand students, OUJ is transforming itself from a radio/television DE college into a modern online institution. OUJ faces national challenges similar to KNOU in that students are expected to 'follow the rules' of the national education system, and if a certain academic standard is not met, there is perceived to be no alternative. The OUJ has embarked on a new project in 2011 to digitize some rare editions of old books held in its library with the opening of the OUJ Library Collections in a desire to make these works accessible to all.

Al-Quds Open University

Al-Quds Open University (QOU) of Palestine began with a temporary office in Amman, Jordan, where early faculty planned the initial course offerings and teaching model of the proposed QOU. In 1991, with relative peace in the region, QOU opened its headquarters in Jerusalem. Despite the unique challenges to the region's stability, today QOU operates 18 branch offices and four study centres throughout Palestine and two educational centres in the Kingdom of Saudi Arabia, serving 57 thousand students. With many Palestinians living in other countries, QOU is working to establish educational centres outside of Palestine to serve expatriates and subsidize services offered in the home region.

Athabasca University

Athabasca University (AU), Canada's Open University, is dedicated to the removal of barriers that restrict access to and success in university-level study and to increasing equality of educational opportunity for adult learners worldwide. The current enrolment is over 40 thousand students located in 87 countries. The main campus is in Athabasca, and three regional offices are located in different parts of Alberta. AU is accredited by the Middle States Commission on Higher Education (MSCHE) and offers undergraduate and graduate programs. AU operates on the following four key principles.

- *Excellence*: Dedicated to achieving the highest standards in teaching, research, scholarship and student service.
- *Openness*: Committed to the mission of guaranteeing access to post-secondary learning to all who have the ability and desire.
- *Flexibility*: The flexible learning model adapts to learner needs. Learners can enrol in most programs and register for most courses at any time of the year and work at their own pace, studying at home, at work or wherever they are located.
- *Innovation*: Continue to adopt and develop new, learner-centred learning models and technology-based alternatives to traditional, classroom-based instructional channels and contexts. Technology is used to make learning accessible.

Open University of Israel

The Open University of Israel (OUI) opened to students in the autumn of 1976. In its initial stages, OUI used the Open University of the UK as a model. It operates 50 study centres throughout the country to serve the needs of 41 thousand students. Students do not enrol in programs but in individual courses. There are no time constraints placed on students other than the 15-week semester, under which all courses operate. This offers students the flexibility to complete their studies at their own pace, dependent on their personal situation. Program choices are extremely flexible and allow students to choose courses across departments and disciplines to suite their own needs and interests. Face-to-face (F2F) tutorials are offered at study centres and online through the course website. Tutorials are not mandatory but students are encouraged to attend the sessions.

Distance Education, E-learning, and Virtual Universities

There are a number of institutions worldwide that are not 'open' in the classical sense, which would include no entrance prerequisites, but are significant in their DE student enrolments and thus their online expertise to warrant mention in this chapter. Some of them use the term 'open' to describe their system but it refers to availability of courses to rural populations and employed individuals who are not able to attend regular classes at a traditional university campus. These higher education institutions also assist in their regions because the areas do not have enough traditional universities to educate all prospective secondary school graduates. By offering DE programs, these students can further their education even though they were not accepted at a brick-and-mortar educational institution. As a result, the population perceives these institutions to be 'open' in that they now have the opportunity to continue their studies through DE. Ten such institutions with large DE student populations are reviewed herein.

Anadolu University

Anadolu University is not an open university but a dual mode institution (Aydin & Ulutak, 2010) offering DE to over one million students. Its total enrolment is approximately two million students. The university has a significant presence in Turkey, as well as Azerbaijan, Kosovo, Macedonia, and throughout the European Union. The largest campus is Yunusemre Campus, located in Eskişehir, Turkey; but its most unique campus, İki Eylül, houses the Faculty of Aeronautics and Astronautics and has Anadolu Airport on the campus. DE students work online through an LMS, which offers all course materials and the ability to collaborate with peers and dialogue with the instructor and tutors.

Universitas Terbuka

The Indonesia Open University (Universitas Terbuka) operates in a most challenging nation. Indonesia is composed of more than 17,500 islands, many of them very remote. It offers all courses through DE and online platforms to more than 586 thousand students. The university was established in 1984 with a mandate to provide higher education to all citizens and residents of the country regardless of their location. It operates under standard 'open' policies, with one exception in that all students must have graduated from secondary school. Universitas Terbuka (UT) operates 37 regional offices, although it also has close partnerships with the major, traditional universities throughout the nation and often uses their facilities and faculty for examinations and tutorials.

National Distance Education University

The National Distance Education University, known in Spanish as Universidad Nacional de Educación a Distancia (NDEU), is based in Madrid, Spain. It envelopes equal opportunity within its mission, and although students over 25 without secondary school matriculation may apply for admission to an undergraduate program, they must write an entrance exam. NDEU offers special one-year programs, University Access Courses, which help to prepare students for the entrance exam. It operates 61 study centres within Spain and 13 in the EU, Americas, and Africa. The centres offer face to face (F2F) assistance with registration and materials, tutoring sessions, computer labs, and laboratories. NDEU offers an extensive 'Welcome Plan' to assist new students in adapting to and understanding DE and online learning. These activities and tutorials introduce students to the obligations necessary to succeed and matriculate. With an enrolment of 260 thousand students, it is the largest university in Spain.

Open University of Catalonia

Headquartered in Barcelona, the Open University of Catalonia (UOC) oversees 23 regional centres throughout Catalonia, six centers in Spain, and one each in Italy, Andorra, and Mexico, serving 60 thousand students. UOC operates according to the criteria of the Bologna Declaration, which stresses not only knowledge and skills but also values and attitudes necessary for competence in the workplace. The university embraces new technologies offering apps and access through mobile devices to all course material, as well as actively participating on social media sites. UOC also promotes open access and is continually increasing the number of open educational resources they offer online.

Arab Open University

The Arab Open University (AOU), established in 2002, is headquartered in Kuwait and serves the needs of 22 thousand students in the Middle East, operating in eight countries (Kuwait, Jordan, Lebanon, Bahrain, Saudi Arabia, Egypt, Oman, and Sudan). AOU has partnered with the Open University of the UK, and graduates of AOU receive a second certificate of achievement from the OU. Prospective students must be graduates of the secondary school system. The AOU has adapted to its own cultural situation by offering a blended approach to DE. It is unique in that students are required to attend a certain number of face-to-face (F2F) sessions during the course of their studies. All programs are taught in English and AOU offers a foundation English program to help students bring their English level up to an academic standard before beginning their studies.

Hellenic Open University

Headquartered in Patras, Greece, Hellenic Open University (HOU) has an enrolment of approximately 21 thousand students. Courses are offered in print form with audio and visual supplements, and students are expected to work through the course material in one semester. Approximately five F2F tutorials are offered during a semester, and although not mandatory, students are encouraged to attend the sessions. HOU operates within a constructivist approach which promotes active learning and student interaction with the course material and with peers. Although not a great deal of Internet technology is used to date, the HOU works closely with the Educational Content, Methodology and Technology (e-CoMeT) Laboratory Unit of the university to research and develop new DE strategies and tools.

Universidade Aberta

The Universidade Aberta (UAb) is located in Portugal with headquarters in Lisbon. Its name translates into English as the Open University. Students must be 21 years of age and hold a secondary school diploma, but students 25 years of age and older can seek admission without secondary school credentials. They are required to write an entrance exam. It specializes in online learning and serves 13 thousand students. UAb operates under the European Credit Transfer and Accumulation System (ECTS), which is a student-centred philosophy but stipulates that full-time students must complete a mandatory number of courses each semester. The university has placed a new emphasis on lifelong learning through a completely digital approach to course offerings.

Egyptian E-learning University

The Egyptian E-learning University (EELU) is a relatively new institution which began operations in 2009 with a mission to provide DE anytime, anywhere, using all modern technological advances. Enrolment is approximately 1,500 students. EELU offers all courses online including lectures, course material, and video conferencing. Instruction is in English. Students are expected to take at least one course during each semester to remain in good standing. Semester breaks are allowed if approved by the program chair. Students must attend a formal F2F final exam, which normally constitutes 50% of their final grade in any given course. EELU is based in Cairo, with a vision to offer DE to not only the nation but the entire region.

African Virtual University

The African Virtual University (AVU) began as a World Bank project in 1997 until it was transferred to a consortium of African governments in 2003. It is now an intergovernmental organization made up of fifteen countries: Ghana, Mozambique, Kenya, Senegal, Ivory Coast, Democratic Republic of Congo, South Sudan, Benin, Tanzania, Republic of Guinea, Sudan, Burkina Faso, Mali, Niger, and Mauritania. The AVU headquarters is located in Nairobi, Kenya. It also operates a regional office in Dakar, Senegal. It hopes to increase the availability of quality higher education throughout the region to students in remote areas and professionals who cannot take the time to attend traditional universities.

The University of Philippines Open University

The University of Philippines Open University (UPOU) is a branch of the University of Philippines. Established in 1995, its headquarters are located in Los Baños, Philippines. It works to improve access to higher education through course offerings delivered through current Internet technology. Seven UPOU learning centres are located throughout the country to assist students who are studying at a distance. These centres also offer tutorials on basic computer and Internet literacy. If students are not residing near a learning centre all materials are offered online at the Virtual Learning Centre through UPOU Networks, a content management system offering open educational resources to students and the general public.

Conclusion

The open and distance education organizations described in this chapter are providing flexibility for citizens in their countries and other parts of the world to obtain an education so that they can improve themselves and, at the same time, contribute to society. These ODL institutions are giving learners a second chance to obtain an education, especially those with special needs, the disadvantaged, those that have family responsibilities, and those who live in remote locations with limited or no means of transportation. Many of these ODL institutions are taking advantage of emerging technologies to deliver education so that learners can learn from any location and at a time convenient to them. The communication capabilities of the technology allow learners to interact with each other and with the instructor or tutor so that learners are not isolated and they get a sense of community.

Because of the flexibility offered by open and virtual universities, there will be an increase in these universities. Many countries are looking at ODL institutions as an efficient way to educate their citizens for the good of society. Some countries are starting to digitize learning materials so that students can learn using emerging technologies. Allowing students to use technology to learn will prepare them for the digitized world where all learning materials, including textbooks, will be electronic. At the same time, the young and upcoming generations of students will demand that learning materials be delivered using technology because technology is second nature to them, and they like to interact with it. Citizens in some countries cannot afford to go to a physical school, and the only way to educate them is by delivering learning materials and providing support by using technology. Some citizens, because of family responsibilities, cannot leave their communities to get an education. Registering in open and virtual universities is the only way they can get educated.

Open and distance education institutions must continually innovate themselves to meet the needs of the 21st century learners who use technology on a daily basis and in a world where there is information explosion requiring learning throughout one's life. The only way to provide lifelong learning is to have flexible education delivery systems which is the mission of open and distance education.

Note

1 The authors would like to thank Dr. Yasser Dakroury of the Egyptian E-learning University for the information he provided to complete this chapter.

References

AIOU. (2014). Allama Iqbal Open University. Retrieved from http://www.aiou.edu.pk/RegionalOffices.asp

Aydin, C. H., & Ulutak, N. (2010). Open education resources of Anadolu University, Turkey. Proceedings of the MIT LINC 2010 Conference, Cambridge, USA. Retrieved from http://linc.mit.edu/linc2010/proceedings/session10Aydin.pdf

Dabbagh, N. (2005). Pedagogical models for eLearning: A theory-based design framework. International Journal of Technology in Teaching and Learning, 1(1), 25–44.

Geith, C. (2008). Teaching and learning unleashed with Web 2.0 and open educational resources. In EDU-CAUSE (Ed.), The tower and the cloud: Higher education in the age of cloud computing (pp. 219–226). Berkeley, CA: EDUCAUSE.

Khoja, S., Sana, F., Karim, A., & Rehman, A. (2008). Implementing constructive pedagogical model in dynamic distance learning framework. In D.M.A. Hussain, A.Q.K. Rajput, B. S. Chowdhry, & Q. Gee (Eds.), Wireless networks, information processing and systems (pp. 191–201). Berlin, Germany: Springer.

Lorentsen, A., Bygholm, A., Wilt, J., Heiner, M., Schneckenberg, D., Kokkeler, B., . . . Opsomer, A. (2001). Report working group 7: Pedagogical models and online pedagogy (Grant Agreement number: 2001-3453/001-001 EDU-ELEARN). Retrieved from http://reve.europace.org/docs/cevu/online_pedagogy.pdf

17

E-learning and Mobile Learning Development in the State of Qatar

Martha Robinson, Mohamed Ally, and Mohammed Samaka

Introduction

The State of Qatar's National Vision 2030 (QNV 2030) defines long-term outcomes for this oil-rich and gas-rich state. It aims at transforming Qatar into an advanced nation, capable of sustaining its own development and providing a high standard of living for its people for the foreseeable future. The vision rests on four development "pillars": human, social, economic, and environmental (General Secretariat for Development Planning, 2008).

The pillar of Human Development recognizes the need to prepare the Qatari people to participate in an increasingly competitive knowledge-based globalized world by creating an educated population and a capable and motivated workforce through educational curricula that reflect current and future needs of the labour market; educational and training opportunities that address the diversity of individual needs within the population, including complex technical requirements, creativity, and innovation; and high-quality certification and training programs to develop the workforce. The pillar of Economic Development foresees economic diversification that results from a knowledge-based economy characterized by innovation, entrepreneurship, and excellence in education.

The National Vision provides a goal towards which national strategies and implementation plans can be developed. The National Development Strategy 2011–2016 recognizes that the goals of QNV 2030 require institutional and organizational capacity building and a shift to a higher valued economic activity advanced by a skilled labour force (General Secretariat for Development Planning, 2011).

To move towards these lofty goals, sector-specific strategies have been developed. In the education sector, the Supreme Education Council (SEC) develops projects that align with the Education and Training Sector Strategy 2011–2016 and Qatar National Vision 2030.

This chapter will discuss the development of e-learning and mobile learning in Qatar, its progress to date, and the challenges that remain. It will begin with a description of the education reform that has spurred e-education and an overview of the ICT infrastructure available in the country, followed by a description of e-learning and mobile learning initiatives.

Education Reform

In view of QNV 2030, the National Development Strategy 2011–2016 recognizes the need for a comprehensive education and training system that is integrated, "stretching from early childhood education through to higher level education and additional training. Engrained in this system is the concept of lifelong learning, with individuals encouraged to acquire education and update their skills throughout their lives" (General Secretariat for Development Planning, 2011, p 13). The Strategy targets a variety of learning contexts: general education (K–12), higher education, technical education and vocational training, and public education and information.

Such comprehensive reforms in education were unheard of until recent years. Throughout the 20th century, teaching and learning in Qatar consisted of very traditional, teacher-centered, bricks-and-mortar school experiences, where lectures and rote memorization were the norm. Beginning in 2001, however, the Education for a New Era reform initiative heralded a shift in education policy and a will to examine new approaches. A standards-based Independent School Model was adopted in 2004, based on four principles: autonomy, accountability, variety, and choice. The traditional curriculum and approach gave way to one that is more learner-centred and takes advantage of innovations in educational technologies and scientific research methods. "Qatar's children were able to access learner-centered classrooms within improved facilities where better-prepared and better-trained teachers guide them in accordance with internationally benchmarked standards" (Brewer et al , 2007)

Prior to the Education for a New Era reforms, distance education was not widely known in Qatar and not recognized by education authorities. In other regions of the world, lessons learned from adult learning and distance learning have been incorporated into the development of e-learning approaches. Learner characteristics, support needs, effective exposition, and assessment approaches identified in traditional correspondence-type distance learning have been modified through the past century to develop current practices in e-learning. Without this history in their own country, educators in Qatar moved into uncharted territory with respect to the needs and experiences of Qatari learners when they chose to pursue the promise of e-learning and mobile learning. Given this fact, the story of the development of e-learning and mobile learning in Qatar in recent years is one of promise, expectation, innovation, and expansion of cultural outlook.

Current State of ICT in Qatar

The shift to a knowledge-based economy and, more specifically, to e-learning and mobile learning development depend on the ICT infrastructure and broadband connectivity of nations, institutions, and individuals that pursue them. It is important, then to understand the ICT context in Qatar. Qatar was ranked the 23rd most networked nation out of 144 nations surveyed for the World Economic Forum's *The Global Information and Technology Report 2013* (GITR; World Economic Forum, 2013). Qatar's mobile penetration stands at 131 percent, and mobile network coverage has reached 100 percent of the population. Figure 17.1 illustrates the increased penetration of computers, Internet, and mobile phones in Qatar in recent years, as reported by Qatar's National ICT Landscape 2013 (ictQatar, 2013).

Despite this positive trend, however, the National ICT Plan 2015, *Advancing the Digital Agenda*, recognizes the challenges that remain in the pursuit of the National Vision 2030. It indicates that current broadband connectivity is not yet sufficient to meet the country's needs.

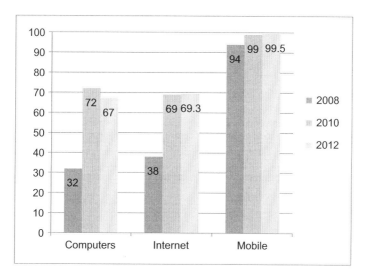

Figure 17.1   ICT Penetration in Qatar

Adapted from ictQatar, 2013

It goes on to state that, "though Qatar is leapfrogging outdated technologies, keeping pace with demand is difficult, especially as new technologies and forms of media demand greater bandwidth and more sophisticated equipment" (ictQatar, 2011a). Infrastructure remains a challenge to be addressed.

Governance in Education

In October 2011, *Computer News Middle East* selected Qatar's Supreme Education Council (SEC) to receive its annual award for ICT in Education in recognition of the SEC's numerous major projects to improve the quality and ease of access to educational resources and its implementation of cloud technologies and mobile computing to transform education (Computer News Middle East, 2011). This is quite a leap for a nation where the first intraschool network was announced only six years earlier (Supreme Education Council, 2005b). This transformation was the result of a clear direction, a supportive institutional structure, and sufficient resources. Two government institutions contribute towards the utilization of ICT to enhance education in Qatar. These are the Supreme Education Council and the Supreme Council of Information and Communication Technology (ictQatar). Their stated goal is the achievement of best-in-class use of ICT resulting from an integrated approach throughout the education and training sector, including effective use of ICT in student education, teacher education, and education administration. Projects include the development of a learning management system, e-content, and electronic devices for each student (ictQatar, 2011a). The responsibilities of each organization, as set out in the 2015 National ICT Plan, are:

SEC

- advanced learning management systems;
- developing IT standards and frameworks that will be applied to schools across Qatar;
- creation of a national e-library;
- curriculum-based digital content for the K–12 public schools;
- ICT training and professional development for educators; and
- enhance information sharing between schools.

ictQATAR

- e-maturity assessment tool which measures the extent to which ICT is integrated and adopted in each school;
- e-content for educational purposes, including a curriculum on cyber safety; and
- e-learning and lifelong learning for all sectors, including government, business, healthcare, and education (ictQatar, 2011a).

E-learning in Qatar

The history of e-learning in Qatar is a brief and eventful one. In August 2006, ictQatar and the SEC announced the signing of an agreement to implement an e-education strategy designed to move Qatari education from a "traditional content-driven, teacher-centered instructional environment" to a "standards-driven, student-centered learning environment" (SEC, 2006a). The manager of e-education at the time explained,

> We want to be a leading nation in educational excellence through technology. . . . From our perspective, the digital divide is more than the question of ICT access and e-literacy. The digital divide addresses the ability to use ICT to access, analyze, evaluate, and synthesize information to construct understanding and functional knowledge.
>
> *(SEC, 2007)*

The Supreme Education Council's current e-education strategy aims to integrate advanced technology in education at all schools and to create a better learning environment in the context of Qatari cultural values and traditions. The Strategy comprises five areas:

1. Infrastructure: connectivity, computers and other smart devices to be used in the teaching process.
2. Learning and management systems: Learning Management System, School Management System, and Content Management System.
3. Learning and instructional resources: E-content and an e-library that contain human–computer interactive materials to engage, support self-learning, promote higher order cognitive skills, contextualize learning, and provide up-to-date information.
4. Professional development: provide teachers with extensive training to adopt ICT for innovative pedagogical approaches.
5. Leadership and planning: guide school leadership in planning to incorporate effective ICT use as an essential transformative tool for education and training. (SEC, 2012a)

The following section will describe the path of development in each of the first four areas.

1. Infrastructure

Qatar's National ICT Plan 2015 recognizes as one of its goals the need to leverage ICT to advance social benefits in health, education, and society. In education, the benefit will derive from "modernizing learning spaces and promoting the use of ICT to enhance the learning experience" (ictQatar, 2011a, p. 11). Progress has been made to date, as illustrated by the statistics shown in Table 17.2, from Qatar's ICT Landscape 2011 (ictQatar, 2011b):

Table 17.2 ICT in Education in Qatar

	2008	*2010*
Average number of PCs per 100 students	12.8	15.5
Primary and secondary schools with Internet access	73%	98%
Schools with broadband access	59%	93%
Individual PC penetration	32%	72%
Individuals' (mainstream) Internet access	63%	82%
Individuals' (transient workers) Internet access		8%
Mobile phone penetration	93%	99%

Adapted from ictQatar, 2013

Table 17.3 Usage-to-Ownership Ratios for Interactive Learning Devices in Schools

Data projectors	0.65
Interactive white boards	0.64
Video players	0.41
Audio/video conferencing	0.26
Digital still cameras	0.26
Digital video cameras	0.22
Mobile phones/PDAs	0.20

Recent ICT milestones include the following:

- In 2009, all Independent Schools in Qatar were linked with a broadband wireless Internet connection (SEC, 2009).
- By 2010, nearly 100 percent of school teachers, university educators, and university students, and 96 percent of school students had access to PCs for educational or personal purposes.
- Also in 2010, 71 percent of K–12 school teachers had received training on using and implementing ICT with their students.

In schools, interactive learning devices are readily available, though the usage-to-ownership ratios indicate potential for improved utilization (see Table 17.3).

2. Learning Management System

Knowledge Net (K Net). In 2006, the Supreme Education Council introduced the Knowledge Net (K Net) portal in eight Independent Schools to provide a framework from which to build a web-based learning environment. It allowed for three-way communication between students, teachers, and parents, providing a standard interface for sharing education applications and student data and instant messaging, email, and discussion boards to facilitate communication between parents and teachers. Microsoft's Learning Gateway was chosen as the platform (SEC, 2006c). Other initial features of the portal allowed users to

- review lesson plans, grades, study guides, and homework assignments;
- communicate directly with their peers through chats and discussion boards;

- access a virtual online library and resources center; and
- view the latest school news, school events, and important school announcements;

The portal received a positive response from educators and parents and was expanded in the 2006/2007 school year to twelve schools (SEC, 2006a). Teachers viewed increased parent engagement in their children's progress as one of the benefits of the K Net (SEC, 2008). Other reported benefits include economies gained from the students and teachers using the K Net to upload assignments, class notes, and information. Some teachers also began to share experiences and practice with each other online.

In 2009, with a client base of 37 schools, new features were added to the K Net to improve the user experience. These included a teacher's section that allowed collaboration and exchange of lessons and experiences, and direct parent access to student and school data. Additional training was provided to support teachers in integrating the portal into their teaching practice.

Learning Management System. In 2012, a new Learning Management System (LMS) was launched in 30 Independent Schools (SEC, 2012c). It provides the means to access

- student performance;
- teacher's agenda, e-mail, learning resources, tasks, calendars;
- communication for parents with the school; and
- e-content and the e-library.

In addition, all students and teachers (93,000 students and 15,000 teachers) of Independent Schools in Qatar were provided with an official and free e-mail address and Internet storage space, to be integrated with the LMS (SEC, 2012d).

To expand public knowledge and access to information, the SEC launched five portals during the 2012–2013 academic year, targeted at the various stakeholders in education, and more specifically e-education. These consist of the following:

- Public Portal, which covers all details related to e-learning as well as news and events.
- Innovative Teacher Portal allows collaboration and knowledge exchange between all Independent School teachers.
- SEC/Schools Collaboration Portal allows sharing of resources, news, circulars, advertisements, and documents between the SEC and all Independent Schools.
- School Portal provides each Independent School with its own Internet presence to share its vision, mission, news, and events.
- Statistical Portal provides reports and statistics related to the assessment of the SEC performance.

3. Learning and Instructional Resources

eSchoolbag. In 2006, the eSchoolbag program was implemented at Al Wakra School for Girls. It consisted of a tablet PC that supported digital inking technology, note taking and mind mapping, virtual geometric construction tools, and software for editing and sharing. The package also included customizable e-contents for science, math, and English mapped to the Qatari curriculum standards (SEC, 2006b).

In the second year of the eSchoolbag program, Robinson (2008) addressed the students' perceptions of the eSchoolbag and found that the diversity in educational values, fluency in English, and use of technology among the students' homes had an impact on the students' confidence in and satisfaction with the electronic device. As a result of the findings, the recommendation is that designers of e-learning in Qatar take into account this diversity and recognize that students do not all have equal access to support and assistance with the eSchoolbag at home. Required support must be available through the school. In addition, as core courses were taught in English, it was deemed important that the level of language used in the resources be suitable to adolescents for whom English was a second language. A third recommendation was that students should begin to develop skills and strategies required for e-learning, such as independence, confidence, and technical knowledge, at earlier grades, before they received the devices. Consistent access to hardware, software, and connectivity both at school and at home were also seen as important, as, without these, some students would benefit from transparency and ease of use of the technology, while others would be hindered by its complexity. A final recommendation was to ensure the means for communication, collaboration, and interaction were integral to the eSchoolbag, to avoid feelings of isolation in the students who are accustomed to a collective society.

Initiative to provide device for each student. In 2012, the SEC announced its intent to provide a personal mobile device for each student and teacher in Independent Schools to allow access to learning, communication, and collaboration capabilities inside and outside the school. Integration of the device into all aspects of the student's academic life is a key feature of the initiative. Pilot implementation took place in six Independent Schools over a period of six months, with male and female students from grades 9 to 11. Math, science, and foreign-language-learning outcomes are a particular focus of this new initiative as is access to an electronic library containing books, magazines, scientific journals, and audio-visual resources. Devices of different brands, all using the Windows 7 operating system, were distributed to students during the initial period. Teachers were trained on the use of the Microsoft Interactive Classroom, educational applications, and cyber-safety and student monitoring online (SEC, 2012b, 2012c, 2012d).

E-content. In order to facilitate access to electronic resources that are culturally and academically appropriate and aligned with Qatari standards, the SEC is creating digital content and related services in all areas of the curriculum in both Arabic and English. The content will include images, videos, and audio recordings (SEC, 2012c). This content is intended to support students' review and enrichment and to assist teachers in sourcing suitable materials to enhance their lessons.

E-library. An electronic library will further support access to digital resources through a formalized library management system and audio, video, and print resources intended to support students and lifelong learners (SEC, 2012b).

4. Professional Development

Under the Education for a New Era reform, many teachers received training on integrating ICT into teaching and learning (GSDP, 2011). Specialized training was provided in an attempt to help teachers adopt innovative teaching methods through integrating ICT into teaching and learning. Training included time management, planning, assessment (SEC, 2006c), and digital skills (SEC, 2007). Between 2008 and 2010, the proportion of teachers who received ICT training rose further, from 44 percent to 71 percent (ictQatar2011b), and in 2012 it was reported that teachers from 100 Independent Schools would be trained to use the LMS.

A second professional development opportunity, the Teacher's Net, was established in 2005 as "a meeting place for all teachers in Qatar to exchange views and information on teaching matters" (SEC, 2005a). Its purpose was to help teachers work together, exchange ideas on curricula, best practices, teaching resources, lesson plans, and pedagogy. It also provided teachers with a place to find suitable professional development programs, to document and disseminate the work of outstanding classroom teachers, and to help provide teachers with the knowledge and skills required to teach effectively.

Private Schools

While the adoption of e-learning strategies has been centrally mandated and supported by government policy in Independent Schools, implementation in private schools has been varied. Some schools enjoy the funding, human resources, and organizational mission to implement e-learning, while others are limited by a lack of infrastructure, financial constraints, and teacher expertise. For example, Qatar Academy, a private K–12 school in Qatar's Education City, has established a one-to-one laptop program with Windows Netbooks and MacBooks from Grades 2 to 10. Students in Grades 2 to 5 use individually assigned classroom laptops to collaborate, research, and present their work, while students in the higher grades use the MacBooks for learning, productivity, and file sharing. Access to files, e-mails, and content is supported by a school-wide wireless network and an online learning management system. In addition, the school has ten computer labs, mobile learning equipment, and audio and video recording equipment.

Launched in the 2011–2013 academic years, eMES is the first e-learning project in Indian CBSE education. The project, an initiative of the Modern English School (MES), comprises interactive classrooms with SMART boards, projectors, computers, and ICT. The aim is to offer e-learning gateways for students and staff to access digital resources and teaching support in an effort to integrate digital curriculum and methodologies into the school's academic curriculum. The implementation was supported through training sessions for teachers and by the establishment of awareness, management, and IT delivery teams to oversee the effort. Due to the size of the institution this is the largest Wi-Fi school campus in Qatar, serving more than 10,000 students (M.E.S. Indian School, n.d).

At the American School of Doha, technology is perceived as ubiquitous, necessary, and embedded, providing the tools students use to create, innovate, and problem solve "within and beyond school walls" (American School of Doha, n.d.). During the 2009–2010 school year, the school piloted several technologies, including 1:2 laptop ratio, tablets in science and math, SMART boards, and a small iPod Touch lab. A five-year plan was developed to implement a 1:1 device program from Grades 3 to 12. In subsequent years, netbooks, tablets, and interactive projectors have been added on a grade-by-grade basis.

Such are examples of schools that have the infrastructure, funding, and organizational will to implement e-learning. While these schools embrace e-education and promote it, e-education and ICT is notable in others by its absence.

Challenges in Implementing E-learning

By September 2012, 50 Independent Schools had begun implementing the Learning Management System components into their curricula, and performance reports during the year indicate steady growth in the adoption of e-education practices (SEC, 2013). In January 2013, the Supreme Education Council recognized several schools for their progress in integrating e-learning. By the 2014–2015 academic year, all Qatari schools will be expected to implement the e-learning experience in their classrooms. While the reaction to date has been positive among early adopting schools and they have been recognized and encouraged in their efforts, challenges remain, namely, teacher preparedness and e-education strategy integration with other education sectors.

Professional development, training courses, and a teacher's portal provide effective support for teachers who are digitally literate and interested in ICT. However, a significant number of teachers are seen as "far removed from the digital world" (El Ghanem, 2012). While teacher training and development has been an integral part of the adoption of e-education strategies since the early initiatives, the need for continued training and support will remain for the foreseeable future, since a large proportion of teachers in Qatar are expatriates from neighbouring Arab countries with relatively little formal training and experience with e-learning and, due to labour policies in Qatar, the turnover of teaching staff is relatively high.

A further challenge remains the discrepancy of experience and support for ICT within the home, with some families actively supporting students' use of computers and the Internet, while some families remain hesitant to allow their children access to such a wide information base.

To educate and empower parents and students to benefit safely and responsibly from online resources, the National Committee for Internet Safety (NCIS) has introduced 'cyber safety' initiatives in schools and begun dialogues with content creators and network providers to enable safe Internet use (ictQatar, 2012).

E-learning and Mobile Learning in the Workplace

Originally launched in May, 2007, the Qatar National e-Learning Portal offers online courses for ICT professionals and partner organizations, to encourage lifelong learning and professional development. By February, 2012, the portal had served nearly 8,000 learners from the government and more than 60 current partner organizations having completed 37,000 online technology and business courses (ictQatar, 2012)

The principal entity charged with promoting national-level employee development through e-learning is ictQatar. To build on the portal's success to date, current activities include

- promoting wider utilization of the 3,000 web-based training courses available on the portal;
- empowering organizations (especially SMEs) with enterprise learning management systems;
- supporting government and private sector organizations in their e-learning efforts;
- raising awareness of the benefits of e-learning; and
- providing technical support and training for organizations to administer and manage the portal (ictQatar, 2011a).

As learning technology emerges, Qatar is providing funding for research and development on the use of mobile technology in education and training. Qatar University completed a project that investigated the use of mobile technology for workplace learning (Samaka & Impagliazzo, 2013). A recent research project that was funded by the Qatar Foundation: Qatar National Research Fund is investigating the use of mobile technology to train the Qatar oil and gas workforce on communication skills so that workers can communicate effectively on the job. Preliminary results from the research project indicate that use of mobile technology for workplace training provides flexibility for learning and young workers are comfortable using the technology for learning (Ally et al., 2014; Ally, Samaka, Ismail, & Impagliazzo, 2013; Samaka & Impagliazzo, 2013).

Towards the Vision: Directions for the Future

The National Vision and sector strategies provide a roadmap to continue the progress towards a digitally mature population. The extent to which the opportunities offered by e-learning and mobile learning are accepted and implemented will depend on continued government support and direction, and further alignment of goals and strategies across education sectors. The National Development Strategy notes that, despite the progress in the first few years of implementation, it remains unclear whether these ICT opportunities are used to their full potential. A continuing training programme for teachers is likely required for students to fully benefit from ICT-supported learning. Also, no integrated strategy links ICT use in K–12 education with higher education and technical education and vocational training. Developing an integrated ICT strategy for education and training will be the starting point of an even more important role of ICT in this sector. (GSDP, 2011)

Acknowledgment

This publication was made possible by NPRP Grant #4-125-5-016 from the Qatar National Research Fund (a member of Qatar Foundation). The statements made herein are solely the responsibility of the authors.

References

Ally, M., Samaka, M., Ismail, L., & Impagliazzo, J. (2013, October). Use of mobile learning apps in workplace learning. *Bulletin of the IEEE Technical Committee on Learning Technology, 15*(4), 6–9.

Ally, M., Samaka, M., Impagliazzo, J., Mohamed, A., & Robinson, M. (2014). Workplace Learning Using Mobile Technology: A Case Study in the Oil and Gas Industry. In M. Kalz, Y. Bayyurt, & M. Specht (Eds). *Mobile as Mainstream–Towards Future Challenges in Mobile Learning*, pp. 269–281, doi 10.1007/978-3-319-13416-1.

American School of Doha. (n.d.). *Technology at ASD*. Retrieved from http://www.asd.edu.qa/page.cfm?p=675

Brewer, D. J., Augustine, C. H., Zellman, G. L., Ryan, G., Goldman, C. A., Stasz, C., & Constant, L. (2007). *Education for a new era: Design and implementation of K–12 education reform in Qatar*. Santa Monica, CA: RAND Corporation.

Computer News Middle East. (2011, November). *ICT Achievement Awards 2011, 238,* Retrieved from www.cnmeonline.com

El Ghanem, N. (2012) Qatar to bring e-Learning to all schools by 2014. *Al-Shorfa*. Retrieved from http://al-shorfa.com/en_GB/articles/meii/features/2012/09/12/feature-02.

General Secretariat for Development Planning. (2008). *Qatar national vision 2030*. Qatar: General Secretariat for Development Planning. Retrieved from http://www.gsdp.gov.qa/portal/page/portal/gsdp_en/qatar_national_vision/qnv_2030_document

General Secretariat for Development Planning. (2011). *Qatar national development strategy 2011–2016: Towards Qatar national vision 2030*. Qatar: General Secretariat for Development Planning. Retrieved from http://www.gsdp.gov.qa/portal/page/portal/gsdp_en

ictQatar (2011a). *Qatar's national ICT plan 2015: Advancing the digital agenda*. Doha, Qatar: Supreme Council of Information & Communication Technology. Retrieved from http://www.ictqatar.qa/en/documents/document/qatar-s-national-ict-plan-2015-advancing-digital-agenda

ictQatar (2011b). *Qatar's ICT landscape 2011*. Doha, Qatar: Supreme Council of Information & Communication Technology.

ictQatar (2012). *ictQATAR recognizes outstanding achievement in adopting e-learning* (press release). Retrieved from http://www.ictqatar.qa/en/news-events/news/ictqatar-recognizes-outstanding-achievement-adopting-e-learning

ictQatar (2013). *Qatar's ICT landscape 2013: Households and individuals*. Doha, Qatar: Supreme Council of Information & Communication Technology.

M.E.S. Indian School. (n.d.). *eMES learning*. Retrieved from http://www.mesqatar.org/admin/elearning.php

Robinson, M. (2008). *The experience of Gulf Arab students new to e-learning* (Master's thesis, Athabasca University, Canada). Retrieved from http://auspace.athabascau.ca/bitstream/2149/3059/1/martharobinsonThesis.pdf

Samaka, M., & Impagliazzo, J. (2013). Developing a platform for mobile learning using mLearn. *Proceedings of the International Conference on E-Technologies and Business on the Web (EBW2013)*, Bangkok, Thailand, pp. 258–262.

Supreme Education Council. (2005a). *Teachers meet in cyberspace* (press release). Retrieved from http://www.sec.gov.qa/En/Media/News/Pages/NewsDetails.aspx?NewsID=1974

Supreme Education Council. (2005b). *Online learning center* (press release). Retrieved from http://www.sec.gov.qa/En/Media/News/Pages/NewsDetails.aspx?NewsID=2043

Supreme Education Council. (2006a). *ictQATAR, SEC to implement e-education strategy* (press release). Retrieved from http://www.sec.gov.qa/En/Media/News/Pages/NewsDetails.aspx?NewsID=2252

Supreme Education Council. (2006b). *Al Wakra goes digital* (press release). Retrieved from http://www.sec.gov.qa/En/Media/News/Pages/NewsDetails.aspx?NewsID=2145

Supreme Education Council. (2006c). *12 independent schools to adopt Knowledge Net learning system* (press release). Retrieved from http://www.sec.gov.qa/En/Media/News/Pages/NewsDetails.aspx?NewsID=2280

Supreme Education Council. (2007). *ictQATAR borne with vocation to make technology part of learning* (press release). Retrieved from http://www.sec.gov.qa/En/Media/News/Pages/NewsDetails.aspx?NewsID=2351

Supreme Education Council. (2008). *School Knowledge Net extended to 25 schools by October 2009* (press release). Retrieved from http://www.sec.gov.qa/En/Media/News/Pages/NewsDetails.aspx?NewsID=2494

Supreme Education Council. (2009). *Wireless networks at Independent Schools* (press release). Retrieved from http://www.sec.gov.qa/En/Media/News/Pages/NewsDetails.aspx?NewsID=2825

Supreme Education Council. (2011). *Education and training sector strategy 2011–2016* (executive summary). Retrieved from http://www.sec.gov.qa/En/about/Documents/Stratgy2012E.pdf

Supreme Education Council. (2012a). *SEC enables e-education programs* (press release). Retrieved from http://www.sec.gov.qa/En/Media/News/Pages/NewsDetails.aspx?NewsID=3156

Supreme Education Council. (2012b). *Thirty independent schools apply e-learning portal LMS project* (press release). Retrieved from http://www.sec.gov.qa/En/Media/News/Pages/NewsDetails.aspx?NewsID=3173

Supreme Education Council. (2012c). SEC provides an email address for each student and teacher in Independent schools (press release). Retrieved from http://www.english.education.gov.qa/content/resources/detail/16815

Supreme Education Council (2012d). *Five educational portals on Internet to serve all stakeholders in learning process* (press release). Retrieved from http://www.sec.gov.qa/En/Media/News/Pages/NewsDetails.aspx?NewsID=3237

Supreme Education Council. (2013). *Independent schools show outstanding practices in e-education applications* (press release). Retrieved from http://www.sec.gov.qa/En/Media/News/Pages/NewsDetails.aspx?NewsID=3272

World Economic Forum. (2013). *The global information and technology report 2013 (GITR)*. Retrieved from http://www3.weforum.org/docs/WEF_GITR_Report_2013.pdf

18

Implementing Mobile Learning Devices Into Tertiary Classrooms
A UAE Case Study

Troy Priest and Kevin Schoepp

Introduction

In the spring of 2012, the UAE's Minister of Higher Education and Scientific Research, Sheikh Nahayan Bin Mubarak Al Nahayan, announced the launch of the largest mobile learning initiative in the world of higher education to date. The initiative was to include, in a collaborative manner, all three of the UAE's federal tertiary institutions and begin with approximately 13,000 students and faculty. Though remaining a face-to-face classroom learning environment, the initiative involved the allocation of iPads to all participants because of the opportunities provided by these mobile devices. The rationale behind this bold initiative was to help students better achieve 21st-century learning outcomes through the ubiquitous use of mobile learning devices. The North Central Regional Educational Laboratory defines 21st-century skills as digital-age literacy, inventive thinking, effective communication, and high productivity (Burkhardt et al., 2003). This approach is in line with the country's Vision 2021 (UAE Government, n.d.), which states that all Emiratis will be offered a first-rate education, one which allows them to reach their full potential, and one which prepares them to assume leadership roles in an innovative, knowledge-based economy. This chapter chronicles the planning, implementation, and evaluation of the first 18 months of this mobile learning initiative through the lens of Zayed University, one of the three participating institutions.

Context

Zayed University is a burgeoning 15-year-old comprehensive institution with a commitment to an American-modeled general education program and a set of institutional learning outcomes, which mirror commonly conceptualized 21st-century skills. Teaching approximately 8,500 male and female students in a gender-segregated environment, it is situated within the federal higher education system along with United Arab Emirates University (UAEU) and the Higher Colleges of Technology (HCT). The institution is an English-medium university serving the local Emirati population, who are mostly native-Arabic speakers, with two campuses in the UAE's major metropolitan centers of Dubai and Abu Dhabi. Accredited by the Middle States Commission on Higher Education, one of six US regional accreditors, ZU aims to become the leading university in the region.

Approximately 80% of the students begin their studies in a developmental English language program known as the Academic Bridge Program (ABP). Depending upon their level of English language proficiency, students spend anywhere from half of one semester to two full academic years in this program before entering the baccalaureate program. The baccalaureate program is divided into a three-semester core general education curriculum delivered by the University College (UC), followed by five semesters in a major. The majors are offered by six colleges, the College of Sustainability Sciences and Humanities, the College of Business, the College of Education, the College of Communication and Media Sciences, the College of Arts and Creative Enterprises, and the College of Technological Innovation. At any one time, the student population is roughly evenly distributed between the three institutional divisions.

It was within the ABP where the university launched the mobile learning initiative and began collaboration with UAEU and HCT. The plan is for a staged implementation, where students will have iPads within the ABP, and then, semester-by-semester, students with iPads will progress up through the general education program and then into the majors. Complete implementation across the university will take a minimum of 4.5 years. This staged rollout is recognized as one of the key success factors for a mobile learning initiative (Warschauer, 2011).

The Academic Bridge Program

The ABP is an integrated-skills English Language Program with approximately 3,000 students and approximately 150 faculty across both Abu Dhabi and Dubai campuses. Over the past 10 years, the program's curriculum and assessment system has become highly standardized to promote student success and measure students' linguistic and academic competencies. Students entering at the lowest level are approximately A1 as defined by the Common European Framework of Reference (CEFR).[1] These "basic users" complete two semester courses during their first year in the ABP and move to four termed courses in their second year. During their time in the ABP, students study 20 hours of academic English per week with a heavy emphasis on reading and writing skills. The exit requirements for the ABP and entry into the baccalaureate program are successful completion of the ABP's highest course and an International English Language Testing System (IELTS) score of 5.0.[2] Students leave at approximately B2, or as "independent users" of English.

Beyond the linguistic challenges, students are often ill-prepared for academic life in an American-styled tertiary educational institution. The ABP has found that students face various other challenges, including "dependence on teacher, lack of independent learning skills, lack of critical thinking skills, inability to apply learned skills in new contexts, lack of study skills, and lack of motivation" (ABP Curriculum Document, 2012). These challenges indicated a need for 21st-century skills. Prior to the announcement of the mobile learning initiative, the ABP began investigating and piloting challenged-based and project-based curricular innovations that added authenticity and creativity to our existing skills-based, performance-based language curriculum. However, with the introduction of iPads, the integration of 21st-century skills, project-based learning, and challenged-based learning into the language curriculum became a priority as it became apparent that the iPads could be leveraged to support these alternative pedagogies.

Pedagogical Rationales

In the context of this mobile learning initiative, it is important to understand the pedagogical rationales that underpin our mobile learning initiative and our second language curriculum. They share a common foundation that focuses on constructivist learning principles—active, engaged, and reflective learning through which learners construct their own understanding, principles which are believed to foster 21st-century skills (Warschauer, 2011). Without this pedagogical underpinning, as the initiative moves up into the rest of the university, the iPad could become a distraction which hinders learning (Sana, Weston, & Cepeda, 2013), rather than a tool which can help foster innovative and engaging pedagogies.

There was a strong pedagogical rationale for beginning the mobile learning initiative within the English language program, namely that the language classroom has long been at the vanguard of interactive and collaborative learning environments. Language classroom pedagogy, though driven by its own literature, strongly adheres to constructivist learning principles. These principles are now being put forward as the foundation for mobile learning pedagogy and for the development of 21st-century skills (Warschauer, 2011). There is an inherent fit between second language instruction and effective pedagogical practices integrating mobile learning devices.

There are two main theories of second language learning that provide the pedagogical rationale for effective mobile learning pedagogy and that can be framed within broader constructivist learning principles. The first theory has become known as the *input hypothesis* or the *monitor model*. Krashen (1982) asserted that language is acquired as learners engage in meaningful interaction in the second language, and that a learner requires language input just beyond their current level in order to advance. Krashen calls this L+1. The second pertinent theory comes from Long via the *interaction hypothesis* (Long, 1985, 1996, as cited in Brown, 2000), which posits that authentic interaction and negotiated meaning in the target language, not just comprehensible input, are keys to effective language learning. It is the role of the teacher to provide authentic language learning activities with collaborative tasks that are pitched just beyond the existing proficiency of the student. Both of these theories clearly reflect constructivist understanding that instructors create learning opportunities which are relevant to the students and encourage students to be authentic problem solvers through an active, collaborative, and conversational process (Jonassen, 1999). The primacy of interaction and the importance of input just beyond current skill level also mirrors Vygotsky's (1978) zone of proximal development, which is

> the distance between the actual developmental level as determined by independent problem solving and the level of potential development as determined through problem solving under adult guidance, or in collaboration with more capable peers.
>
> *(p. 86)*

The concepts of collaboration and problem-solving are recognized as key 21st-century skills. Given the similar pedagogical foundation of the constructivist approach, the language classroom seemed the logical place to begin the mobile learning implementation. It has provided us with many *early wins* and *best practices* which we are now showcasing as part of an ongoing faculty development program.

Though interactive and constructivist in nature, language classrooms integrating a mobile device still require a model or framework to guide the effective implementation and professional development opportunities for faculty. To this end, the SAMR model, which progresses from the bottom up (see Figure 18.1)—*Substitution, Augmentation, Modification,* and *Redefinition* (Puentedura, 2013) was used as the guiding framework because of its simplicity and use of examples of the model in action. We were also able to work directly with Dr. Puentedura early in the implementation phase. Its straightforwardness has allowed it to become embedded into our conversations and professional dialogues about effective integration of iPads. At its core, the model offers a way of thinking about using technology, or in our case, iPads, within the regular classroom learning environment, while maintaining a focus on sound pedagogy and the promotion of 21st-century learning outcomes. At the lowest level of the SAMR model, *Substitution,* computing technology

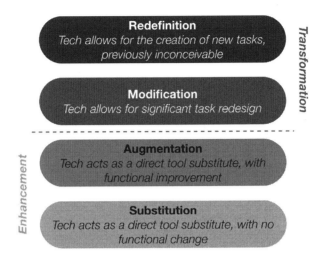

Figure 18.1 SAMR Model

Reprinted with permission from Ruben R. Puentedura, Hippasus; from "SAMR and TPCK: An introduction," by R. Puentedura, 2013.

simply replaces what was previously used. An example would be a .pdf version of a textbook with no enhancements over a traditional paper-based text. As there is no 'added value' in this example, faculty would legitimately be able to ask *why bother*? At the second level, *Augmentation*, the technology serves as a substitution, but it does offer some degree of functionality that enhances learning opportunities. An electronic textbook which allows the creation of shared notes would be an accurate example of augmentation. *Modification,* the third level, is where true transformation of the learning environment takes place. In a modified classroom, students can work on common tasks such as writing an essay, but may do it in a collaborative manner using a tool such as Google Docs. At *Redefinition,* the classroom is truly transformed into a constructivist learning environment as the tasks and activities students undertake offer learning opportunities that were not previously imagined without the technology. For example, students use the video camera on the mobile device with physics apps to measure velocity and view and plot trajectory of objects in motion.

Pilot Project

In April 2012, when the mobile initiative was announced, there was very little research available on the best use of mobile devices in a tertiary ESL context. The relatively short lead in time to the fall 2012 implementation made it difficult to collect data and conduct research into the pedagogical opportunities of mobile devices. This presented a significant challenge.

Whereas Wollongong University conducted a four-semester investigation into the pedagogical opportunities provided by mobile devices in order to avoid a technology-driven pedagogy (Herrington et al., 2009), the ABP had just five months from the announcement of the introduction of iPads to the actual rollout itself, and two of these months were taken up by summer vacation. With such a short time period to prepare, the program decided to devote the time and available resources to training faculty on the use of the device itself, and to launch an immediate exploratory pilot project.

The pilot investigated the technical and pedagogical implication of iPads in the classroom. Over 90 students, seven sections, and eleven teachers participated in the pilot that lasted for eight weeks and explored both the technical and pedagogical implications of the mobile devices. Feedback from the pilot was used to make informed pedagogical decisions about which applications could be best leveraged to achieve curricular outcomes.

The pilot team also collaborated with the Computer Services Department (CSD) to investigate and test various technical issues such as ways for teachers and students using the classroom projector to share content to the class through mirroring tools (such as Reflections and Apple TVs). It became clear from the pilot that the ability for students to share and collaborate through instantaneous mirroring could have a transformative effect on the classroom. Using these mirroring tools, teachers could have students exhibit their work with the rest of the class quickly and easily. The students' "audience" now included their peers in the class rather than just the teacher. This motivated many students to work more diligently knowing their peers would review their work. Teachers immediately noticed that the quality and completeness of the students' work was improved. These mirroring tools also allowed the teacher to move about the classroom and away from the front of the room while still controlling what was projected at the front of the classroom. This allowed the teacher to present information using iPad while at the same time moving around the room checking students' work, mentoring, and so forth.

Technological Considerations

Long before the announcement of the implementation and the development of the exploratory pilot, campus-based technical challenges existed. The most pressing was that the new Abu Dhabi campus did not have ubiquitous Wi-Fi and had very limited coverage in all but a few classrooms and common areas. Teacher offices had hardwired ports but no Wi-Fi. With iPads only able to connect to the Internet via Wi-Fi, this meant teachers who were expected to use the iPads in the classroom did not have Wi-Fi access in their offices where they spend much of their time preparing their lessons. As a result, the CSD team had to come up with a series of workarounds. To address the Wi-Fi issues on the Abu Dhabi campus, CSD prioritized the installation of a robust wireless network in all ABP classrooms capable of handling 20 plus devices per classroom. A case was also made to procure MacBook Pros for ABP faculty. One rationale for this is MacBook's ability to create a network stable and secure Wi-Fi hotspot using the office wired connection. This allowed faculty to create a password protected wireless connection for their iPads.

Although mirroring the iPads and projecting them using the classroom projector via the iPad's AirPlay afforded many pedagogical opportunities, it created additional technical challenges for CSD. During the pilot, teachers tested Apple TVs in the classroom that used AirPlay to mirror the device through the projector. The first challenge was actually purchasing Apple TVs in the UAE as they were not yet on the market. Again, workarounds had to be devised, including the piloting of third party applications such as Reflections and AirServer.

Another decision by all three institutions to provide a uniform suite of paid applications to all foundations' students and faculty posed serious logistical challenges. Since these applications were being purchased by the respective institutions and not the users, an unprecedented gifting system for apps had to be created.

Collaboration Between Institutions

A national mobile learning steering committee was formed by the three institutions shortly after the decision was made to adopt iPad. This steering committee was charged with coordinating the preparations for the implementation of these mobile devices. Reporting to the steering committee were four national working committees: pedagogy, content, technology, and procurement. Throughout the next several months these committees met to coordinate the implementation of mobile devices across the three institutions' 20 campuses.

Months before the announcement of the implementation, the national steering committee had been in discussions with Apple regarding their support. Apple was actively involved from the beginning in the planning and preparation of the project and offered technical support, help with procurement of devices, and in professional development support by the Apple education team.

In spring 2012, the three institutions began a "train the trainer" program. The institutions selected a group of enthusiasts, called iChampions, from the three institutions to explore the pedagogic opportunities of iPads, who would then go back and cascade training to faculty within their respective institutions. Apple and the three institutions organized a series of cross-institutional professional development conferences. As the implementation started in the foundation programs across the institutions, the pedagogic focus was on English language instruction and mathematics. Through collaboration, the iChampions explored and shared ways to incorporate challenge-based learning and project-based learning into the foundations' curricula.

Content and Resources

From the announcement of the implementation, the ABP decided that all teachers and students had access to paper copies of all course materials for the first semester, even though digital versions were made available for most levels. This was decided for two reasons. First, the commercial books used by the ABP at that time had extremely limited interactivity. Indeed, if we applied the SAMR model, it could be said that the digital version of the materials were actually "subtracting" functionality (i.e., the paper versions offered more functionality than did the new nonannotatable versions of the e-textbooks). Second, as there was little research on e-readers or e-reading within an English-language-learning context, the ABP decided to utilize both paper and electronic resources.

However, during the spring semester of 2012, the ABP allocated resources to develop a variety of iPad-mediated materials. This included converting existing in-house materials to interactive PDFs and eBooks; creating new language-rich iPad training materials for students and teachers; and creating new materials specifically for the iPads. By fall 2012, when the rollout began, each of the ABP's six levels had iPad-mediated materials. These materials were created with a focus on sound English language learning pedagogies while leveraging the features of iBooks Author and third party applications. The use of embedded third party applications and native iBooks Author applications, or widgets, allowed the materials to be more media-rich with the inclusion of interactive picture galleries, videos, audio files, and interactive maps. Other widgets allowed students to reorder content by dragging and dropping content into the correct order, labeling images, create and collate glossaries of vocabulary in the text, answer multiple choice questions, etc., all while receiving instant feedback. Other applications allowed multiple students to collaborate by working on a single text simultaneously. These materials also included project-based activities, which required students to use tools and applications that fostered creativity. For example, rather than writing a traditional book report for their reading course, students created iMovies and interactive Keynotes to demonstrate their understanding of the text.

Professional Development

During the ABP pilot in spring 2012 a series of professional development opportunities were planned for faculty. However, with the exception of the teachers on the pilot, key faculty involved in the planning process of the mobile learning initiative, and a few early adopters of iPad within the department, the vast majority of the 150 ABP teachers did not have iPads.

The purchase of a large number of iPads took time and faculty received their university-provided devices in early June. This posed obvious challenges for the faculty development efforts from April to June. One solution was to provide a series of "faculty familiarization sessions", where 20 or so faculty at a time could explore the interactivity and features of the iPad. Immediately after the deployment of iPads to faculty, the ABP hosted a daylong faculty professional development training session on these mobile devices and various key apps. While initial training often focused on the lower levels of the SAMR model, substitution and augmentation, in order to get faculty comfortable and confident using the iPads, the goal was always to transition to the more impactful upper levels of the model, modification and redefinition. Understanding of the SAMR model allowed us to phase in professional development opportunities that targeted *Substitution* and *Augmentation* and begin to move towards *Modification* and *Redefinition* because it is only there where transformation takes place. The shared understanding of SAMR helped make conversations about this transition far simpler.

Returning faculty had two months to familiarize themselves with the device and reflect on the training and SAMR model. In the two weeks before the start of the academic year, the ABP organized an intensive professional development series. The focus of the sessions was to go beyond app training and investigate the ways apps and other tools on the mobile learning device could be used and sequenced in workflows to achieve curricular outcomes.

After classes began in fall 2012 and teachers were asked to incorporate the device into their lessons, the professional development and support needs of faculty for the first few months required a three-pronged approach. A series of workshops on effective use of mobile devices to achieve curricular outcomes were organized. These workshops were developed based on teachers' needs and feedback from the faculty. The ABP also organized a "brown bag" series where teachers could share ideas, successes, and failures in an informal environment. An iPad Help Center was also set up as a place where teachers could go for technical or pedagogical help. The iPad Help Center also provided on-call assistance to teachers during their class time.

Rollout into the UC and the Emergence of the CEI

As the entire ABP began to teach with iPads during the fall 2012 semester, planning and professional development was underway within the University College because students with iPads would begin their first semester of general education courses in spring 2013. Departments within UC engaged in weekly professional development sessions focused on their unique disciplinary requirements throughout the semester. While professional development was first focused on iPad basics, it quickly transitioned into pedagogically focused learning. As Warshauer (2011) has shown, long-term and sustained professional development that centers on pedagogy is far more likely to lead to a successful mobile learning initiative.

The UC was fortunate on two fronts because they were able to turn to the ABP and its emerging pool of experts, as well as to the recently relaunched Center for Educational Innovation (CEI), the university's faculty development office. The CEI was able to provide basic iPad training and then lead and organize pedagogically based workshops. Near the end of the first semester, the CEI organized the largest professional development event in the history of the institution. Across two days, more than 90 faculty and staff delivered over 160 workshops, with many of these dedicated to mobile learning. In the spring of 2013, the UC began using iPads within their first semester courses. They have developed a faculty-led mobile learning leadership team and have started to transition to iBooks resources within their curriculum.

Now that the urgency of implementation has ended, professional development offerings have decreased and shifted from the ABP into the CEI. The CEI realized the essential role that the scholarship of teaching and learning must play in any large-scale mobile learning initiative in higher education; it cosponsored a regional mobile learning research symposium, which will lead to a special edition of the journal *Learning and Teaching in Higher Education: Gulf Perspectives.* To prepare for the continued rollout of iPads into the majors, the CEI also launched a competitive iPad pilot targeting the colleges. Though still one academic year away, there were far more faculty submissions to participate in the pilot than there were available iPads. Eventually, the pilot included 13 faculty and nearly 300 students. It will be expanded to additional faculty and a further 200 students due to the success of the pilot project. While the current faculty pilot participants are obviously the *innovators* and *early adopters* (Rogers, 1995), they are expected to become mobile learning leaders within their respective colleges.

One way in which the CEI is capturing and disseminating the emerging best practices within the pilot, the UC, and the ABP is through a set of mobile learning showcase videos[3] in which key faculty are given the opportunity to share successful classroom practice and explain the ways in which they feel the iPads have transformed their classroom. Housed on the CEI website, these short three-minute videos highlight some of the innovative ways faculty throughout the university are integrating mobile learning into their teaching. This provides a safe and nonthreatening way for skeptical or curious faculty to hear directly from colleagues who are working at the same institution, teaching the same students, and facing similar challenges. This ongoing communication among peers will be a significant driver in the success of the project.

Research Into Faculty Perceptions

At the beginning of the fall semester 2012, we had a unique opportunity to collect baseline data on faculty attitudes, beliefs, and skill levels related to the iPad. This data was collected using a modified version of Jordan's (2010) Faculty Attitudes Toward Online and Blended Learning survey. The same survey was administered again at the start of the second semester for a pre- and postcomparison, and on both occasions more than 60 faculty completed the survey.[4] Backed by an intensive faculty development program, we had hypothesized that the faculty as a whole would have started to progress up the SAMR model. Though we do not have an exact measure of SAMR, there were two survey questions that do provide insights into this model. The first was labeled the *Stages of Technology Adoption* (see Figure 18.2), which included six stages with descriptors ranging from *Stage 2: Learning the process* (I am currently trying to learn the basics. I am sometimes frustrated using technology including iPads. I lack confidence when using technology including iPads) to *Stage 6: Creative application to new contexts* (I can apply what I know about technology including iPads in the classroom. I am able to use it as an instructional tool and integrate it into the curriculum).[5]

The other item was labeled *Technology Integration Phases* (see Figure 18.3), which comprised five phases ranging from *Stage 1: Familiarity* (I know the importance of technology including iPads. I have some basic skills but do not think I have sufficient expertise to use technology without assistance. I rarely require the use of technology to complete assignments) to *Stage 5: Facilitation* (I share my knowledge of technology including iPads through modeling, peer coaching, and mentoring. I encourage students and coworkers to experiment with different applications and technologies).

For both instruments the results indicated that there was substantial progression through the developmental levels, more than we had anticipated, in fact. For example, with the adoption scale, 34% of faculty placed themselves at the high-end stages of *Adaptation* or *Creative Application* at the beginning of the semester. At the start of the second semester, a full 57% placed themselves at these stages. The lower end perspective measured through the integration scale, where we initially

Stages of Technology Adoption

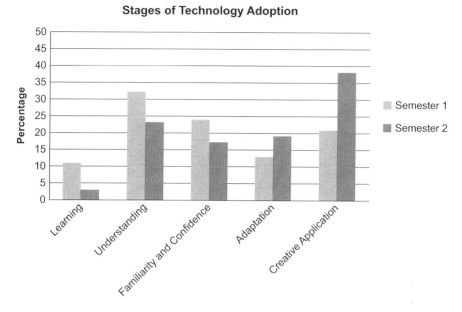

Figure 18.2 Stages of Technology Adoption

Technology Integration Phases

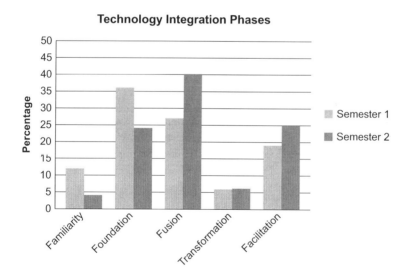

Figure 18.3 Technology Integration Phases

had 48% of faculty at the two rudimentary phases, we only had 29% at the beginning of Semester 2. Given the timelines of three years plus, often associated with educational change initiatives (Hall & Hord, 2001), we are quite pleased with the development that has occurred. Significant progress had been made and many faculty appear to be transitioning or have transitioned to the upper levels of the SAMR model.

Four other items within this survey instrument provide some important insights into the perceptions of faculty in terms of their level of preparedness and comfort in integrating the

Table 18.1 Faculty Preparedness and Comfort

Survey Item	Semester 1	Semester 2
I have had adequate training in technology use, including iPads.	54%	75%
I have a sufficient level of technical support at my campus for iPads and associated technology.	73%	76%
I feel comfortable using iPads for classroom instruction.	59%	77%
I feel prepared to effectively integrate technology (iPads) into the curriculum in my classroom.	46%	75%

iPad. Table 18.1 shows the percentage of faculty who indicated they either agreed or strongly agreed with the statements from a 5-point Likert scale. Large increases are evident except for technical support that began as a highly rated item. The data seems to indicate that at the start of the second semester, fully three quarters of the faculty feel pedagogically prepared, supported, and able to work well with iPads for instructional purposes. This supports the earlier assertion that faculty are progressing up through the SAMR model. In addition, it is evidence that the intensive professional development programs that were underway during the spring, summer, and throughout the semester appear to have been a success. We have seen this firsthand through the types of professional development that has been requested and delivered. Where at the start it was rudimentary and basic, much of it is now centered on innovative pedagogical practices such as problem-based learning.

Next Steps

The momentum of this first year must be maintained. In order to achieve this various projects and initiatives through the ABP, the CEI, and the CSD are underway. The ABP is embarking on an ambitious in-house materials-creation project mediated through iBooks for the upper two levels. The materials and topics are currently being developed to incorporate more 21st-century themes such as entrepreneurship, sustainability, and service learning. These books will exploit the interactive widgets provided by the iBooks Author application and third-party providers.

The ABP is also formalizing project-based learning in its assessment system at all levels with the development of the integrated-skills project. These projects require students to draw on and develop 21st-century skills, such as creativity, critical thinking, collaboration, and problem solving by creating media-rich, iPad-mediated projects. Along with 21st-century skills, students are assessed on language skills such as reading, writing, listening, and speaking, as well as lexical and grammatical accuracy.

The ABP in collaboration with the CEI is currently collecting information and exploring the pedagogical implications of the mobile devices through the formation of action learning groups. These groups allow teachers to explore and collaborate on effective use of mobile devices in teaching and learning.

The CEI has recently completed a teaching and learning professional development series into project-based learning, is planning to repeat the series, and is planning other institution-wide series specific to mobile learning. Another way the institution is moving forward is to emphasize research into mobile learning. Through the internal research funding system and in collaboration with the CEI, faculty research into mobile learning will be given a priority and an external partnership with a major research institute is being pursued. The goal is to create a large-scale longitudinal research project developed through a design-based research methodology. Such a methodology is ideal because it partners teachers and practitioners with researchers that can provide the research expertise and contextual knowledge required to conduct larger scale projects (Anderson & Shattuck, 2012). The key technical issue is that the CSD will have the Abu Dhabi campus wireless project completed by fall 2013. However, solutions to effective mirroring still need to be found.

Conclusion

Though this massive mobile higher education learning initiative began as a mandate, it has proven to be a grassroots success. As Hall and Hord (2001) have stated, mandates that include continued communication, considerable professional development, and an ongoing longitudinal support can succeed. In addition, the speed at which it all began provided a necessary sense of urgency that can be a key success factor in any mobile learning initiative (Ally, 2013). At this stage, with the initiative more than one year old, the main sense of urgency has dissipated, the semester-by-semester rollout is ongoing, and faculty development is becoming formalized through the CEI. If mobile learning is to remain one of the institutional hallmarks, future success will require consistent faculty development and an ongoing commitment to evaluating the effectiveness of the initiative. Faculty want evidence that the innovative pedagogical practices being promoted help motivate learners, keep learners engaged, and, most importantly, increase student learning and foster 21st-century skills.

Notes

1 An expanded explanation of the CEFR is available at: http://www.cambridgeenglish.org/images/126011-using-cefr-principles-of-good-practice.pdf
2 IELTS scores are further explained at: http://www.ielts.org/institutions/test_format_and_results/ielts_band_scores.aspx
3 Mobile learning best practices: http://www.zu.ac.ae/main/en/cei/Mobile_Learning/
4 The survey has been completed by ABP faculty twice, but only once by UC faculty because they began implementation in Semester 2. Reported results are only for ABP because they offer comparison data.
5 *Stage 1: Awareness* has not been included in this analysis because it was never selected.

References

ABP Curriculum Document. (2012). Unpublished document. Zayed University, Abu Dhabi, UAE.

Ally, M. (2013, April). *Mobile learning: From research to practice to impact education.* Paper presented at Mobile Learning, Gulf Perspectives, Abu Dhabi, UAE.

Anderson, T., & Shattuck, J. (2012). Design-based research: A decade of progress in education research? *Educational Researcher, 41*(1), 16–25.

Brown, H. D. (2000). *Principles of language learning and teaching.* White Plains, NY: Longman.

Burkhardt, G., Monsour, M., Valdez, G., Dawson, M., Lemke, C., Coughlin, E., Thadani, V., & Martin, C. (2003). *enGauge 21st century skills for 21st century learners.* North Central Regional Educational Laboratory. Retrieved from http://pict.sdsu.edu/engauge21st.pdf

Hall, G. E., & Hord, S. H. (2001). *Implementing change: Patterns, principles, and potholes.* London, UK: Allyn & Bacon.

Herrington, J., Herrington, A., Mantei, J., Olney, I., & Ferry, B. (2009). Using mobile technologies to develop new ways of teaching and learning. In J. Herrington, A. Herrington, J. Mantei, I. Olney, & B. Ferry (Eds.), *New technologies, new pedagogies: Mobile learning in higher education* (pp. 1–14). Wollongong, New South Wales, Australia: University of Wollongong. Retrieved from http://ro.uow.edu.au/

Jonassen, D. (1999). Designing constructivist learning environments. In C. M. Reigeluth (Ed.), *Instructional-design theories and models, volume II: A new paradigm of instructional theory* (pp. 215–239). Mahwah, NJ: Erlbaum.

Jordan, D. (2010). *Faculty attitudes toward online and blended learning (FABOL).* Unpublished survey. Stockton, CA: University of the Pacific.

Krashen, S. (1982). *The input hypothesis: Issues and implications.* London, UK: Longman.

Puentedura, R. (2013). *SAMR and TPCK: An introduction.* Retrieved from http://www.hippasus.com/rrpweblog/archives/2013/03/28/SAMRandTPCK_AnIntroduction.pdf

Rogers, E. M. (1995). *Diffusion of innovations* (4th ed.). New York, NY: Free Press.

Sana, F., Weston, T., & Cepeda, N. J. (2013). Laptop multitasking hinders classroom learning for both users and nearby peers. *Computers and Education, 62,* 24–31.

United Arab Emirates Government. (n.d.). *Vision 2021.* Retrieved from http://www.vision2021.ae/downloads/UAE-Vision2021-Brochure-English.pdf

Vygotsky, L. (1978). *Mind in society: The development of higher psychological processes.* Cambridge, MA: Harvard University Press.

Warschauer, M. (2011). *Learning in the cloud: How (and why) to transform schools with digital media.* New York, NY: Teachers College Press.

19

E-learning Implementation at an Open University

The Case of Universitas Terbuka (The Indonesia Open University)

Dewi Padmo and Sri Harijati

Introduction

In many countries, information and communication technology (ICT) has become an integral part of the learning delivery system. The Indonesia Open University (Universitas Terbuka, or UT) is a distance learning institution and realizes that ICT plays an important role in the administration, management, and delivery of learning. The services of UT cover all of the Indonesia provinces as well as some overseas countries. With such a large coverage area, utilization of ICT at UT has become very important. This chapter will share UT's experience in utilizing ICT, specifically e-learning, as one of the academic services it provides faculty and students.

Research suggests that educational institutions that seek to implement ICT as a learning innovation should pay attention to the answers they receive to questions such as how, what, and why (Mahdizadeh, Biemans, & Mulder, 2008). Furthermore, Mahdizadeh et al. (2008) mentioned that when universities promote ICT use, they should understand teachers' and learners' attitude toward it. Therefore, when utilizing ICT to implement e-learning, teachers' and students' e-readiness should be considered. Bowles (2004) defined e-readiness as an organization's readiness to use e-learning in many aspects. Bowles (2004) also stated that an organization's readiness to take advantage of e-learning should be declared before the organization introduces e-learning. For UT, concerns related to the wide use of ICT include the limited ICT infrastructure in Indonesia as well as IT literacy and the readiness of human resources (including faculty and students).

Context and Challenges

One of the main reasons for using ICT at UT is the geographical aspect. Indonesia is one of the largest archipelago countries with a population of over 240 million, the fourth most populous country in the world. The country is mostly water (81%) with about 17,508 islands divided into 33 provinces, 497 districts, and some 69,065 villages (per January 2009; Ministry of Home Affairs, 2012). Indonesia has five major islands: Java, Sumatra, Kalimantan, Sulawesi, and Papua. Java is the most populous island, and more than half of the population of Indonesia (65%) lives on that island. Although the majority of Indonesians are Moslem, Indonesia consists of various ethnic, linguistic, and religious groups. With such a large and diverse population, ICT would seem to be the perfect solution to connect all people in the country. Unfortunately, ICT access in Indonesia is still limited and mostly concentrated in big cities.

Public access to ICT requires an infrastructure, a regulatory framework, and financing. Among the three, infrastructure plays the key role for widening access. Public access to ICT can be viewed from rates of Internet penetration—that is, the percentage of Internet users within a region in comparison to its population. Despite the fact that 57% of the world population lives in Asia, Internet penetration in Asia is only about 27.5%, while the world average is at 34.3%. Specifically for Indonesia, although Indonesia is within the top five Internet users in Asia, its penetration rate is only 22.1% (as of June 2012) and even lower if we look at the penetration of Internet subscribers (1.9%). It appears that China has the highest number of people who actively use the Internet, followed by India and Japan. Within ASEAN countries, Singapore seems to have the highest penetration (75%), followed by Malaysia (60.7%). These data indicate that the ICT infrastructure in Asia, and particularly in Indonesa, is still very limited, hindering wide access of the public to the Intenet and thus to the ample open educational resources available in the network (Internet World Stats, 2012).

It is interesting to note that the growth of Internet users in Indonesia is probably mostly the result of the high mobile phone penetration, which is very high (110%), with the number of subscribers passing 260 million by early 2012, up by almost 200 million from just five years earlier (Evans, 2012). The wide use of mobile devices has also made Indonesia one of three countries with the highest number of Facebook users at almost 48 million (Internet World Stats, 2012).

The Internet access challenge was also revealed by a web accessibility survey conducted by PANdora Network in 13 of Asia's countries (Baggaley et al., 2007). The survey found that the time taken to access web pages between major Asian cities (browser loading times) was up to four times slower than commonly prescribed as acceptable, and pages frequently failed to load. At surveyed institutions, all web hits went through over 20 intermediate web servers before reaching their target, or failing to reach their destinations altogether. By comparison, access or hits by Canadian users may only go through six hops to reach a destination site. The survey revealed that Asian web hits are commonly routed through countries such as the US and Russia. Thus, improved local web routes are needed to address this problem.

Gradually, the Indonesian government is also building the Internet infrastructure in the outermost, farthest, and left-behind regions, through the Ministry of Communication and its Internet Service Plans Circumference (PLIK) and Mobile Internet Service Plans Circumference (MPLIK) programs. With these initiatives, especially with the District Internet Car Service Center at all districts in Indonesia, by 2014 the number of Internet users in Indonesia has reached 153 million, which is 61.2% of the population (Noor II, 2014). The development of mobile technology seems to have compensated for the lack of physical ICT infrastructure by providing people access to the Internet. In fact, this has given rise to the huge potential market for the use of mobile devices in Indonesia. Data show that the penetration rate of the mobile phone (number) in Indonesia has reached over 110%.

Universitas Terbuka at a Glance

Universitas Terbuka (UT) is a state university and the only university in Indonesia that is entirely based on a distance education system. It was established in 1984 and was designed to be a flexible and inexpensive university, focusing on serving people who do not have the opportunity to attend conventional, face-to-face higher education institutions for various reasons, including lack of funding, living in isolated and rural areas, and working full time. With distance education, it is expected that UT will increase access to higher education and at the same time promote equity of quality higher education to all citizens of Indonesia.

There are three policies in place to widen access to and ensure equity in higher education. The first policy governs operation on a nation-wide basis. The operational system is managed by a head office (HO) in Jakarta and 37 regional offices (ROs) located throughout the country. The ROs are responsible for carrying out the daily operational activities, including student registration, face-to-face tutorials, some administrative counseling, and examinations. Thus, ROs are an important part of UT's system of organization and management.

The second policy governs access, equity, and the selection of technology. UT is designed to be a flexible and affordable university. The challenge for UT has been to provide quality instruction that is accessible to all students with different characteristics, levels of economy, access to ICT, as well as learning habits. It is based on the findings of many studies combined with the availability and accessibility of different kinds of technologies to different students. Some UT students have limited access to technology and limited proficiency in the use of computer and Internet technologies. Other UT students do not have access to a computer and the Internet, and are computer illiterate. Currently, UT is using print media as the basis for the design and delivery of its multimedia learning packages, and a range of learning support services assists the design and delivery of the learning materials.

UT distance learner students are expected to study independently using the provided course materials. Students, as needed, may take advantage of the various learning support services available to them. The learning support services include tutorials (face to face and online), nonprint (offline) and online supplementary learning materials, dry laboratory, online test exercises, digital library, e-bookstore, and online examination. In short, the design of the instructional system is that of a "supermarket" and provides a place for students to take advantage of different learning support services according to their circumstances.

The third policy governs and accommodates the different needs of students by offering various study programs. UT offers more than 1,000 courses within 33 study programs under four faculties and one school: the Faculty of Economics, the Faculty of Social and Political Sciences, the Faculty of Mathematics and Natural Science, the Faculty of Teacher Training and Educational Sciences, and the Graduate School. The Faculty of Teacher Training and Educational Sciences offers only in-service training programs for practicing primary and secondary school teachers. Starting in 1990, when UT was appointed by the Indonesian government to upgrade primary teacher qualification, the study program of Primary School Teacher Trainings (for classroom teachers) is the biggest program, with a total student body of almost 468,000 students in 2012.

As a result, UT has been able to reach many students in Indonesia who would otherwise not have access to higher education. This outcome is reflected in the large number of students and the spread of their age groups, study programs, and locations. In total, UT has a student body of 585,700 active students. Table 19.1 shows the number of students by faculty in the second semester of 2012.

With regard to student characteristics, UT's students are mostly working adults (92%) and female (67%). While some studies suggest that female students are underrepresented in higher education, this is not currently the case at UT. UT has a higher number of female students than male students. Another important piece of data is the range of students with regard to age. Studies have shown that distance education can serve the education needs of people who have passed "traditional" school age.

Table 19.2 shows that UT successfully caters to older students and that 80% of UT's students are above the typical age of the average university student (i.e., over 24 years old). The

Table 19.1 The Number of Students (2012.2)

Faculty	No. of Students	%
Teacher Training	467,969	79.90
Science	4,696	0.80
Social Science	87,289	14.90
Economics	23,834	4.07
Graduate School	1,912	0.33
Total	585,700	100

Table 19.2 Students' Profile by Age (2012.2)

Age	No. of Students	%
= <24	114,730	19.59
25–29	153,801	26.26
30–34	102,400	17.48
35–39	57,108	9.75
40–44	63,720	10.88
– >45	93,941	16.04
Total	585,700	100

Table 19.3 Students' Profile by Location (2012.2)

Sumatra	167,588	28.6
Java	225,938	38.6
Kalimantan	59,621	10.2
Nusa Tenggara	42,546	7.2
Sulawesi	73,328	12.5
Moluccas	8,829	1.5
Papua	6,536	1.1
Abroad	1,314	0.2
Total	585,700	100

older student is someone who, for whatever reason, did not previously have the opportunity to attend higher education. This may be due to the student's economic and/or geographical situation. Many students and alumni state that UT provides a second chance for individuals to obtain a university degree without having to leave work, home, or their town.

Another example of how UT addresses equity in higher education is by the representation of students throughout the country. Table 19.3 shows that UT students come from all islands (small islands are combined with the closest big island). Although 38% of students live in Java, UT has students in all subdistricts and inhabited islands in Indonesia. This is significant and has been acknowledged by the government as well as people around the country. Throughout Indonesia, you can easily meet a UT student or someone that has a UT student in his or her family or neighborhood.

The History of Universitas Terbuka's Online Learning Services

An open university, UT has relied on technology since its beginning. However, the use of technology for learning purposes only began in 1996 when UT decided to develop an ICT-based learning support service, utilizing the Internet that came to Indonesia in mid-1995. Through its Media Research Center (a center that was in charge of research and development related to the use of media and ICT), UT initiated a pilot project for online tutorials in the form of mailing-list-based tutorials. The tutorial was delivered using a mailing list for a group of students in a certain course that was administered by tutor. This trial served in order to identify the readiness of tutors, students, and technical support in managing online tutorials. The mailing-list-based tutorials were used for almost 4 years (1996–2000). At the end of 2000, the total number of courses provided with mailing-list-based tutorials was around 80 courses.

In 2000, a web-based Learning Management System (LMS) became available and the term *e-learning* became popular among Indonesians. UT then moved its online tutorial services into an open-source LMS platform called Manhattan Virtual Classroom (MVC). Using MVC, the number of tutorial courses also increased. By 2003, 201 courses were accompanied by online tutorials. Although MVC was better than a mailing-list-based tutorial, it was not completely satisfactory. It was not compatible with the existing student record system (SRS) of the university. This incompatibility caused difficulty in identifying and verifying participants enrolled in online tutorials. There were many participants who were not registered as UT's students. In addition, students' performance in tutorials (assignment scores) could not easily be integrated into their examination scores. At the time, many new open source LMS became available. Based on a technical evaluation of several LMSs, in 2005 MVC was replaced by a better and user-friendlier LMS called Moodle. With Moodle, only registered students can participate in UT's online tutorials, and any scores given by the tutors can be automatically integrated with students' examination scores. Scores are processed in the Examination Center and stored in the SRS. Moodle continues to be used with many modifications and additions that better suit the growing features of UT's online learning services. The number of courses accompanied by online tutorials has also increased. Starting in 2013, online tutorials will be provided for all courses (around 1,000).

It is important to note, however, that because of some students' limited access to the Internet, participation in online tutorials is not mandatory except for students in the graduate school. In graduate programs, online tutorials are designed at the same time as the face-to-face tutorials. To encourage students to participate in online tutorials, UT has a policy that students who participate in online tutorial will get a participation score that contributes to their final grade. In 2002, the participation score percentage of contribution to the online tutorial final grade (including tutorial assignments) was set at 15% of the final grade. In 2005, the participation score contributed 50% of the final grade. For the graduate school, students' participation in online tutorials is compulsory, and it contributes 60% of the final grade. To further development of online learning at the graduate level, in 2012 UT started two programs, a Master of Management and a Master of Public Administration, that are completely online or e-learning.

In 2002, UT began to provide students with web-based supplementary learning materials for its courses. The web-based supplementary learning materials (known as web-supplements) were designed to provide students with current and up-to-date content to enrich the learning materials (most of which are print). About 120 courses were provided web-supplements by 2009 (Padmo, Mutiara, & Kurniati, 2009); and by 2012 no less than 752 courses were web-supplements. These supplements are now called open coursewares because they are open for public access. Open coursewares are UT's contribution to the global movement to provide open

Figure 19.1   Guru Pintar Online Portal

Reprinted with permission from Guru Pintar Online.

educational resources (OER). In addition to the OER repository, for the past four years, UT has been developing and uploading video-based materials to its Internet TV portal and a comprehensive Digital Library. This library includes a Virtual Reading Room that contains full-text digitized print materials. All of the online learning support services are accessible through the UT Online Learning Center portal (www.student.ut.ac.id).

Teacher education is UT's biggest program, and UT has a dedicated portal for teachers. This portal, Guru Pintar Online (http://gurupintar.ut.ac.id), serves teachers in Indonesia and aims to facilitate continuous learning of teachers. The portal contains a forum where teachers can interact with each other, an instructional teaching clinic where teachers can learn from other teachers through video-based real cases, as well as numerous materials developed by both UT and other linked resources. The cover page of the Guru Pintar Online portal is shown in Figure 19.1.

Design and Management of Online Tutorials as E-learning

As previously mentioned, the form of e-learning at UT is currently dominated by the application of online tutorials for each course as part of the learning process. Online tutorials are designed as one of many learning support services provided to students that are directly associated with the courses they take within a semester. Within UT's system, students are allowed to take a maximum of 10 courses per semester; and students may also take zero courses without any notification nor penalty. When a student wants to take part in an online tutorial, the student activates his or her online account using the student number and specified password. Once the account is activated, the student can log in to the student's personal tutorial online web page that shows the student's list of registered couses. As mentioned earlier, the online tutorial is delivered using Moodle. Each course has its own virtual tutorial class facilitated by a team of tutors (although some courses may only have one tutor).

The implementation of online tutorial requires a preparation process that includes tutor recruitment and training, development of tutorial materials, as well as monitoring and evaluation. The preparation and management of the online tutorial service is the responsibility of each faculty (e.g., vice dean for student affairs) and is set up each semester to maintain a specific ratio of tutors and students. For undergraduate programs, the ratio of tutor and students in each online tutorial class is a maximum of 1:100, but for graduate programs the ratio is 1:60. The main reason there are such high ratios is that a number of students do not actively participate in the online tutorial. Many students are silent participants and do not participate except to submit assignments. In some cases, there are non-starters, which means a student has registered but they fail to participate or do not submit assignments. Finally, high ratios are appropriate because the online tutorials are designed as asynchronous tutorials. This is different from face-to-face tutorials which are designed to maintain the ratio of one tutor for every 20 students in each tutorial class.

Tutor recruitment is based on tutor competencies. As prescribed in the university quality assurance standards, tutors must hold at least a master's degree in a relevant subject. Most tutors are UT's own academic staff, but others may come from other universities. As the number of online classes increases, more online tutors are hired from other universities on a contract basis. New tutors must complete a training program before they begin a teaching assignment. Most external prospective tutors are nominated by the regional offices, which have direct contact with various local face-to-face universities, and are appointed by the deans. Tutor training is organized by the Center for Instructional Activities, which is also responsible for the accreditation of all UT's tutors.

Tutor training aims to equip tutors with various knowledge and skills, including the concept of online tutorials (and also face-to-face tutorials, in some cases), pedagogy of online teaching and learning, technical operation/navigation of the Moodle application, and development of online tutorial materials using standardized format. More importantly, as online tutorial is a new method for most tutors, training also educates tutors about the difference between face-to-face teaching and online teaching, including online tutorials. Teaching online not only requires tutors to provide learning materials and experiences through an online medium, it also requires tutors to consider the art, strategies, and approaches most suitable for the online classroom. According to Mishra and Koehler (in Ward & Benson, 2010), an online tutor should be able to demonstrate both technological pedagogy and content knowledge. This means an online tutor must be able to integrate teaching substance (content) with using online tutorial applications.

According to UT's policy, the online tutorial should provide at least eight initiation materials covering different topics to trigger discussions. An online tutorial for one semester is broken down into eight tutorial "sessions," each of which spans for a one week discussion period. This means that for each discussion topic, the online tutor provides an opportunity for the student to interact with the tutor and other students for one week at a minimum (Belawati, 2013). Tutors are also required to give assignments, and the three highest assignment scores obtained by students would contribute to students' final grades (combined with the scores of their final examination).

Another important component in the implementation of the online tutorial is the development process of online tutorial materials. Respective faculties develop online tutorial materials using a standardized format. The contracted online tutors are asked to use the standardized online tutorial materials, so that the academic quality of the tutorial can be maintained throughout all tutorial classes (some courses have more than one online tutorial class facilitated by different tutors). Every year online tutorial materials are reviewed and revised in order to keep the material updated. This process aims to ensure the quality of the online tutorial material. The standardized format of online tutorial material includes the following: the concept map of the course, the design and matrix of activities for each of the eight tutorial "sessions," eight initiation materials, enrichment material from open educational resources (OER), and three assignments. The standardized online tutorial material becomes a reference for each tutor in conducting the online tutorial so that the tutorial activities will be in line with the learning objectives. The online tutorial is basically available to help students study the print materials, which are the main source of learning.

As mentioned previously, some courses may have more than one online tutorial and may involve more than one tutor for the same course. Successful implementation of tutorials is supported through technical and mechanical activities, and by nontechnical activities such as communication and coordination among tutors. This is where the course manager and online tutorial manager play important roles. The responsibilities of the course manager for online tutorials are as follows:

- ensure the technical readiness of the online tutorial system/application,
- assign students and tutors to tutorial classes,
- ensure that all tutors are keeping the tutorial running smoothly in accordance with the schedule,
- ensure the quality and quantity of the tutorial materials, ensure that all tutors have developed and uploaded the discussion materials on time,
- ensure that tutors are keeping the discussion alive and are responding to students' questions and/or comments,
- communicate technical problems with the technical support team at the university's computer center, and
- anticipate problems that might arise during the online tutorial process.

In addition, the online tutorial manager reminds online tutors to motivate students to participate in online discussion. Coordination between tutors and online tutorial managers is necessary to obtain feedback and suggestions from the tutors. In short, the online tutorial manager provides quality control for the entire online tutorial process.

Student Participation in Online Tutorials

As mentioned earlier, the number of courses complemented with online tutorials continues to increase (Table 19.4). Table 19.4 shows that student participation rates in online tutorials are also increasing. The increase in participation within the past five years has been significant, about

Table 19.4 Student per Course Participation in Online Tutorial

Program	Number of Students per Course in Semester							
	2007.1	2007.2	2010.1	2010.2	2011.1	2011.2	2012.1	2012.2
Master of Fishery Management	52	—	64	55	64	80	254	232
Master of Public Administration	876	25	349	893	349	1,824	1,724	1,925
Master of Management	370	—	346	903	346	1,743	1,806	2,044
Master of Mathematics Education[1]	—	—	—	—	—	616	819	815
Faculty of Mathematics and Natural Sciences	785	999	1,772	2,734	2,304	4,100	4,288	51,320
Faculty of Economics	8,670	9,970	15,740	20,870	22,191	37,844	41,179	5,843
Faculty of Social Sciences	10,088	12,851	24,825	32,798	35,876	57,922	62,657	82,589
Faculty of Education	1,948	1,906	5,887	6,818	6,089	10,635	14,244	29,399
TOTAL	22,789	25,751	48,983	65,071	67,219	114,764	126,971	174,167

[1] The Master of Mathematics Education program opened Semester 2 in 2011.

a 664% increase, starting from about 22,789 students per course in Semester 1 of 2007 to 174,167 students per course in Semester 2 of 2012. The increasing participation rates may seem high, but they are still comparatively low compared to the total number of UT student-course registrations. In Semester 2 of 2012, the total number of registrations was more than two million students per course (assumption each student registered four to five courses each semester).

It is assumed that low participation is the result of various aspects, especially those related to the lack of access to Internet and the student's lack of study habits when using the Internet.

Closing Remarks

The implementation of e-learning at UT through online tutorials continues to increase, both in number of courses and number of students who participate in online tutorials. However, implementation of online tutorials faces hurdles, such as a limited ICT infrastructure, that has lowered the availability and accessibility of the Internet. While Internet access in Indonesia is a problem the government continues to improve the accessibility of the Internet in the outermost regions, territories, and the furthest behind regions. There is an increasing number of Internet users in Indonesia, from 2 million in 2000 to 55 million (22.1%) of the population in 2012.

Computer illiteracy is an obstacle for students if they wish to participate in online tutorials. Many students are not able to operate a computer or utilize the online tutorial application. Inability to operate a computer affects the student's confidence and comfort level with participation in online tutorials. Efforts are underway to reduce the barriers faced by students in participating in online tutorials. UT has taken several steps, including the provision of a computer laboratory in every regional office, hotspots in all UT's premises, technical training to operate the computer as well as to navigate within the Moodle LMS, and of course providing students with "online tutorial guidance" that is distributed in print and also uploaded to the UT online learning website.

Tutors still face technical problems in operating the online tutorial applications (Moodle). In some instances, it was found that some tutors are reluctant to use the various features in Moodle. As a result, the tutorials do not provide an enriched learning experience to the optimum allowed by the application. Tutors' lack of online teaching skills (the strategies and arts of online pedagogy) seems to be the most common problem. Some studies suggest that this constraint will be less of a problem as tutors' experience increases. Another issue concerns tutors' lack of discipline in organizing online tutorials in accordance with the tutorial schedule. Several tutors were late in uploading the discussion materials, were unable to respond to questions promptly, and some were unable to provide positive reinforcement to students. Nevertheless, with regular and consistent reminders from the course managers, the problems with tutors have gradually decreased. It is expected that tutor maturity will improve the implementation and quality of online tutorials.

In conclusion, the e-learning implementation experience of UT suggests that

- adopters of e-learning should pay attention to students' characteristics and also evaluate the ICT infrastructure available in order that the e-learning can be implemented effectively,
- e-learning implementation requires tutor and student preparation in order to acquire the skills and knowledge needed for successful e-learning, and
- the management of e-learning goes beyond a focus on technical requirements. There are management aspects that are non-technical (such as, coordination between tutors and course managers), may be manual, and require individual approaches to solve problems and successfully implement and manage e-learning.

References

Baggaley, J., & Batpurev, B. (2007). Technical evaluation report 60—The world-wide inaccessible web part 1: Browsing. *The International Review of Research in Open and Distance Learning, 8*(2). Retrieved from http://www.irrodl.org/index.php/irrodl/article/view/438/917

Belawati, T. (2013, February 4–6). *Universitas Terbuka, Indonesia: Meeting the diverse needs of the Indonesia distance learners.* Presentation material for the 2013 Summit of the Open and Distance Learning Australian Association (ODDLAA).

Bowles, M. (2004). *Relearning to e-learn: Strategies for electronic learning and knowledge.* Melbourne, Australia: Melbourne University Press.

Evans, P. (2012). *Indonesia—Telecoms, mobile, broadband and forecasts.* Retrieved from http://www.budde.com.au/Research/Asia-Mobile-Broadband-and-Digital-Economy-Overview.html?r=51

Ministry of Home Affairs, Geography of Indonesia. (2012). Retrieved from http://www.indonesia.go.id/en/ministries/ministers/ministry-of-home-affairs/1652-profile/170-kementerian-dalam-negeri-.html

Internet World Stats. (2012). http://www.internetworldstats.com/

Mahdizadeh, H., Biemans, H., & Mulder, M. (2008). Determining factors of the use of e-learning environments by university teachers. *Computer & Education, 51,* 142–154.

Noor II, A. R. (2014). 2014, Pengguna Internet di Indonesia tembus 153 juta. http://inet.detik.com/read/2011/10/05/073623/1737117/328/2014

Padmo, D., Mutiara, D., & Kurniati, S. (2009). Development of learning and supplementary materials. In A. Zuhairi & E. Nugraheni (Eds.), *Universitas Terbuka: A journey towards a leading open and distance education institution 1984–2008* (pp. 37–56). Jakarta, Indonesia: Universitas Terbuka.

Ward, C. L., & Benson, S.N.K. (2010). *Developing new schemas for online teaching and learning: TPACK.* Retrieved from http://jolt.merlot.org/vol6no2/ward_0610.htm

20

Maximizing Study Hours With Cloud-Based and Mobile-Based E-learning

A Case Study at a Full-Online University in Japan

Hiroshi Kawahara, Miwako Nogimori, and Sayaka Matsumoto

Introduction

Cyber University is Japan's first full-online undergraduate institute, certified by the Ministry of Education, Culture, Sports, Science and Technology (MEXT) in 2006. All course credits are counted toward college degrees, yet the students are neither required to come to classrooms nor to take examinations at designated times and places. The students can earn bachelor's degrees in information technology (IT) and business administration in 4 years. All classes and course materials are offered online and on demand, and all course activities, including assignments and exams, are conducted through web communication as well. Because of its on-demand attendance system and the practical curriculum, Cyber University attracts students who seek college degrees in fields directly related to their present work so that they can apply their new knowledge and skills immediately to their jobs at hand.

Hence, most of the full-time students at Cyber University are also full-time workers. They must find time to attend classes, to read, write, and interact with their classmates just like the students at universities based on face-to-face education. The key difference is that the Cyber University students have to manage all their study hours on their own, since there is no fixed class schedule for them to follow. Therefore, personal time management to set aside certain blocks of time per week for studying is critical for our students to achieve their academic goals. As a matter of fact, one of the most serious student issues at Cyber University is not financial problems, but squeezing extra hours out of their busy life for studying and working on academic tasks in order to satisfy course requirements for earning credits.

Cloud computing as various forms of service has been well adopted in IT industry, and utilization and benefits of such new forms of computing resources to e-learning have been reported (Dong, Zheng, Yang, Li, & Qiao, 2009). However, network and content service models—such as iCloud, by Apple and Kindle, by Amazon.com—may not have been recognized enough as effective tools that can be applied to enrich e-learning environments. The key concept here is device-free, time-free, and space-free accessibility to the learning content and synchronization of all user records.

Cyber University developed a cloud-based e-learning system named "Cloud Campus" in which Moodle, the learning management system (LMS) and iPad/iPhone applications are tightly integrated and synchronized. The goal was to provide as many additional study hours as possible to the students by making the learning contents and communication tools accessible to them with minimum effort.

In the following sections, the key components and technologies of the "Cloud Campus" will be described, followed by a discussion of how the system could effectively contribute to maximize the students' study hours from the students' perspective.

Cloud for E-learning

"Cloud Campus": A Fully-Integrated Multidevice E-learning System

Cloud computing has been recognized literally as computing resource services that can be procured though the Internet, but the service content is not necessarily well defined. The National Institute of Standard and Technology (NIST) definition of cloud computing includes five essential characteristics (Mell & Grance, 2009). In the software service model called SaaS (Software as a Service), the NIST definition states that the applications are accessible from various client devices through either a thin client interface, such as a web browser (e.g., web based e mail), or a program interface.

"Cloud Campus," the Cyber University's new device-and-OS-free e-learning system, was released in 2012 (Kawahara, 2012). Moodle was chosen to replace our own proprietary LMS, which had been operating since 2007. This made the LMS compatible with both Windows PC and Mac, and almost all browsers available in the market as well. Cyber University also developed a web-based courseware viewer application named "CC Viewer," which can be used as SCORM-compatible resources for Moodle. For content production, we created an original tool called "CC Producer" available as a web application to our students and instructors. With this application, they can easily develop their original video contents with slides.

For messaging, scheduling, and documentation management services, we adopted Google technologies for both internal and external uses. Moodle and Google services are made accessible with single sign-on system (SSO) to provide seamless web service to the faculty and students.

For iPad and iPhone/iPod Touch, Apple's Safari browser is the standard application for each platform. However, browsing and interacting with web pages designed for an ordinary PC interface on those mobile devices is tedious, and it would not serve the purpose of mobile convenience very well. Therefore, we have developed "CC Handy for iPad" and "CC Handy for iPhone," iOS-based integrated learners' applications separately optimized for iPad and iPhone. More detail of the features and its integration with Moodle will be discussed in the next section.

As shown in Figure 20.1, we have made a complete cloud-based e-learning platform that can serve from content production to delivery.

"CC Handy": Mobile Learning Applications for iPad and iPhone

With our "CC Handy for iPad" and "CC Handy for iPhone," students can access almost all of the course contents, materials, and activities, except for paper assignments, hands-on exercises, and final examinations (see Table 20.1). In other words, the mobile applications were made to provide the same "everyday" course materials and learning experiences as those available on PC.

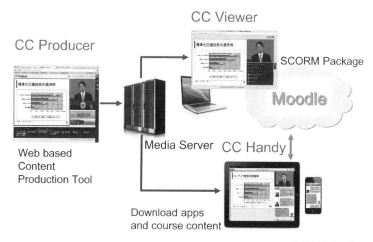

CC Viewer

CC Producer

SCORM Package

Moodle

Web based
Content
Production Tool

Media Server CC Handy

Download apps
and course content

© 2014 Cyber University

Figure 20.1   From Content Production to Delivery: Cyber University's Cloud-Based E-learning Platform

Table 20.1 Course Activities Accessible from PC and Mobile Devices

Activities	PC	Mobile
Lecture	√	√
Quiz	√	√
Forum	√	√
References (PDF)	√	√
Taking Notes	√	√
Papers	√	
Hands-on exercise	√	
Online examination (video monitored)	√	

The most important features of mobile learning are availability of the device itself and accessibility to the learning content. In the process of application development, we examined the students' needs for accessibility to the course contents and for synchronization of all course activities with other devices on a per-student basis. As a result, we found that the students spent most of their study time viewing the course contents, which are in the forms of slides with video and/or web-based training modules. As a matter of fact, the course contents at Cyber University are usually designed to run for 10 to 20 minutes per chapter, and each "class" usually contains four chapters. We also found that students prefer being able to work on class activities on the mobile devices as well—like taking quizzes immediately after viewing the chapters, reading and responding to forum comments, or viewing reference materials prepared by the instructors.

Figure 20.2 depicts the Moodle activities that are mapped onto the iPad application interface. As a cloud service, class activities conducted either on Moodle or on the iPad application are synchronized instantly. The iPhone application has the same features as the iPad application with modified user interface layout because of its 3.5-inch screen size as opposed to the 9.7-inch screen of iPad.

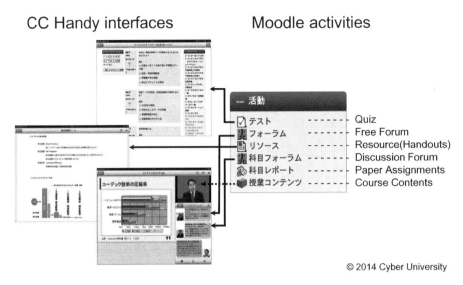

Figure 20.2 iPad Application and Moodle Activities Are Synchronized on "Cloud Campus"

Integrated Learning Application Interface for iPad

On the Moodle web page, the course content (a SCORM package), forum, test, and resource are separate entities. It would not be an issue to access each of those class activities and resources with a browser on a PC screen. One can even open a separate window for word processing or for searching information. However, the mobile learning application must allow students to have access to most of the resources by just a single flick.

Figure 20.3 shows the window layout of Cyber University's iPad application made for "Cloud Campus." The major portion of the window is provided for the lecture content, which consists of

Figure 20.3 The Integrated Student's Application Interface for iPad

the video player screen and slide show window. Each slide is shown according to the time stamp embedded in the video clip.

The window below the video screen is the forum discussion display. In the forum, the instructor and the students can exchange messages freely on certain topics and course subjects. Each message is displayed in the forum as a bubble with a thumbnail picture to identify the speaker. These SNS (social networking service) timeline-like forum discussions are synchronized with the Moodle forums so that one can participate in any forum with any learning device.

Downloadable Course Contents and Synchronization of Study Records

Wi–Fi networks as well as 3G and even 4G mobile networks in some areas of large cities are now widely available and have contributed to the rapid growth of smartphone and tablet PC users. However, we are not yet at the point where a wireless network is available anytime and anywhere. In order to take full advantage of the convenience of mobile devices, we had to isolate the content viewing process from the network instability so that students can continue their learning even while they are traveling from one place to another. To deal with this, we made all course contents and materials downloadable (see Figure 20.4a). If a student plays downloaded content while the mobile device is off-line, the viewing and activity records are all kept by the device application (see Figure 20.4b). These records are transmitted to and synchronized with the records on Moodle when the network connection is resumed (see Figure 20.4c).

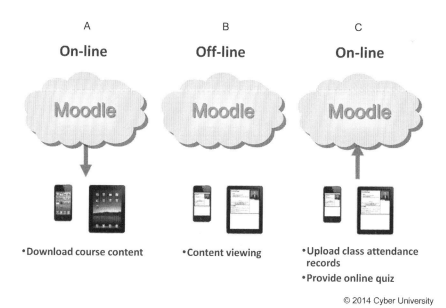

A	B	C
On-line	**Off-line**	**On-line**

- Download course content
- Content viewing
- Upload class attendance records
- Provide online quiz

© 2014 Cyber University

Figure 20.4 Online/Off-line Communications on iPad and iPhone

Biometric Authentication for Student Identification

Student authentication is an inescapable issue, especially in distance education. Since Cyber University is a 100% online university, it is not feasible to physically gather students for face-to-face class meetings or for end-of-term exams like other online universities do. In order for our students to receive course credits by taking quizzes, participating in discussion forums, submitting course papers, and taking online examinations, they have to identify themselves at each of these instances.

Cyber University has been utilizing biometric authentication system based on face image structures (Kawahara, 2010). Whenever a student tries to take a quiz or participate in a class discussion after viewing all the chapters assigned for the class, the "Face Authentication" log-on interface is activated automatically. The system identifies the student's face each time with the "master picture" registered beforehand to ensure that the activity is done by the right person. Even when the students use their mobile devices to access "Cloud Campus" there is no exception. For this purpose, we extended the use of the same biometric authentication system and made it compatible with the built-in cameras on iPad and iPhone (see Figure 20.5).

For final examinations that require even more stringent authentication, we utilize "face monitoring" along with the "face authentication" system. While a student is taking a final exam, and automatically activated web camera keeps sending the test-taker's snapshots to the server every 15 to 25 seconds, which are then identified with the "master picture" after the exam.

Figure 20.5 "Face Authentication" Identifies the Student Before Providing Quiz Problems

Cloud-Based and Mobile-Based Learning in Practice: Student Survey Results

In this section, we will discuss how the new cloud-based and mobile-based e-learning system contributed to maximize students' study hours, based on a student survey conducted in Academic Year 2012, among all registered students at Cyber University (those who had been renting free iPads from the University were especially encouraged to participate). At the time of the survey, 351 course contents with more than 13,000 chapters had been available on iPad and iPhone applications.

The survey was conducted to address the following key questions:

- Does the cloud-based and mobile-based learning system encourage students to study at other places than home?
- Do students find more study hours per week with the mobile devices?
- Do the students find the furnished mobile learning application to be as effective as the one for PC?

For the spring semester of 2012, 277 of the full-time students who had been using iPads in addition to their PCs participated in the survey. The following are questions and answers to respond to the above concerns.

Q1: Where do you mostly use your iPad? (More than 2 answers are allowed.)

As we had expected, many of the students (145 out of 262) reported that they use their iPads during their commute and/or while traveling. Interestingly, most of the students (207 out of 262) answered that they use their iPad at home, which is their ordinary place for e-learning (see Figure 20.6).

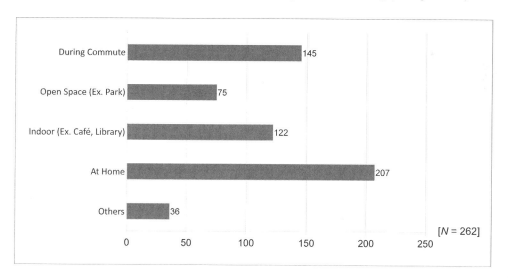

Figure 20.6   iPad Use Locations (multiple answers allowed)

Q2: Have you found an increase in your study hours with iPad? If so, how many hours per week?

More than 60% of the students found that their study hours had increased since using the iPad application (see Figure 20.7). Almost one quarter of the students thought that their study hours had increased by more than four hours per week.

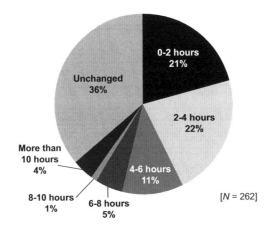

Figure 20.7   Increase of Students' Study Hours per Week

Q3: Do you think that reviewing the class contents with iPad is easier than with PC?

Needless to say, more than 80% of the students found the accessibility to the content with iPad superior to that with PC (see Figure 20.8). One of the benefits of e-learning is that the students can repeatedly review the course materials as many times as they want. The survey addressed the effectiveness of the mobile learning with respect to the conventional learning experience with browsers on PC.

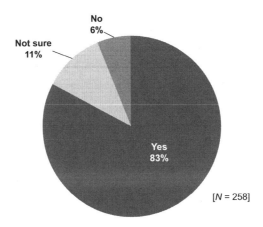

Figure 20.8   Is the Class Review Easier With iPad Than With PC?

Q4: Which did you use more often, PC or iPad?

Approximately half of the students used their PCs more often than iPads, as shown in Figure 20.9. This means that PCs still play the role of the main e-learning device, while approximately 30% of the students found iPad as their preferred device for learning. Interestingly, 19% of the students reported that they use PC and iPad simultaneously. This seems to be a new way of e-learning with multiscreens. For example, a student can review a course content on iPad while commenting on a forum discussion from his or her PC (and the data is reflected instantly by cloud synchronization). This is a perfect combination of passive (iPad) and active (PC) learning interface (see Figure 20.10).

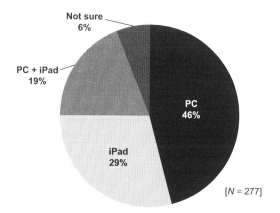

Figure 20.9 Most Frequently Used Devices

Figure 20.10 Multiscreen Learning With PC and iPad

Additional Students' Comments

The students also made several remarks that would offer additional input regarding the values of the mobile learning. The following are a few examples.

"The iPad application's quick start–up also leads immediate start of learning process, which is more productive than PC."

"Whenever I feel like studying, I can start with iPad. This increases my frequency of content access."

"When I come home late, I don't feel like starting–up my PC. It's good to be able to find time to study during the break at work or on the commuting train."

"I found it very useful to view the course instruction content on the iPad while I do coding on my PC in my programming course."

Multidevice Learning Practice

One of the purposes of cloud-based learning is to allow a student to freely choose the accessing devices depending on his or her learning situation at a time, while his or her study progress is constantly tracked and logged. Since the learning records on all devices are synchronized in the cloud, a student can choose to use PC, iPad and/or iPhone without losing continuity of his or her learning progress.

We obtained our students' attendance logs from one of the lecture courses along with their accessing device records. Figure 20.11 shows the students' use patterns of PC and/or iPad during

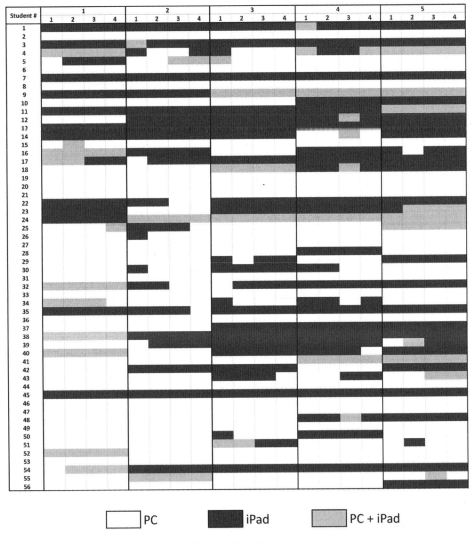

Figure 20.11 Students' PC and iPad/iPhone Use Patterns

the five classes in the course. (Each class content consists of four chapters.) Forty-one students out of 56 had been using their mobile devices to participate in these classes. Each content chapter is shaded as white for PC-access, black for iPad-access, and gray for both PC and iPad-access. It is clear from the block patterns that few students demonstrated consistent use of single device; most of them used multiple devices in a random manner. They all had access to the same course materials, but chose different learning devices based on their situation at the time.

We also observed from the access logs that the students frequently used the mobile application not only for viewing the course content but also for taking quizzes and making comments in the class forums. This device-agnostic usage of "Cloud Campus" clearly indicates that the mobile learning application supports the students' learning activities as effectively as the one for PC.

Conclusion

We found that noncompromised mobile learning applications associated with a cloud-based e-learning system, where learning records are fully synchronized among accessing devices, allowed the students to extend their study hours. The mobile devices such as the iPad seemed to be the most effective learning tool at remote sites. However, the maximum use of such a "handy" device was actually found at home, where the PC is expected to be the primary learning device. As a result, the students at Cyber University reported that they could extend their study hours as much or more than 10 hours a week.

The survey results along with the students' independent comments indicate not only that mobile devices brought a significant increase in study hours for the students, but also that the students found another way to make the most of the cloud-based learning: utilizing a mobile device in conjunction with PC for multiscreen learning. While approximately half of the students found PC as the main device, nearly 30% of the students found iPad to be the main, and nearly 20% found the simultaneous use of PC and iPad to be an effective learning environment. We also found that the iPad application is preferred for reviewing the course materials over use of the PC. Having the cloud-based learning system along with the mobile applications made available for formal lecture courses, most of the students took advantage of the device-free learning environment where they chose learning devices in random manner.

Thus, we found the "Cloud Campus" to be effective in terms of providing more study hours to the students. The learning effectiveness with multi-applications featured for specific skill learning and laboratory works should be explored next. Our e-learning system development effort will be shifted to enhance quality of learning experience.

References

Dong, B., Zheng, Q., Yang, J., Li, H., & Qiao, M. (2009). An e-learning ecosystem based on cloud computing infrastructure. In A. Ignasio, C. Nian-Shing, Kinshuk, & S. Demetrios (Ed.), *The Ninth IEEE International Conference on Advanced Learning Technologies 2009* (pp. 125–127). Los Alamitos, CA: IEEE Computer Society.

Kawahara, H. (2010). Student authentication for course credit in distance learning. *Journal of Multimedia Education Research*, 7(1), S57-S63.

Kawahara, H. (2012, August 20). *Cloud and mobile based e-learning—Increase in study hours and class communication*. Proceedings of the 10th International Conference for Media in Education 2012 (ICoME), Beijing Normal University, Beijing.

Mell, P., & Grance, T. (2009). *The NIST definition of cloud computing*. Retrieved from National Institute of Standard and Technology website: http://csrc.nist.gov/publications/nistpubs/800-145/SP800-145.pdf

21

E-learning in India

Ramesh C. Sharma and Sanjaya Mishra

Introduction

Soon after independence in 1947, the Government of India had the challenge of bringing uniformity in educational systems and providing education to large segments of the population. The education system was marked with regional imbalances. In 1947, the literacy rate in India was 14 per cent while female literacy was very low (8 per cent). There were around 20 universities and 500 colleges. To address to the issue of illiteracy among adults, some of the initiatives undertaken were as follows (Government of India, 2008):

- Social education (taken up in the First Five Year Plan 1951–1956) for providing literacy, extension, general education, leadership training, and social consciousness.
- Gram Shikshan Mohim (1959), for providing basic literacy skills to rural people in the State of Maharashtra.
- Farmer's Functional Literacy Project (FFLP; 1967–68) targeted at popularisation of high-yielding varieties of seeds.
- Nonformal education (NFE; 1974–1979) for people in the age group of 15 to 25 years.
- National Adult Education Programme (NAEP; 1978) to eradicate illiteracy.
- National Policy on Education (1986) and the Revised Plan of Action (1992).
- National Literacy Mission (1988), as a Technology Mission to impart functional literacy.

The Government of India has, in addition to some of the above mentioned schemes, taken additional measures to improve literacy rates in India, such as offering free education to poor people and creating more schools and colleges at districts level. These measures have resulted in an increase in the literacy rate from 65.38 per cent in 2001 to 74.04 per cent in 2011 (Government of India, 2011).

These developments were also a result of the increase in the number of educational institutions. From 20 universities and 500 colleges in 1947, India had 523 universities (43 central, 265 State owned, 80 State–private owned, 130 deemed to be universities, and 5 institutions under State legislation) and more than 33 thousand colleges (University Grants Commission, India, 2012).

Developments in ICT

ICT is one of the most important tools used to enhance teaching, learning, and other administrative transactions in education. With the advent of Web 2.0, the ICT tools have enabled teachers of today to change from knowledge-generators to knowledge-facilitators. There is a need for integrating ICT into the curriculum and with pedagogy. The learning process can be made more learner-centric with such an integration. Utilising ICT for teaching and learning has also another dimension of capacity building of the teachers. Teachers should not only be able to integrate technology into the curriculum, they need to have an understanding of how to use ICT tools for various functions. ICT applications have been found to enhance knowledge transfer beyond formal communication lines (Osman et al., n.d.). Over a period of time, India has shown tremendous growth in different ICT indicators. With new technology adoption and development, lowering of tariffs for telephony (both fixed and mobile), India has emerged as one of the fastest markets in consumer products and services.

A major boost for the IT sector came with the setting up of a National Task Force on Information Technology and Software Development by the Prime Minister of India in 1998 (Sharma, 2001). This task force had the mandate of developing a long-term national policy on information technology. Some of the recommendations in the policy (Government of India, 1999) having a direct bearing on educational institutions are as follows:

Recommendation #13

ix. Government in association with IT HRD companies will aim to achieve 100% IT literacy at senior secondary level (10 + 2) in 5 years and at secondary level in 10 years.

x. All institutes offering engineering education, including Polytechnics and ITIs, will ensure that within 3 years all engineering students in the country will acquire IT knowledge to be able to serve in IT enabled Services sector besides serving in IT industry directly.

Recommendation #45

iv. Institutes of national importance such as IITs and IIITs will be encouraged to establish Virtual Institutes, particularly in the area of Advanced Post Graduate and Continuing Education programs in IT, to support IT education and Research at other institutions in the country.

To bring out direct reforms and formulate policy guidelines, another milestone was the constitution of the National Knowledge Commission (NKC) on June 13, 2005, as a high-level advisory body to the Prime Minister of India. It was mandated to focus on certain key areas, such as education, science and technology, agriculture, industry, e-governance, and so forth. The setting up of NKC put the country on the path of becoming a knowledge society. In its duration of three-and-a-half-year terms, NKC submitted around 300 recommendations pertaining to five key areas of the knowledge paradigm—access to knowledge, knowledge concepts, knowledge creation, knowledge application, and development of better knowledge services (more details can be found at http://knowledgecommission.gov.in/focus/default.asp).

One of the results of deliberations of NKC was the setting up of a National Knowledge Network (NKN). This NKN is supported with an ultra-high-speed CORE, augmented with a distribution layer at corresponding speeds of the CORE. The partner institutions can now get a speed of 1 Gbps or higher. It has its applications in health, education, science and technology, grid computing, bio informatics, agriculture, and governance.

While these developments were taking place, India was witnessing another advancement in the field of mobile telephony. According to "The Mobile Economy India 2013" report, released by the GSM Association (2013), India is the second largest market for mobile connections in the region, and by the end of 2013, around 107 million subscribers will be enjoying 3G connections, which will be growing to more than 400 million by 2017. These developments have commercial implications too. Snapdeal (http://www.snapdeal.com/), which is one of India's leading online marketplaces, with 25,000 units selling per day and shipping to 4,000+ cities and towns in India, has around 18 million registered users. The company has issued a statement: Thirty per cent of all orders on Snapdeal are now being placed over mobile phones (PTI, 2013). This shows that Indian mobile users are now going increasingly for online shopping.

The report "Measuring the Information Society 2013," released by the International Telecommunication Union, places India at 121st rank among 157 countries in relation to progress in ICT. This ranking is done on the basis of an ICT Development Index (IDI) comprising 11 indicators. The report further analyses the placement of countries on the basis of this ICT Development Index (IDI), and for 2012 figures, India is one of the least connected countries (LCC). "In these LCCs, most ICT access and use is limited to basic voice and low-speed data services. While a number of LCCs have reached relatively high levels of mobile-cellular penetration, more advanced ICT services, including broadband Internet access, remain very limited" (ITU, 2013, p. 42, Box 2.9).

Since ICT comprises two main components, information technology and communication technology, it would be prudent to examine the developments on both these fronts. Over the past two decades, we have witnessed impressive growth in both these areas. The software industry and ITES (information technology-enabled services) sector has reported good business, both domestic and internationally.

According to the report "Computer Software and Information Technology (IT) Services Exports: 2011–12," released by the Reserve Bank of India (2013), there is an annual growth of 14.5 per cent of exports of software services. "India's export of software services and ITES/BPO services during 2011–12 is estimated at 2,484.3 billion (US$ 51.8 billion), showing an annual growth of 14.5 per cent. Exports of Computer Services and ITES/BPO services accounted for 75.2 per cent and 24.8 per cent, respectively of the total software services exports" (RBI, 2013, p. 1).

National Policy on Information Technology 2012: The Way Forward for Going Online

The Government of India approved a National Policy on Information Technology in 2012 with the purpose to use ICT for meeting the economic and developmental concerns of the country. The policy has its grounding in the belief that ICT can transform the lives of people and is a key driver of the knowledge-based economy. Some of the thrust areas of this policy are as follows:

- To increase revenues of IT and ITES (Information Technology Enabled Services) Industry from 100 Billion USD currently to 300 Billion USD by 2020 and expand exports from 69 Billion USD currently to 200 Billion USD by 2020.
- To promote innovation and R&D in cutting edge technologies and development of applications and solutions in areas like localization, location based services, mobile value added services, Cloud Computing, Social Media and Utility models.
- To make at least one individual in every household e-literate.
- To leverage ICT for key Social Sector initiatives like Education, Health, Rural Development and Financial Services to promote equity and quality.

- To make India the global hub for development of language technologies, to encourage and facilitate development of content accessible in all Indian languages and thereby help bridge the digital divide.
- To adopt Open standards and promote open source and open technologies.

(Government of India, 2012, p. 1)

The developments in the field of information and communication technologies, the opening up of the telecom sector for more spectrum, the lowering of tariffs, and the formulation of IT policies has acted as a catalyst for e-learning in India. It was found to be an effective medium to cater to the educational needs of the learners, providing them the avenues to learn anytime and anywhere, or all the time and all the places!

Social Media and Social Networks

Like elsewhere, India also joined the bandwagon of social media and social networks. Educational communities soon turned into online communities for collaboration and networking. The members of such online communities created web identities, had a net presence felt, and with the help of the Internet, they are now able to stay tuned with each other. We were able to see the transformation from information sharing to information communicating. Social media like Facebook, LinkedIn, and microblogging applications became an important conduit for academics for direct interaction with others through multichannels in the form of one-to-many, one-to-one, many-to-one, and many-to-many. Teachers and trainers creating, uploading, and sharing videos on social networks like YouTube, photo management over Flickr, and sharing presentations over slideshare.net has provided certain benefits to academia, such as expressing themselves, establishing relations, developing leadership qualities, and value for social norms and ethics. There are certain risks associated with social media and social networks, such as cyberbullying, which we are not going to discuss here, being out of scope of this chapter. In a nutshell, social networks have given birth to a new type of online entities where real meets with virtual and new educational apps are being developed as a next wave of growth.

E-learning Initiatives

Let's have a look at some of the prominent examples of e-learning initiatives in India (Sharma, 2013):

- Netvarsity (http://www.netvarsity.com) was one of the earliest initiatives in India by the NIIT (National Institute of Information Technology) for offering online programmes.
- Institute of Professional Studies at Allahabad University (http://www.allduniv-ips.in/portable_lab.php) is creating infrastructure for mobile learning for imparting English proficiency and workplace skills. Titled "Transforming Learning Through M-education" they provide access to information with the help of a portable device (tablet) based language lab.
- Akshaya project (http://akshaya.kerala.gov.in/) is a Government of Kerala initiative, having three components: Ensuring broad-based access to Information and Communication Technology (ICT) for every citizen, providing basic functional skills (100 per cent household e-literacy), and making available content relevant to the local population in the local language.

- BalSahara (http://www.cdachyd.in/) deals with information on children falling into two categories: children in need of care and protection, and children in conflict with law. This initiative allows to evaluate and examine the status of child homes and to make policy decisions about children's education, case history, diet, medical condition, and so on.
- Pan African e-Network Project (http://www.panafricanenetwork.com/) is labelled as a shining example of south–south cooperation, and is a joint venture of India with the African Union to support tele-education, telemedicine, e-commerce, e-governance, infotainment, resource mapping, and meteorological services. With a budgetary cost of INR 5429 million (i.e., over US$125 million), the Ministry of External Affairs, Government of India, is the Nodal Ministry. Telecommunications Consultants India Ltd (TCIL), as the turnkey implementing agency, would design the network, procure, and install the equipment, along with providing consultancy to the Government.
- National Repository of Open Educational Resources (http://nroer.in/home/) is an initiative of the Ministry of Human Resources Development, Government of India. This digital repository of open educational resources offers resources for all school subjects in multiple languages. It provides the content in a wide variety of formats such as concept maps, videos, audio clips, talking books, multimedia, learning objects, photographs, diagrams, charts, articles, wikipages, and textbooks.
- Hole-in-the-Wall Learning Solution (http://www.hole-in-the-wall.com/) is an initiative of the Hole-in-the-Wall Education Limited (HiWEL) to bridge the digital divide through innovative technologies to the underprivileged groups. It has so far delivered over 600 learning stations.
- Educating Women (http://www.jvwomensuniv.com/) is an initiative of Jayoti Vidyapeeth Women's University to provide 'education for community development', leading to women's empowerment and awareness of women's rights and law to all people.
- Amrita Vishwa Vidyapeetham Virtual Lab (http://amrita.vlab.co.in/) is an initiative of Ministry of Human Resource Development under the National Mission on Education through ICT. It offers state-of-the-art computer simulation technology to create real-world environments and problem-handling capabilities.
- Indian Institute of Technology, Mumbai (http://www.iitb.ac.in/) offers online video courses and off line recorded video lessons for students to learn. Under the National Mission on Education through ICT, 1,000 teachers are being trained at a time via online workshops.
- Indian Institute of Technology, Delhi (http://www.iitb.ac.in/), was established in January 1959 (through an Act of Parliament) in collaboration with the British Government to offer instruction in applied science and engineering of a standard comparable to the best in the world. As an institute of excellence in scientific and technical education and research, it generates new knowledge by engaging in cutting-edge research and to promote academic growth by offering state-of-the-art undergraduate, postgraduate, and doctoral programmes.
- Indira Gandhi National Open University (http://www.ignou.ac.in) has integrated ICT into curriculum, and instructional design and delivery. E-Gyankosh has been developed for content sharing. In addition, Flexi-Learn provides online courses.
- Yashwantrao Chavan Maharastra Open University (http://www.ycmou.com) provides the facility of e-books in addition to online services and online courses.
- Symbiosis Centre for Distance Learning (http://www.scdl.net), established in 2001, is one of the largest autonomous distance learning education institutes in India with an active student enrolment of more than 2,54,000 across 48 countries including India, US, UK, Middle East, Russia, Germany, Singapore, and Japan. It offers post graduate diploma, diploma and

certificate programs across industry sectors including business management, international business, information technology, banking and finance, supply chain management, customer relationship management, insurance management, education management, business and corporate law, and entrepreneurship development. SCDL uses a "blended learning" methodology for all its programs, combining three forms of instructional delivery for learning, namely, published/printed self-learning material, e-learning, pre-recorded DVD lectures and faculty interaction (chat sessions and virtual classroom facility) and online and on-demand examinations.

- MedVarsity (http://www.medvarsity.com), established in April 2000, is India's first medical e-learning venture by Apollo Hospitals Group, a leader in healthcare in the Asia Pacific Region. It offers information technology based quality education to the health care providers (HCP) at any distance and to facilitate cutting-edge research in delivery of medical education. MedVarsity also undertakes and encourages research in the development of new information technology tools relevant to medical education and its virtual delivery.
- Tamil Virtual University (http://www.tamilvu.org) is an Internet-based resource that offers information about the history, art, literature, and culture of Tamils.
- Punjab Technical University (http://www.ptu.ac.in/) offers multimedia-rich interactive learning experiences to students.
- Birla Institute of Technology and Sciences (http://vu.bits-pilani.ac.in) deals with designing and developing web-enabled multimedia courses as full degree programs for off-campus students. To explain the concepts to the students, multimedia-based soft-teachers and Java-based "concept applets" for educational resource development are deployed. To provide skill-based and practical training to the students in a lab environment, an introductive virtual lab framework has been put in place for practice-intensive courses. Other facilities like desktop IP-based video-conferencing, scheduled video over IP, and video-on-demand over IP facilities are also integrated into the learning support system.

Conclusion

E-learning in India is fast emerging. There are cases and examples from all sectors: governmental, nongovernmental, private ventures, business houses, independent academics, and others. Realising the importance of e-learning, the University Grants Commission of India had established a dialogue on "Enhancing Higher Education Through E-learning" with the Commonwealth of Learning (COL) in 2003. Six areas were identified for review of e-learning development in India: standards and specifications; hardware and software; connectivity; user studies; content-related issues; and private–public partnership (Mishra & Sharma, 2005). Major recommendations of the group (University Grants Commission [UGC], 2003) were as follows:

(a) UGC should create a system to support the use of e-learning by all institutions of higher learning in India, in an ambitious timeframe. Specifically, the system should be learner centered, cost effective, affordable, inclusive, widely and easily accessible, scalable and up-gradable.

(b) The goal of the system should be to change the teaching–learning paradigm; increase access with equity for higher education; make education relevant to sustainable human developments; and enhance the quality of higher education through e-learning.

(c) A national infrastructure should be developed for e-learning; policy guidelines should be developed based on the goals of e-learning and bridging the digital divide; and the efforts towards development and use of e-learning should be recognised and rewarded.

(d) National standards for e-learning materials should be set up; different stages of design, production, delivery, evaluation and revision of e-learning materials must be identified.

Resistance to adoption of e-learning has been noted. Parihar (2004) reported about the fear of the teachers for their dislocation, perceived unreliability of networked services, and being unsure of security provisions in online contents. Mishra and Sharma (2005) suggested developing teacher competencies in the use of web technologies to promote e-learning. The National Knowledge Commission also recommended filling the gap in the skills to use computing devices of the teachers who have hitherto remained untouched by the digital revolution and have not been able to join the mainstream of the knowledge economy. An inherent component of e-learning is 'learning'. To augment learning, we need to focus on certain issues, like support—financial, pedagogical, or methodological. For e-learning programmes to be successful, there is a need to create suitable learning environments, bring out pedagogical changes, and create relevant teaching and learning materials. For e-learning to be successful in regions, we need to focus on methodologies of registration, examination, certification, and content development in regional languages. Vinaykrishnan, Rathod, and Lad (2012) also support multilingual content creation, such as specialized Indian language calendar, portal, electronic publishing, newsletter, newspapers, manuals, brochures, online documents, and so forth. Those e-learning programmes are poised to sustain not only educational demands and emerging technologies, but also provide suitable employment to the learners.

References

Government of India. (1999). *National task force on information technology and software development: IT action plan part III—long term national IT policy.* New Delhi: Government of India. Retrieved from http://it-taskforce.nic.in/actplan3/

Government of India. (2008). *Efforts to eradicate illiteracy in India.* Retrieved from http://pib.nic.in/newsite/erelease.aspx?relid=42161

Government of India. (2011). *The Indian census.* Retrieved from http://censusindia.gov.in/default.aspx

Government of India. (2012). *Cabinet approves national policy on information technology 2012.* Retrieved from http://www.pib.nic.in/newsite/erelease.aspx?relid=87875

GSM Association. (2013). *The mobile economy India 2013.* Retrieved from http://www.gsmamobileeconomyindia.com/GSMA_Mobile_Economy_India_Report_2013.pdf

ITU (International Telecommunications Union). (2013). *Measuring the information society, 2013.* Retrieved from http://www.itu.int/en/ITU-D/Statistics/Documents/publications/mis2013/MIS2013_without_Annex_4.pdf

Mishra, S., & Sharma, R. C. (2005). Development of e-learning in India. *University News, 43*(11), 9–15.

Osman, W.R.S., et al. (n.d.). *PSP's research digest: Information communication technology—Benefits among Y generation a road map towards vision 2020.* Available online from http://politeknik.gov.my/webjpp2/penyelidikan/jurnal/abstrak/11-Syahrizad-1-PSP-full_edit.pdf

Parihar, S. M. (2004). Geo-informatics in higher education, *Information for Development, 2*(2), 25–28. Retrieved from http://issuu.com/i4d_magazine/docs/i4d_february_2004_issue

PTI. (2013). *Snapdeal says 30 pct orders are being placed through mobile phones.* Retrieved from http://www.indianexpress.com/news/snapdeal-says-30-pct-orders-are-being-placed-through-mobile-phones/1184654/

Reserve Bank of India. (2013). *India's exports of computer services 75.2 per cent of total software services exports in 2011–12: RBI survey.* Retrieved from http://rbi.org.in/scripts/BS_PressReleaseDisplay.aspx?prid=29029

Sharma, R. (2001). Online delivery of programmes: A case study of Indira Gandhi National Open University (IGNOU). *The International Review of Research in Open and Distance Learning, 1*(2). Retrieved from http://www.irrodl.org/index.php/irrodl/article/view/18/356

Sharma, R. (2013, February 20–22). *Open educational resources: Strategies to enhance networking and collaborative opportunities.* Keynote delivered at India-Canada International Conference on Open and Flexible Distance Learning, Mumbai, SNDT Women's University.

University Grants Commission, India (UGC). (2003, November 17–19). *Report of the UGC-COL dialogue on enhancing higher education through e-learning*. New Delhi: India International Centre.

University Grants Commission, India. (2012). *Annual Report 2010–11*. New Delhi, India: Author.

Vinaykrishnan, P., Rathod, V., & Lad, K. (2012). Intelligent and multilingual e-learning model for India. *International Journal of Societal Applications of Computer Science, 1*(1), 7–10. Retrieved from http://www.ijsacs.org/vol1issue1/paper2.pdf

22

Using Mobile Phones for Teacher Professional Development in Bangladesh

Views of Secondary School Teachers and Teacher Facilitators

Robina Shaheen and Ashok Paul Kumar

Despite increasing efforts, investment, and support by external funding agencies, teacher training remains one of the biggest challenges in many developing nations (Banks, Moon, & Wolfenden, 2009; Moon, 2007; Dembélé & Bé-Rammaj, 2003). This is likely to 'become greater' as countries move towards achieving the Education For All (EFA) targets (Lewin, 2002). Few would contest that countries "that have achieved high learning standards have invested heavily in the teaching profession" (UNESCO, 2005, p. 3). However, while many countries would aspire to achieve the 'high learning standards', few may either have the means or the priority to make the investments required to develop their teachers' professional capacity.

Efforts through international partnerships, consisting of academic institutions, local governments, and international donor agencies have led to experimenting with many innovative ways of dealing with the problem of developing teachers' professional capacity at scale and with impact. A more recent example of such an initiative has been the English in Action (EIA) project, working in Bangladesh since 2008. EIA is a long-term project (e.g., 9 years), with the goal to contribute to the country's social and economic growth by assisting 25 million people and 80,000 primary and secondary English teachers to improve their communicative English language (EL) skills (Power, Shaheen, Solly, & Woodward, 2012; Shaheen, Walsh, Power, & Burton, 2013; Walsh et al., 2012).

English in Action has adopted a school-based teacher development model rather than rely on traditional and lengthy forms of training (UNESCO, 2005). Features of this model include some of the grounding principals within effective professional development models (Adelman, Donnelly, Dove, Tiffany-Morales, et al., 2002; Dembélé, 2005; ESSPIN, 2012; National Foundation for the Improvement of Education, 1996; Porter, Garet, Desimone, Yoon, & Birman, 2000). Some of these features include

- face-to-face meeting(s);
- classroom focused materials;
- in-school support from another teacher (peer support);

- in-school support from the head teacher;
- meetings outside that are close to the school where a teacher can meet with others working on the same ideas (cluster meetings);
- visits to the school by someone more skilled than the teacher; and
- some kind of audio–visual support that can show what other teachers have done in the classroom perhaps with commentary (e.g., the 'tutor in the pocket' or 'classroom in your pocket') (Power & Thomas, 2007).

One of the unique features of the EIA teacher professional development model is the use of mobile phones to support teacher facilitators in delivering training and teachers during teaching. Technology appears to be a vital component of the new emerging models of teacher professional development (TPD) to deal with the issue of training teachers effectively on a large scale (Banks et al., 2009; Moon, 2007). It is claimed that 'significant economies of scale' could be achieved through use of new forms of ICT (UNESCO, 2005). In a synthesis of six case studies from across African countries, three issues were identified as of particular importance for those working in teacher development, curriculum reform, time structure (e.g., rethinking period of initial training), and exploiting technologies (Moon, 2007).

In recent years, ICT tools have become more powerful and flexible, (Soloway et al., 2001). A research report from the UK's Department for International Development demonstrated the values of mobile communication systems for teacher education (Leach, 2006). Moon (2007) strongly argued that by "exploiting . . . communication technologies" and building them into "play and practice around teacher education" the "opportunity and entitlement for education and training can be significantly enhanced" (p. 366). Kukulska–Hulme (2006) is of the view that language learning can particularly benefit from ownership of mobile devices, such as phones and media players. Today there are over 5.9 billion mobile phone subscriptions worldwide (UNESCO, 2012), and ownership in developing countries is continually increasing. Fotouhi-Ghazvini, Earnsha, and Haji-Esmaeili (2009) emphasized that

> mobile learning has significant potential to be very influential in developing countries. Because of its ubiquitous nature and comparatively low cost, the mobile phone system appears to be the most practical way of delivering m-learning for the foreseeable future. Mobile learning with its any time/place/pace learning will conveniently accommodate different modes of language learning for different groups of learners. Being a relatively inexpensive technology, mobile phones can be easily integrated into mainstream education in developing countries, where underprivileged societies such as tribal and rural people can use it as a supplementary educational source.
>
> *(p. 391)*

They defined mobile learning (m-learning) as "micro learning through mobile devices that can be used anywhere, anytime, by either being connected using the mobile web or free standing" (Fotouhi-Ghazvini, Earnsha, & Haji-Esmaeili, 2009, p. 391). In Bangladesh, there were expected to be 95.5 million subscribers by the end of 2012, covering 60% of the population (BTRC, 2012). Waycott and Kukulska-Hulme (2003) investigated the use of handheld devices to support adult learners studying on an Open University course. They reported that the 'anytime, anywhere' access to learning resources is an 'important advantage' for learners to study at their own convenience.

In 2012, 4,000 teachers were provided a Nokia mobile phone together with a speaker for use in classrooms, followed by another 8,000 in 2013 (see Figures 22.1 and 22.2).

Figure 22.1   Virtual Guide on Nokia Mobile

Photo credit: English in Action/Faysal Abbas

Figure 22.2   Classroom Video on Nokia Mobile

Photo credit: English in Action/Faysal Abbas

Teachers are provided with audio–visual (AV) resources on micro-SD cards, which they are able to access any time through their mobile phones. These AV resources include authentic videos of pedagogic techniques, carried out by Bangladeshi teachers in their own classrooms. The audio files developed are linked to the government prescribed textbooks.

Teachers are provided support to help them use the provided materials. This is done through one-day initial teacher workshops (ITW) followed by seven bimonthly cluster meetings, conducted over a period of 16 months. In this, the teacher facilitators (TF) are required to use their Teacher Facilitator Guide, which has detailed 'cluster meeting (CM) plans' to help teachers deliver the modules from their Teacher Guide. The TFs follow the CM plans during the CMs to prepare teachers on using the audio, video, and print materials upon their return to the classrooms. Many of the pedagogic techniques that teachers are expected to use for teaching English have been 'decentralised' by embedding them into the audio and video materials uploaded onto the SD card inserted into the mobile phone (Leelan & Shaheen, 2012; Woodward, Solly, & Uzzaman, 2012). This was done with a view to reach an increasing number of teachers where direct firsthand contact with them by expert ELT specialists would be impossible.

During the cluster meetings, every teacher has a mobile phone inserted with SD card containing the audio and video materials, with headphones, provided by the project. The teacher facilitators work with the teachers and provide training during cluster meetings. They work with them through group, pair, and individual work using the mobile phones (see Figure 22.3a–22.3c).

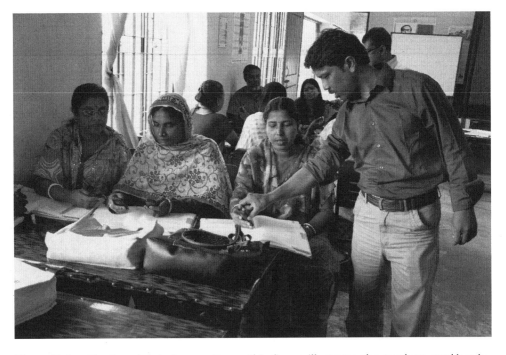

Figure 22.3a Teachers in cluster meetings. This figure illustrates the teachers working in groups using the mobile phones during cluster meetings.

Photo credit: English in Action/Faysal Abbas

Figure 22.3b Teachers in cluster meetings. This figure illustrates the teachers working in groups using the mobile phones during cluster meetings.

Photo credit: English in Action/Faysal Abbas

Figure 22.3c Teachers in cluster meetings. This figure illustrates the teachers working in groups using the mobile phones during cluster meetings.

Photo credit: English in Action/Faysal Abbas

Figure 22.4 EIA teacher participating in the cluster meeting. This figure illustrates a project teacher following the guidelines in the teacher guide and using the mobile phone.

Photo credit: English in Action/Faysal Abbas

The Cluster Meetings are built around the video sequences that teachers have on their mobile phones and are planned such that teachers are able to watch them collectively. This is based on both pedagogical and practical grounds. A fundamental tenet of EIA training is that learning is a social process (Woodward et al., 2012). The TFs work with the teachers to watch the video with them on their mobile phones and direct their attention to certain elements of the video, pause, repeat, and ask focused questions. They are also required to do a detailed analysis of the video through questions and answers. The teachers operate their own phones, focus on the content of the video, and work as a group. When teachers are viewing the videos in pairs on phones, the TFs need to ensure that all teachers are watching the same section.

An initial feedback on the use of the aforementioned techniques during cluster meetings was gathered from secondary school teachers and teacher facilitators during their second cluster meeting. This was held in November and December 2012, about four months after their first introduction to the program.

Two questionnaires, one for the teachers and one for the TFs, were specifically designed for this purpose in collaboration with the English language-teaching experts working on the project and involved in designing the audio and video materials. The purpose was to identify teacher and TF views on the use of mobile phones during training within cluster meetings, particularly viewing of the video clips as part of the teachers' professional development. There were 37 secondary school teachers, 8 female and 29 male, aged 26 to 59 from the Dhaka region, and 7 TFs, 3 female and 4 male, aged 32 to 47 from the Dkaka and Chittagong region. Once received, the data was entered into an Excel spreadsheet and analysed to generate frequencies. The findings are discussed next.

Teacher Facilitator Views on Mobile Phones as Training Devices During Cluster Meetings

The TF views are categorised into facilitation/group management and use of mobile phone functions. The TFs appeared less satisfied over some aspects of the mobile phone than teachers. Almost three-quarters stated it was easy to organise and ask the entire group of teachers to watch the video together on their phones. However, less than half agreed it was easy to manage the group as each teacher used his or her individual mobile phone. Opinion was divided amongst TFs over teachers remaining focused when watching videos on their mobile phone. Slightly less than half strongly agreed that it was easy for teachers to remain focused while watching video on their mobile phones. Similarly, opinion was further divided over initiating whole-group discussion with teachers as they individually used their mobile phones. One-third of the TFs strongly agreed that using individual mobiles was helpful in initiating whole group discussion (see Table 22.1).

The majority of the TFs agreed it was easy to get teachers to pause parts of the video using their mobile phones; however, no one strongly agreed. Just over two-thirds strongly agreed it was easy to get teachers to repeat parts of the video using their mobile phones while about one-third disagreed or strongly disagreed. The majority of TFs strongly agreed (70%) that videos shown on the mobile phone could be clearly seen by teachers; hence, the picture quality was good (see Table 22.2), which is contrary to the number of teachers strongly agreeing (less than half), discussed later.

Table 22.1 TF Views on Group Management and Facilitation While Using Mobile Phones to Watch Videos

Statements	Number of TFs responding				
	Strongly agree	Agree	Neutral	Disagree	Strongly disagree
Asking the entire group of teachers to watch the video together on their phones was easy to organise	5	2			
It was easy to manage the group using individual mobiles to watch the videos	2	3		2	
Teachers remained focused when watching videos on their mobiles	3	4			
Using individual mobiles was helpful in initiating whole group discussion (N = 7)	2	1	2	2	

Table 22.2 TF Views on Use of Mobile Phone and Its Functions

Statements	No. of TFs responding				
	Strongly agree	Agree	Neutral	Disagree	Strongly disagree
It was easy to get teachers to repeat parts of the video using their mobiles	4		1	1	1
The video shown on the mobile could be clearly seen by teachers (good picture quality) (N = 7)	5	2			

Teacher Views on Receiving Training Using Mobile Phones During Cluster Meetings

The findings from the teachers have been categorised into use of mobile phones and its functions, use of video contents/teacher participation, and group management by TFs.

Most teachers, three-quarters, strongly agreed they liked the use of mobile phones during the cluster meetings (see Table 22.3); however, opinions were divided amongst the teachers in terms of ease of using the functions on the mobile, including ease with which they could repeat, pause, and play the video, the picture quality, and adequacy of the sound system.

The majority of teachers (just over two-thirds) strongly agreed they could analyse the video using the mobile phone and were able to remain focused when watching the video on their phone (see Table 22.4). However, slightly less strongly agreed that it was easy to follow the instructions/contents when the mobile phone was used. Opinions were divided in terms of ease with which teachers felt they could participate in whole-group discussions and the disturbances caused when the mobile phone was used to watch and analyse videos.

More teachers strongly agreed (just over half) it was easy for TFs to use the mobile with the teachers to analyse the videos and to hold discussions, as shown in Table 22.5.

The teachers were also asked for any further comments they wished to make in relation to the use of mobile phones for training; however, only eight commented and those comments were mostly related to being satisfied with the overall project. Respondents indicated, "CM is quite fruitful"; "CM is quite successful"; "I am satisfied about the program"; and ". . . the technique of mobile is unique and its use makes the class diversified, funny and it reduces monotony" (Teacher 1).

However, there were also other comments. The teachers wanted to see examples of what they were taught in the CM 'being used in the class.' They also wanted fewer teachers in the cluster meeting. The teachers also said that the TFs should be accessible to them, outside cluster meetings, in case they faced problems when applying their learning.

Table 22.3 Teacher Responses to Use of Mobile Phone and Its Functions During Cluster Meetings

Statements	No. of teachers responding				
	Strongly agree	Agree	Neutral	Disagree	Strongly disagree
I like the use of mobile phone in the cluster meeting	28	9			
I could pause the video on the mobile	21	12	3	1	
I could easily repeat the video on the mobile	19	16	2		
The videos watched on the mobile were clear (visible)	17	16	2	1	
The sound system of the mobile was good (N = 37)	15	19	2	1	

Table 22.4 Teacher Responses to the Use of Video Contents on the Mobile Phone and Teacher Participation During Cluster Meetings

Statements	No. of teachers responding				
	Strongly agree	Agree	Neutral	Disagree	Strongly disagree
I could analyse the video easily using the mobile phone	25	11	1		
I was able to remain focused when watching video on mobile phone	25	11	1		
It was easy to follow the instructions/ contents when mobile was used	23	11	3		
There were fewer disturbances when mobile was used to watch and analyse videos.	18	16	2		
I could easily participate in whole group (all the participants in CM) discussions when watching the video on the mobile (N = 37)	18	17	1	1	

Table 22.5 Group Management by TFs

Statements	No. of teachers responding				
	Strongly agree	Agree	Neutral	Disagree	Strongly disagree
It was easy for TFs to get teachers to analyse videos using mobile phones	21	16			
It was easy for TFs to hold discussions with teachers during CM when they used mobile phones (N = 37)	21	16			

Use of Mobile Phones, Audio-Video Materials by Teachers in Their Classrooms and as Part of Their Professional Development

For the current phase, it is too early to assess the extent to which the teachers are using the provided materials and technology, or the impact of this on the classroom practice and language proficiency of teachers and students. However, in order to obtain initial feedback, a specifically designed questionnaire was administered to 18 secondary school English teachers, 12 male and 6 female, from the Dhaka area. The data were collected during the second cluster meeting, held in November 2012. The specific purpose of this was to gather initial experiences of teachers using mobile phones and the accompanying audio and video materials. The data were collected

Robina Shaheen and Ashok Paul Kumar

five months after the project inception when teachers received the mobile phone, speakers, and materials. Excel and SPSS were used to analyse the quantitative data, while qualitative responses were hand listed and categorised accordingly. The findings are presented next.

Mobile Phone Use

The teachers at this stage of the project are expected to use the provided mobile phones for playing the audio in the classrooms and the audio/video for their professional development. In this regard, most reported using the device for this intended purpose, with 17 reporting using the mobile phones to watch videos while slightly less using the device to play audio in the lessons and improve their own English. Few of the teachers are using other functions on the mobile phone, such as taking photos, making videos, calls, and using Internet, as shown in Table 22.6.

Most teachers reported being satisfied ($n = 13$) with the training received on how to operate the mobile phone. Similarly, 13 teachers reported being satisfied with the training received on how to use the mobile phone during their teaching, while five teachers said they were not satisfied. The findings indicate that one-time training is not sufficient for some teachers.

Use of Audio Materials During Teaching

The teachers are expected to use the materials as much as possible during their teaching in order to develop their expertise and confidence as well as to identify issues, which they may want to discuss in their cluster meeting. In this, most teachers ($n = 17$) reported playing the audio files on their mobile during their English lessons. However, the frequency with which teachers use audio appears low. Only 5 reported having used audio lessons 15 to 30 times over a five-month period. This is about once a week. These results show low use of the audio materials and perhaps suggest low levels of motivation and confidence amongst teachers. The findings may also indicate to the teacher's attitude and the degree to which these materials are regarded as helpful in supporting their teaching.

Some teachers have reported using the audio lessons repeatedly. Seven teachers reported playing audio three times in a single lesson, and five reported playing it two and four times, respectively. It must be mentioned that during training, teachers are encouraged to do this to develop interaction and achieve 'effective technology integration' (Manochehri & Sharif, 2009). This is done by using the pause and play function on the mobile phone.

Table 22.6 Purpose of Using the Mobile Phone

Purpose of using the mobile phone	No. of teachers reporting using the phone
To watch professional development videos about improving classroom teaching	17
To play audio lessons in the classroom	16
To listen to audio material for improving own English	15
To make and receive calls and send SMS	3
To use Internet	3
To listen to music	2
To take photos/record video	2
(N = 18)	

240

Teachers ($n = 16$) have reported that using audio lessons encourages the students to participate more. Some teachers ($n = 10$) have reported that they encourage further interaction amongst students by asking questions while playing the audio. All this indicates perhaps to the increasing confidence in the teacher's own ability to use the mobile phone and the audio materials.

The audio files provided to secondary school teachers are specified for use at certain points in a lesson. Teachers are reporting using these, for example, for listening comprehension ($n = 11$), pronunciation ($n = 2$), and reading passages ($n = 2$). Some have also reported using these to start the lesson ($n = 1$). This shows a diversion, nevertheless innovative use, of the audio material to capture student attention.

The primary purpose of the audio–video materials is to support teachers in improving their teaching of English. Eighteen teachers have reported that using audio helps them in teaching English better and students in learning English better. Teachers suggest that audio files are a direct support to their own teaching, by enabling them to teach listening comprehension, pronunciation, making teaching attractive, improving their self-confidence, and enabling 'good' preparation before teaching (see Figure 22.5). The teachers also report that playing the audio over reading text passages from textbooks makes a difference to the children, as it helps their pronunciation, 'reduces monotony', enables them to learn correctly and increases attention. In addition, audio lessons enable teachers to monitor the class; hence, students 'remain relatively quiet'.

Some teachers' comments on the benefits of using audio materials include the following:

"[Children] speak like foreigners."
"Teacher can monitor the class properly while audio is playing."
"[Students] become more delighted, studious, and active."

Figure 22.5 Primary school teacher using a mobile and speaker in her classroom.

Photo credit: English in Action/Faysal Abbas

Teachers also believe audio files help them to teach English better by being attractive to students. As a result, students become more attentive, interested, active, and 'excited' about the 'new things in class'. Furthermore, audio files help them understand, enable learning 'easily', improve their pronunciation, and increase active listening skills. More teachers are reporting using these materials because both they and their students are enjoying English lessons more when audio is used ($n = 17$). The reasons given for children's increased levels of enjoyment are mostly related to the availability of new equipment and techniques ($n = 17$).

Some of the teachers' comments related to using audio are given below:

"Students are happy to find something new apart from the traditional method."
"Pronunciation of the audio is beautiful and attractive."
"Students can correct themselves by knowing the proper pronunciation."
"They are enjoying the new voice in the audio."
"They can speak correctly."
"Students are realizing that English learning is not difficult to learn and getting interested to learn it."

The Ease and Difficulties of Using Audio

Most teachers indicated they do not have difficulty in using the audio files, with 16 saying that they find them easy to use in their classrooms and that the files make teaching English easier. Seventeen teachers said the children have difficulties when they teach English using audio, and seven said they face difficulties in using the audio in their classroom. Some of the difficulties faced included distraction for other classes ($n = 2$), problems with students not immediately understanding (e.g., needed to be replayed; $n = 2$), limited time ($n = 1$), and large classrooms (difficulty with volume management; $n = 1$). The teachers also reported having difficulties with the mobile device itself and the connection to the rechargeable speaker. Almost half of the problems reported were related to the play and pause buttons on the mobile phone while fewer reported keypad and the picture on mobile not working properly (see Table 22.7).

Some of the teachers' comments related to the difficulties faced include the following:

"Difficult to manage in limited time (You have to play it at least 4 times to make students understood)."
"Students could not understand it immediately. It has to be played several times."
"In large classroom, students in the back side cannot hear properly. On the other hand, if the volume is high student at the front face problem and it also disturb the class nearby."

Table 22.7 Problems Faced by Teachers When Using the Mobile Phone

Problems faced	No. of teachers reporting having the problem
Using pause and play buttons	5
Picture on mobile not working properly	2
Keypad is not working	2
Content deleted	1
Problem with connecting mobile to speaker (cord)	1
Problem with speaker volume	1
($N = 17$)	

Some of the problems outlined by the project teachers are also documented in the literature, including Anuradha and Tai (2010), who reported on a project using mobile phones in India where teachers also faced problems such as 'irregular power'. They also did not feel that they were 'useful' with some saying that they were a "waste of time" involved "heavy work load on the part of the teacher" and "not so important from the examination point of view" (p. 463).

Use of Video and Audio Material for Teacher Professional Development

Most teachers reported they listened to the TPD audios ($n = 13$), which helped them improve their own English ($n = 13$). Seventeen teachers said they watched the videos and 16 said the videos helped them in their classroom teaching by enabling them to teach more effectively, ($n = 5$), motivating students ($n = 1$), making lessons interactive ($n = 1$), and preparing students for listening activities ($n = 1$).

Few teachers reported they had difficulties understanding and following the guidance given by the virtual guide, Santa. Instead, these videos helped them in their classroom teaching by enabling them to teach more effectively ($n = 5$), motivating students ($n = 1$), making lessons interactive ($n = 1$), and preparing students for listening activities ($n = 1$).

Some of the teachers' comments in relation to videos included the following:

"To make warm-up attractive."
"Learning the correct way of teaching."
"I have learned how to prepare students for pre, post, and while listening."

Some teachers ($n = 7$) reported they found the videos very useful in helping them improve their English teaching, while three said that they found them quite useful. The teachers mostly reported things they liked about the videos, including way of teaching ($n = 9$), teacher student pronunciation ($n = 2$), while some (6) liked 'everything'. Only one teacher reported disliking the videos because the screen was too small.

Most teachers ($n = 16$) listened to an audio from the English Language for Teachers (EL4T) folder on their mobile phone to improve their English. Six reported listening to less than 10 EL4T lessons, a third ($n = 4$) listening to 15 to 20 lessons, and five listening to all or almost all the lessons. All teachers found lessons linked to the government prescribed textbook (*English for Today*) more useful ($n = 16$), and all reported that these lessons helped them to develop their own English ($n = 18$).

Conclusion

In this chapter, the background to the English in Action project, being implemented in Bangladesh, has been discussed. In addition, the teacher professional development model used and the delivery of materials to a large number of teachers through the use of mobile phones has been described. While the project has shown impact after its pilot phase, it is too early to assess the impact for the current phase. However, the initial feedback received from teachers and teacher facilitators, as presented in this chapter, indicates teachers are keen to explore the use of mobile phones and audio-video materials, because of its novelty and increase in student interest.

The mobile phone is also used as a training device by the project. While teachers and teacher facilitators remain positive, they are also reporting issues with the actual device, particularly in terms of using the pause and play buttons and managing a large group of teachers who are using the mobile device at the same time.

References

Adelman, N., Donnelly, M. B., Dove, T., Tiffany-Morales, J., Wayne, A., & Zucker, A. (2002). *The integrated studies of educational technology: Professional development and teachers' use of technology.* Arlington, VA: SRI International.

Anuradha, R., & Tai, K. (2010, June 22–24). *Effective use of audio-visual equipment and materials in classroom teaching.* Second International Conference on Education Technology and Computer (ICETC), Shanghai, China.

Bangladesh Telecommunication Regulatory Commission (BTRC). (2012). *Mobile phone subscribers in Bangladesh.* Retrieved from http://www.btrc.gov.bd/

Banks, F., Moon, B., & Wolfenden, F. (2009, June 8–10). New modes of communication technologies and the reform of open and distance learning programmes: A response to the global crisis in teacher education and training. 23rd ICDE World Conference on Open and Distance Learning, Maastricht, The Netherlands.

Dembélé, M. (2005). Breaking the mold: Teacher development for pedagogical renewal. In A. Vespoor (Ed.), *The challenge of learning: Improving the quality of basic education in sub-Saharan Africa* (Chapter 7, pp. 167–194). Paris, France: Association for Development of Education in Africa.

Dembélé, M., & Bé-Rammaj Miaro II. (2003, December 3–6). *Pedagogical renewal and teacher development in sub-Saharan Africa: A thematic synthesis.* Association for the Development of Education in Africa Biennial Meeting, Grand Baie, Mauritius.

ESSPIN. (2012). *Report of a small scale evaluation of ESSPIN's support to Kwara State's literacy and numeracy programme.* Abuja, Nigeria, Africa: ESSPIN.

Fotouhi-Ghazvini, F., Earnsha, A. R., & Haji-Esmaeili, L. (2009, September 7–11). *Mobile assisted language learning in a developing country context.* International Conference on CyberWorlds, Bradford University, United Kingdom.

Kukulska-Hulme, A. (2006). *Mobile language learning now and in the future. Från vision till praktik: Språkutbildning och Informationsteknik (From vision to practice: language learning and IT).* Sweden: Swedish Net University (Nätuniversitetet).

Leach, J. (2006). *DEEP impact: An investigation of the use of information and communication technologies for teacher education in the global south.* London, UK: Department for International Development (DFID).

Leelan, M., & Shaheen, R. (2012, October 15–18). English in Action: Usability and sustainability of audio-visual materials for English language teaching in Bangladeshi schools. *Proceedings from 11th World Conference on Mobile and Contextual Learning (mLearn 2012),* Helsinki, Finland.

Lewin, K. M. (2002). The costs of supply and demand for teacher education dilemmas for development. *International Journal of Educational Development, 22*(3/4), 221–242.

Manochehri, N., & Sharif, K. (2009). *Impact of classroom technologies on individual learning behaviour—A case study.* New York, NY: McGraw-Hill.

Moon, B. (2007) School-based teacher development in sub-Saharan Africa: Building a new research agenda. *Curriculum Journal, 18*(3), 355–371.

National Foundation for the Improvement of Education. (1996). *Teachers take charge of their learning: Transforming professional development for student success.* Washington, DC: Author.

Porter, A. C., Garet, M. S., Desimone, L., Yoon, K. S., & Birman, B. F. (2000). *Does professional development change teaching practice? Results from a three-year study.* Washington, DC: U.S. Department of Education.

Power, T., Shaheen, R., Solly, M., & Woodward, C. (2012). English in action: School based teacher development in Bangladesh. *The Curriculum Journal, 23*(4), 503–529.

Power, T., & Thomas, R. (2007). The classroom in your pocket? *The Curriculum Journal, 18*(3), 373–388.

Shaheen, R., Walsh, C., Power, T., & Burton, S. (2013 April 27–May 1). *Assessing the impact of large-scale teacher professional development (TPD) in Bangladesh: English in Action (EIA).* American Educational Association Annual Meeting, San Francisco, California.

Soloway, E., Norris, C., Blumenfeld, P., Fishman, B., Krajcik, J., & Marx, R. (2001). Log on education: Handheld devices are ready-at-hand. *Communications of the ACM, 44*(6), 15–20.

UNESCO. (2005). *Education for all: The quality imperative.* Paris, France: Author.

UNESCO. (2012). *Working paper series on mobile learning.* Paris. France: Author.

Walsh, C., Shaheen, R., Power, T., Hedges, C., Katoon, M., & Mondol, S. (2012, October 15–18). Low cost mobile phones for large scale teacher professional development in Bangladesh. *Proceedings from 11th World Conference on Mobile and Contextual Learning (mLearn 2012)*, Helsinki, Finland.

Waycott, J., & Kukulska-Hulme, A. (2003). Students' experiences with PDAs for reading course materials. *Personal and Ubiquitous Computing*, 7(1), 30–43.

Woodward, C., Solly, M., & Uzzaman, A. (2012, October 15–18). Delivering a personalized and reflective approach to teachers' professional development through the use of video on mobile phones. *Proceedings from 11th World Conference on Mobile and Contextual Learning (mLearn 2012)*, Helsinki, Finland.

23

Managing the Change During E-learning Integration in Higher Education

A Case Study From Saudi Arabia

Khalid Al-Shahrani and Len Cairns

Introduction

Information and Communication Technologies (ICTs) that are already familiar components in business environments are finding their way into education at all levels in many parts of the world. Such technologies, however, *disrupt* education (Bonk, Lee, Kim, & Lin, 2010; Christensen, Horn, & Johnson, 2008), as they require changes in the teaching approaches and the structure of the institutions (McPherson & Nunes, 2008). People, on the other hand, can resist change because it challenges them and drives them out of their comfort zone (Latchem & Jung, 2010). Therefore, managing the change during the transition phase is crucial (Kotter, 1996) and a challenging task for any leader (Tibi & McLeod, 2010). Universities experience such challenges during the transition from a traditional way of teaching to more e-learning-based teaching and learning, and this chapter has taken one Saudi Arabian University as a case study.

Despite the importance of e-learning leadership, it is not an issue that features much in the literature of e-learning (Jameson, 2011; Satyanarayana & Meduri, 2007). However, the impact and necessary elements of any change facilitation in an organization depend, to a large extent, on leadership support and management. This chapter examines the role of leadership in the change process surrounding the implementation of e-learning at one Saudi Arabian University, as a change from previous practices forms the site and context.

Recent Developments of E-learning in Saudi Arabia

The higher education sector in Saudi Arabia has undergone tremendous development in the last 10 years. The number of universities has jumped from eight in 2005 to 24 public and 10 private in 2012, including the Saudi e-University (SEU). Established in 2011, SEU is government-funded and approved by the Saudi Ministry of Higher Education to provide graduate and undergraduate degree programs along with lifelong education based on e-learning and distance education technologies (SEU, 2013). SEU came as the result of the development of e-learning initiatives in Saudi higher education, which included the establishment of the National Centre for eLearning and Distance Learning (NCeL) and e-learning Deanships in almost all Saudi universities. This development was parallel with rolling out the traditional distance learning programs, which had been operating in a number of local universities for the last decade. The National Commission for Academic Accreditation & Assessment (NCAAA) established Quality Standards for Distance Education Courses (NCAA, 2012) as a guide for Universities in this relatively new endeavour. The concept of establishing an organizational unit (the e-learning Deanship) with a Dean as leader emerged as a particular Saudi government approach within this set of e-learning developments.

E-learning Management and Leadership in the Transition Phase

Leadership is critical in managing successful institutions in any domain. E-learning in higher education is no exception. Mapuva (2009) stated that "institutional leaders are a determinant factor, given their decision-making which could either make-or-break the e-learning projects by either facilitating or impeding its implementation within their institutions" (p. 103). He continued that the direction and thrust of institutions towards learning programs were mainly determined by the leadership of that institution, which largely determines the extent to which e-learning is implemented in learning and teaching. Implementation is mainly based upon the leadership's commitment to, and realisation of, e-learning goals in their institutions.

Another main task that institutional leaders need to deal with is management of change (McPherson & Nunes, 2006; Tibi & Mcleod, 2010). Managing resistance effectively throughout the change phase has been reported in the literature as the corner stone for any change to be successful (Bridges, 2010; Kotter, 1996). Such resistance is inevitable in the transition phase when traditional universities move toward more online/virtual learning, which requires a fundamental change in the structure of the institution as well as teaching approaches (McPherson & Nunes, 2006; O'Neill, Singh, & O'Donoghue, 2004). There is a need for a leadership that deals with any resistance that may accompany such change in a cautious and assuring manner, given the growing number of universities that are migrating to increasingly digitalized learning environments. As universities endeavor to make this move, academics and e-learning leaders need to take into account the difficulties associated with these fundamental changes to the structure of their institution and the changing landscape of higher education at large (O'Neill et al., 2004; Tibi & Mcleod, 2010). This process of change is particularly difficult and requires strong and supportive leadership as well as changes to the organizational culture (McPherson & Nunes, 2006). It involves changing faculty's attitudes, values, and conceptions of teaching (O'Neill et al., 2004; Tibi & Mcleod, 2010). This may be best achieved when all stakeholders of institutions are involved in the process of change over considerable time (McPherson & Nunes, 2006). Other factors that contribute to leading successful change include clear and frequent communication and professional development opportunities. This is likely to lead to a better management of resistance as well as forming the basis of further successful change (Tibi & McLeod, 2010).

Leadership styles might be different in Middle Eastern, Asian, and Western countries. Latchem and Jung (2010) believed that leadership in open and distance learning (ODL) in Asia sometimes comes from governments. This is probably true, as most universities in Asia and the Middle East are still dependent upon government support and therefore are excessively influenced and regulated by government policies (Latchem & Jung, 2010). Such government-driven initiatives can be both supportive and controlling or even frustrating for innovation, depending on the issues and areas of concern. E-learning has, in many nations, been an area where the scope and need for infrastructure developments on large scales has necessarily involved significant government intervention and drive. Dhanarajan (2002) supports this claim and attributed most of the advancement of ODL in India to the commitment and farsighted policies of the Indian government. E-learning in Saudi public universities has been supported and regulated through the Ministry of Higher Education (MoHE) and its affiliated NCeL. However, despite the importance of top-level support for e-learning developments, this alone is not sufficient to make all the necessary changes within organizations charged with the development and implementation of the desired outcomes and programs (Cook, Holley, & Andrew, 2007). Collegial support and learning communities are significant factors in encouraging faculty to reflect on their practices and possibly adopt new technologies (Palloff & Pratt, 1999). In all cases, there is a need for e-learning leadership that maintains a balanced approach, one that is not highly centralized and provides diverse and flexible professional development opportunities for all faculty members who are expected to adopt e-learning approaches in their University teaching.

Methodology

This chapter draws on a PhD study that was conducted between 2009 and 2013 in an Australian University. The data presented in this chapter were collected from a Saudi Arabian University, which will be referred to as (SAU). Data were elicited mainly from interviews with four e-learning staff members and four faculty members. The faculty-member participants came from different faculties, including science, languages, education, and medicine. The e-learning staff participants included the e-learning Dean, the e-learning Manager, and two e-learning Specialists who were all involved in the e-learning Deanship entity. Interviews were conducted individually in a face-to-face setting on the SAU campus and lasted for approximately 30 minutes each. Data were transcribed and imported into Nvivo®, software developed in Australia for analyzing qualitative research. The study adopted a multisteps analysis process using two approaches. That is, 1) it adopted Miles and Huberman's (1994) principles of analyzing qualitative data, and 2) it used the Activity Theory (AT) model (Engestrom, 1987) to identify the unit of analysis of the study, which acted as a lens through which the Activity system was discussed and interpreted.

E-learning Evolution at SAU

One of the main goals of the e-learning Deanship at SAU according to its Strategic Plan for E-learning is to 'establish e-learning for everyone'. Among the steps outlined in the plan to achieve this goal is to "furnish continuous support, training, incentives, rewards, and encouragement for faculty in the valuable integration of technology into the teaching and learning activities". However, the focus of the Deanship during its earlier stages (between 2006 and 2008) was on the technical aspects of e-learning. 'In the first phase we were asking questions like what LMS should be used and similar technical questions about the hardware and software' (e-learning Dean). SAU faculty might require the technical training at the early stages of e-learning implementation, which can be seen as a prerequisite for pedagogical-driven different and new teaching practices. Lareki, de Morentin, and Amenabar (2010) asserted that e-learning training for university teachers need to be adjusted to respond to teachers' needs at their different stages of development.

The e-learning Deanship at SAU appeared to have recognized faculty's needs beyond the early technical aspects. Therefore, as the basic e-learning infrastructure developed, the Deanship started to provide, during later stages, training that included some pedagogically specific instruction including an on campus 'full week course in this notion of learner-centred learning . . . provided by an academic from another local university last year' (Teacher-4). It also provided SAU faculty, via first-hand experience, a chance to be online learners as explained by Teacher-2:

> I am enrolled in a distance online learning course in the USA paid for by [SAU] along with another 50 teachers from the university, and I'm very glad for that. This course is about the effective use of e-learning and maintaining the quality for teaching online. I think there are plenty of training chances at [SAU], but I think it should be made compulsory. You know, it is still voluntary, not everyone will come.
>
> *(Teacher-2)*

The e-learning staff showed a reasonable pedagogical awareness of the importance of not focusing on the technology per se but rather encouraging faculty to use e-learning as the means for different, yet effective, teaching. 'I think the technology itself is not the main issue in using e-learning in teaching, it is what you do with it is the most important issue' (e-learning Dean). The e-learning manager explained the Deanship view about e-learning:

> We [e-learning staff] tried to make technology and education meet at the right level and that was also mentioned clearly at least to the e-learning staff that technology should be in the background. This means we do not use technology for its own sake, this is an educational project. Technology is not our first concern; it should be used just as a tool.
>
> *(e-learning Manager)*

It can be said that the role of the Deanship has evolved from focusing on the technicality of e-learning to a more pedagogical-informed approach. The SAU university appeared to have invested in developing teachers' and students' skills through extensive support and training. Teachers' experience of being online learners themselves can also change their conceptions of teaching (Al-Mahmood & McLoughlin, 2004). Such *studentship* experience allows teachers to be reflective on their own beliefs and practices. Recently, Kukulska-Hulme emphasized that teachers need space and opportunities where they can be involved in concrete experiences that generate "personal conviction" about any particular technology they use (Kukulska-Hulme, 2012, p. 247). In this manner, the opportunity provided by SAU to teachers to experience being online learners in the American University, as mentioned by Teacher-2, can be a concrete experience that might lead to personal conviction.

E-learning Deanship Activity System

The Activity Theory model (Engestrom, 1987), which is also referred to as Activity System, has six aspects: subject, object, tools, community, rules, and division of labor. The model was adopted to depict the activity structure of e-learning Deanship at SAU in order to examine the dynamics within and between the elements of the activity system (see Figure 23.1). It is not the individual aspects of the model that constitute the subject of analysis, it is the relations between them and the contradictions within and between activity systems as a whole (Engestrom, 1987). *Contradictions* is a term used in AT to describe misfits within elements of one activity and between different activities (e.g., technology) and rules or change and local culture. However, AT does not see such contradictions as problems but rather as potential development spots in the activity (Engestrom, 2001). Therefore, the aim of the analysis is to find contradictions within the e-learning Deanship activity system and whether or not they have been dealt with.

Tools

E-learning Artefacts

iPads, data-show projectors
Internet
E-learning labs
Web-based applications (e.g.,
Blackboard, *Elluminate Live*,
Tegrity)

E-learning Training

On-campus training
Online courses provided by
international universities
Online technical support
Targeted training for Deans

E-learning Awards

SAU e-learning prize
Appreciation certificates
Highlighting teachers'
success stories

Subject

E-learning staff

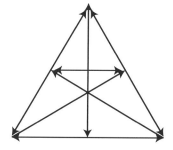

Object
Assist teachers, students,
and staff in eLearning
transitioning phase

Outcome
Making e-learning an
integral part of teaching
and learning

Rules
SAU E-learning Strategic Plan
SAU E-government Strategic
Plan
Course guidelines
SAU norms and culture

Community
Faculty members
Faculty Deans
University admins
Students

Division of Labor
Teachers' roles
E-learning specialists'
roles
Students' roles

Figure 23.1   E-learning Deanship Activity

Adapted and used with permission from Yrjö Engeström.

Emerged Challenges

Taking the e-learning Deanship as the unit of analysis, the activity system model revealed three contradictions among the different aspects of the activity. The first contradiction was between some of the activity tools (e.g., Internet connection) and the object of the activity. That is, the Internet connection interrupted e-learning implementation, especially at the earlier stages, which the Deanship tried to overcome by providing other alternative options as well as reporting any faults to the Internet provider. The second contradiction occurred between the community of the activity and its object—that is, the slow uptake of e-learning by faculty and students at the earlier stage of e-learning implementation. This has been overcome through local and international training for faculty and students. The e-learning staff also provided extensive technical support: 'We were accepting support requests till 12 a.m. midnight' (e-learning Manager). The e-learning specialists also provided immediate help to faculty and visited them in their offices when needed. Figure 23.2 shows a help page that was added in all courses for both teachers and students in Arabic and English.

The third contradiction arose within the community of the activity. That was between the e-learning staff and some academic staff across some faculties. Resistance to adopt e-learning occurred across faculties. In fact, the Deanship itself was, at times, conceived as a *threat*: 'We posed as competitors' (e-learning Manager). This may have resulted from the different change of pace

Figure 23.2   Blackboard Screen-Shot Showing E-learning Support Page for Faculty and Students

between the e-learning Deanship and some other faculties. 'Some faculties thought we did what we were doing to make them in a difficult position' (e-learning Manager). Coates, James, and Baldwin (2005) believed that introducing technology into university teaching creates new relationships, especially between teachers and other university staff. This often results in an overlap of responsibilities of teaching. It is this overlap of responsibilities that has been perceived differently within the community of the Deanship activity (e.g., e-learning staff and faculty Deans). Knoster (1991), as cited in Latchem and Jung (2010), stressed the importance of maintaining a balance between the pace and the extent of change, to avoid creating incoherence and disintegration within the target environment.

Managing the Change

According to the SAU website, the e-learning Deanship is the body that manages e-learning at SAU and develops the skills and abilities of university faculty and staff that are required for e-learning integration in teaching and learning. At the heart of this mission is managing the change that e-learning brings to the overall culture of teaching and learning at SAU. When asked about the main challenges in integrating e-learning at SAU, the e-learning Dean stated clearly:

> Well, the biggest barrier we faced and still facing is the human factor in the change management process. Honestly, the change is a very difficult issue we are facing. How can we deal with the opposition that we sometime have? How can we deal with some of the very enthusiastic staff? How can we deal with people who might have different goals from using e-learning? How can we deal with the negative people?
>
> *(e-learning Dean)*

Integrating e-learning in teaching often results in new and complex divisions of labor between faculty, e-learning staff, and students. Faculty may no longer be the sole organizers of the learning materials of their courses. They need the technical expertise of instructional designers and other e-learning staff to prepare for teaching on e-learning environments (Coates et al., 2005).

However, this change challenges teachers' status quo, which may result in teacher resistance. This makes managing change during the transition phase crucial (Kotter, 1996) and a challenging task for any leader (Tibi & Mcleod, 2010). SAU is no exception in experiencing this challenge during its transition from a traditional way of teaching to a more e-learning-based teaching and learning.

McPherson and Nunes (2006) believed such resistance from the university teachers was expected and possibly unavoidable. It was a result, they contend, of the fact that teaching in e-learning enhanced environments requires fundamental changes in the teaching approaches and the structure of the institutions. Some of the changes referred to by McPherson and Nunes seemed to be happening at SAU. The Dean of e-learning gave a relevant example: 'Those who have good positions in the university but not necessarily have the desire to change, started to think of the *new players* [who integrated e-learning in their teaching] who can attract the attention of the university community' (e-learning Dean). Therefore, such resistance might have some cultural interpretations. E-learning Specialist-2 observed that 'some of the university teachers, especially the professors, regard themselves as the elite in their society and therefore might find it difficult to be taught by others'. To respond to this contradiction in the SAU activity, the Deanship adopted strategies, such as targeted training for senior groups.

> It happened few times that we did specific training for certain groups such as Deans and Department Heads. That training is also different from the training we offer faculty as it focused more on the value and benefits of e-learning.
>
> *(e-learning Manager)*

Another change management strategy was 'to do some public relations across university and continue to give assurance to all parties involved of the main goals of the e-learning Deanship' (e-learning Manager). The Deanship also chose a faculty member from each faculty as an *e-learning coordinator* and provided them with additional training. Their designated role was to liaise between the Deanship and each faculty and to be a first point of contact for their colleagues in relation to integrating e-learning in teaching.

In addition to the abovementioned support, the Deanship adopted different approaches to motivate SAU faculty and students to be more creative in integrating e-learning in their teaching and learning. An *e-learning Award* was one of the Deanship initiatives toward that aim. It included incentives for faculty and students comprising an amount of cash, Laptop computers, and certificates of appreciation as well as highlighting success stories on the university website. The strategy of highlighting faculty's success stories served two purposes. First, it worked as recognition of teachers' efforts. Second, it showed other teachers some examples for e-learning use from their own context. The e-learning Specialist at the Faculty of Medicine (e-learning Specialist-1) explained how the Deanship highlighted the experience of one Professor from the faculty:

> One of our professors who used e-learning in teaching Surgery in the previous semester, gave an introductory session for medicine staff about his experience titled Is E-learning Suitable for Clinical Use? So, that was another story from one of their colleagues that encouraged them further to be more active with e-learning in their teaching.
>
> *(e-learning Specialist-1)*

Students were also included in the e-learning prize: 'I have two postgraduate female students who won SR5000 [approx. $1,300] for each of them' (Teacher-3). Faculty, on the other hand, expressed their gratitude towards the Deanship and university: 'Look, every one of us needs appreciation, regardless of our age' (Teacher-1). However, there might have been other motives driving teachers' use of e-learning that were not made explicit during interviews for any reason (e.g., motivation to win the e-learning prize, get more qualification to be recognized nationally or internationally, and/or the sense of accomplishment after being recognized). Indeed, it could be any one of these factors or all of them.

Professional development opportunities for teachers, as well as other university staff, coupled with accessible and multiple support channels seemed to be the main factors managing the change rather effectively (Tibi & Mcleod, 2010). Change is not an easy process and relies on both the e-learning leadership and socio-cultural context of the organisation (McPherson & Nunes, 2006), especially in a context where e-learning is not yet fully established. The change itself within the organization is a dialectical process, as it involves changing teachers' conceptions and practices (O'Neill et al., 2004) while at the same time, the teachers' beliefs are affected by the perceptions of the institutional support. Therefore, there is a pressing need for e-learning leadership that ensures the alignment of e-learning policies and organizational cultures with the objective of e-learning implementation in educational organizations. Whilst acknowledging the role of individual teachers in making effective use of e-learning, teachers need leadership that facilitates their efforts in all stages of e-learning implementation.

Conclusion: The Future of E-learning Deanships in Saudi Arabia

By 2015, e-learning Deanships initiatives would have almost completed a decade of managing e-learning in Saudi universities. Therefore, studies that review the nation-wide initiative and the future of such Deanships are invaluable. However, we believe that there is an ultimate need for within-faculties leadership of e-learning. In other words, leadership and management for e-learning need to emerge organically from within faculties. Ultimately, the role of e-learning Deanships will need to change as faculties and departments build the e-learning capacities of their teachers and students. Teachers and students are also changing as a part of the rapidly changing society, both locally and across the increasingly globalized world. Therefore, e-learning Deanships in Saudi Arabia need to be restructured so that the focus shifts gradually to excellence and innovation in teaching. It is helpful to think of e-learning Deanships as an evolving activity system with its tools, community, and object. This also means that it must set new object(s) that are of a more challenging and innovative nature. As the expertise of the community (in this case faculties and teachers) develops and their requirements change, the object of the activity needs to be revised and developed so it continues to meet the community's demands and aspirations.

References

Al-Mahmood, R., & McLoughlin, C. (2004). *Re-learning through e-learning: Changing conceptions of teaching through online experience*. Paper presented at the the 21st ASCILITE Conference, Perth, Australia. Retrieved from http://www.ascilite.org.au/conferences/perth04/procs/al-mahmood.html

Bonk, C., Lee, M., Kim, N., & Lin, M. (2010). Wikibook transformations and disruptions: Looking back twenty years to today. In S.C.Y. HH Yang (Ed.), *Collective intelligence and e-learning 2.0: Implications of Web-Based Communities and Networking* (Vol. 2, pp. 127–146). New York, NY: Informatoon Science Reference.

Bridges, P. W. (2010). *Managing transitions: Making the most of change*. Philadelphia, PA: Da Capo Press.

Christensen, C., Horn, M., & Johnson, C. (2008). *Disrupting class: How disruptive innovation will change the way the world learns*. New York, NY: McGraw-Hill.

Coates, H., James, R., & Baldwin, G. (2005). A critical examination of the effects of learning management systems on university teaching and learning. *Tertiary Education and Management, 11*(1), 19–36.

Cook, J., Holley, D., & Andrew, D. (2007). A stakeholder approach to implementing e learning in a university. *British Journal of Educational Technology, 38*(5), 784–794.

Dhanarajan, G. (2002, December 6). *Open and distance learning in developing economies.* Paper presented at the UNESCO Conference of Ministers of Education of African Member States (MINEDAF VIII), Dar es Salaam, Tanzania.

Engestrom, Y. (1987). *Learning by expanding: An activity-theoretical approach to developmental research.* Helsinki, Finland: Orienta-Konsultit Oy.

Engestrom, Y. (2001). Expansive learning at work: Toward an activity theoretical reconceptualization. *Journal of Education and Work, 14*(1), 133–156.

Jameson, J. (2011). Distributed leadership and the visibility paradox in on-line communities. *An Interdisciplinary Journal on Humans in ICT Environments, 7*(1), 49–71.

Kotter, J. P. (1996). *Leading change.* Boston, MA: Harvard Business School Press.

Kukulska-Hulme, A. (2012). How should the higher education workforce adapt to advancements in technology for teaching and learning? *The Internet and Higher Education, 15*(4), 247–254. doi:10.1016/j.iheduc.2011.12.002

Lareki, A., de Morentin, J.I.M., & Amenabar, N. (2010). Towards an efficient training of university faculty on ICTs. *Computers and Education, 54*(2), 491–497. doi:http://dx.doi.org/10.1016/j.compedu.2009.08.032

Latchem, C., & Jung, I. (2010). *Distance and blended learning in Asia.* London, UK: Routledge.

Mapuva, J. (2009). Confronting challenges to e-learning in higher education institutions. *International Journal of Education and Development Using ICT, 5*(3), 101–114.

McPherson, M., & Nunes, M. (2006). Organisational issues for e-learning: Critical success factors as identified by HE practitioners. *International Journal of Educational Management, 20*(7), 542–558.

McPherson, M., & Nunes, M. (2008). Critical issues for e-learning delivery: What may seem obvious is not always put into practice. *Journal of computer assisted learning, 24*(5), 433–445.

Miles, M., & Huberman, A. (1994). *Qualitative data analysis: An expanded sourcebook.* Los Angeles, CA: SAGE.

NCAAA. (2012). Standards for quality assurance and accreditation of higher education programs offered by distance education. Retrieved from http://www.ncaaa.org.sa/siteimages/ProductFiles/40_Product.pdf

O'Neill, K., Singh, G., & O'Donoghue, J. (2004). Implementing elearning programmes for higher education: A review of the literature. *Journal of Information Technology Education, 3*(2), 313–322.

Palloff, R., & Pratt, K. (1999). *Building learning communities in cyberspace.* San Francisco, CA: Jossey-Bass.

Satyanarayana, P., & Meduri, E. (2007). The qualities of leadership required in distance education. *Asian Journal of Distance Education, 5*(1), 4–7.

SEU. (2013). *Saudi e-University: Vision and mission.* Retrieved from https://www.seu.edu.sa/sites/en/AboutSEU/Pages/VMG.aspx

Tibi, S., & McLeod, L. (2010). Faculty members' perceptions about the management of organizational change. *Learning and Teaching in Higher Education: Gulf Perspectives, 8*(1), 1–16.

24

Issues and Implications of Integrating E-learning at Arab Universities

Ali Al-Musawi and Mary Lane-Kelso

Introduction

The developments of the 21st century in Information and Communication Technology (ICT) are considered to be distinctive landmarks of human creativity. These technologies have affected all life sectors, especially education, and have led to a new mode of education delivery—e-learning. In turn, e-learning has revolutionized educational learning styles and methods in higher education (HE) by extending the boundaries of learning beyond the traditional classroom into the homes and work places of society (Relan & Gillani, 1997; cited in Khan, 2005, p. 4). At the same time, e-learning has added new possibilities to education, which make it more engaging and motivating with the addition of sound, images, movement, and illustrations; in addition to multimedia, the robustness of these new communication and information resources promotes more information freedom, academic democracy, and equitable educational opportunities.

E-learning and Education

Learning using ICT is an innovative way to provide information to learners that is responsive to their different characteristics—intelligence, age, gender, experiences, capabilities, and preferences in a technology–rich environment. Instructors and learners interact in a dynamic educational environment without physical presence. Thus, designing this virtual campus technological environment is characterized by the following (Khan, 2005, p. 3; Grable, Overbay, & Osborne, 2005):

1. Openness and flexibility according to the time, place, and speed with which the student wishes to receive learning.
2. Accessibility to the largest number of learners.
3. Accessibility for students at the lowest possible cost and effort.
4. Accessibility to abundant digital and human resources.
5. Accessibility to multiple technologically rich modes of content and interactions.

The potential of ICT in education lies in its ability to develop human and academic resources and increase the cost effectiveness of the outcomes. In addition, ICT is considered as the fastest way for information and knowledge growth, making it a tool to lead the change of the traditional education characterized by limiting factors. Traditional education is treated as a closed system that occurs within the classroom, campus, book, and specific field visit. Despite the lecturer's instructions for their students to prepare papers using the library and to engage in field learning activities, many traditional classrooms are confined within walls that contain the thoughts of lecturers, authors of the textbook, and comments of the students. Thus, the classroom remains limited for these students and only open to those in its physical location (Khan, 2005, p. 4).

E-learning, in general, improves oral and visual communication between university students, fosters a computing culture, and develops positive attitudes toward learning in general through daily interaction (Grable et al., 2005). It helps to build a common cultural of understanding and a dynamic dialogue between cultures. It leads to the bridging of intellectual, scientific, and humanistic exchange at a time that ICT has become one of the most important components/ tools of an era of globalization.

E-learning improves learning significantly, especially that which occurs as a result of the student's own search for knowledge and information, facilitated by technological tools. It becomes a positive force seeking out practical and realistic solutions to the chronic problems in education. We believe that the use of e-learning not only helps to increase student interaction with the information given to them but also increases their interaction with each other and with their lecturers. Therefore, e-learning, through the use of modern technologies, plays three distinctive roles in education (Al-Musawi, 2011). First, in the instructional communication medium, education is designed with illustrative multimedia and interactive formats. These new forms of communication use digital technologies to disseminate the traditional educational audiotapes and videotapes, slides, transparencies, and textbooks, which, limited in their traditional use by time and place, can now be used to communicate to different parts of the campus and the surrounding community. Second, as an open learning resource, e-learning presentations display information, sources of knowledge and skills, and scientific/academic data in unprecedented ways. It allows acquisition of knowledge and skills more easily and in a variety of preferred learning styles. Third, the delivery of content includes multiple methods from multiple sources, so the instructor is no longer the sole source of information. Finally, e-learning allows multiple ways for instructors to interact with students as well as students interacting with other students, which allow collaboration, self-pacing, and more student-centered activities. Synchronous/ asynchronous learning, blended learning, and mobile learning extend the experience and enrich the process of learning (Ismail, Almekhlafi, & Almekhlafy, 2010).

While the use of e-learning facilitates new methods in university teaching, students, too, can discover new ways of learning when time and space constraints are removed. Resources, which include human resources, can allow students to reach out to experts they would not have access to in traditional classrooms. Based on the pace of understanding, comprehension, and application, e-learning can meet individual intellectual and ability needs as well as better respond to their unique cultural and social backgrounds.

In the following sections, we will discuss, in detail, e-learning integration and its future implications to the institutions at the HE sector.

Integration of E-learning in Higher Education

In general, ICT enhances the universities' independence by enabling them to make more of their own educational decisions. Adapting to the e-learning mode of teaching and learning provides planners in educational institutions with accurate information through documents, rationale, and administrative and statistical data details in order to make systematic and rationalized decisions. In addition, it allows other universities to share their experiences in the field of important administrative decisions and shows content and the results of these experiences. The systematic planning for e-learning in the universities provides information about required standards, quality assurance, new technological tools, best educational practices, funding sources and levels, and the available human resources (Al-Musawi, 2007). It also helps to employ research recommendations and considers the needs of the labor market while providing alternative scenarios to compare global technological planning and its interactions at the local level. In turn, this allows educational planners to better weigh advantages and disadvantages of others and better inform their decision-making process.

As in other areas of the world, implementing e-learning in HE would require a change in society and, sometimes, in a culture. The main factors that encourage individuals to think differently about the effectiveness of technological applications and form positive attitudes toward e-learning may include providing them with training to create positive roles to help others understand e-learning and its benefits, and disseminating information on e-learning within the university. This should promote changing attitudes and create a collaborative environment eager for its use in education (Al-Musawi & Akinyemi, 2002). In addition, the administrational leadership should distribute a positive statement of the extent to which e-learning can improve teaching and learning methods and solve organizational and educational problems at the university. This leads to extend its legitimacy throughout the institution. Furthermore, initial models (prototypes) should be designed, developed, produced, and presented to help lecturers achieve the required level of competence in the future to deal with e-learning.

Implications of Integrating E-learning in Higher Education

Change is difficult under normal circumstances, but when altering the direction of a coveted societal sector that is by nature traditional, such as education, it can prove quite dramatic. There are consequences to the changes that are taking place, and some are not as easily anticipated as others. Following are some of the implications that have been witnessed so far.

First: The Changing Role of University Faculty

University faculty must keep pace with the rapid changes in the areas of education, information, and communication technologies. University faculty should utilize all teaching tools that include the Internet and the new technologies as to ensure best practices and help learners access educational materials and facilitate self-learning. Faculty need to be trained to manage Internet conference sessions and interactive debate/dialogue through the networks using audio-video and chat tools. Faculty should be trained to assist learners to retrieve information from databases stored on computer servers of educational institutions.

Faculty should also be instructional designers who can facilitate learning as well as teach students. They need to be aware of how to use e-learning in order to raise the cost effectiveness of the educational process and to cut costs. Faculty should meet the learners' needs, respond to their individual differences, and contribute to design remedial e-lessons so that learners can access information directly on the Internet (Al-Musawi, 2007; Al-Musawi & Abdelraheem, 2004). Faculty should give learners the opportunity to evaluate themselves, increase their motivation toward learning, and participate positively using multimedia. Faculty needs to be trained how to access multiple kinds of authentic resources of knowledge and make them available to the learners. They need to be familiar with using networks in the management and control of information in light of the ever-increasing quantity of knowledge.

As a result, we can designate the following kinds of skills required from 21st-century faculty (Al-Musawi, 2011; Al-Sarrani, 2010; ISTE, 2012):

1. Technological expert: one who masters the skills of the operation and maintenance of computer hardware/software, multimedia/hypermedia, Internet, and networks and uses and reproduces them in the presentation of information and designs, develops and integrates e-activities in the teaching/learning process.

2. Instructional designer: one who masters the skills of design and production of virtual and multimedia/hypermedia according to the learners' characteristics, academic content, and learning methods through technologies of simulation, programming languages, and computer animation and integrates them into teaching.

3. Distance education lecturer: one who masters the use of educational software/hardware and audiovisual communication media to equip, design, and broadcast recorded/live distance educational lectures, conferences, and seminars through ICT.

4. Information and resources specialist: one who possesses the skills to apply the principles of computer and Internet in education in order to gather information from learning resources and the mechanisms of their revision, organization, processing, selection, evaluation, and retrieval and then links them to the educational curriculum and scientific theories/concepts.

5. Communication consultant: one who possesses the skills of dialogue, conversation, listening, and writing and can maintain positive relationships with learners using e-tools, chat, and electronic discussion forums.

6. Facilitator of cooperation: one who masters the skills of forming educational teams and collaborative/cooperative groups and is able to manage and facilitate collective dialogue between team members.

7. Problem-solver: one who is able to resolve conflict, recognize potential problems, find solutions with compromise, and stimulates critical and creative thinking toward educational issues.

8. Self-developer: one who possesses the skills to apply the principles of computer in continuing professional self-development to become an educated person who keeps abreast of technological innovations and educational techniques.

9. Coach: one who is able to transfer knowledge and expertise to others, employs electronic training methods and smart/virtual classrooms to retrain colleagues, and provides the necessary support for them to solve problems using e-learning and integrate it into education.

10. Legal advisor: one who practices the skills to apply netiquette (online ethics) and intellectual property rights, is familiar with copyright issues, protects the privacy of others, and provides solutions for digital divides and electronic piracy.

11. Evaluator expert: one who improves the selection and use of computer and Internet software and evaluates learners' work; designs e-tests and scales to judge their academic works and assignments; aligns to recognized standards of the field; updates e-portfolios and electronic records, databases, and schedules; and tracks progress electronically.

12. Researcher: one who masters the use of statistical and research packages to conduct field studies and measure the impact of e-learning on student achievement, and relates it to the content of e-curriculum, e-courses, and e-books.

13. Long-term planner: one who masters the skills of strategic e-learning planning on the medium-and long-term; chooses computer, media, and Internet hardware and software; and acquires, purchases, stores, classifies, organizes, indexes, and monitors them; studies the market to see prices and review updates.

Second: The Changing Role of the University Student

The International Society for Technology in Education (ISTE, 2012) has listed six areas of competency required of student mastery of the knowledge society based on the use of e-learning. For example, at Sultan Qaboos University, we have adopted these to help guide the expectations of our students. The first area is creativity and innovation, where students need to demonstrate creative thinking, construct knowledge, and develop innovative products and processes using technology. The second is communication and collaboration, where students need to use digital media and environments to communicate and work collaboratively, including at a distance, to support individual learning and contribute to the learning of others. The third is research and information fluency, where students need to apply digital tools to gather, evaluate, and use information. The fourth is critical thinking, problem solving, and decision-making, where students need to use critical thinking skills to plan and conduct research, manage projects, solve problems, and make informed decisions using appropriate digital tools and resources. The fifth is digital citizenship, where students need to understand human, cultural, and societal issues related to technology and practice legal and ethical behavior. The sixth is technology operations and concepts where students need to demonstrate a sound understanding of technology concepts, systems, and operations.

Third: The Changing Role of the Technology Resource Specialist

In general, in light of technological developments, the university support specialists need competencies to design instruction and analyze learners' characteristics and the university's educational/virtual environment to serve the teaching/learning process. They should employ educational innovations in e-learning, such as electronic and digital libraries, e-books, and electronic publishing; serve the university educational environment; and deal with lecturers/learners as its activation incorporates efficient utilization of ICT. In addition, they should provide training and consultancies on the integration of e-learning in education along with technical support for equipment and software, resources, and networks. They have to plan, design, and evaluate e-learning software/hardware, and supervise their organization, acquisition, classification, upkeep, and records. They should acquire the skills to contribute to the flexibility of technological change on campus and dissemination of educational innovations. Moreover, they have to upkeep the network functioning and security, promote e-learning culture and ethics, and maintain security, privacy, and intellectual property for electronic products and software (Al-Musawi, 2000; ISTE, 2012).

Fourth: The Adoption of Standards or Guidelines to Utilize E-Learning at Universities

These criteria include developing an administrative and regulatory technology plan of e-learning activation and providing technological centers with qualified specialists. In addition, technical specifications for technologies to be acquired and updated and rules, guidelines, and procedures that regulate the uses of e-learning at the university should be established. Technological infrastructures should be prepared supported by connections of fiber optic and wireless networks that are sufficient for administrative, educational, and research purposes. Electronic educational portals at the university, along with electronic software, forum lists, and databases for student, administrative, and academic information systems should be prepared and managed. Furthermore, preparation of multimedia laboratories, mobile labs, and classrooms with appropriate media technologies should take place. Other criteria include preparing the learning and educational content management system's inclusive virtual classroom management and providing quality and evaluative measures based on the use of e-learning (Khan, 2005, p. 10).

Fifth: The Use of E-learning in Professional Development and Training

The use of e-learning in training can be gradually approached to attain Internet-based training (e-training) through the creation of a technology plan for the university that outlines continuous improvement for all faculty and staff. Universities should take steps such as raising the awareness of administrators, lecturers, and students of the importance of e-learning in the training, development of human resources, and academic and administrative development as well as methods of managing continued professional development (Kamal, 2013). They should retrain human resources and improve their skills and competencies in order to employ ICT in the university administration. In this domain, the concerned authorities need to design, develop, and produce orientation sessions and training workshops including their materials, media, and programs according to the needs of lecturers, administrators, and students. They have to guide faculty and students using best practices for integration of technology with training centers and support specialists.

To address these issues, we provide the reader with the following detailed literary background on e-learning and its prospective roles in Arab HE. In the following sections, we will discuss integration issues at these institutions and offer some suggestions to ensure a successful process.

Integrating E-learning at Arab Universities

Many Arab universities are aware of the impact of ICT on their respective countries' overall economies, as well as on their individual citizens, that affect social development of their communities. The purpose of focusing on Arab universities is to share some lessons that have been learned and to highlight the need for continued collaborative efforts. Universities in the Arab World are in the process of e-learning development and their leaders have understood that there is a need to move thoughtfully and gradually with its approach. Most universities in the region have understood this and have introduced e-learning as a way to support traditional education on campus (Akinyemi, 2003). This step is a way toward moving to the future accommodation of more learners, who will be taught online, via the network, combined with part-time college attendance, a delivery mode known as 'blended learning'. However, some Arabic academic institutions have already adopted electronic 'enrichment' to support its face-to-face traditional courses and interactions. For example, Saudi Arabia has established the National Center for E-learning and Distance Learning to "have the most accurate design using the best tools and pedagogy to achieve the society and community needs in the higher education sector". The Center sponsors a biannual e-learning conference and offers professional programs to develop lecturers' skills (MOHE, 2013).

In many universities, there are clear efforts to help support the metamorphosis into the e-learning environment that include the following suggestions (Akinyemi, 2003; Ismail et al., 2010; Sadik, 2008):

1. Introduce specialized software to facilitate the design of teaching/learning courses and online classroom management.
2. Connect networks and provide technological infrastructure within universities.

3. Conduct training workshops and courses to disseminate e-learning and present its benefits, show how to adapt and employ it in the teaching/learning process, and increase the number of faculty using it.

4. Establish smart and e-classrooms, multimedia laboratories, and technology-rich environments, and provide students with laptops or tablets at a subsidized cost.

5. Construct electronic portals and information systems for student registration and management of electronic databases. For example, a portal designed and implemented by the Arab Bureau of Education for the Gulf States is distinctive of its type in terms of inclusiveness, content, and services.

6. Develop technology integration plans that reflect futuristic strategies and visions identifying policies, legal frameworks, and procedures associated with the use of e-learning.

7. Conduct and promote e-research and studies and publish these on the uses of e-learning and ICT in the educational process.

8. Establish open and virtual universities guided by best practices based on electronic, open, and blended learning methods of distance education delivery.

9. Introduce e-mobile administrative services and official announcements.

10. Initiate procedures of electronic supervision, training, guidance and counseling, and microteaching.

11. Design digital libraries, electronic journals subscriptions, and participate in utilizing electronic textbooks in courses.

It is important to stress that even though these suggestions propose an ambitious move in the e-learning direction, it should be noted that introducing e-learning in the Arab HE institution should depend on "adaptation" to the educational reality rather than to its "adoption". Planning for technology integration is a crucial step to ensure ownership of the process. There is no "one size fits all" for countries when education extends to e-learning. There needs to be clear recognition of the unique background, traditions, and culture of individual societies (Akinyemi, 2003).

Planners should not blindly adopt e-learning teaching/learning methods from the Western context and apply it to the Arabic context and societies. They must ensure its suitability for the Arabic environment and reformulate it to outfit the components of the new culture. It is among the issues that have plagued Arab education in the last century. The scenario of imposing numerous educational approaches without paying attention to their suitability to the new educational environment in the Arab world is all too familiar and often unsuccessful. Previous attempts have failed due to the different societal contexts, values, and goals.

It is clear that the Arab Universities have a long way to go in order to optimally utilize ICT in HE institutions and to make the shift toward serving large segments of students using teaching methods based on e-learning. This is critical based on the large numbers of secondary schools' outcomes, which offsets a lack of financial, human, and technical resources available to HE institutions. Based on this, we can conclude that taking the "technological" approach in the Arab world universities is a step forward that considers the good of the Arab society, not just a good way to remain contemporary. Similar to other countries or regions, Arab universities need to increase the cost effectiveness of their educational sectors, reduce wastage of their financial and technical resources, raise the internal efficiency of university systems, improve the level of learning outcomes, and respond to the requirements of the labor market (Al-Musawi & Akinyemi, 2002). The e-learning approach to education can assist with all these improvements.

E-learning can be used in the existing Arab universities, which are originally based on traditional methods, to provide students with learning resources and media and to support classroom meetings. It can be also used to deliver foundation courses, which are usually crowded with students. In advanced stages, it can be used to award degrees for short-term academic programs directed to students at continuing education and community courses, and conduct training sessions for managers and heads of academic departments (Al-Musawi & Abdelraheem, 2004). However, some Arab universities have been established with educational standards based entirely on e-learning and award degrees to full academic programs, such as Arab Open University, Al-Quds Open University, and Syrian Virtual University.

Arabic Research in the Field of E-learning Integration

There are a number of Arab research studies on integrating e-learning in university education (Al-Musawi, 2007; Al-Musawi & Abdelraheem, 2004; Al-Musawi & Akinyemi, 2002), but most of them are theoretical as a result of the lack of actual e-learning applications. Most Arab-conducted research studies are quantitative and focus on levels of equipment and the efficiency in the design, production, use of software, and future requirements for technological applications. However, there are some research efforts that are beginning to study the impact of teaching students using e-learning. Researchers have conducted research using both quantitative and qualitative approaches as well as descriptive field analysis to study the applications of e-learning in the Arab HE institutions.

The results of these studies have reported positive trends towards e-learning and increased improvement in the academic achievement of students when integrating e-learning in their education. Findings also showed the need for future expansion in e-learning initiatives combined with low-cost and portable equipment. They also reported an urgent need to train human resources and suggest establishing specialized university programs in educational technology and e-learning. Other findings showed the need to recruit more faculty members who were specialized in these areas in order to activate in-service training for professionals in the field. Lastly, research studies reported the need to support e-learning budgets and funding of future research.

Issues of Integrating E-learning

There are many advantages to integrating e-learning in Arab higher education, and there are also difficulties and obstacles which need attention. Issues and difficulties that have emerged from e-learning initiatives in HE institutions are explained in this section.

General Issues

There are many general issues to consider in the Arabic context. Boldly moving forward with e-learning requires large expenditures on new facilities and equipment, which can alter the balance of spending for university budgets. There are fears that are expressed when integrating e-learning. For example, educationalists express concerns about dehumanizing faculty and students while exalting technology, social isolation of learners with the loss of face-to-face communication skills, and the psychological effects of e-learning such as affiliation by unfavorable e-groups and attitudes (Ismail et al., 2010; Mouakket, Nour, & Al-Imamy, 2007). Parents, on the other hand, are deeply concerned about the kids' technology addiction, moral and ethical decline brought about by unlimited access to unsavory websites and ideas, and losing traditional ways of thinking and living in favor of contemporary fads and fashions.

Practical Issues

In practice, there are doubts about the real need for e-learning in the traditional universities that are founded and equipped to support face-to-face education and provided with their human, financial, and physical resources and facilities (Al-Musawi & Akinyemi, 2002). Faculty members have their own technophobia originated from the fear that e-learning can replace them, which may generate psychological resistance. This resistance can also be due to technological ignorance or to fears of loss of academic independence and authority. In addition, there is lack of belief in the quality of teaching with e-learning that creates doubts about its effectiveness. On planning and technical levels, many Arab universities lack the infrastructure and Internet accessibility. They tend to have long-term technological planning to adopt e-learning with no strategic vision for the process of its integration. In many instances, there is little administrative support and financial resources with scarcity of technical expertise and human resources. There are no legal frameworks and/or precise criteria for the academic evaluation to deal with cases of fraud, plagiarism, and electronic piracy. Furthermore, many universities suffer from the lack of mechanisms to control the quality of courses and graduates, incentives for academic accreditation of university e-learning initiatives, and procedures to guide electronic security and the flow of information, confidentiality, privacy, and protection of intellectual property rights.

Cultural Issues

Culturally, the impact of technology on Arabic identity is obvious specifically in terms of using Arabic language versus other languages and interacting with other "foreign" cultures because of globalization (Ismail et al., 2010; Mouakket et al., 2007). This is partially attributed to scarcity of software corresponding to the needs of Arabic university curricula and the Arabic electronic content, as the volume of online content in this language does not exceed 3%.

In addition, the "digital divide" in the Arab HE institutions is evident between those who use e-learning applications and those who do not use them among lecturers and students and males and females. Gender equity is another important issue that needs Arab universities' attention. For example, recent research found statistically significant differences with regard to gender equity and technology access in Saudi Arabia and recommends that further studies should be conducted to investigate how gender differences may affect women faculty's access to e-learning (Al-Sarrani, 2010; Kamal, 2013). As a whole, Akinyemi (2003, p. 1861) emphasized the "need for intensive and aggressive research on the different facets of web-based instruction with special purpose of protecting and preserving the Arab socio-cultural values and heritage."

Language Issues

The information and communication era requires creative language teaching skills commensurate with the requirements of the global communication and technological knowledge. Teaching language—at all levels—must go hand in hand with technological advances that have become the basis of sciences and disciplines. The use of technology and its multimedia in language teaching/learning helps students to perform self-learning and use computers/Internet; it provides an atmosphere of active learning, which depends on the use of sound with image and movement, display of some practical applications, and practice of the language (Sadik, 2008).

E-learning studies (Goh, Ng, Raja, & Wan, 2004; Ismail et al., 2010; Mouakket et al., 2007) suggest the willingness of lecturers to accelerate the integration of e-learning into teaching to improve the teaching/learning of the Arabic language. However, these studies found that time savings and motivation were prerequisites for further introduction of e-learning into the teaching of the Arabic language. These studies noticed that the Arab faculty members who did not use English in their teaching found this lack of English proficiency as the most important barrier to hindering the benefits from e-learning in their academic work. In addition, it was found that the use of e-learning was very important in teaching the Arabic language as a second language, so that instructional materials could become more understandable for non-Arab students in order to gain more experience, and enable them to benefit easily from the information. These studies have confirmed that the technology-based learning improved writing in Arabic and enhanced non-Arab student achievement in this language in terms of constructing phrases, structuring sentences, and creating styles.

In general, word processors, for example, provided students with greater flexibility of writing techniques. It supported the ability to formulate words and link them with each other, and to test tens, and even hundreds, of different formulations of text linkages. Al-Musawi (2000) provided an inquiry-based model on the introduction of technology in Arabic language teaching about how the keyboard enabled students to distinguish letters, how the computer screen helped students to link letters between words and spell them correctly, and the word processor helped students to improve their calligraphy and comprehension. He questioned the likelihood that computer writing could replace handwriting. He also questioned the possibility of an increased frequency of alternative correct words using the word processor and the impact of audio input in computer applications on the development of the students' language skills. Some examples would be in listening, speaking, reading, and the correct pronunciation of letters, linking them, and forming words into proper structures.

Gleaned from what has been said above, the following sections will explain the future requirements of e-learning integration in the Arab HE institutions.

Prospective Integration of E-learning in the Arab HE

Rationale for Integration

Justifications for integration are represented in the need to cope with this burst of knowledge in HE, to prepare citizens capable of dealing with the effects of globalization through lifelong learning, and to provide them permanently with learning resources and information. Additionally, opportunities must be given to the greatest number of learners to access different HE levels in order to achieve the principle of equal educational opportunities and education for all and to broaden the base of education to ensure a reduction of cost, time, and effort in order to get a high level of educational quality. This approach is necessary because the emergence of new technological innovations may undoubtedly reduce the need for substantial financial resources. The use of e-learning helps to design effective educational activities through digital libraries, virtual museums, electronic laboratories, and virtual field educational trips to help students gain new experiences that would be risky in reality. They also help students to imagine and carry out educational adventures in order to become innovative persons well prepared to future technological needs (Grable et al., 2005).

Requirements of Integration

Perhaps what Arab university education needs at the present stage is careful planning, strategic administrative decision with a comprehensive view to integrate e-learning in HE institutions, and gradual progress that is carefully studied to adapt it to their needs, reality, and socio-economic and scientific requirements. HE institutions in the Arab world need to plan for the technological infrastructure, training, financial, technical and human resources, and legal framework to integrate all efforts to strengthen the trend toward an e-learning-supported education system. When active planning has been achieved, these institutions can safely ensure the effectiveness of teaching methods used and assure the quality mechanisms of learning in university systems, thus ensuring the efficiency and quality of their graduates. This system will enable students who wish to study from distance to pursue HE, especially in terms of their qualifications, recognition, ratification, and accreditation.

In order to institute a proper ground for the integration of e-learning in HE, one must first build an institutional culture to accept and embrace e-learning that is accepted by lecturers and students by raising motivation and offering encouragement and administrative support, as well as the provision of incentives. Here, the institution should follow specific mechanisms, such as holding campaigns, lectures, workshops, and symposia to prepare faculty members, students, and staff for ways to deal with e-learning.

Psychological Factors for Integration

Technology is not self-explanatory and the educational process is primarily humanistic. Technology does not react emotionally to the student, and lecturers can understand students and analyze their characteristics and feelings that are associated with social realities and surroundings. This is important in HE. Therefore, the presence of the lecturer in e-learning must be carefully planned to provide role and social models and transfer the ideals that cannot be acquired through student interaction with technology. It remains that the lecturer is the cornerstone of HE.

We believe that e-learning can be a medium sometimes, or a resource of information at other times, or a mode to deliver knowledge—as noted above. However, education, as a communication process, is not complete until all its components, led by the sender (the lecturer, here), are provided. We also believe that the role of the lecturer, when employing e-learning in HE, remains essential, but that it is also a changing one. This shift in role will require the lecturer to design materials in electronic forms. The lecturer should be more democratic, since her or she is no longer the sole source of available knowledge. Other sources, available through technological means, exist. The lecturer's role increasingly becomes that of a guide, facilitator, and assistant to acquire, revise, and correct the student's acquisition of knowledge. Initial indications for the introduction of e-learning in HE demonstrate that the need for a lecturer, and the human element in general, may increase in the future, because we need to design educational materials in a better way. We need someone to provide them over the network in an effective and appropriate way who is trained and qualified at a high level.

Formats of Integration

Arab universities can adapt one or more of the following formats to integrate e-learning in their educational processes:

1. Distance learning: a technological system wherein students learn so as they are not under the direct supervision of the lecturer most of the time but under the responsibility of an academic institution dealing with its organization. All learning resources and educational ingredients are provided through a systematic distance learning program for students, who are not physically attending colleges and educational institutes, by means of technology to

enable them to obtain the same educational opportunities available to students attending colleges and institutes.

2. E-learning: the use of electronic networks and the Internet supported by technological and electronic means that allows interaction between lecturer and student. This interaction may include video tutorials, computer software, electronic systems, technology tools, and social media. The capacity of the institutions of HE can be increased through the acceptance of numbers of students who are able to study off-campus using e-learning by being linked with academic institutions that continuously employ these media to ensure the standards of the educational process and quality.

3. Technological portable devices: using mobile telephones linked to the Internet, personal digital assistants, tablets, and laptops in learning so that individuals can move these devices with them to give them the opportunity to learn anywhere; this is now called 'mobile learning' (m-learning, in short).

4. Electronic portal: a portal developed through electronic means that may include virtual research centers, media resources, the e-curriculum, e-books, and virtual libraries as a mechanism to facilitate the continuous flow of information, expertise, and resources within and between HE institutions using ICT, and employing innovations. The purpose of portals is to activate administrative processes of training, education, communication, research, knowledge, and creativity to promote individual and collective academic action. This coordination and networking is an actual realization of real e-learning-based education, which lead to the achievement of the goals for the comprehensive development of the university.

5. Electronic training: a system that includes training, workshops, courses, and registration information, such as dates of workshops, and electronic sessions, topics, and methods of interaction (synchronous in the presence of trainers or asynchronous in their absence).

6. Electronic book: a digital book that is characterized by portability, searchability, and accessibility. In addition, sound, image, and video properties can be added. It can be provided with hyperlinks, rich resources of information, images, and multimedia. It is less expensive than the traditional book because it reduces the price of paper and printing. It also saves space, since it can be organized in digital libraries.

In sum, e-learning can support Arab universities' open education in various forms. It can raise the efficiency of HE institutions in terms of both quantity and quality; it gives decision makers the ability to cope effectively with urgent educational issues to ensure economic viability and cost reduction in the long term.

Conclusion

It is clear that the strong start of the Arab World in ICT will continue in the near future. The resolution of resulting problems remains subject to the human ability to rationalize technological innovations and use them for good purposes and human welfare. We feel compelled to say that educational and curriculum planners in Arab universities must attend to the requirements of the new Arab generation, who have grown up in the flow of information coming from space, computers, and the Internet; young Arabs have a great deal of information skill, which must be appreciated by educators and curriculum planners. These skills should be developed within and outside the school. Lecturers need to be trained to keep abreast of these developments and not insist on pursuing traditional methods in the design and implementation of curricula and teaching materials. In this chapter, we have reviewed some of the key issues to help planners and lecturers to search for solutions related to the use of e-learning in HE with a focus on the status of Arab universities and issues.

Additional Readings

Mitchell, A. C. (2002). Developing a learning environment: Applying e-learning and TQM to distance learning. In M. Khosrowpour (Ed.), *Web-based instructional learning.* Hershey, PA: IRM Press.

Pimmel, R. (2001). *Cooperative learning instructional activities in a capstone design course. American Society for Engineering Education.* Retrieved from http://onlinelibrary.wiley.com/doi/10.1002/j.2168-9830.2001.tb00621.x/abstract

Tsai, P., & You, M. (2005). *The implementation of graphic organizers for instructional activities of creative design in elementary school—An Example of 'My Map Book.'* Retrieved from http://www.iasdr2009.org/ap/Papers/

Young, M. R., Klemz, B. R., & Murphy, J. W. (2003). Enhancing learning outcomes: The effects of instructional e-learning, learning styles, instructional methods, and student behavior. *Journal of Marketing Education, 25*(2), 130–142. doi:10.1177/0273475303254004

References

Akinyemi, A. (2003). Web-based learning and cultural interference: perspectives of Arab students. In A. Rossett (Ed.), *Proceedings of World Conference on E-Learning in Corporate, Government, Healthcare, and Higher Education 2003,* 1858–1862. Chesapeake, VA: AACE. Retrieved from http://www.editlib.org/p/12239

Al-Musawi, A. (2000). Technology effectiveness in improving teaching, learning, and communication skills: Literature review and implications to Arabic education. *Contemporary Education Journal, 54,* 221–244.

Al-Musawi, A. (2007). Current status of educational technologies at Omani HE institutions and their future prospective. *Education Technology Research and Development (ETR&D), 55*(4), 395–410. doi:10.1007/s11423-007-9041-x

Al-Musawi, A. (2011). Redefining e-learning role in education. *Creative Education, 2*(2), 130–135. Retrieved from http://www.scirp.org/journal/PaperDownload.aspx?paperID=5414. doi:10.4236/ce.2011.22018

Al-Musawi, A., & Abdelraheem, A. (2004). E-learning at Sultan Qaboos University: Status and future. *British Journal of Educational Technology, 35*(3), 363–367. Retrieved from http://www.academia.edu/5223533/E-learning_at_Sultan_Qaboos_University_status_and_future

Al-Musawi, A., & Akinyemi, A. (2002). Issues and prospects of e-learning in Oman. *Proceedings of ED-MEDIA 2002-World Conference on Educational Multimedia, Hypermedia & Telecommunications, 1,* 17–18. Retrieved from http://www.aace.org/dl/index.cfm/fuseaction/ViewPaper/id/10017/toc/yes

Al-Sarrani, N. (2010). *Concerns and professional development needs of science faculty at Taibah University in adopting blended learning* (Doctoral dissertation, Kansas State University).

Goh, Y., Ng, A., Raja. B., & Wan, A. (2004, September 25–26). *Technology and foreign language learning: Student perceptions on the feasibility of using WBI (web-based instruction) to supplement the on-campus foreign language courses in UiTM.* Paper presented at the International Online Conference on Second, Foreign Language Teaching, and Research, pp. 147–160.

Grable, L., Overbay, A., & Osborne, J. (2005). Instructional activities, use of e-learning, and classroom climate: What lies beneath. In C. Crawford et al. (Eds.), *Proceedings of Society for Information E-Learning & Lecturer Education International Conference 2005* (pp. 858–862). Chesapeake, VA: AACE. Retrieved from http://www.editlib.org/p/19123

International Society for Technology in Education-ISTE. (2012). *The standards for learning, leading, and teaching in a digital age.* Retrieved from http://www.iste.org/standards.aspx

Ismail, S., Almekhlafi, A., & Almekhlafy, M. (2010). Lecturers' perceptions of the use of e-learning in teaching languages in United Arab Emirates' schools. *International Journal for Research in Education (IJRE), 27,* 37–56.

Kamal, B. (2013). *Concerns and professional development needs of faculty at king Abdul-Aziz University in Saudi Arabia in adopting online teaching* (Doctoral dissertation, Kansas State University).

Khan, B.H. (2005). *Managing e-learning strategies: Design, delivery, implementation and evaluation.* Hershey, PA: IGI Global.

Ministry of Higher Education (MOHE). (2013). *About the National Center for E-Learning and Distance Learning.* Retrieved from http://www.mohe.gov.sa/en/aboutus/Institutions/Pages/Distance-education.aspx

Mouakket, S., Nour, M., & Al-Imamy, S. (2007). Investigation of information e-learning use by non-English speaking academics. *University of Sharjah Journal of Pure & Applied Sciences, 4*(2), 25–45.

Sadik, A. (2008). *Arabic language learning technology.* Qatar UNESCO office seminar. Retrieved from http://www.slideshare.net/alrefa3ia/ss-6381870

25

E-learning for Continuing and Professional Development

Angela Kwan and Mary Wilson

E-learning for Continuing and Professional Development

Continuing and professional development (CPD) occupies a unique place in e-learning, since often CPD courses are funded directly by organizations for their staff and developed under this organizational direction. CPD is intended to improve performance at work. If CPD is to be successful in changing behavior and improving performance on a sustainable basis, it must be designed to meet the needs of both individuals and the organizations they work for, and must be delivered in a quality manner.

In the past seven years, the Commonwealth of Learning E-Learning for International Organizations (COL eLIO) unit has served about 7,000 adult professional learners, helping them to enhance their capacities in writing, operational data management, and national debt management. Based on our experience with these professionals and the international organizations that employ them and our reading of some of the classic literature of adult education and distance education, we have identified several factors that learners need and value, and which providers of e-learning for CPD should be aware of. The factors broadly include course design, learner experience, and administrative support. Each of these three areas will be explored in this chapter.

Since we work as an external consulting organization, our experience is somewhat different than that of an internal training/human resources development department. However, we believe there are many similarities arising from the situation of learners themselves. Those participating in CPD do so as part of a typically busy work life. Support for learners, both from the administrative and teaching side, is critical for success. The development and successful delivery of continuing professional education requires balancing many different needs; those needs may be identified by managers, by staff members themselves, by course designers, and by tutors.

The examples we draw on in this chapter are largely based on our experience designing, delivering, and supporting writing courses for staff in international organizations.

Course Design

Course development involves several considerations. These include designing based on a theoretical understanding for practical knowledge, designing for relevance to the workplace, designing contextualized learning experiences, and designing based on learners' current knowledge and experience.

Designing Based on a Theoretical Underpinning for Practical Knowledge

COL eLIO's training design is consistent with adult learning principles, and with best practices in open/distance education. (In our view, while e-learning is a specific mode of distance education, it is still distance education when delivered with no face-to-face student/tutor contact. We use that term to describe it, and find the literature of distance education helpful in discussing it.) The course content, including activities, assignments, and assessments, is based on the idea that adult learners learn best when what they are learning is relevant to their needs.

Seven Underlying Principles Guide the Course Methodology and Design

1. Adult learners bring life experience and knowledge to their study. They demand relevance and practical experience, and are goal oriented (Knowles, 1980).

   These basic principles of andragogy are well-supported by the course methodology. Course learners examine and reflect on work they have done—not work done for the course, but authentic tasks completed in their professional lives. Course examples are drawn from authentic institutional documents. This focus ensures relevance and encourages learners to draw on their own experiences.

2. Learning cognitive and intellectual skills can be seen as a process of apprenticeship. Viewing learning in this way bridges the potential gap between learning and use (Brown, Collins, & Duguid, 1989; Lave & Wenger, 1991; Johnson & Pratt, 1998).

   Our courses are practice based and require learners to apply new tools to authentic tasks. Practice with authentic tasks is an important part of apprenticeship; so is observation of expertise. Examples within the course materials and coaching from tutors help learners increase their expertise and challenge them to apply what they have learned.

3. Working with expert practitioners, those who are learning can accomplish more at a higher level than is possible for them working on their own (Lave & Wenger, 1991).

   Although courses are designed for flexible study anywhere in the world, learners are not isolated. Throughout the course, each learner works with a tutor. The tutor assists the learner in accomplishing authentic tasks through supportive feedback. In the case of writing courses, learners are guided by their tutors to edit documents to a level of effectiveness and clarity they would likely not be able to achieve without support. The tutor accomplishes this using the same tools and techniques taught in the course, thus providing the learner with an example of an expert writer in action. Having had this experience with the tutor, the learner will be prepared to repeat the process using the tools they have acquired to improve their day-to-day writing.

4. Reflection is a valuable way for learners to consolidate new knowledge and to apply it in new ways (Kolb, 1984; Rowntree, 1994; Schön, 1983).

   Our courses provide learners with opportunities to reflect on their own work and the work of others, to learn from those reflections, and to apply them to new experiences. Activities throughout the courses provide learners with guided opportunities for reflection. In our writing courses, for example, they are encouraged to reflect on their own experiences of effective and ineffective writing, and to analyze their own writing with these experiences in mind. They are asked to think from the perspective of the intended audience of their documents, identifying what is necessary and what is not to produce a convincing document.

This is consistent with the principles of effective course design for distance education and, in particular, with the vision of distance education course materials as a reflective action guide. The course materials provide support to learners as they pursue personal projects (Rowntree, 1994).

5. Respect for learners is fundamental to successful learning (Knowles, 1980).

    Tutors for our courses are experienced in working with adult professionals in a wide range of fields. The one-to-one relationship established between tutor and learner is based on mutual respect and recognition of expertise. Course materials, too, convey respect for the learners through the use of authentic, organization-specific examples of varying levels of complexity.

6. Course materials and course delivery are enhanced when learners are given both autonomy and support (Holmberg, 1989; Moore, 1993; Rowntree, 1994).

    COL eLIO courses are designed to allow learners flexibility within a predesigned framework. Guidelines are provided for assignments, but learners select relevant tasks within those guidelines. A timeline for optimum completion is provided, but it contains enough flexibility to encourage learners to set a schedule that works for them.

    The tutor's role in providing feedback to the learners is at the heart of this approach. Feedback is entirely individual and based on a broadly framed competency-based marking scheme. Tutors provide detailed feedback based on the learner's goals, strengths, and weaknesses.

7. Education at a distance is enhanced when interaction and dialogue is encouraged (Arseneau & Rodenburg, 1998; Holmberg, 1989; Moore, 1993; Rowntree, 1994).

    The psychological and communication gap that can develop between tutor and learner in a distance education course is not an inevitable consequence of physical separation. This psychological and communication gap, which Moore (1993) called the transactional distance, can be overcome by a course structure that encourages both learner autonomy and interaction. Interaction in our courses is of several types:

- Learners interact with the course materials themselves, entering into an internal dialogue with the tutorial content.
- Learners interact with their tutor, entering into an ongoing and largely learner-driven dialogue. Tutors are available to provide responses to questions, suggest further resources, and act as sounding boards. Tutors also at times lead the conversation, particularly through feedback on assignments, guiding learners to consider issues they may not otherwise have identified.
- Learners may interact with other learners completing the course, through group e-mails or within course management software. This learner-to-learner interaction is typically offered as an option within courses. In our experience, few course learners take advantage of it unless it is made mandatory; in our National Debt Management course, participation in a group forum is a requirement for satisfying all course completion criteria.

Designing Courses for Relevance to Context

Strong course design requires careful identification of learner needs. Specific course design for CPD begins prior to needs assessment—or, put another way, the needs assessment process often begins before course design at the earliest proposal stage. In our experience, the organization requesting CPD has already identified needs that they hope training will meet. These needs must be validated in the earliest phase of course design. This follows the usual process of identifying the desired state and current state and then documenting gaps between the two—a typical part of the instructional design process. The process can be complicated in the case of CPD courses, however, since visions of the desired state may be held passionately, rather than unanimously, by managers championing the project and by potential learners. Typically, the course design team includes both an instructional designer and course writer with expertise in the content area; this expertise makes it possible for them to balance the needs of various groups. Building in opportunities for learners to work with their own examples helps to ensure that specific learner needs are addressed (Rowntree, 1994).

We find on-site needs assessment to be the most practical, and would recommend it when course developers are working with a company or organization with a single, accessible location. On-site visits give us an opportunity to see people in their work environment, to see the range of tasks they accomplish each day, and to observe experts in the organization in action (Lave & Wenger, 1991). In many cases, the courses we design are intended for delivery around the world, to individuals working for the organization in very different contexts. Such extensive site visits are impractical. We find it useful to consult organizational websites and online information, and in particular corporate intranets when they are made available to us, to determine differences between regional or country offices and corporate headquarters.

We strive to design learning experiences that provide an opportunity for structured practice, helping learners to develop their expertise in the performance of tasks they actually do at work (Johnson & Pratt, 1998; Knowles, 1980; Lave & Wenger, 1991). When we are planning a writing course, for example, we begin by collecting documents written by the organization's staff. We meet with as many managers and staff as possible throughout the organization. In each meeting, we ask those we meet to provide us with examples of successful documents and ask them what makes each document successful. We further ask what challenges they find in their attempts to create similar documents, and the challenges they notice others having. We begin our work with a strong understanding of the basics of clear communication and professional writing, but we strive to ensure that the course goals we identify are actually relevant for the specific workplace. Beginning with an examination of the work that is actually done, both successful and unsuccessful, helps us do this.

Since we build our courses based on examples of successful and unsuccessful documents produced in the organization, they are contextualized to the learners' environment. Course materials identify the strengths and weaknesses of examples, making the expert thinking involved in their creation apparent (Lave & Wenger, 1991; Schön, 1983). Further, though, we design assignments and activities that require learners to bring examples from their own practice. See Table 25.1, a summary of the course assignments for *Writing Effectively for WHO*, for an example.[1]

Designing Content That Builds on Learners' Prior Knowledge and Experience

Designers for e-learning face a challenge that those teaching face-to-face do not usually experience. We produce the course materials in advance and thus will not have an opportunity to discover individual learners' previous experience as the course unfolds. Tutors in online CPD usually do not have the option of changing materials in response to learners' needs.

To address this, we work to incorporate reflective activities into the course materials. These activities ask learners to reflect on their own earlier experiences and examine documents they have produced through the lens of course material (Kolb, 1984; Rowntree, 1994; Schön, 1983). This arguably does not take the place of a face-to-face, one-on-one discussion with an attentive instructor; it does, however, encourage learners to think deeply about the course materials and

Table 25.1 Course Assignments, Writing Effectively

Module 1: Completed by all learners	• Assignment 1: Analyze a document you have written and submit the analysis and the document for feedback. • Assignment 2: Create a portfolio of good and bad examples of course content drawn from your own writing at work. • Assignment 3: Write a description of the type of writing you do most frequently at work, and identify your personal goals for the next module.
Module 2: General correspondence (typically selected by administrative staff)	Submit a portfolio of four documents, selected from: • E-mail, memo, or letter • Meeting minutes • Briefing notes or notes for the record
Module 3: Report and proposal writing (typically selected by professional staff)	• Plan a report or proposal of four to ten pages, including analyzing readers and creating an outline. • Draft the report or proposal. • Prepare a briefing note based on the report or proposal.

Learners may submit each assignment up to three times, incorporating tutor feedback into successive drafts.

begin the process of incorporating course content into their own work. Tutors and learners are also given flexibility to modify assignments when modification can make the assignment more relevant for the learner's professional development.

Learner Experience

Our goal in course design, in tutoring and in administrative support, is to support the learner's experience and their engagement with the course materials. This begins with the creation of a course that is relevant to the learners' needs in the workplace, and continues with encouragement of their active involvement in the course both through the materials themselves and through tutor and administrative support (Holmberg, 1989; Moore, 1993; Rowntree, 1994).

Providing Opportunities to Learn by Doing

In our experience, it is rare for learners to have time away from work to complete CPD courses via e-learning, although they might be able to attend face-to-face courses on work time. Instead, they are usually completing the course at work and often without specific time allocated for it. It is therefore helpful to have the course divided into shorter segments, and to focus on practice rather than lengthy didactic passages (Schön, 1983).

Our course materials provide multiple opportunities to learn by doing. In writing courses, for instance, content pages include examples and demonstrations of the points in question and are followed by exercises. Examples are drawn from the collection of institutional documents discussed in the course design section above. Often, activities for practice help prepare learners to complete module assignments.

In the national debt management course where learners are required to record and manage debt using a purpose-designed software package, they follow the step-by-step process for logging in, opening files, entering data, computing figures and compiling reports. Screen shots of the software are streamed as a video for learners to watch the processes. Then they try out the steps through computer-aided help and eventually do it live on a training dataset, submitting screen shots of their own work for tutors' assessment and feedback.

Building One-on-One Tutoring Relationships

In our experience, the active presence of a tutor in online CPD is critically important for learner success.

Tutors play several roles: They are guides to the materials, answering questions and clarifying confusion; they are cheerleaders, reminding busy professionals of deadlines and time limits for course completion; and they are coaches, providing extensive feedback on assignments, encouraging learners to apply course content, and pushing them to reflect critically on their own work (Arseneau & Rodenburg, 1998; O'Rourke, 2003). Some of our courses include the possibility of participation in discussion with other learners; in most cases, though, the primary focus is on interaction with a single tutor.

Coaching for Improvement, Rather Than Grading to an Imposed Standard

In our CPD courses, the focus is on improvement, rather than attaining a particular external standard (Lave & Wenger, 1991; Schön, 1983). In writing courses, for example, learners are writers at all levels of expertise, from experts hoping to polish a particular aspect of their writing, to technical experts in other fields who find themselves in new roles with extensive reporting requirements, to new administrative staff learning the basics of business writing in English or French. Learners are successful in their assignments when they demonstrate a good effort to apply the course content, and to incorporate feedback from their tutors on assignment drafts.

Although we do use a learning management system, and in some courses learners could participate in discussions if they wished, the primary focus of the tutor–learner relationship is on the course assignments. Assignments provide what Papert (1980) called an object to think with: in this case, an authentic document, produced by the learner, that can provide a focus for discussion of concepts. Learners draft assignments, and tutors read them in detail, encouraging revision and incorporation of feedback. Tutors in this way play the role of a more experienced colleague, providing advice and feedback on a document that is relevant to the workplace (Lave & Wenger, 1991).

The opportunity to submit multiple drafts of an assignment, incorporating feedback after each draft, also helps learners learn the reality of writing in a professional environment. As report writers and correspondents in international organizations, these professionals will often be required to revise their work in response to feedback from colleagues and managers. The structure of our writing courses reminds learners that the need for revision is a normal part of the writing process, not a weakness to be overcome.

Stimulating Development of Critical Thinking Within the Area of Study

Because learners are working with their own documents, in their own context, with a tutor as a coach rather than an absolute authority, they are encouraged to think critically about the course materials and their own application of those materials (Schön, 1983). Tutors are all experienced, professional-standard writers who have extensive exposure to documents created by those in these international organizations. The learners themselves, though, are the authorities on what is required in their specific location, and for a particular document.

Empowering Learner Autonomy: Flexibility Within a Predetermined Framework

We strive to provide learners with flexibility within the course format, recognizing that this is necessary to meet the needs of learners with varying levels of professional expertise and varied backgrounds (Knowles, 1980). This is apparent particularly in the portfolio option for the correspondence module (see Table 25.1). Tutors also work flexibly with learners. A report, as defined in these courses, can be anything from a short project report to a section of a potential scholarly publication, depending on learner needs.

Administrative Support

Administrative support or learner support is a critical success factor in e-learning. It tends to be overlooked by many CPD providers as such processes are often overshadowed by the focus on technology. Open and distance learning "loyalists" have tirelessly advocated for the importance of such systems and processes in providing an ultimate quality learning experience to learners.

Administrative support, or learner support, covers a range of targeted services that eLIO provides through our courses. Our ideal for quality learner services is informative, communicative, and supportive. It appeals to people's need for customized and applicable learning and includes the celebration of learning successes, acknowledging busy and mobile learners for staying on course and accomplishing goals.

We use "administrative support" and "learner support" interchangeably, because good learner services embrace both. The administrative services focus on logistics, with clear timelines, prompt delivery of courseware, and accurate transmission of information. The softer learner support services include the encouragement, the counseling and attention given to each learner by administrative staff, not just by tutors.

The image of open and distance learning (ODL) includes a high drop-out rate; professional development or corporate training often struggles to provide a solid return on investment. One of the key contributing factors to both problems is the lack of learner support. When learners and instructors are separated and isolated in their individual locations, the lack of support (out of sight, out of mind) can easily lead to noncompletion and waste of an opportunity. With adult professional learners trying to balance work, life, and family, it is a constant battle to commit to professional development even when it is meeting users' needs and goals.

Realizing the challenges, the eLIO administrative and learner support system is designed to engage stakeholders and learners in the learning journey when they are separated and dispersed. The eLIO support system aims at creating a 360° support system embracing learners, tutors, and administrators to maintain regular monitoring of learning pace, progress, and problems (Kwan, 2011). The tracking system flags individuals falling behind and alerts the administrators to take timely actions. This human touch in personalized reminders helps keep learners on track.

The eLIO administrative system underpins the notion that learning is most effective when courses are paced and not rushed; planned and not randomized; incremental and not forced. The system uses several tools to provide learners with informative, communicative, and supportive services. Tables 25.2 through 25.6 detail the specific tools used at various course stages.

Preparing Learners for Application and Registration

Support for learners is critical before the course begins. These tools help learners decide if the course will be useful for them, and if it is possible for them to complete it in the course timeframe.

Table 25.2 Application and Registration

Nature	Tools used
Informative: to tell potential learners about the course • Use clear and plain language to give a clear purpose and outcome statement. • Clearly state eligibility requirement and the time and efforts required for successful learning.	• Course advertisements Usually a one-pager outlining course objective, course outlines, and outcomes on organization intranet or training sites. Gives contact information for further questions. • Course Registration Form A PDF template or link to an online form. Form must be simple to fill out and obtain key data like contact details (for sending materials and making contacts) and personal details (like office grade, gender, job title, and mother tongue in aid of tutor allocation).

Table 25.3 Course Startup

Nature	Tools used
Informative: To provide key course data • Provide clear and targeted information on dates and expectations. • Provide answers to frequently-asked questions. • Sent as PDF documents to learners' work e-mail addresses, and also posted on course sites.	• Welcome e-mail Our welcome is always person to person from an eLIO administrator; tutors also send welcomes. Learners can be assured of a human being attending to their learning interests and questions • Key Dates Sets out an ideal learning schedule for each learner. The schedule can be modified and adapted to suit individual's schedule. • Course Regulations Gives clear assessment, grading, and extension policies and states the code of conduct for learners and tutors. • FAQs Antitcipate and answer course/learning related questions for quick references. • How to Guides (e.g., how to study at a distance, how to get help, how to get resources, how to submit assignments).

Preparing Learners for Course Start

Support at course start-up sets the tone for tutor–learner relationship and ensures that learners have the information they need to get started. Since learners may be unfamiliar with e-learning and studying at a distance, information needs to be very clear.

Preparing Learners to Access Materials and Tutor

Many of our courses are delivered using the Moodle learning management system. eLIO chose Moodle, an open source LMS, as an online platform to support learning interaction and record management. It has proven to be robust, reliable, and user-friendly. Our virtual classes on Moodle often span the four corners of the world from Africa to Europe and Asia, the Pacific, Australia, and the Americas.

Whatever system is used, it is important to ensure that learners have access to course materials, their tutor and administrative support, and are able to find everything they need. This orientation process helps those new to e-learning feel confident in their ability to succeed.

Table 25.4 Accessing Course Materials

Nature	Tools used
Informative, communicative, and supportive • Moodle LMS provides a single location for dispersed learners, tutors, and administrators to come together to collaborate and support each other for success in the learning initiative. • eLIO administrators play a major role in informing, communicating with, and supporting learners as well as tutors. • Supporting tutors is important because they are learners' main point of contact as well as their individual counselor and mentor during the course.	• Moodle Learning Management Platform creates a virtual classroom for learners and tutors. Provides a single location for accessing information and resources; submitting and downloading assignments; tracking progress; communicating with peers, tutors, and administrators individually or in groups. An eLIO administrator sets up the course site and introduces learners to Moodle. • Moodle Orientation Week Usually from 3 days to a week to orientate learners and tutors to the functions of the virtual learning environment, to meet people, and to access learning materials. • Grace period From two weeks to a month, this is a period for familiarization on courseware, learning technologies, self-directed e-learning, tutor, administrators, and fellow learners. Withdrawal before end of grace period incurs no penalty. This is a fair treatment to adult professional learners for CPD.

Table 25.5 Accessing Tutoring and Learner Support

Nature	Tools

Supportive, communicative, and informative
• This is the exciting phase when substantive learning happens through all sorts of interactions and engagement between learner and materials, learner and systems, learner and peers, learner and tutors, and learner and administration.
• eLIO creates a 360° support system so that each learner will enjoy a timely and targeted support whenever he or she needs it, either through the system, their tutors, peers, or eLIO administrators.
	• Moodle LMS. eLIO employs the following plug-ins in Moodle for supporting learners:
	  ◦ Bulletin Board—for course administration to broadcast important notices. The message posted goes directly into learners' e-mail inbox and is archived on Moodle.
	  ◦ E-mail—enables one-to-one e-mail and one-to-multiple e-mails. Used most frequently by tutors to communicate with individual learners.
	  ◦ Discussion Forum—engages the learning groups in peer to peer interaction as well as tutor to learner exchanges. Seldom used as part of our course design.
	  ◦ Calendar—highlights key dates of activities
	  ◦ Assignments—provides a record of assignment submission, and when they are received, marked, and returned to learners for review.
	• Monthly Progress Report (MPR)
	During the course, eLIO course administration requires each tutor to report on the performance of each of the learners. The MPR is in the form of an Excel file or a wiki in which tutors provide a snapshot of where each learner is at in the course. Through these regular updates, eLIO can spot learner(s) struggling with course requirements or timing and coordinate remedial action(s).
	• Review of the TMAs (tutor marked assignments)
	The assignments promote a dialogue between learners and tutors. Learning deepens when TMAs are detailed, discursive, and developmental. To quality assure and to standardize TMAs, eLIO randomly selects TMAs for quality checks by an external advisor.

Table 25.6 Celebrating Course Completion

Nature	Tools
Communicative and informative This is the phase when eLIO celebrates with learners who have achieved their learning goals through their own commitment and dedication with the support provided by eLIO. eLIO congratulates those who have successfully completed, and consoles those who fail to complete.	• E-mail eLIO sends each individual a congratulatory or consolatory message. This message echoes the message they receive from their tutor. • Survey Monkey We use this online tool to invite course learners to comment freely on four aspects of course experience: materials, assessment, tutoring, and administration. This provides the data for Phase 1 assessment of the Kirkpatrick evaluation model. • Moodle Grader Report The Grader Report gives each learner a transcript of their results and allows eLIO to run an overall result report as a training record for organizations. • Final Training Report eLIO presents to each stakeholder of the training cohorts the completion picture in terms of gender and country participation and their success rate. Learners' feedback and performance data is collected across several cohorts, putting eLIO in a position to undertake in-depth program evaluation to inform the continuous improvement of the course content, delivery, and support.

Supporting Learners During the Course

Much of the one-to-one support for learners during the course comes from their tutors. Administrators also play a key role in ensuring continuous course access and providing reminders to learners who have fallen behind their intended schedule. Administrators also play an ongoing role in tutor support.

Celebrating Course Completion

Learners in international organizations often work hard to complete their courses, balancing home, family, and work in difficult situations. Successful course completion is a time to celebrate accomplishments through overcoming many hurdles like time, workload, travels, and personal issues.

Conclusion

Our experience teaches us that e-learning can be an effective mode of delivery for CPD—effective both for organizations and for staff members. To be effective, course design, learner experience, and administrative support all require careful planning and commitment from the organization providing e-learning design, development, and delivery services. For COL eLIO, the reward for this work is in the experience of thousands of successful adult learners throughout the world.

Note

1 The full course may be seen at www.colelearning.net/who

References

Arseneau, R., & Rodenburg, D. (1998). The developmental perspective: Cultivating ways of thinking. In D. D. Pratt & Associates (Eds.), *Five perspectives on teaching in adult and higher education* (pp. 105–149). Malabar, FL: Krieger.

Brown, J. A., Collins, A., & Duguid, P. (1989). Situated cognition and the culture of learning. *Educational Researcher, 18*(1), 32–42.

Holmberg, B. (1989). *Theory and practice of distance education* (2nd ed.). London, UK: Routledge Studies in Distance Education.

Johnson, J., & Pratt, D. (1998). The apprenticeship perspective: Modeling ways of being. In D. D. Pratt & Associates (Eds.), *Five perspectives on teaching in adult and higher education* (pp. 83–103). Malabar, FL: Krieger.

Kolb, D. A. (1984). *Experiential learning: Experience as the source of learning and development.* Englewood Cliffs, NJ: Prentice Hall.

Knowles, M. S. (1980). *The modern practice of adult education.* New York, NY: Adult Education Company.

Kwan, A. (2011). *eLearning: We are watching* (Blog post). Retrieved from http://www.col.org/blog/Lists/Posts/Post.aspx?ID=121

Lave, J., & Wenger, E. (1991). *Situated learning: Legitimate peripheral participation.* Cambridge, UK: Cambridge University Press.

Moore, M. G. (1993). Theory of transactional distance. In D. Keegan (Ed.), *Theoretical principles of distance education* (pp. 22–39). London, UK: Routledge.

O'Rourke, J. (2003). *Tutoring in open and distance learning: A handbook for tutors.* Vancouver, BC: Commonwealth of Learning. Available online from http://www.col.org/resources/publications/Pages/detail.aspx?PID=238)

Papert, S. A. (1980). *Mindstorms: Children, computers, and powerful ideas.* New York, NY: Basic Books.

Rowntree, D. (1994). *Preparing materials for open, distance and flexible learning.* London, UK: Kogan Page, published in association with the Institute of Education Technology, Open University.

Schön, D. A. (1983). *The reflective practitioner: How professionals think in action.* New York, NY: Basic Books.

26

Using the Unified Theory of Acceptance and Use of Technology and Dewey's Theory of Experience to Interpret Faculty Experience of E-learning at one School of Public Health

Terry Kidd

Introduction

As with many in other professional fields of study, faculty in public health have been thrust into e-learning as a means to respond to preparing their workforce to meet future health challenges (Dodds, Laraia, & Carbone, 2003; Edouard et al., 2009; Institute of Medicine (IOM) 2003; University of Texas System, 2005; World Health Organization [WHO], 2006).

While scholars and policy makers in public health equally recognize the importance of face-to-face training, only scholars recognize that traditional methods alone cannot meet the educational or workforce development needs of public health. Therefore, in order to meet this shortage and focus, e-learning has been shown to be a viable solution for improving the current and future public health workforce (Dodds et al., 2003; Billot, 2007; Edouard et al., 2009; Escoffery et al., 2005; MacDonald, Alexander, Ward, & Davis, 2008; Mokwena, Mokgatle-Nthabu, Madiba, Lewisa, & Ntuli-Ngcoboa, 2007; Umble, Shay, & Sollecito, 2003; WHO, 2006). To date, few e-learning studies have been conducted in public health (Billot, 2007; Mokwena et al., 2007). According to Laraia, Dodds, Benjamin, Jones, and Carbone (2008), little is known about the successes of online learning in public health, including their experiences in e-learning; their psychological and emotional response to the process; their perceptions of barriers, challenges, and benefits associated with the process; or their role as faculty. This study sought to explore the experiences of faculty in public health as they engaged in e-learning to inform public health educational practices and workforce development initiatives online.

E-learning—Review of Literature

With advances in information and communication technologies, e-learning has been propelled to the forefront of higher education, providing educational and access solutions to students from diverse geographical locations (Allen & Seaman, 2010). As the number of e-learning-type courses continues to rise, institutions will need faculty who are willing to accept and participate in online learning, specifically, developing and teaching these courses (Allen & Seaman, 2010; Sugar, Martindale, & Crawley, 2007). This section will discuss five areas of e-learning: (a) faculty experience and response to e-learning, (b) psychological and emotional response to e-learning, (c) faculty role in e-learning, (d) roadblocks and rewards to e-learning, and (e) e-learning in public health.

Faculty Experience and Response to E-learning

Previously, faculty who participated in e-learning activities stemmed from a pool of faculty who historically taught traditional courses and did so on a voluntary basis, expecting compensation and other extrinsic rewards (Allen & Seaman, 2010). However, in more recent years, faculty have been expected to participate in e-learning as a part of their regular duties (Appana, 2008; Fish & Gill, 2009; Mitchell & Geva-May, 2009; Reeves & Reeves, 2007). Despite this expectation, faculty have been hesitant to convert their traditional courses to an online format (Appana, 2008; Fish & Gill, 2009; Mitchell & Geva-May, 2009; Reeves & Reeves, 2007). These authors found that many faculty felt uncertain and uneasy towards the e-learning process due to perceived assumptions regarding the quality of learning and student learning outcomes. This uncertainty came from assumptions concerning the nature and mode of learning (Appana, 2008), subscribing to myths and misconceptions about online learning (Fish & Gill, 2009; Li & Akins, 2005), lack of competency in technology and online learning methods (Maguire, 2005), and institutional incongruence with relation to faculty, attitudes, beliefs, and practices (Mitchell & Geva-May, 2009; Simpson, 2010).

While the use of traditional faculty to teach online may appear to be a quick and uncomplicated solution to the need for faculty participation in e-learning, issues relating to faculty experience and challenges they encounter need to be explored in order to facilitate and support successful courses and programs (Bruner, 2007; Kyei-Blankson, 2009; Tallent-Runnels et al., 2006).

In an earlier discussion, Maguire (2005) found that faculty uncertainties for e-learning were aimed at issues of quality, student learning outcomes, and academic engagement. Allen and Seaman (2010) contend similar findings that faculty assumptions regarding course quality, student learning outcomes, lack of support, training, and engagement were reasons as to why they did not participate in e-learning, despite the growing literature on student learning outcomes and faculty involvement. Previous work on faculty response and participation in e-learning (Conceição, 2006) expand these dimensions to include adequate resources, technical and instructional support, quality professional development specifically for technology integration, e-learning, learning methods, as well as incentives and organizational support. Tallent-Runnels et al. (2006) found that faculty lagged behind in accepting e-learning due to the prevailing assumptions of course quality and lack of training and professional development to deliver instruction online. Reeves and Reeves (2007) and Paulus et al. (2010) concurred and found that faculty jumped into teaching online without sufficient training or consideration for instructional planning, design, or assessment methods.

Psychological and Emotional Response to E-learning

The pathway of course migration to online environments often begins with the assumption that instructional designs, grading procedures, and other methods that typically work in the traditional classroom would remain the same in online settings. When faculty come to terms with the reality that these two environments are entirely different and that traditional teaching methods would not be suitable, they suddenly become frustrated (Bruner, 2007; Clark-Ibanez & Scott, 2008; Conceição, 2006), realizing the need for change. Consequently, acceptance of e-learning has challenged traditional, well-established teaching methods and faculty responsibilities (Clark-Ibanez & Scott, 2008; Conceição, 2006; Grosse 2004). Such a transition for faculty is not easy and has been labeled as "daunting," "painful," and "stressful" due to the extensive preparation time and revision of teaching methods (Grosse, 2004).

Despite faculty's emotional reaction to e-learning, this modality of teaching and learning presents a learning curve that may be difficult for faculty to undertake. As noted by Gerlich (2005, p. 8), e-learning presented a "steep learning curve associated with learning to teach online." Because of the many tools, intense work, and strategies associated with e-learning, faculty are sometimes left frustrated and exhausted (Bruner, 2007; Conceição, 2006; Kyei-Blankson, 2009; Paulus et al., 2010; Sugar et al., 2007).

Faculty Role in E-learning

Due to the complex nature of e-learning and the manner in which teaching online differs from teaching in traditional environments, some faculty may need to rethink their role in e-learning (Conceição, 2006; Panda & Mishra, 2007). Previous research by Scagnoli (2001) identified that faculty who engaged in e-learning moved from content subject matter experts to course facilitators with new roles that were framed around the activities that took place in e-learning. Collins and Berge (as cited in Palloff & Pratt, 2001) continued this research and were able to divide the roles of the online instructor into four distinct categories: pedagogical, social, managerial, and the technical. The pedagogical role revolved around instructional facilitation. The social role involved creating a friendly social environment necessary to place online. The managerial role involved agenda setting, pacing, objective setting, rule making, and decision making within the course. The technical role dealt with understanding the functionality of software, hardware, and peripherals needed to engage in e-learning. Coppola, Hiltz, and Rotter (2002) identified three faculty roles based upon three prevailing functions: cognitive, affective, and managerial. They defined the cognitive role as a role that connected with the mental processes of learning, information storage, and thinking. The affective role is defined as a role influenced by relationships between students, faculty, and the classroom environment. The managerial role is described as course management. Emphasizing these roles, Coppola et al., (2002) and Liu, Bonk, Magjuka, Lee and Su (2005) concur and suggest that successful faculty who engage in e-learning redefine their roles into three distinct areas: pedagogical, social, and technological.

Roadblock to Faculty Participation in E-learning

As researchers seek to understand faculty involvement in e-learning, issues of barriers and benefits are important to document, discuss, problematize, and frame. A seminal report from Allen and Seaman (2010) suggests that faculty issues serve as major roadblock to the acceptance of e-learning, including the acceptance that online learning provides a valid learning medium. Such roadblocks, as Pajo and Wallace (2001) suggested, provide a context for framing them. These roadblocks can be attitudinal (no faith in technology, unwillingness to work with technology, concerns about student access), personal (lack of knowledge, skills, training, role models, and time), or organizational (inadequate technical support, hardware, software, instructional design, no recognition of the value of e-learning, policy).

Given this reality, literature provides context for framing roadblocks to e-learning around three perspectives: individual psychological, technical, and organizational. Individual psychological roadblocks refer to the internal and psychological challenges associated with a lack of knowledge and skills to engage in e-learning; intellectual reluctance; belief in misconceptions, assumptions, and myths related to online learning's internal incongruence with organizational culture; negative predisposition and attitudes toward e-learning; loss of autonomy and control over curriculum; and time to learn technology tools and software (Conceição, 2006; Conrad & Pedro, 2009; Covington, Petherbridge, & Warren 2005; Fish & Gill, 2009; Li & Akins, 2005; Macy, 2007; Maguire, 2005; Mitchell & Geva-May, 2009; Panda & Mishra, 2007; Tallent-Runnels et al., 2006). Technical roadblocks refer to the inadequate technical support, inadequate hardware and software, malfunctioning hardware and software, slow Internet connections, and unreliable technology tools (Macy, 2007; Nkonge & Gueldenzoph, 2006; Panda & Mishra, 2007). Organizational roadblocks refer to shortages of stipends, limited recognition by departments and institutions in promotion and tenure decisions, minimal instructional design support, poor ICT access and infrastructure, lack of training and faculty development, lack of institutional and administrative support, lack of time, increased workload, incidental costs, lack of quality of equipment, concerns of intellectual property, conflict of faculty culture with institutional culture, lack of institutional image, failed market competition, and lack of organizational fit between policy and organizational practices (Andersen, as cited in Green, Alejandro, & Brown, 2009; Appana, 2008; Macy, 2007; Maguire, 2005; Mitchell & Geva-May, 2009; Orr, Williams, & Pennington, 2009; Parthasarathy & Smith, 2009; Simpson, 2010).

Rewards Associated With E-learning

Several studies have highlighted potential rewards to e-learning (Appana, 2008; Clark-Ibanez & Scott, 2008; Conrad & Pedro, 2009; Li & Irby, 2008; Maguire, 2005), including increased opportunities for and access to learning (Fish & Gill, 2009), flexibility of scheduling for instructors and students (Keeler & Horney, 2007), improved faculty–student interaction (Appana, 2008; Clark-Ibanez & Scott, 2008), increased student participation (Conceição, 2006; Reeves & Reeves, 2007), facilitation of higher order thinking (Conrad & Pedro, 2009), opportunities for new markets (Mitchell & Geva-May, 2009; Parthasarathy & Smith, 2009; Simpson, 2010), improved costs (Simpson, 2010), anonymity (Appana, 2008), student interaction and satisfaction (Covington et al., 2005; Sugar et al., 2007), and growth in faculty skills in technology and pedagogy (Appana, 2008; Conrad & Pedro, 2009; Kyei-Blankson, 2009; Reeves & Reeves, 2007; Tallent-Runnels et al., 2006).

E-learning in Public Health

E-learning in public health emerged in the mid-1990s (Bruce, Gresh, Vanchiswaran, & Werapitiya, 2007; MacDonald et al., 2008; Umble et al., 2003). These programs were designed to provide experienced public health practitioners with the knowledge and skills needed to lead effective assessment, assurance, and policy development activities in public health practice. As schools and universities explored the Internet's potential for traditional academic learning, more schools of public health sought online alternatives to meet educational and workforce demands (Bruce et al., 2007; Reeves & Reeves, 2007). Stone, Barber, and Potter (2005) and Billot (2007) profiled earlier work of e-learning in public health and found that e-learning served as a means to train public health professionals in areas such as health promotion, nutrition, community health assessment, and suicide prevention measures. Edouard et al. (2009) suggested that teaching online through e-learning-based instructional activities helped facilitate access to public health knowledge, which could be used to extend an institution's geographical, cultural, and contextual reach.

Of the few studies relating to e-learning or e-teaching that exist in the public health literature, few concentrate on the need to teach online to help alleviate the workforce shortage, demand, or on the need to train better quality workers (Bruce et al., 2007; Laraia, Dodds, Benjamin, Jones, & Carbone, 2008). Others concentrated on program evaluation of online master's of public health programs, leaving out the experience of public health faculty who engage in e-learning (Bruce et al., 2007; Escoffery et al., 2005; Laraia et al., 2008; MacDonald et al., 2008; Umble et al., 2003). To fill this gap, Laraia et al. (2008) and Edouard (2009) conducted research that established a need for continued studies of e-learning in public health. Their findings suggest that little is known about the success of online programs in preparing students to practice public health or in preparing faculty to setup successful online programs. Therefore, this article presents a phenomenological study as a way to seek in-depth information pertaining to the experiences of public health faculty who engage in e-learning.

Theoretical Framework: UTAUT and Dewey's Theory of Experience

Two concepts emerged from this study: the first being adoption and the second being experience. The Unified Theory of Acceptance and Use of Technology model (UTAUT) (Venkatesh, Morris, Davis, & Davis, 2003) provides a platform as to how attitudes towards technology, self-efficacy, and computer anxiety play an important role in shaping one's use and experience with a technological innovation. In this study, teaching online constitutes a technological innovation. Although UTAUT provides a discussion as to how experience influences the use of technology, the discussion of the experience construct is limited. Dewey (1938) was used to expand the concept of experience relating to this study. Experience, according to Dewey (1938) is composed of two principles. The first is the principle of continuity and the second is interaction. Continuity refers to past events influencing the present and how one's experience of an event, observation, or moment is unique and profoundly influenced by one's experience of past moments. The principle of interaction refers to present experiences arising from interactions between past experiences and present situations. Dewey (1938) also lets us know that experience is an "interaction" between the external environment, whether objects, people, or surroundings, and the individual's internal state, including knowledge, skills, and attitudes are shaped by prior experiences. Taken together, the principles of continuity and interaction means that what individuals may observe or learn from a given experience is influenced by their prior experiences and by the physical and social settings of the previous and current experience. This theory combined with UTAUT provides useful insights into understanding the experiences of public health faculty as they engage in e-learning, the outcomes of those experiences, and any potential learning opportunities that may come from the overall experience (Dewey, 1938, p. 28).

The Study: Research Design and Methodology

The purpose of this study was to explore the experiences of faculty involved in e-learning in public health. The motivation for doing this study was the result of the authors' own experiences as online instructors and concerns about issues of faculty and organizational development. The authors believe that experience is a valid source of knowledge and that faculty's everyday e-learning experiences contain rich insights into various phenomena (Moustakas, 1994).

This study addressed the following research question: "How do public health faculty describe their experiences developing and teaching online courses (e-learning)?" To respond to this question, a phenomenological study of the e-learning experiences of five public health faculty members was conducted. This type of research allows the reader to begin to understand and empathize with the phenomenon of e-learning and, in turn, determine the extent to which interpretations make meaning for them (Moustakas, 1994). A phenomenological research design was considered most suitable for this study because it provided a clear process for setting aside the researcher preconceptions about the phenomenon of e-learning (Moustakas, 1994). As such, the goal of this phenomenological study was to explore the phenomenon of e-learning by public health faculty by obtaining verbal and written descriptions of their perceptions and experiences of the process.

Phenomenology was first developed as a philosophy by Husserl (Moustakas, 1994). Husserl introduced the phenomenological concept of the "lived experience" to describe the social world and events as it is experienced. This study followed the empirical phenomenological research methodology based on Moustakas's (1994) approach, which focuses on a situation in which the investigated experience occurred. The researcher looked for descriptions to construct structures of the experience. From these descriptions, the underlying structures and essence of how public health faculty engaged in e-learning were extracted.

Selection of Participants

Two sampling strategies for selecting participants were employed: the gatekeeper technique and criterion-based sampling. Although no formal gatekeeper was needed for this study (Richardson et al., 1965, as cited in Seidman, 1998), an informal gatekeeper, a senior organizational leader, was contacted via e-mail and used in this capacity to identify public health faculty who developed and taught online courses (Richardson et al., 1965, as cited in Seidman, 1998). Criterion-based sampling involved selecting participants who met predetermined criteria (Moustakas, 1994; Ritchie & Lewis, 2003), specifically, who (a) developed and taught an online course at a school of public health, (b) was willing to participate in digitally recorded interviews and written narrative protocols, and (c) granted the researchers permission to publish data.

Participants

A total of five public health faculty members (two women, three men), teaching at a school of public health, agreed to participate in this phenomenological study. Selected participants were from different academic disciplines, including biostatistics, epidemiology, environmental and occupational health sciences, health promotion and behavioral sciences, and management, policy, and community health. The faculty status of participants included four full professors and one associate professor. Four of the participants were administrators; two came from other campuses within the system. The e-learning experience of participants ranged from 1 year to 8 years. To maintain the confidentiality of study participants, pseudonyms were used to refer to the five faculty members who participated in the study. Table 26.1 displays a profile of the five participants.

Data Collection and Analysis

Data were collected using a variety of methods, including written narratives; semistructured, open-ended interviews conducted at the participants' site of preference; follow-up interviews; interview notes; and artifact examination. The researcher followed the essential processes that characterize phenomenological analysis: epoche, phenomenological reduction, imaginative variation, and synthesis of meanings and essences.

Table 26.1 Profile of Study Participants

Pseudonym	Faculty Status	Administrative Capacity	Age of Participant	Academic Discipline	Years of Experience Teaching	Years of Experience Teaching Online	Communication Technology	Number of Learners per Course	Course Length	Location
BIO01	Full Professor	None	70	Biostatistics	40	4	Blackboard	50	15 weeks	Main Campus
EPI02	Full Professor	Regional Dean	55	Epidemiology	35	1	Blackboard	20	8 weeks	San Antonio
EOHS03	Full Professor	Division Director	53	Environmental Occupational Health Sciences	25	1	Blackboard VSEE Skype	20	15 weeks	Main Campus
EOHS04	Associate Professor	Associate Dean	65	Environmental Occupational Health Sciences	36	4	Blackboard VSEE	50	15 weeks	Main Campus
HPBS05	Full Professor	Regional Dean	60	Health Promotion Behavioral Sciences	30	1	Blackboard	30	15 weeks	Austin

Epoche was the process in which the researcher set aside everyday understandings, prejudgments, and biases about e-learning. During the phenomenological reduction phase, this task was to look at the phenomenon of e-learning with a fresh look and to describe it in textual language—the focus was on the e-learning experience and its meanings. During this stage, the researcher uncovered, defined, and analyzed the elements and essential structures of the phenomenon of e-learning as experienced by the public health faculty. Data were then grouped into clusters, and repetitive, irrelevant, or overlapping data were removed, leaving only the textual meanings and invariant constituents of the phenomenon of e-learning. Next, the imaginative variation was performed on each theme; this entailed describing the structural elements of the phenomenon and the variation of possible meanings and perspectives of the phenomenon from different vantage points. The next step involved an intuitive-reflective integration of the composite textual and composite structural descriptions to develop a synthesis of meanings and essences of the experience (Moustakas, 1994). Triangulation, including member checks, peer examination, long-term observation, participatory modes of research, reducing researcher bias via the bracketing process, and detailed accounts of participants' experiences were used to increase the trustworthiness, confirmability, and transferability of this inquiry (Merriam, 1998; Moustakas, 2004).

Discussion of Themes

Five faculty members agreed to participate in an intensive data-collection process involving written narratives; intensive, multiple one-hour interviews; an analysis of their online courses; and their course documents or evaluations. Data from written narratives, artifacts, and interview notes were analyzed using the inducted grounded analysis technique (Blasé & Blasé, 1999). Categories, themes, and patterns emerged inductively from the data. Interview data were analyzed using the phenomenological technique the Stevick-Colaizzi-Keen Method (Moustakas, 1994). Based on the intensive data-collection and analysis process, three salient themes that were common across the experiences emerged: (a) rhetoric of fear, (b) transformation, and (c) negotiation between organizational spaces and institutional support. Themes and descriptions are summarized in Table 26.2.

Table 26.2 Summary of Textural–Structural Thematic Descriptions

Themes	Descriptions
Rhetoric of Fear	Apprehension due to lack of preparation
	Fear of the unknown
	Fear of interpersonal intimacy
	Relationships of students and safety
Transformation	Transformation of thought and intellectual capacity (internal psychological capacity)
	Transformation of instructional and pedagogical practice (behavioral practice)
	Transformation of identity and the concept of the faculty self (identity and role)
Negotiating Between Organizational Spaces and Institutional Support	Instructional & Organizational Support
	Spaces and Institutional Support
	Faculty Development and Training
	Resources

Rhetoric of Fear

Fear, as described by participants, was to be afraid or apprehensive about a possible or probable situation or event. Participants experienced fear in the process and activities of e-learning, describing their fear in terms of being apprehensive to new experiences of e-learning brought on by their lack of experience and preparation for e-learning. This led to a "painful, time-consuming" process, which made e-learning "daunting" due to the amount of preparation and facilitation. Illustrating this point, Dr. EPI02 said, "I knew it was going to be an enormous amount of work; I felt inadequately prepared; I had never even used Blackboard, so my expectations were a combination of excitement, dread, and fear. I thought to myself, how am I going to get this done?" Likewise, she also stated that, "It can be a bit scary, learning a number of new things." Describing this theme, Dr. BIO01 said:

> My lack of training and support for reassurance left me to spend much of my time developing and teaching these online courses without any guidance or support. This made me feel like I was not developing the online course correctly. I felt that administration abandoned [us] in this endeavor.

A second component to Dr. BIO01s' experiences of fear dealt with administration. He said:

> Administration does not support online course development efforts, therefore I for one became apprehensive, once I figured there was little to no support offered. I did it all by myself, not knowing the outcome.

Dr. EPI02 described a similar experience that stimulated fear relating to the lack of reassurance for e-learning, saying, "I oftentimes find myself second guessing if I am doing something right or wrong. I don't know how the course will come out." Likewise, when experiencing unknown outcomes relating to e-learning Dr. EOHS04 perceived a similar experience, saying, "The feeling of being unsure as to how the online course would turn out or if the quality of the course content would diminish leading me to become apprehensive about developing online courses."

When experiencing fear in the process and activities of e-learning, Dr. EOHS04 said, "I still have a fear that I will not be able to do a good job developing and teaching online courses, because I was not formally trained." Dr. EOHS04 also said, "I had some concerns about making it [the online course] work in the sense that students could understand what I was trying to teach through an online interface. This was a fear of mine." Dr. EOHS03 agreed, saying, "Lurking in the back of my mind is the fear I would fall behind and that I wouldn't be able to catch up."

Dr. EOHS03 further described fear relating to e-learning relating from the stand point of safety brought on by the lack of interpersonal intimacy and relationships with students. He said:

> All that was interesting [developing and teaching online courses] but it taught me to learn the personality of the person not necessarily seeing their face, however I then came back to Houston and within the first few weeks the students would stop by and speak and of course I didn't recognize them, but they recognized me and that always worried me. You know, I have an office in the back of the building that has one door and there's nowhere to escape. They could corner you and you didn't know if they were going to kill you or not.

Transformation

Transformation, as described by the participants, involved an act of enlightenment and a meta-morphosis. Transformation took place in three forms: (a) transformation of thought and intellectual capacity, (b) transformation of instructional and pedagogical practice, and (c) transformation of identity and role.

Transformation of thought and intellectual capacity. When participants experienced transformation of thought and intellectual capacity, there was a shift in attitudes, beliefs, and skills relating to e-learning. Previous assumptive thinking and negative predispositions of e-learning changed. In depicting transformation, Dr. EOHS04 said:

> Well, I was skeptical of whether online courses could provide a comparable or engaging experience for students. . . . With that in mind, when I developed my own online course I relied on and continue to rely on lectures that were recorded in the classroom. I felt that what I had to say was so important that students had to hear it and could not be sent to a reading in other learning activities and be expected to know what I thought was important about the topic and understand it in sufficient depth. So that was one apprehension I had. Again, my beliefs were that it probably wasn't as good. How did that change. Well, I was wrong, although my delivery of the course material has been changed greatly in the last five years. I learned that students can answer the material and never meet. I learned that and this is my own personal thought—I've learned that to do this well you can't just be a content expert but you have to have a real understanding of what it is like being an online student and to relate to that challenge.

Similarly, Dr. HPBS05 experienced a transformation in her negative thinking. She said:

> I sort of looked down on it [teaching online], that it was, I don't know, like the kind of course you would send away for that you would read a whole bunch of materials and take tests, that's kind of what I thought it was going to be. I didn't realize that it would be multi-faceted and interactive. You know I had no idea, I just thought I knew that a faculty course went well so I thought I would give it a try. I sort of had low expectations. I thought the students would just read stuff. So I would say I have really low expectations, and then I was pleasantly surprised.

Transformation of instructional and pedagogical practice. When participants experienced transformation of instructional and pedagogical practice, there was a change in teaching behavior, from traditional didactic methods to methods suitable for e-learning. In depicting this transformation, Dr. EPI02 described her experience, saying:

> I had to plan everything much more in advance, incorporated only one guest lecture (as opposed to many), and had to think through in greater detail the materials and scope of the entire course. I developed learning objectives for each module, so I had to think through the purpose and desired skills for each module. Overall, as many online instructors learn, the amount of time spent online responding to students, grading, developing materials, etc. is greater with online than in-class teaching. My greatest benefit is about to come, as I am about to teach it for the second time this summer. It will be so much easier to work on enhancement/improvement than in overall development.

Likewise, Dr. EOHS03 said:

> Both faculty and students must understand that, at least at the beginning, this [developing and teaching online courses] is going to require more up-front work and definite changes in their time management. This wasn't just a matter of posting PowerPoint on blackboard and hoping for the best however, it is actually going to involve some fundamental changes in approaches to teaching and learning.

In addition, Dr. EOHS03 said:

> It [developing and teaching online courses] allowed me to think through the building blocks of the course. You know in graduate school, we never had any formal training in teaching, this allowed me to do that—mapped it out in a series of sequential didactic modules. This was a transformation of a face-to-face course to online. The content is largely there—having said that the activities had to be changed—the way in which the content was delivered had to be changed and greatly adapted to an online format. So there were a number of changes, but what helped was the fact that I had done a face-to-face and it was the first time.

Lastly, Dr. EOSH03 added:

> E-learning offers a wealth of opportunities, but you've got to take the time up front in the beginning to create enough and allow enough time to become versed in the theory and activities. I love it, and learn on the job, but spending a few weeks reading about the theory, the framework, looking at sample courses. It is really helpful because then that unleashes your own creativity rather than if you do it in a rush. It has tremendous potential, but you got to pay attention to the base and grounding of what it's all about. Personally, I had a blast developing the course—more fun than in many years.

Transformation of identity, role, and responsibility. When participants experienced transformation in identity, role, and responsibility, there was an evolution in how faculty saw themselves as faculty and their role as faculty in e learning (from the "sage on the stage" to "knowledge facilitator"). Dr. EOHS03 described that this new shift was essential in order to be successful in e-learning. He said, "Faculty must successfully transition (and accept) from the traditional 'sage on the stage' format, teacher-centered, to more of a facilitator role (student centered)." In describing this experience, Dr. EOHS03 said:

> With developing and teaching online courses, faculty in public health will have to evolve into a new role. No longer can faculty use traditional means of teaching. With online, you have to design the course, then develop the course, the revise and manage the course, then you have to learn technology and the course management system, and then master the discussion board and use it well. This will require more time, more energy, and more patience.

Dr. HPBS05 emphasized this role, she revealed:

> I know a lot of people are thinking in that way that we should just put the courses online and they would be sort of self-generating and you know that you finish it—then that would be teaching as far as I am concerned. You really have to learn how to manage this new style of teaching.

Dr. BIO01 described a similar experience and felt that faculty needed to change with the times and with the new age of teaching, brought on by the digital age. He said:

> Faculty in public health can no longer see themselves as the expert giving information to students, but more a guide, showing students where the information is, how to understand it, and ultimately collaborating with the student on how to use it.

Dr. EOHS03 emphasized understanding the complexities of the new role as faculty developing and teaching online courses and that faculty could not accomplish the tasks of e-learning on their own without realizing their new role. He felt that now faculty would have to "design" learning environments, instead of "having" class. Illustrating this point he said:

> Once I understood that this was going to take a lot of pragmatic shifts both in my role as a teacher as well as the students as learners, I realized it was a lot of work. The one thing that helped the most was working with the instructional design team on fixed schedules.

Negotiating Between Organizational Spaces and Institutional Support

Negotiation with organizational spaces was a process where participants navigated, bargained, and made deals with the organization to accomplish the activities of e-learning. This was manifested through an interactive exchange with various forms of support. Support, as described by participants, was the act of giving moral, psychological, or tangible resources such as supplies, money, or necessities to accomplish a task. Participants experienced support in a variety of ways, most notably in a context that hindered the e-learning process. This included (a) instructional and organizational support, (b) availability of quality resources, and (c) faculty development and training. The experiences with support were described as nonexistent, token, not of real value, unsupportive, unhelpful, important, critical, and needed.

Instructional and organizational support. Participants described their experiences with support in the metaphorical style of roadblocks as a constant back and forth with the administrative culture of the organization. These roadblocks emerged as ill-defined policies as to who were screened and selected to develop and teach online courses, procedures as to how to find support and or technical assistance, lack of incentives or a policy for incentives such as release time, inadequate resources to improve e-learning skills, no real support office to handle instructional design coaching for teaching online, and lack of personnel to assist with e-learning. The following is a narrative from Dr. EOHS04, detailing lack of support from administration:

> I can look back on my duties developing and teaching online activities, and wish I could make things better and different and spend more attention to them. None of the prior administration at this school provided resources or support to the academic teaching part of the school at all. We have a token office. There was some attention given to upgrading the visibility of that position and increasing those responsibilities, and so forth. But no budget came with it. Very little assistance came with it. Expectations from administration weren't clear. I never had any authority, nor was the director of the office given any, either.

Dr. EPI02 described a similar experience relating to support for the regional campuses. She said:

> More support for regional campuses would be helpful. It's difficult not having access to the main campus's resources and personnel. Some of the workshops provided some great ideas,

but it would be nice to have a few translated for us, with specific examples—the opportunities and technology get overwhelming.

A similar experience relating to support can be found in the experience of Dr. BIO01. He said:

Early on, there was among the "disconnects" from the promise, rewards, and the actuality. This is normal for systems, I guess. Also, uneven access to help and personnel changes left lapses and thus no support.

Another important finding relating to support was the perceived lack of organizational commitment from administration. An excerpt from Dr. EOHS04:

Administration must decide if the school should invest in e-learning. We did not anticipate the resources needed to support course development and implementation. It seems obvious that faculty need training and assistance in moving out of the classroom to online. However, I don't know what level of support is appropriate. Administration needs to be committed to online, supporting faculty who develop and teach online.

Dr. EOHS03 shared a similar experience that speaks to the support:

Administration should make sure that as they are calling for more online courses that they go beyond advocating for those types of courses because they result in increased student enrollment and increased tuition-based formula funding. That they go beyond that and understand what opportunity that offers as long as it's done well. I'm saying that if administration is going to encourage us as faculty to do more online courses, then they need to have enough understanding of what e-learning is and allow the faculty to develop these courses the right way. And that means ample time up front getting faculty at the time to be grounded in the theory of e-learning and give them enough time to develop courses. So otherwise you were going to get what you get, which is, I'm going to post my PowerPoint and post an exam, and that's not e-learning.

The process of e-learning became further complicated by the lack of organizational support and the silencing of faculty voices. Dr. BIO01 felt that "his voice of concern was left on deaf ears." He explained:

There was not time allowed to pilot test the material. When I asked for one semester first to do this develop–pilot test revise–then implement, it was rejected out of hand. When I pointed out this was not consistent with either good curriculum development or even good methodology, this was met by an expletive, and was told "move on with it."

Availability and quality of resources. Availability and quality of resources dealt with access to technology tools and personnel, including current hardware and software, peripherals, instructional design support, and stipends. Participants indicated that administration should provide and ensure a means of instructional design support. This can be illustrated in the following narrative by Dr. EOHS03. He said:

I didn't actively solicit any help other than the instructional design staff at the school because there weren't really any other resources available. The one-on-one instructional training provided from the instructional design staff was very helpful. I do consider the school given access to resources—the instructional design staff was a resource. But obviously if the instructional design team hadn't been at the school, I would not have had access.

Dr. HPBS05 shared a similar experience that spoke to staff personnel as a resource:

If I had to start from scratch then it would have been a huge challenge. Starting with a model is so much better. So if people could be given extra money or hire and really develop—because it's so much work to do, then I think people could go from there. I think that it is what the faculty who I used did. She had a really gifted TA to develop the class. I think that is really helpful. Also, make sure there is a TA for these classes. Because the TA can trouble-shoot, do the grading, and other things. So to do it without a TA is kind of tough. So a TA in this case is important—just to keep feedback going on participation.

Faculty development and training. The issue of faculty development and training in formal or informal settings, with emphasis on more informal one-on-one instructional coaching was critical to the experience and process of public health faculty who engaged in e-learning. Topics that were found to be important to the participants can be divided into three broad categories: (a) technology tools, (b) instructional design, and (c) pedagogical and teaching practice. Technology tools dealt with software and course management system training. This training allowed faculty not only learning the mechanics and functions of software programs but also how to use the technological tools to package and distribute content via Blackboard for teaching. This can be illustrated in the following narrative from Dr. EPI02 who said, "I had to have a crash course in learning new technologies, Blackboard and Camtasia." Relating to faculty development, informal training sessions were seen to be of more value and preferred over the formal sessions. This can be illustrated in the following narrative from Dr. HPBS05, who said:

I think other than one of the instructional designers coming for a lecture and showing us Blackboard, that was it. So nope, I just got online and started learning. Then I think that is how most faculty are doing it. I know there are modules, but I also asked people, and the students are the ones—oh, and the faculty who I shadowed to learn how to develop and teach online courses had a teaching assistant.

Dr. EPI02 had a similar experience and narrative. She said:

I would say that my training opportunities were more informal consultations with an instructional design and other faculty. The only formal training was a Blackboard session held by the instructional designer, which was very helpful, and I had some helpful notes. I took advantage of informal consultations with the instructional designer and other more experienced faculty, and then I got assistance with IT for Camtasia, as well as talking to students who had taken online courses.

Although participants at this particular school of public health saw formal and informal faculty development as helpful, some participants had mixed emotions. Dr. EPI02 revealed the following:

More support for regional campuses would be helpful. Some of the workshops provided some great ideas, but it would be nice to have a few translated for us, with specific examples—the opportunities and technology get overwhelming.

296

Similarly, Dr. EOHS04 had a similar experience and narrative. He said, "I hate to sound very arrogant, but I don't feel like I had a great deal of help. Formal training was not that plentiful."

As informal coaching sessions were important to e-learning, faculty development in pedagogy and teaching were also essential to e-learning and in helping faculty grow as teachers in both their online and face-to-face classroom. Dr. EOHS04 revealed this importance:

> It's assumed for whatever reasons that everyone walking in with a PhD and their name next to a course can be an effective teacher without any training. I doubt that any of our faculty have had instruction in pedagogy and teaching. You basically walk in a classroom and do what you saw your instructors do in the past. So when we think about preparing faculty to teach online many of those skills all faculty should have. Though our concept of providing faculty development and support for teaching might begin with online, most don't know what they are doing and should be teaching. It should be improved across the board.

Analysis of Three Themes Using Dewey's Theory of Experience and Unified Theory of Acceptance and Use of Technology

This study shows that new issues relating to internal psychological capacity, teaching practices, and identity have emerged because of the use of online technologies and the transformative process of e-learning. Themes found in the literature related to the experience of faculty who are involved with e-learning are similar to the findings in this study: (a) the changing role of the instructor; (b) the work intensity because of the length of engagement during course design and delivery; (c) the complexity of e-learning; (d) the transformation of thinking, attitudes, and beliefs; and (e) the organizational infrastructure and resources that facilitate and/or hinder e-learning. However, this study's findings raised new issues that have major implications for schools of public health and, to a broader context, other institutions of higher learning as they implement e-learning initiatives. What the literature did not offer and what this study suggests is that the e-learning experience brings new dimensions and experiences to public health teaching practices, and that faculty exhibit (a) emotional anxiety and fear; (b) a psychological transformation that leads to changes in attitudes, beliefs, and teaching behavior; and (c) a struggle and negotiation with organizational spaces and institutional support where faculty learned self-directedness in order to accomplish the tasks of e-learning. These dimensions are influenced by and contingent upon three prevailing perspectives: an individual, technical, and organizational perspective that are absent from the face-to-face teaching experience. In essence, a congruence of interactions between the individual perspective (knowledge and abilities needed to develop and teach online courses), a technical perspective (the availability and capacity of technology tools to facilitate e-learning), and an organizational perspective (a social, technical, and political system that influences faculty's ability to engage in e-learning) resulted in a transformative process, where public health faculty challenged their assumptions and thinking concerning e-learning, their identity as faculty in an e-learning environment, and, ultimately, their teaching behavior and practices, as they emerged as online teachers.

Dewey's Theory of Experience and the Unified Theory of Acceptance and Use of Technology (UTAUT) provided a basis for exploring and interpreting the e-learning experience of public health faculty, the elements that influenced those experiences, and the outcomes resulting from those experiences. This conceptual framework precisely describes the interactions, feelings, and lived experiences of the participants involved in this phenomenon. It is clear that e-learning for public health faculty was complicated not by choice, but due to the current complex realities of the social, technical, and political systems in place that support e-learning.

Terry Kidd

When exploring and analyzing outcomes of faculty e-learning experience, Venkatesh et al. (2003), Cron, Slocum, VandeWalle, and Fu (2005), and De Vries, Midden, and Bouwhuis (2003) suggested that the UTAUT model provides a platform as to how attitudes toward technology, self-efficacy, and computer anxiety play an important role in shaping one's use and experience with technology, and whether the experience is positive or negative based on failing or succeeding in one's efforts to participate in a particular innovation. These authors suggest that for some, failing at one's efforts results in negative emotions and future efforts relating to innovation. In reference to innovation that involves technology, which includes e-learning, these authors suggest that an individual's failure to successfully learn a technology or participate in an innovation may induce a negative cycle of nonuse and emotions. This negative cycle may affect self-confidence and trust in technology and may have implications for self-efficacy when using technology—in this case, e-learning. As the current study sought to explore the experiences of public health faculty who engage in e-learning, these constructs play an important role in analyzing the elements that shaped the faculty experience in the e-learning process.

Rhetoric of Fear

The experience of faculty in e-learning was shaped and influenced by their previous experiences and interactions with teaching, learning, technology, organizational spaces, institutional support, and faculty from the traditional academic context. As such, faculty thinking, beliefs, and assumptions regarding e-learning and technology were influenced by this previous context. Based on past interactions with faculty and organizational spaces that helped shape their thinking about teaching and learning in general and e-learning, participants from this study found themselves in a condition where there was a biased lack of experience with e-learning. This lack of experience, brought on by a lack of preparation and training, the perceived workload, as well as influences of prior interactions with faculty from previous institutions to believe and subscribe to myths and assumptions regarding e-learning, led faculty into a state of apprehension, anxiety, and fear resistance toward e-learning; in essence, as they navigated the e-learning process, cognitive dissonance emerged. This caused the process and activities of e-learning to be a painful and daunting experience. This construct of fear is a major theme generated from the participants' narratives and is what UTAUT refers to as anxiety, which refers to the anxious or emotional reaction associated with the use of a particular technology, in this, case e-learning. Anxiety, according to UTAUT, influences attitudes toward technology, which is defined by the degree to which an individual believes he or she should use a particular technology—in this case, e-learning.

This study shows that the influence of past experiences and inadequate preparation or awareness of e-learning directly influences self-efficacy, which UTAUT defines as the degree to which an individual judges their ability to use a particular technology to accomplish a particular job or task. Given that previous belief in negative suppositions and psychological models that subscribed to myths and assumptions of e-learning, faculty experienced negative expectations in a combination of excitement, dread, and fear regarding e-learning. These expectations ultimately clashed with the practices and activities of e-learning, resulting in fear and apprehension revealing itself in the e-learning process, interactions with students, and in interaction with organizational spaces and with institutional support.

When interacting with students online, fear and apprehension emerged as to how faculty would build rapport and relationships with students and which ultimately bring into question one's own physical safety, as one described a situation of being "killed" because he did not know the faces or personalities of the students whom he had taught online. Given these circumstances and previous experiences influencing current experiences and interactions, faculty would once again have to find equilibrium with the complex realities of e-learning.

In this study, fear was experienced as a result of a lack of experience and awareness of e-learning. As such, this psychological element manifested itself in how faulty experienced e-learning, thereby suggesting that attitudes towards technology, self-efficacy, and computer anxiety (emotional reaction) play an important role in shaping one's experience with e-learning. This produces attitudes that influence individual self-efficacy related to e-learning and levels of anxiety and fear associated with the tasks of e-learning. As such, administrators within schools of public health and other institutions should devise systems of emotional support to create a climate of trust, respect, and encouragement as faculty engage in e-learning.

Transformation

This study suggests that faculty experience a transformation in the process and activities of e-learning. This metamorphosis takes place in the psychological and intellectual realm of individuals and in their identity as online faculty. Central to this metamorphosis was faculty development and training. Changes in psychological and intellectual capacity, including thinking and attitudes, created a new experience, allowing faculty to shift from previous negative and biased beliefs regarding learning, instructional delivery, and technology to attitudes and beliefs commensurate to engage the process of e-learning, thereby shifting and reconstructing previous mental models of instructional delivery and student learning. In addition to transformation in thinking and knowledge regarding e-learning, faculty experienced a transformation in behavioral outcomes relating to their teaching practice as a result of the congruence of e-learning and interaction between the three prevailing perspectives: an individual, a technical, and an organizational perspective. This change presented a new experience for teaching practices.

An additional component to the transformation theme is the notion of identity. New identities emerged as faculty engaged in the process of e-learning. With this new identity there was a shift and the evolution in how faculty saw themselves and their role as faculty. In depicting this transformation, new roles that emerge can be collectively framed around four constructs: pedagogical, managerial, social, and technical.

Transformation in thinking, teaching behavior, and identity made it possible for faculty in the context of this study to engage in the process of e-learning. Such affordance allows faculty the ability to gain necessary tools and knowledge to engage in e-learning, build self-efficacy, reduce anxiety, and transform negative feelings and attitudes towards e-learning.

Negotiating Between Organizational Spaces and Institutional Support

The experience of faculty involved in e-learning depicted a struggle and a negotiation between organizational spaces, (i.e., institutional support, administration, and resources). Organizational spaces, according to this study, can be defined as the relational perspective and influence of the socio-political and technical environment on the health, psychological, and behavioral capacities in and around the organization. Such capacities and environments represent an interaction between the faculty and policy, organizational culture, administrative culture, instructional resources, and organizational resources. UTAUT defines this element as facilitating conditions, the degree to which an individual believes that an organizational and technical infrastructure exists to support the use of a system or innovation (Venkatesh et al., 2003). This construct and overall experience within the process of e-learning was influenced by the individual's ability to deal with and challenge the complexities of the organizational space and ultimately their relational perspective of instructional and organizational resources. Using Dewey (1938) as a lens, past experiences and current interaction with various organizational entities influenced how faculty perceived and experienced various spaces within the organization. Each participant described his or her past experiences with the institution and organizational spaces provided as a negative hindrance or obstacle. Based on the current interaction of faculty with the institution and the relational perspective of organizational spaces within the institution, those in the process of adopting e-learning experienced institutional support as a negative, complex set of roadblocks. These roadblocks represented a wall or barrier that they had to overcome to successfully engage the e-learning process.

Implications

This study relates to previous research regarding faculty participation and experience in e-learning in notable ways. First, the study confirms that fear, transformation, and the negotiation with organizational spaces and institutional support are important moderators and facilitators to the individual, technical, and organizational perspectives that influence e-learning and the subsequent experience. These elements work to reduce fear, anxiety, and apprehension; present opportunities for transformation; and provide opportunities to build mental models associated with e-learning that are free of assumptions and negative dispositions. The results further confirm previous studies about the characteristics of successful online instructors in e-learning as they transition from traditional instructional environments to e-learning.

Additionally, this study provides valuable insights as to how faculty engage in e-learning. This can help administration understand what faculty perceives as beneficial or helpful as they engage in e-learning. Understanding how public health faculty, and to a broader context, faculty in general, engage in e-learning may help institutions to identify, plan for, and provide support services to increase online faculty with success in e-learning.

Conclusion

A key concept throughout this study has been change. Changes in thinking, changes in teaching behavior, and changes in identity are necessary to successfully adapt and engage within a new and distinct paradigm of learning. Salient features of the essence of public health faculty involved in e-learning dealt with fear, transformation, and organizational spaces and their relationship to continuity and interaction with the internal individual knowledge and skills needed to engage in e-learning (individual perspective/performance expectancy); continuity and interaction of technology tools used to support faculty in e-learning (technical system/effort expectancy); and continuity and interaction of the organizational, social, technical, and political infrastructure used to support faculty in e-learning (organizational perspective/facilitating conditions). These insights present an opportunity for change. Without such, engaging in e-learning and to a broader extent innovation, the process will become difficult, daunting, and stressful, thereby adversely influencing one's experience of the process.

References

Allen, I. E., & Seaman, J. (2010). *Learning on demand: Online education in the United States, 2009.* Needham, MA: Sloan Center for Online Education.

Appana, S. (2008). A review of benefits and limitations of online learning in the context of the student, the instructor and the tenured faculty. *International Journal on E-Learning, 7*(1), 5–22.

Billot, D. (2007). Developing and testing a module promotion and health education as part of a distance learning online. *Public Health, 19*(1), 53–65.

Blasé, J., & Blasé, J. (1999). Principals' instructional leadership and teacher development: Teachers' perspectives. *Educational Administration Quarterly, 35*(3), 349–378.

Bruce, L., Gresh, K., Vanchiswaran, R., & Werapitiya, D. (2007). Protecting health and saving lives: The part-time Internet-based master of public health program at the Johns Hopkins Bloomberg school of public health. *TechTrends: Linking Research and Practice to Improve Learning, 51*(6), 26–31.

Bruner, J. (2007). Factors motivating and inhibiting faculty in offering their courses via distance education. *Online Journal of Distance Education Administration, 10*(2), 1–24.

Clark-Ibanez, M., & Scott, L. (2008). Learning to teach online. *Teaching Sociology, 36*, 34–41.

Conceição, S. (2006). Faculty lived experiences in the online environment. *Adult Education Quarterly, 57*(1), 26–45.

Conrad, D., & Pedro, J. (2009). Perspectives on online teaching and learning: A report of two novice online educators. *International Journal for the Scholarship of Teaching and Learning 3*(2), 1–17.

Coppola, N. W., Hiltz, S. R., & Rotter, N. (2002). Becoming a virtual professor: Pedagogical roles and asynchronous learning network. *Journal of MIS, 18*(4), 169–190.

Covington, D., Petherbridge, D., & Warren S. (2005). Best practices: A triangulated support approach in transitioning faculty to online teaching. *Online Journal of Distance Learning Administration, 8*(1), 1–10.

Cron, W. L., Slocum, J. W. Jr., VandeWalle, D., & Fu, Q. (2005). The role of goal orientation on negative emotions and goal setting when initial performance falls short of one's performance goals. *Human Performance, 18*(1), 55–80.

De Vries, P., Midden, C., & Bouwhuis, D. (2003). The effects of error on system trust, self-confidence, and the allocation of control in route planning. *International Journal of Human Computer Studies, 58*(6), 719–735.

Dewey, J. (1938). *Experience and education.* New York, NY: Macmillan.

Dodds, J., Laraia, B. A., & Carbone, E. (2003). The development and delivery of a masters in public health nutrition degree program using distance education. *Journal of American Dietary Association, 103*(5), 602–607.

Edouard, G., Billot, D., Moussiliou, P. N., Francis, G., Khaled, B., & Serge, B. (2009). E-learning and north-south collaboration: The experience of two public health schools in France and Benin. *Pan African Medical Journal, 3*(5), 1–7.

Escoffery, C., Leppke, A. M., Robinson, K. B., Mettler, E. P. Miner, E. P., & Smith, I. (2005). Planning and implementing a public health professional distance learning program. *Online Journal of Distance Learning Administration, 8*(1), 1–13.

Fish, W., & Gill, P. B., (2009). Perceptions of online instruction. *Turkish Online Journal of Educational Technology, 8*(1), 53–64.

Gerlich, R. N. (2005). Faculty perception of distance learning. *Distance Education Report, 9*(17), 8.

Green, T., Alejandro, J., & Brown, A. H. (2009). The retention of experienced faculty in online distance education programs: Understanding factors that impact their involvement. *International Review of Research in Open and Distance Learning, 10*(3), 1–15.

Grosse, C. U. (2004). How distance learning changes faculty. *International Journal of Instructional Technology and Distance Learning, 1*(6), 25–35.

Institute of Medicine. (2003). *The future of the public's health in the 21st century.* Washington, DC: National Academy Press.

Keeler, C. G., & Horney, M. (2007). Online course designs: Are special needs being met? *American Journal of Distance Education, 21*(2), 61–75.

Kyei-Blankson, L. (2009). Learning to teach and teaching online: Faculty-faculty interactions in online environments. In I. Gibson et al. (Eds.), *Proceedings of Society for Information Technology & Teacher Education International Conference 2009* (pp. 947–952). Chesapeake, VA: AACE.

Laraia, B., Dodds, J., Benjamin, S., Jones, S., & Carbone E. (2008). Can distance education prepare future public health nutritionists? A case study. *Journal of Nutrition Education and Behavior, 40*(1), 34–38.

Li, Q., & Akins, M. (2005). Sixteen myths about online teaching and learning in higher education: Don't believe everything you hear. *TechTrends: Linking Research and Practice to Improve Learning, 49*(4), 51–60.

Li, C., & Irby, B. (2008). An overview of online education: Attractiveness, benefits, challenges, concerns, and recommendations. *College Student Journal, 42*(2), 449–458.

Liu, X., Bonk, C. J., Magjuka, R. J., Lee, S. H., & Su, B. (2005). Exploring four dimensions of online instructor roles: A program level case study. *Journal of Asynchronous Learning Networks, 9*(4), 29–48.

MacDonald, P. D., Alexander, L. K., Ward, A., & Davis, M. V. (2008). Filling the gap: Providing formal training for epidemiologists through a graduate-level online certificate in field epidemiology. *Public Health Reports, 123*(5), 669–675.

Macy, R. (2007, August 1). *The transition from face-to face to online teaching. Campus 2007 Technology.* Paper presented at the Campus 2007 Roadmap to IT leadership conference Renaissance Hotel, Washington, DC.

Maguire, L. (2005). Literature review-faculty participation in online distance education: Barriers and motivators. *Online Journal of Distance Learning Administration, 8*(1), 1–15.

Merriam, S. B. (1998). *Case study research in education: A qualitative approach.* San Francisco, CA: Jossey-Bass.

Mitchell, B., & Geva-May, I. (2009). Attitudes affecting online learning implementation in higher education institutions. *Journal of Distance Education, 23*(1), 71–88.

Mokwena K., Mokgatle-Nthabu, M., Madiba, S., Lewisa, H., & Ntuli-Ngcoboa, B. (2007). Training of public health workforce at the National School of Public Health: Meeting Africa's needs. *Bulletin of the World Health Organization, 85*(12), 949–954.

Moustakas, C. (1994). *Phenomenological research methods.* Thousand Oaks, CA: Sage.

Nkonge, B., & Gueldenzoph, L. (2006). Best practices in online education: Implications for policy and practice. *Business Education Digest, 15*, 42–53.

Orr, R., Williams, M. R., & Pennington, K. (2009). Institutional efforts to support faculty in online teaching. *Innovative Higher Education, 34*(4), 257–268.

Pajo, K., & Wallace, C. (2001). Barriers to the uptake of web-based technology by university teachers. *Journal of Distance Education, 16*(1), 70–84.

Palloff, R., & Pratt, K. (2001). *Lessons from the cyberspace classroom.* San Francisco, CA: Jossey-Bass.

Panda, S., & Mishra, S. (2007). E-learning in a mega open university: Faculty attitudes, barriers, and motivation. *Educational Media International, 44*(4), 323–338.

Parthasarathy, M., & Smith, M. A. (2009). Valuing the institution: An expanded list of factors influencing faculty adoption of online education. *Online Journal of Distance Learning Administration, 11*(4), 1–13.

Paulus, T. M., Myers, C. R., Mixer, S. J., Wyatt, T. H., Lee, D. S., & Lee, J. L. (2010). For faculty, by faculty: A case study of learning to teach online. *International Journal of Nursing Education Scholarship, 7*(1), 1–18.

Reeves, P. M., & Reeves, T. C. (2007). Design considerations for online learning in health and social work education. *Learning in Health and Social Care, 7*(1), 46–58.

Ritchie, J., & Lewis, J. (2003). *Qualitative research practice: A guide for social science students and researchers.* Thousand Oaks, CA: Sage.

Scagnoli, N. I. (2001). Student orientations for online programs. *Journal of Research on Technology in Education, 34*(1), 19–27.

Seidman, I. (1998). *Interviewing as qualitative research: A guide for researchers in education and social sciences* (2nd ed.). New York, NY: Teachers College Press.

Simpson, C. M. (2010). Examining the relationship between institutional mission and faculty reward for teaching via distance. *Online Journal of Distance Learning Administration, 13*(1), 1–13.

Stone, D., Barber, C., & Potter, L. (2005). Public health training online: the national center for suicide prevention training. *American Journal of Preventive Medicine, 29*, 247–251.

Sugar, W., Martindale, T., & Crawley, F. (2007). One professor's face-to-face teaching strategies while becoming an online instructor. *The Quarterly Review of Distance Education, 8*(4), 365–385.

Tallent-Runnels, M. K., Thomas, J. A., Lan, W. Y., Cooper, S., Ahern, T. C., Shaw, S. M., & Liu, X. (2006). Teaching courses online: A review of the research. *Review of Educational Research, 76*(1), 93–135.

Umble, K. E., Shay, S., & Sollecito, W. (2003). An interdisciplinary MPH via distance learning: Meeting the educational needs of practitioners. *Journal of Public Health Management Practice, 9*(2), 123–135.

University of Texas System. (2005). *The future of public health in Texas: A report by the Task Force on the Future of Public Health in Texas.* Austin, TX: Author.

Venkatesh, V., Morris, M. G., Davis, G. B., & Davis, F. D. (2003). User acceptance of information technology: Toward a unified view. *MIS Quarterly, 27*(3), 425–478.

World Health Organization. (2006). *The world health report 2006: Working together for health.* Geneva, Switzerland: Author.

27

A Blended Learning Approach to Team-Oriented Work in Large Classes

A Facebook Case Study

Salys Sultan

Computer-mediated learning enhances both the teaching and the learning processes; students appreciate the timely feedback, the increased accessibility of faculty, the resources outside of normal class hours, and their ability to get more out of the class (Berge & Collins, 1995). The role of a well-designed, computer-mediated system that affords communication among its members should support the human roles dedicated to synchronizing the individual process and group process as well as support both synchronous and asynchronous use (Turoff, 1991). In the asynchronous approach, it is possible to integrate an individual problem-solving process and the group problem-solving process in such a manner to take advantage of collective intelligence.

Blended learning is a mixture of computer-mediated learning and face-to-face environments. A contemporary blended learning environment usually consists of a learning management system (LMS) that students use to access resources for the courses using the Internet. Studies (Halimi, Seridi, & Faron-Zucker, 2011; Sultan, 2012a, 2012b) have shown that while LMSs provide students with a more convenient and flexible learning environment, they are still limited by the capability of the instructional team, the students' interest in using the LMS, and their knowledge of the communication affordances of this platform.

Research has shown that a lack of social interaction was the most severe barrier as perceived by students overall when using computer-mediated learning systems (Muilenburg & Berge, 2005). The authors' findings indicated that social interaction is strongly related to online learning enjoyment, effectiveness of learning online, and the likelihood of taking another online class. The authors noted that further work should be conducted to determine if improving social interaction in an online learning system would lead to a more effective educational experience.

Social media are the online media for social interaction, based on Web 2.0 technology, which has the typical characteristics of user-generated content and online interpersonal interactions (Chen, Diao, & Zhang, 2011). This research presents a case study of a blended learning environment that uses Facebook to facilitate group work in a first-year bachelor's course and presents preliminary results surrounding student involvement and social learning practices. It investigates how Facebook can be used to improve social interaction with the computer-mediated component of the blended environment and facilitate work in groups with a special focus on the development sequence: forming, storming, norming, and performing (Tuckman, 1965).

Related Work

Schlimmer et al. (1994) discussed how a team-oriented practicum enhanced student retention and significantly improved student–faculty involvement in first-year computer science courses. In the late 1990s, Dr. Guy Bensusan was an early adopter of online learning. He taught on Interactive Television at Northern Arizona University. His classes were live in Flagstaff and televised at eight sites across Arizona. He used a bulletin board system called ScreenPorch (Bensusan et al., 1995), and by creating a separate page for each group and assigning student logins to their group's pages, took all the confusion out of setting up online groups in a class of over 200. His work focused on designing learning experience before class, for class, and after class.

With the advent of social networking tools came the promotion of the sharing learning resources, and supporting distance learners in carrying out social interactions through collaborative learning. Charlton, Devlin, Marshall, and Drummond (2010) were the first to investigate the use and autonomous adoption of social networking technologies in students' communication strategies during the duration of a group-based project. The authors examined the role that 'status awareness' (knowledge of the current activities of one's teammates) had on the outcome of that collaboration.

One of the potential negative effects of online courses is a loss of social relationships and of the sense of community that is usually present in a classroom. This is where social networking tools can make an impact. This research investigated the use of Facebook as the online platform for a blended learning environment with a special focus on group work and the group development sequence. We examined how students in a first-year bachelor's course use this Web 2.0 tool for addressing the challenges associated with forming groups in large classes with an online learning component.

The Online Classroom

In this section we will describe the design and development of the Online Classroom (OC), the online component of a blended learning environment at the University of the West Indies.

The OC is the web-facilitated component of a blended learning environment (Sultan, 2012a). The OC provides students with electronic access to course materials for undergraduate first-year IT courses through the use of a learning management system (LMS) and a social networking site. The OC is built on the Moodle LMS and provides different features, including a weekly outline layout, lecture postings, a Q&A forum, a latest news section, an upcoming events calendar, an online chat room, and several types of quizzes. The first time the OC environment was used with a group of students one of the main suggestions that came from the feedback sessions was the need for a tool/feature where the students could collaborate with each other during the semester on matters relating to the course. The existing chat room feature only worked for synchronous communications, and the forum feature was not as user friendly to them. Instead of working on a new collaborative module for the LMS, we decided to integrate an existing social media tool that the students were already familiar with—Facebook. The use of Facebook versus individual break-out rooms within the LMS itself was also driven by the fact that Facebook provided some social and contextual cues to the participants that are sometimes limited in computer-mediated communication. Since this was a beginner's course, many of the students were now acquainting themselves with each other for the first time. Students (depending on the privacy levels set) would be able to orient themselves with their group mates by inspecting the respective profiles online. This was also the case for the instructional team. Furthermore, many LMSs require the students first acquire the skills to navigate and use their features. Since the majority of the students were already familiar with Facebook and its features, they were able to get acquainted much faster for their group work. The group interaction feature was called Group Discussions, and the students enrolled in the OC were connected to a dedicated Facebook page created specifically for the course using their existing Facebook profiles. For the remainder of this chapter, the terms Group Discussions and the Facebook feature are used interchangeably.

Facebook provided students with an electronic means of posting their ideas and work. Students can use the *like* feature to indicate when they were in agreement with the post or solution and the *comment* feature to suggest changes. At the time of this study, the *seen by* feature did not exist in Facebook, but the researchers believe that this would also be a useful feature in group work in the future as it records and displays the ID of student members and course coordinators who would review items but may not explicitly contribute on the page.

The course's main Facebook page was moderated by the lecturer and a dedicated online tutor. The main page was also linked to individual pages representing smaller student groups within the class. Only students belonging to a particular group, the course lecturer, and the online tutor could contribute content to the respective group pages.

The Study

In January 2012, 120 students enrolled in a compulsory first-year programming course, which lasted 13 weeks. For the delivery of the course, a blended learning environment was used, with the OC as the online component. The course's assessment included five assignments, four in-class written examinations, student participation (in-class and online), and a final two-hour written exam. Course-work assessments contributed 40 percent of the final grade and the two-hour written final exam 60 percent of the grade. The majority of the students enrolled in the course were familiar with the OC because they had used it during the previous semester, and the only new feature added was the integration of the social networking site for student collaborations.

For the course assignments, students were assigned to groups comprising four or five students to work on them. Students were placed into groups based on their academic performance history (so that each group had an average grade history of B) and according to their student enrollment status: full-time day, part-time day, or evening student to facilitate groups being able to get together in real-time if necessary. Full-time students pursued the most number of credits, and their classes were scheduled during the daylight hours. Part-time students took fewer credits than their full-time colleagues, and their classes also took place during the day. Evening students took the fewest credits, as they were people who were working full time, and their classes took place after working hours. Both full-time and part-time day students attended the same class sessions, and the evening students attended a different session, but all sessions were managed by the same lecturer, and the students used the same OC for the online component of the course.

The groups were structured based on a team-oriented group structure where each member was assigned a primary business role within the group (Chen et al., 2011). These roles were explained at the start of the course. Each group for this course represented a single software development company, and the four roles were Project Manager, Business Analyst, Programmer, and Tester/Debugger. The Project Manager was only responsible for coordinating the group's tasks, such as meetings, work distribution, and supervising task completion, and presenting the group's solution on the date it was due. The Business Analyst was responsible for analyzing the problems assigned to the group, clarifying any ambiguities, and preparing a high-level solution using structured tools such as pseudocode or a flowchart. The Programmer then took the high-level solution and coded it, using the Java development environment, which was the main software development platform for the course. The Tester/Debugger was responsible for the preparation of test cases and ensuring the solution met its objectives. In some groups, two students were assigned as programmers, and in others there was only one programmer. These roles were selected based on the average available IT job market opportunities in Trinidad and Tobago and the significance they play in the software development process. The job roles were rotated for each course assignment, so by the end of the semester students would have assumed each role at least once. This approach was taken to ensure that each student had the opportunity to develop the necessary skills used in the different roles. Other than gaining an appreciation for the different skills required for each role, our intention was also to provide the students with clear guidelines as to what is expected of them for each assignment; specifically, the steps involved in generating a solution and how each role contributed to these steps. The group assignments were posted on the OC in Week 1 of the course, and they were also announced in class so students were given the opportunity to meet their group members face to face. Students were then asked to use their respective group or company pages in Facebook to manage group-related tasks. While they received ample information concerning their roles and group processes, they were not provided with any further instructions on how the group's Facebook page should be used or how often they should use the small-group pages. Participation both in-class and online was encouraged, and as an incentive a percentage of the student's course-work mark was awarded for participation.

For the purpose of this study, we investigated the following research questions:

1. What were the groups' pages used for as it relates to the group formation sequence?
2. How often did the groups use their pages?
3. How were the features of Facebook used to achieve different group-related tasks?
4. Was there any relationship between the group's enrollment status and the use of the Facebook feature?
5. Was there any relationship between the extent of the groups' activities online and the students' performance in their final exams?

Results and Discussion

Students started using the OC from the first week of class. The new Facebook feature was explained, and a listing of group assignments was posted so that each student knew which group or company they belonged to. A total of 25 groups were formed: 21 groups comprised full-time students, one group comprised part-time students, and three groups comprised evening students. Out of the 25 groups, eight groups used their group page in Facebook throughout the semester, four groups used it for half of the semester, nine groups used it only at the beginning of the semester, and four groups did not use the feature at all.

In this section, the results are summarized and explored in the context of the different stages of the group development sequence: forming, storming, norming, and performing.

Forming

Within two hours of posting the group assignments (which included the student IDs and the corresponding companies they were assigned to), students started using the course's main Facebook page, posting 'inbox me' requests to find the other members in the group. At the end of the first week, each group was using their company page for group-based discussions. There were a few students that did not find any other group members. This was due to late student registrations, settling activities of the respective students, and the fact that some students decided to drop the program for personal reasons. If these changes affected the role composition of the group, the instructional team provided more support and guided the group through the change process. In most cases, the ones that left the group had not started participating as yet, and the established dynamics did not change.

The usage numbers indicate that 84 percent (21/25 groups) of the class used the group's page to find 'missing' members; the students that were not present for the face-to-face introductions. This was expected as one of the main challenges of group work in large classes is locating other group members and forming groups in a timely fashion. In some cases, in previous courses, students were left out of a group because they did not know the other members of their group and how to contact them. Students also had differing schedules, so coordinating a meeting time and place was easier using their Facebook pages.

Most of the full-time students used their Facebook page to set up face-to-face meetings on campus. Since full-time students are on campus for most of the day, meeting in person was an available option and was easy to arrange. After locating their group members, the evening students preferred to exchange ideas over e-mail. This may be because many evening students usually have access to the Internet at work, and some companies ban the use of social networking sites. This made tracking the communications with these groups harder. For the next version of the system, these students would be encouraged to use the communication features native to the LMS more. The part-time students were one of the groups that utilized their page the most throughout the semester. These students represented people that were working part time, so they were not always able to meet face to face and were comfortable using the social networking site. Some students also used their company Facebook page to discuss the different roles in the project team and who would be assigned to which role for a given assignment.

Storming

The Facebook company pages allowed students to set the respective groups' agenda according to their own perspectives. Students broke up tasks and assigned them to others and followed up on solutions that were due. When group members were not providing feedback or were missing in class, online posts were made to prompt these students for responses. In some cases, the students did in fact respond and in other cases the students did not.

The general conduct of students' behaviour did not show any signs of 'flaming.' The authors assumed that since the students knew the instructional team had access to the pages, this form of moderating influenced the type of behaviours exhibited. If there was any conflict arising in a group, the student usually brought it to the lecturer's attention during a class session.

Norming

The students that used the Facebook group pages for more than group formation established a set of norms over time. Once an assignment was made available, the Facebook page was utilized within 24 hours on average. The following is a listing of the more frequent uses of the groups' pages:

- Catching up on material if students were not able to attend a lecture session.
- Presenting and discussing their ideas relating to the assignments.
- Allocating work to each member for each assignment.

- Obtaining feedback on work completed/attempted.
- Providing encouragement and emotional support.
- Posting updates about the current status of work and personal availabilities.
- Discussion of non-course-related stuff, for example, other courses and extracurricular activities.
- Posting of reminders of assignment due dates and upcoming examinations.
- Posting questions to the lecturer and online tutor.

For those students that did not utilize the group's page as much, they also established their working norms such as the use of e-mails and face-to-face meetings to brainstorm ideas but the initiation of these processes started from the group's page.

Performing

For the group assignments, every group presented at least once for the semester, and the timing of the presentation was random. In the week starting February 6, 2012, the first group activity was due. As part of the evaluation process, four groups were randomly selected to present their solutions. The Project Managers were in charge of the presentation of their solutions, and they were also responsible for answering questions from the class and lecturer. Another member from the group was asked to take notes on all the questions asked and corresponding answers provided so that weekly feedback could be posted on the course's main Facebook page.

For this group assignment, at least one member from the selected groups was required to be present in class, and each group had a solution ready to present. It was noted that even though each member had a designated role for each assignment, not all groups used the roles for their intended purposes. Based on discussions with the presenting students, we discovered that, in the first group, only two members were active in producing the solution. In the second group, everyone submitted an individual solution for the assignment, and the final solution was based on the consensus of the majority. In the third group, everyone worked independently on their group assignments and therefore the solution presented was not a group effort. In the fourth group, the roles were used as intended. It was evident that more guidance or supervision was needed for the roles to be used as intended and for providing more instruction or direction in the group process. This form of assessment continued throughout the semester for each assignment. Without empirical evidence, the researchers noted that the students' performance in the final exam at the end of the semester was not significantly different for the day students, but for the evening students there was an overall increase in the pass rate.

The following were some limitations of the study. Researchers were not able to monitor how the groups utilized the online chat feature in Facebook; analysis of group communication was only based on asynchronous communications recorded as postings and comments. When probed during the presentation of the assignment sessions, students explained they did not use the assigned team roles as much as expected. Some possible reasons for this were that some students were not clear on the responsibilities of the different roles; other students were more familiar and comfortable doing everything themselves and discussing their final solutions; and different personalities were more comfortable assuming specific roles. The changing of the roles for each assignment would also pose as a challenge because it would require a reestablishment of new norms. There was also no accountability in place to ensure the roles were in effect other than the in-class presentation of the assignment, which was random. Finally, there was no qualitative follow-up with the group of students who did not use the social networking site at all. This would validate the existing research on the type of learners that are and are not attracted to this form of computer-mediated communication.

Conclusion

This chapter presented the findings of a case study on the use of Facebook as a social interaction tool for team-oriented work in an IT undergraduate course. Some students adopted the use of the social media site, Facebook, quickly and used it for the identification of group members and the establishment of the group norms for the execution of in-course assignments. Other students found that face-to-face meetings or e-mailing was a more feasible approach to interact because of logistical reasons. The results indicate that the use of online social media made the group formation more efficient in the large class. The research also highlighted the need to reinforce the performance of the four group roles within the team and their intended purposes for the roles to be effective. Future work will examine the type of learner that is attracted to using tools such as Facebook to facilitate group work, and what features of similar systems improve the group development process.

References

Bensusan, G. (1995, October–November). Interactive instructional television: The Bensusan Method. *Education at a Distance, 9*(11), 5–14.

Berge, Z. L., & Collins, M. P. (1995). *Computer mediated communication and the online classroom.* Cresskill, NJ: Hampton Press.

Charlton, T., Devlin, M., Marshall, L., & Drummond, S. (2010, April 14–16). *Encouraging interaction and status awareness in undergraduate software engineering projects: The role of social networking services.* First IEEE Education Engineering Conference (EDUCON), Madrid, Spain.

Chen, S., Diao, Y., & Zhang, J. (2011, September 16–18). *Social media: Communication characteristics and application value in distance education.* Second International Conference on Electrical and Control Engineering (ICECE), Yichang, China.

Halimi, K., Seridi, H., & Faron-Zucker, C. (2011, October 19–21). *Solearn: A social learning network.* Third International Conference on Computational Aspects of Social Networks (CASoN), Salamanca, Spain.

Muilenburg, L. Y., & Berge, Z. L. (2005). Student barriers to online learning: A factor analytic study. *Distance Education, 26*(1), 29–48.

Schlimmer, J. C., Fletcher, J. B., & Hermens, L. A. (1994). Team-oriented software practicum. *IEEE Transactions on Education, 37*(2), 212–220.

Sultan, S. (2012a, March 5–7). *Identifying the potential for blended learning in large class sizes with limited resources: A case study undertaken in an IT undergraduate course.* Sixth International Technology, Education and Development Conference, Valencia, Spain.

Sultan, S. (2012b, March 5–7). *An investigation into students' learning styles and their participation in a blended learning environment.* Sixth International Technology, Education and Development Conference, Valencia, Spain.

Tuckman, B. (1965). Developmental sequence in small groups. *Psychological Bulletin, 63*(6), 384–399.

Turoff, M. (1991). Computer mediated communication requirements for group support. *Journal of Organizational Computing, 1*(1), 85–113.

28

Mobile Learning BYOD Implementation in an Intensive English Program

Rasha AlOkaily

Context

The Intensive English Language Program, which is offered by the English Language Center in the University of Sharjah, provides four levels of language proficiency for first-year students. Most classrooms are equipped with a desktop computer and an overhead projector with ample Internet connectivity. There are two computer labs available for the English Language Center, which must be booked in advance for class use. IT technicians are frequently required to visit classrooms or computer labs to deal with hardware or software problems that come up during classes. When this happens, it impedes the flow of the lesson and hinders delivery of the lesson outcomes. This type of setting makes educational technology an add-on rather than an integral part of instruction.

Keeping up with the latest trends in learning and continuously inspiring students to learn are key factors for instructors to ensure the success of the program. Financial restraints and limited resources put a higher demand for creativity and resourcefulness on the part of the instructors. Ideally, with the advent of mobile learning, technology should be at the core of the educational process. It should be used to empower students, foster independence, increase creativity, enable learning 'anywhere, anytime' by reaching the abundance of available resources, and help develop the skills needed for the job market. Therefore, embarking on a bring your own device (BYOD) strategy can provide a suitable solution within the current context.

Key Trends in Education

Salmon (2012) summarized the key trends in education as mobility, connectivity, openness, collective intelligence, and virtual worlds, and commented that, as we move forward, higher education will become increasingly mobile, resulting in students carrying their university 'in their pockets'.

The NMC Horizon Reports: Higher Education Edition (Johnson, 2012, 2013) identify the same trends and add that the role of educators is being redefined by the abundance of online resources (Johnson, 2012) and the Massively Open Online Courses as an alternative to university courses (Johnson, 2013). Moreover, technologies are increasingly cloud based, with a decreasing demand for IT support (Johnson, 2012).

In keeping up with the abovementioned trends, it becomes quite clear that traditional, teacher-centered classes no longer serve the purposes of modern education. The move toward mobility becomes a must. IT leaders are often quoted to say that there is no avoiding mobility; campuses must keep up or be left behind (EDUCAUSE, 2013).

Mobile Learning in Higher Education

The concept of mobile learning has been around for some time now (see Alexander, 2004; Quinn, 2000; Sharples, 2002; Wang, 2004, among others), and attempts to define it vary. A recent UNESCO report on Mobile Learning and Policies identifies a popular definition of mobile learning as "education that involves the use of mobile devices to enable learning anytime and anywhere" (Vosloo, 2012), and the same report adopts a broad definition of mobile devices as "digital, easily portable, and can enable or assist any number of tasks including communication, data storage, video and audio recording, global positioning, and more" (Vosloo, 2012, p. 10). Hence, the general agreement is that mobile devices include smart phones, tablets, MP3 and portable media players, e-book readers, gaming devices, net books, even cell phones that have Internet connectivity. The list is not inclusive and will keep on changing with the rapid developments in technology. The notion of learning anywhere, anytime is a prominent feature of mobile learning that many other available definitions also focus on (see ADL, n.d.; El-Hussein & Cronje, 2010; Traxler, 2007; Woodill, 2011, and others).

Shifting toward mobile learning is not only about the technology. There is more to be said about the approach than the tools. Mobile learning is redefining the role of educators and the focus in the classroom. Implementing it in higher education does not mean merely integrating new technology into teaching; it requires a paradigm shift in the way students learn (Edutopia, 2012). Vosloo (2012, p. 10) also noted that

> discussions about mobile learning should: 1) focus more on mobility and its unique affordances than on technology per se; and 2) include questions about how mobile devices can support not only learning but also broad educational goals such as effective education administration and information management.

It becomes quite clear that mobility is becoming a lifestyle and continuous, personalized learning is the trend. Owners of mobile devices can effortlessly load their choice of apps and other content such as e-books, videos, audio files, and so forth, which transforms their devices into a "portable, personalized learning environment" (Johnson, 2013, p. 15).

BYOD and DNA

BYOD is also known as BYOT (Bring Your Own Technology) or referred to as "the consumerization of IT" (Converge, 2012, p. 6). Vosloo (2012, p. 7) asserted that "for the first time in history, a majority of people can afford to buy personal ICT in the form of mobile devices, in particular mobile phones." College students are tech savvy and use their mobile devices in their everyday and academic lives in the form of daily web searches, social networking, e-mailing, and collaborating (CDW.G., 2012). So why not take advantage of the unprecedented high percentage of mobile device ownership. Probert (2012) commented that it is a communication revolution, and organizations are faced with a choice to either provide devices for people or allow the use of personal devices, the later being a more convenient option. Hence, to engage and excite students we have to integrate the tools and technology they can 'use' and 'relate to'.

Benefits of BYOD

All cited sources in this chapter on the topic of BYOD agree on a number of measurable benefits. Many of these sources are studies done by, or on, institutions who have implemented the BYOD approach; therefore, they know from first-hand observations and statistics the advantages gained by that approach.

The benefits can be summarized as follows:

- Lower cost technology integration
- Engagement
- Teaching 21st-century skills
- Anytime, anywhere access
- Personalized learning
- Learner independence
- High-speed of implementation.

Some Challenges

The success of any program implementation depends on awareness of possible difficulties and ways to overcome them. Hockly (2012) categorized the challenges in three main areas. The first area is *devices and hardware*. There have been concerns over the issue of inequity among students, differences in learning material due to personalized learning, need for IT support, need for a reliable Wi-Fi network, and concerns regarding battery life of the devices. Another area of concern is *safety*, in terms of controlling device access, device safety, and e-safety. Finally, there is a concern regarding *class management* due to different platforms and continuous distractions.

None of these challenges is 'insurmountable'; Edutopia (2012), Hockly (2012), Johnson (2012), McCrea (2012), Probert (2012), and Vosloo (2012), among others, offer ways to overcome these challenges through policy making, professional development/teacher training, and investing in a reliable Wi-Fi network. To reduce the effect of inequity, institutions should consider providing a number of loaner devices to make sure that no students are disadvantaged if they own a less capable device. As for IT support, BYOD tends to reduce the demand on IT technicians since students are technologically savvy enough to deal with daily tech issues, more so because of their familiarity with their own personal devices. They are capable of offering support for each other and their instructor as well.

An important way to overcome the different learning platforms issue in the classroom is through creating device-neutral assignments (DNAs), which can be defined as "assignments and lesson plans that can be completed on any device" (AlOkaily, 2013, p. 2). (See Campo, 2013, for some practical guidelines for creating DNAs to help integrate technology owned by students into lessons.) DNAs also reassure teachers that moving forward in mobile learning through BYOD does not necessarily mean changing the assignments they have already created but rather converting them in such a way that allows students to use different devices and lets them find the relevant app or software to do it (AlOkaily, 2013).

Research Questions, Method, and Implementation

This chapter questions how ready and/or willing students in the University of Sharjah are for mobile learning. Has incorporating a degree of mobile learning in some Intensive English Program (IEP) classes shown any increase in student engagement and achievement? Has it improved the level of instructor–student and student–student communication? Did it result in more learning and more language practice? A number of activities that involve the use of mobile devices were introduced to students, who later took a survey designed by the instructor. The survey contained eighteen statements to evaluate students' benefit and degree of engagement.

The study took place in four classes of the IEP, namely, two level-three International English Language Testing System (IELTS) preparation sections, one writing skills class, and one speaking skills class. Students were encouraged to use their mobile devices for classwork, homework, individual and collaborative assignments, communication, and course management. They were invited to use these devices as tools both inside and outside the classroom to maximize language practice and critical thinking. The given assignments were related to the curriculum and assessed as part of students' overall course assessment. Communications (i.e., instructions and clarifications) regarding these assignments took place online through Edmodo, e-mail, Twitter, and even basic text messaging, which they all received and responded to from their mobile devices. Other engaging activities were introduced and encouraged without being part of any assessment; the sole purpose of which was to increase engagement and general language practice. After midterm exams, students were asked to take a survey to measure the results of incorporating mobile learning in the learning and teaching process.

Dictionary/Thesaurus Apps

Students were required to install a thesaurus and two electronic dictionaries on their mobile devices, an English–English dictionary and an English–Arabic one. They were advised to use these apps to look up meanings of words when doing writing assignments, vocabulary exercises, reading comprehension, and so forth.

Web Search

Quite frequently during lessons, the instructor would raise questions that students did not have a ready answer for. In such cases they were instructed to find out the answer from the Internet. Questions included historical information, people information, image searches, lists of word groups, or movie genres, among other things, depending on the lesson.

Video Projects

Two video projects were assigned. One was a video dictionary where students created a short video (approximately one minute) showing the meaning of a word. They were supposed to introduce a word from their vocabulary list and create a short video where they act out the meaning of the word or act out a scenario in which the meaning becomes clear. Alternatively, for students who did not wish to be in a video for cultural reasons, they were given the option of creating a video or a presentation with pictures and words to show the meaning, part of speech, and example sentences with relevant pictures (see bit.ly/12y9p3w). Videos where then uploaded by the instructor to YouTube.com as 'unlisted' links to protect the privacy of students. The links were shared with students of the same class to provide easy access to all videos (see bit.ly/14wfPQ1). Students used their mobile devices to create the videos and to watch them later for revision before quizzes.

The other video project was to create a food channel for the speaking-skills class. Students were asked to record a video in which they share a recipe by talking about the ingredients and explaining the steps (see bit.ly/ZefpgZ). When all the videos were completed, students watched them in class and assessed them according to a rubric provided by the instructor. Videos were uploaded to YouTube.com as 'unlisted' links as well (see bit.ly/YOdvD9).

Online Practice for IELTS Speaking Test

VoiceThread was used to create three complete IELTS speaking tests with video recordings of the instructor asking each of the IELTS speaking-section questions (see bit.ly/11AlcKL). Students were instructed to download the VoiceThread App on their mobile devices and record their answers to each question. The instructor listened to all answers and gave feedback both individually and to the whole class on common mistakes.

Blogging

In the writing class, students were required to keep a journal with entries every week where they write about anything they liked. The purpose of the assignment was to train them on free writing. To encourage students to blog, the instructor started blogging to give ideas and set an example. Blogger was suggested as a platform for their journals. Students were not familiar with blogging and were skeptical at the beginning. Therefore, they were given the option of keeping a journal in a copy book provided that they try blogging first for a week. As expected, none of the students took the copy book option and were not only blogging regularly but were also reading and commenting on each other's blogs (e.g., bit.ly/12A5vX1 and bit.ly/106OXD7).

Social Networking

The activities on social networking websites were not required from students as part of their course work but were encouraged for purposes of communication and content sharing. Students who had an account on Instagram, Pinterest, or Twitter were posting pictures of what they felt was an interesting activity(e.g., a picture of a drawing on the board that the lesson was about, or taking pictures of their own work and posting them). Each shared picture received *likes* from other friends, not necessarily from the same class. One student shared on Twitter a link to the instructor's blog post because the blog post was about her presentation (see Figure 28.1), and another student shared a picture of a murder scene drawn on the whiteboard, the set of *wh*-questions, and a picture of the worksheet that the lesson was about. Figure 28.2 shows a picture of the whiteboard with a comment from the student and 48 likes from her followers on Instagram.

Social Learning Platform (Edmodo)

Edmodo was the main social learning platform used for communication and learning management for the abovementioned classes. Occasionally, the instructor posted a link to an interesting article and spent five minutes at the beginning of the class chatting with the students who read it. This caused more students to be curious, so they logged on to Edmodo to see what the instructor was talking about with other classmates. Edmodo was also used for posting extra exam practice for students who wanted to go at a faster pace than their classmates. Another important way Edmodo was used was for online quizzes. Students could take the quiz from their mobile phones. Quiz results could be viewed immediately with all relevant statistics.

Figure 28.1   A Screenshot from Twitter

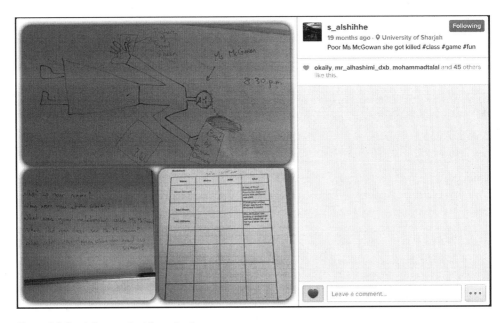

Figure 28.2   A Screenshot from Instagram

Feedback From Students

A survey was designed to evaluate the use of mobile devices in learning and students' readiness to view their mobile devices as tools for learning as much as tools for social connectivity and entertainment. The survey was divided into four parts:

- General questions about mobile ownership and usage,
- using mobile devices for class work and homework,
- learner independence, and
- possible disadvantages.

   Students were informed that there was a survey for them to take, but taking it was voluntary. They were informed through Edmodo during a two–week midsemester break (after the midterm exams). This was done to measure the number of the students who would respond to a notification they received on their mobile phones from the Edmodo App during the break. A surprising number, 45 students out of 57, took the survey. This means 78.9% of the students continued to be engaged, even during the break.

   For easier reference, the results for 'definitely' and 'surely' were combined and presented as a total percentage reflecting responses that agree with the statement.

Part 1: General Questions About Mobile Ownership and Use

Only one student indicated that she did not have a mobile device, but it is believed that the students did not realize that a laptop PC can also be considered a mobile device. In response to the question of what they like to use their mobile devices for (see Figure 28.3), they indicated connectivity to be the main reason. Their next preference was listening to language audio files, followed by keeping a journal, while doing assignments and taking quizzes were the lowest on their preference list.

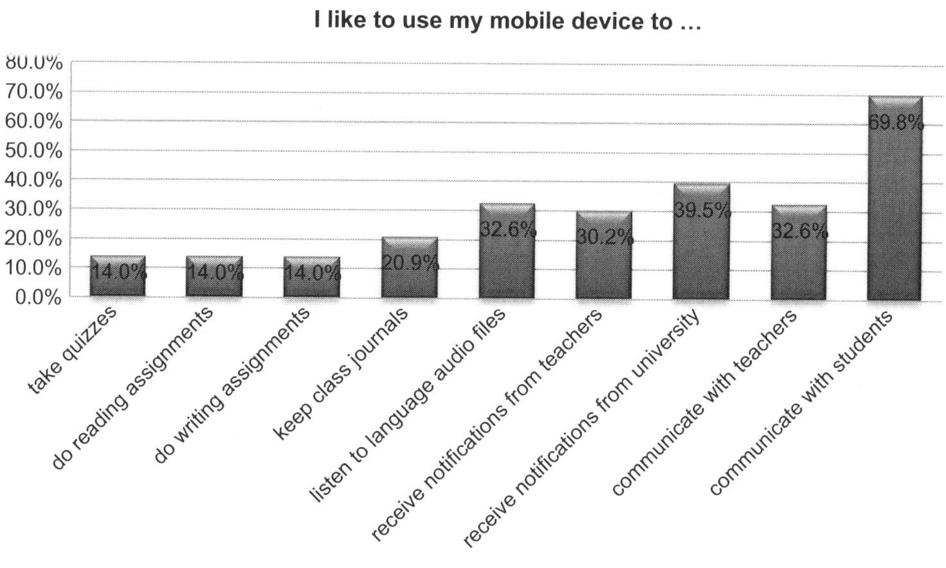

Figure 28.3   Students' Use of Mobile Devices

Part 2: Using Mobile Devices for Class Work and Homework

In this part, the first four statements were aimed at evaluating students' feelings regarding the use of mobile devices in class, whether it increases the quality of the lesson, makes the lesson more interesting, and whether they feel more active when they use their mobile devices in the class (see Table 28.1). An equal percentage (40.9%) of students expressed that they 'definitely/surely' and 'maybe' like to use their mobile devices in class, while only 18% chose 'rather not' and 'not at all'.

When asked if using mobile devices increases the quality of the lesson, similar percentages were received—38% agreed while 44% chose 'maybe'. Higher percentages were found in statements relating to engagement: 51% felt that it makes the lesson more interesting and 62% felt that they become more active when they use their mobile devices in the classroom as part of the lesson. The next statement was added to see if students preferred their own devices over computers provided by the university, and 53% chose their own devices. The same trend continues with the homework-related question since only 42% did not mind doing more homework from their mobile device. For keeping a journal, 51% felt that it became easier to keep a journal if they could write it using their mobile device. This percentage can be explained in view of the fact that only 19 of the 45 students were in the writing class and had to keep a journal as a requirement for their course work. The other 26 students who took the survey did not have to keep a journal and hence did not give an informed response.

The results of Part 1 in the survey can be seen as an explanation for the results of Part 2. In Part 1, students chose connectivity-related uses for their mobile devices in higher percentages than they did productivity-related uses (e.g., assignments, quizzes, journals). The results show that students like to be connected and stay informed, they are more engaged, but only half of them are willing to let their engagement and interest drive them to more production.

Table 28.1 Students' Use of Mobile Device in Class

	Mobile Learning Part 2	Definitely	Surely	Maybe	Rather not	Not at all
1	I would like to use my mobile device for class work.	13.6%	27.3%	40.9%	11.4%	6.8%
2	Using mobile devices will increase the quality of our lessons.	13.3%	24.4%	44.4%	13.3%	4.4%
3	Using mobile devices in the classroom makes the lesson more interesting.	17.8%	33.3%	28.9%	11.1%	8.9%
4	I feel more active in the classroom when I use my mobile device as part of the lesson.	22.2%	40.0%	13.3%	8.9%	15.6%
5	I like using my mobile device rather than using the university computers.	22.2%	31.1%	20.0%	8.9%	17.8%
6	I don't mind doing more homework from my mobile device.	11.1%	31.1%	31.1%	11.1%	15.6%
7	Keeping a journal becomes easier when I can write it using my mobile device.	8.9%	42.2%	26.7%	13.3%	8.9%

Part 3: Learner Independence

To determine whether using mobile devices increases learner independence, students were given statements in the survey to evaluate if they feel able to learn more; find information independently; learn anywhere, anytime; stay connected; and whether they need IT support when using their own devices. Here too, the results for 'definitely' and 'surely' are combined and presented as a total percentage reflecting responses that agree with the statement.

Seventy-three percent felt it enabled them to learn more (see Figure 28.4), 49% could find information independently from the instructor (see Figure 28.5), 77% expressed that they like to learn anywhere, anytime (see Figure 28.6), but only 37% indicated that they do not need IT support with another 32% not sure if they do.

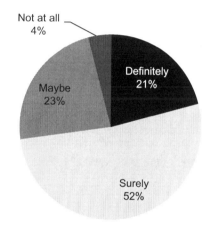

Figure 28.4   My Mobile Device Can Help Me Learn More

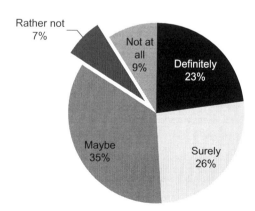

Figure 28.5   I Can Easily Find Information Without Depending Completely on My Teacher

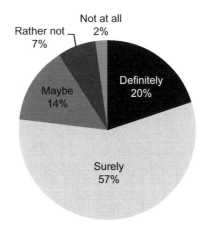

Figure 28.6   I Would Like to Be Able to Learn Anywhere, Anytime With My Mobile Device

The results clearly show an increased degree of learner independence. Students are able and willing to access information and manage it independently of their instructor. They still felt unsure of their ability to deal with technical problems.

Part 4: Disadvantages

The last three statements in the survey were aimed at finding out students' perception of the limitations that hinder the use of mobile devices to its full potential. There was one general statement regarding their general view of mobile learning, and another regarding whether the disadvantages are more than the advantages. Forty-two percent believed the advantages are more, while 44% chose 'maybe', which indicates that they had not had enough experience with mobile learning to be able to give a definite answer. Only 25% thought that mobile devices can be distracting. In a statement where they were asked to identify why using mobile devices was not so easy, 73% chose the response 'Internet connection is weak', and 43% chose 'Internet connection is slow'. Students had the option of adding any other reasons and four students wrote the following:

- "It works by touch."
- Wireless is bad (response edited).
- "Mobile device distracting me to hear the lecture."
- "The screen is too small."

It can be deduced that in order for mobile learning to be implemented in the University of Sharjah, the Wi-Fi connection needs to be improved to better enable connectivity for the increasing number of students' mobile devices. This, of course, is one of the requirements of implementing a successful BYOD program.

Survey Generalizations

A number of generalizations can be made from the survey results:

1. Students already own one (or more) mobile device(s).
2. The main use preference is connectivity, followed by keeping a journal.

3. Students are more engaged but would rather not do extra homework.
4. The majority of students are showing more independence.
5. The general perception is that the advantages of mobile learning outweigh the disadvantages.

Instructor's Observations

The increased engagement of students was evident from the general attitude towards classes. To be more specific, in both IELTS preparation classes, students' engagement increased. They repeatedly asked for more online practice. They felt that the online IELTS speaking practice on VoiceThread gave them extra opportunities to try the test alone, at home, in addition to the speaking practice that was done in class. They showed interest in the various articles posted for them on Edmodo, which meant more reading practice to improve reading speed and comprehension. The initial remark from students upon posting the first article was that they wanted to read it but stopped because they felt it was too difficult. Later, there were more comments by students on the articles that followed. Interest increased when article topics were discussed and commented on in class. Now, students simply read, comment, and enjoy the process of finding out interesting things around the world. Audio files were also posted for them on Edmodo, and they frequently asked for more. This relates to the survey when students showed 'listening to audio files' a preferred use of their mobile devices.

In the writing class, students were keen on updating their blog with the required three entries a week, more so because they received comments from the instructor and classmates. They are more careful about what to write and share experiences that will win them more reactions from classmates. Another major consideration here is that it is by far easier for the instructor to keep up with the students' blogs than the previous method of collecting copy books from students, in which case classmates did not have the chance to see each other's writings. It is the sharing and the publishing that encourages students to try their best. As blogs progressed, the instructor noticed improvements in style and language in varying degrees.

In the speaking class, students had more opportunities to speak because of VoiceThread and because of their ability to create videos of themselves presenting. One student could not come to class to give her presentation, so she was offered the opportunity to upload her PowerPoint presentation on VoiceThread and record herself speaking for every slide of the presentation. Students handed in the video assignments on time in an unprecedented rate compared to face-to-face presentations, in which a number of students would try to delay as long as possible.

The general interaction and rapport between instructor and students were increased. Students felt that they are partners in the learning process rather than passive receivers, which is the ideal that all educators strive to achieve.

Limitations of This Study

The study was carried out mainly in the Women's Campus among female students. The survey was given to students after eight weeks of study with the incorporation of mobile devices. The number of students taking the survey was limited, and results would have been more indicative if there had been more students, both male and female, and a longer period of time for further implementations of mobile learning. The number of online activities and other specially designed activities for mobile learning could have been increased to give students more exposure to mobile learning. The instructor was not able to offer as much as she had hoped for due to certain complications in timetabling, which led, unavoidably, to a hectic teaching schedule on different campuses. This led to limited preparation time per class.

Conclusion and Recommendations for Further Research

The nature of mobile learning and the openness of 21st-century learning need to be investigated against the cultural background of society in the United Arab Emirates. Online connectivity and communication between instructor and students need to be studied to find the best practices that respect the cultural uniqueness of the region. Similarly, requiring students to create and share videos or even pictures needs to be carefully considered to avoid inappropriateness. Publishing on the web means further exposure, and that must be done with caution as to what is deemed culturally acceptable in such situations. In this study, cultural issues were minimal because both the instructor and the students are female, but there were a number of activities that were not included in the study due to a feeling that further investigation should be made to assessed levels of appropriateness. Some examples would be the use of social networking websites like Facebook because of the precaution that in certain social contexts it is deemed as not suitable. Twitter, in this study, has been used in a limited way, and not as part of any class activity but rather as a way for further communication and connectivity with individual students who already had an account. There is a need to draw clear lines and describe successful practices that are considerate of students' culture. Finding out the parameters within which instructors can maneuver would ensure better implementation of mobile learning in the region.

References

ADL (n.d.). *Mobile learning handbook*. Retrieved from https://sites.google.com/a/adlnet.gov/mobile-learning-guide/basics

Alexander, B. (2004, January). Going nomadic: mobile learning in higher education. *EDUCAUSE Review, 39*(5), 28–35. Retrieved from http://www.educause.edu/ero/article/going-nomadic-mobile-learning-higher-education

AlOkaily, R. (2013). Device neutral assignments for mobile learning in an English language classroom. *QScience Proceedings, Vol. 2013, 12th World Conference on Mobile and Contextual Learning (mLearn 2013)*, 29. doi:10.5339/qproc.2013.mlearn.29

Campo, S. (2013, April). *Device neutral assignments: DNA for BYOD*. Retrieved from https://www.smore.com/: https://www.smore.com/r0um-device-neutral-assignments?ref=lboard

CDW.G. (2012). *Bring your own device: Adapting to the flood of personal mobile computing devices accessing campus network*. Retrieved from http://www.edtechmagazine.com/higher/sites/edtechmagazine.com.higher/files/108532-wp-hied-byod-df.pdf

Converge. (2012). *One-to-One 2.0*. e.Republic. Retrieved from http://www.samsung.com/us/it_solutions/innovation-center/downloads/education/white_papers/One-to-One_2.0_-_Handbook.pdf

EDUCAUSE. (2013). *EdTech, focus on higher education*. Retrieved from www.edtechmagazine.com: http://www.edtechmagazine.com/higher/video/educause-2012-mobile-devices-everywhere

Edutopia. (2012). *Mobile devices for learning: What you need to know*. Retrieved from http://www.edutopia.org/mobile-devices-learning-resource-guide

El-Hussein, M.O.M., & Cronje, J. C. (2010). Defining mobile learning in the higher education landscape. *Educational Technology & Society, 13*(3), 12–21.

Hockly, N. (2012, October). Tech-savvy teaching: BYOD. *Modern English Teacher, 21*(4), 44–45. Retrieved from http://www.academia.edu/2065524/Tech-savvy_teaching_BYOD

Johnson, L. A. (2012). *The NMC horizon report: 2012 higher education edition*. Austin, TX: The New Media Consortium.

Johnson, L. A. (2013). *NMC horizon report: 2013 higher education edition*. Austin, TX: The New Media Consortium.

McCrea, B. (2012, November 14). Pros and cons of BYOD and school supplied mobile devices. *Campus Technology.* Retrieved from http://campustechnology.com/Articles/2012/11/14/Pros-and-Cons-of-BYOD-and-School-Supplied-Mobile-Devices.aspx?sc_lang=en&Page=1

Probert, T. (2012, June). BYOD—An education revolution? *Educational Technology.* Retrieved from http://www.universitybusiness.co.uk/?q=features/byod-%E2%80%93-educational-revolution/5227

Quinn, C. (2000, Fall). *mLearning: Mobile, wireless, in-your-pocket learning.* Retrieved from www.linezine.com: http://www.linezine.com/2.1/features/cqmmwiyp.htm

Salmon, G. (2012, July 10). Tech for teaching: five trends changing higher education. *The Conversation.* Retrieved from http://theconversation.com/tech-for-teaching-five-trends-changing-higher-education-7617

Sharples, M. (2002). The design and implementation of a mobile learning resource. *Journal of Personal and Ubiquitous Computing, 6,* 220–234. Retrieved from http://delivery.acm.org/10.1145/600000/594358/20060220.pdf?ip=194.170.95.210&acc=ACTIVE%20SERVICE&key=C2716FEBFA981EF1997E81D9778A2D67CDFB9DE69F1D5833&CFID=205044391&CFTOKEN=73396274&__acm__=1366039200_2015bc02b9d4d1e4f63a2ceaccd20551

Traxler, J. (2007, June). Defining, discussing, and evaluating mobile learning: the moving finger writes and having writ. . . . *International Review of Research in Open and Distance Learning, 8*(2). Retrieved from http://www.irrodl.org/index.php/irrodl/article/view/346/875

Vosloo, S. (2012). *Mobile learning and policies: Key issues to consider.* Paris, France: UNESCO. Retrieved from http://unesdoc.unesco.org/images/0021/002176/217638E.pdf

Wang, Y.-K. (2004). Context awareness and adaptation in mobile learning. *Proceedings of the Second IEEE International Workshop on Wireless and Mobile Technologies in Education* (pp. 154–158).

Woodill, G. (2011, August). *The evolution of the definition of mobile learning.* Retrieved from http://floatlearning.com/2011/08/the-evolution-of-the-definition-of-mobile-learning/

29

Blended Learning and Teaching— A Panacea for Students With Learning Disabilities

Edith Gotesman

We are moving from the teacher-centered to a learner-focused system of education. New developments in learning and technology provide opportunities for creating well-designed meaningful learning environments for diverse learners. With the advent of the computer-based education and online learning methodologies and technologies, providers of education are combining teaching methods to fulfill the needs of their learners. Academic institutions are now increasingly using the Internet and digital technologies to deliver instruction and training. Many instructors are encouraged to design courses in which students can benefit from blended learning, an educational strategy that combines the use of online teaching and learning with the best features of classroom interaction. The use of blended learning was born out of the necessity to accommodate students with learning disabilities who study English for academic purposes (EAP) in higher education. We would like to share our experience in the field by discussing the practical use of blended learning: frontal teaching and the use of assistive technologies (AT) combined with e-learning.

Teaching English for Academic Purposes in Higher Education

In the world of globalization, reading academic texts in English is a basic requirement of higher education. As part of the academic requirements in Israel, all students have to reach an advanced level, exemption, in order to receive a degree. Those students who are unable to read texts in English find themselves at a disadvantage. In order to help those students who have not reached the advanced level of proficiency in reading comprehension, special courses at different levels, from beginning to advanced levels, are provided for all students at the institutions of higher education so that they can meet the requirements.

However, in addition to the regular students, there are those students who have been identified as having language-related disabilities, for example, dyslexia. These students, by definition, struggle to attain literacy in their mother tongue, yet they are required to meet the same standards as those without disabilities. This student population faces failure before they have even begun. The question thus arose: How can we help these students? We reasoned that as they had been unable to learn using regular teaching methods, perhaps the use of AT combined with e-learning could facilitate their understanding of texts in English and also lead to their becoming autonomous learners.

Dyslexia

"In order to establish who our subjects are, we start by defining dyslexia followed by a definition of assistive technology. Dyslexia is a difficulty in the acquisition of literacy skills that is neurological in origin. It is evident when accurate and fluent word reading, spelling, and writing develop very incompletely or with great difficulty" (Siegel & Smythe, 2004, p. 135).

Within the context of our study, we would like to emphasize 'literacy skills,' which include comprehension and not only word recognition and decoding.

Students who have dyslexia often find reading texts extremely difficult in the L1, and almost, if not impossible, in English as a foreign language. Our goal in the college has been to provide these students, who have been diagnosed as having dyslexia and other language-related difficulties, with the possibility of learning to read fluently and coping with the texts to achieve reading fluency and to succeed in their academic studies. After using different teaching strategies, we came to the conclusion that assistive technology, specifically text-to-speech programs, might help these students.

Assistive Technologies

The use of technology has been shown to be effective in many areas, including education. AT has also proved effective in assisting students with learning disabilities to perform better and more accurately, gain knowledge and confidence, gain independence in performing tasks, and in general have better achievements.

Definition and Types of AT

Assistive technology (AT) is defined by Raskind and Higgins (1998) as any technology that enables an individual with a learning disability to compensate for specific deficits. AT covers a wide range of software that helps students read, write, organize information, and spell.

We will present the way AT can be used to assist specific needs (Table 29.1) and show examples of various existing software (Table 29.2).

Research on Assistive Technology and Learning Disabilities

The use of technology has been shown to be effective in a wide range of content areas (Ashton, 2005; Edyburn, 2004; Okolo, Cavalier, Ferretti, & MacArthur, 2000). Research says that use of AT can contribute to strengthening students' skills in decoding, comprehension, and reading with fluency (Elkind, Cohen, & Murray 1993; Higgins & Raskind, 2000), word recognition, reading

Table 29.1 Matching AT to Students' Specific Needs

Student's Individual Need	Assistive Technology
Decoding (sounding out words) Reading comprehension	Text-to-speech programs
Handwriting Directionality	Speech-to-text programs
Expressing words in written form	Word processors Word prediction programs
Encoding (spelling)	Proofreading programs Spell checkers
Organization	Outlining/brainstorming programs

comprehension, spelling and reading strategies (Raskind & Higgins, 1999), spelling (Dalton, Winbury, & Morocco, 1990), organizing, reading and synthesizing information (Anderson–Inman, Knox–Quinn, & Horney, 1996; Anderson–Inman, Knox–Quinn, & Szymanski, 1999), and proofreading and writing (Raskind & Higgins, 1995).

Selecting the Appropriate Technology and Matching It to Students' Individual Needs

According to Raskind and Higgins (1998) and Raskind et al. (1998), selecting the appropriate technology for an individual with a learning disability requires careful analysis of the interplay between the individual, specific tasks or functions to be performed, the specific technology, and the specific context of interaction (see Figure 29.1).

Each individual should make use of the technology that best complements his or her needs. The chosen type of assistive technology could help an individual with a learning disability to function at a level that is commensurate with their intelligence. Table 29.2 presents types of AT to be chosen according to the type of learning difficulty: difficulty in reading, writing, planning and organization of material, spelling, and word prediction.

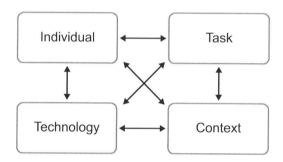

Figure 29.1   The Interplay of Individual, Task, Context, and Technology
Adapted from Raskind, 2006

Table 29.2 AT According to Types of Difficulty/Impairment

Type of Difficulty	AT to Consider	Internet Site
Reading	ReadPlease	www.readplease.com
	TextAloud	www.textaloud.com
	TextAssist	www.textassist.com
	Kurtzweil	www.kurzweiledu.com
	Read&Write	www.texthelp.com
Writing	DragonNaturally Speaking	www.nuance.com/naturallyspeaking
	Intellitalk	www.synapse-ada.com/intellitools/ new/Classroom_Suite_IntelliTools_ Home_Page.htm
Planning and organization	Inspiration	www.inspiration.com
Spelling and word prediction	WordQ	www.wordq.com
	Predictor Pro	www.readingmadeez.com/home.html

Text-to-Speech Programs

Individuals with severe learning disabilities, such as dyslexia, who have difficulty decoding and understanding written text, may comprehend printed content much better when it is read out loud. These individuals may have substantial gains in reading scores and comprehension when the text is read aloud for them. Text-to-speech programs allow the electronic text to be synchronized with audio in order to help people with reading difficulties. These reading programs are very useful not only for dyslexic students, they are also valuable for visually impaired students who can use one of the software features to enlarge font, change background, and/or listen to the text uploaded to the screen of the reader.

Our choice for text-to-speech software was TextAloud. This reading program provides multimodal reading, which means that the text-to-speech is combined with word-by-word highlighting. The program can read digital text aloud. Students can adjust the reading rate and the font size according to their individual needs. The software provides options for voice type. One of its advantages over other text-to-speech programs is that it can turn text files into audio files. Our learning disabled (LD) students use TextAloud to listen to the texts of their articles both in class when they work on assignments and at home when they do homework. TextAloud offers AT&T voices, which sound less artificial and are better understood by students.

E-learning

> E-learning can be viewed as an innovative approach for delivering well-designed, learner-centered, interactive and facilitated learning environment to anyone, anyplace, anytime, by utilizing the attributes and resources of various digital technologies along with other forms of learning materials suited for open and distributed learning environment.
>
> *(Kahn, 2001, p. 3)*

The theoretical framework for our special course is based on Khan's e-learning framework (http://asianvu.com/bk/framework/), *The Octagonal Framework* (see Figure 29.2).

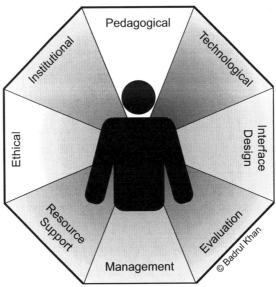

Figure 29.2   Khan's Octagonal Framework

According to Khan (2005), a variety of factors are required to be addressed in order to create a meaningful learning environment, many of which are interrelated and interdependent. Since the learning requirements and preferences of each learner tend to vary, it is essential to use a blend of learning approaches and teaching strategies in order to cater for their needs. Placing the learner at the center of Kahn's framework, we identified the critical issues of the learning environment for our particular group of students and adopted the teaching philosophy which best suits the needs of our students: *blended learning*.

Blended Learning

The widespread adoption and availability of digital learning technologies has led to increased levels of integration of computer mediated instructional elements into the traditional F2F (face-to-face) learning experience (Bonk & Graham, 2004).

Blended learning represents a shift in educational strategy. It is an educational method that combines the benefits of e-learning, computer technology, and the conventional face-to-face teaching methods in order to optimize the teaching and learning process. It intends to take the best of both worlds. Students take advantage of teacher-driven presentation and selection of relevant content, benefit from social interaction, live instruction, and immediate feedback. Blended learning supports personalized learning, thoughtful reflection, and differentiates instruction from student to student across a diverse group of learners. According to Dziuban, Hartman, and Moskal (2004), blended learning should be viewed as a pedagogical approach that combines the effectiveness and socialization opportunities of the classroom with the technologically enhanced active learning possibilities of the online environment.

The Pilot Project Study

Rationale, Problems, and Solutions

Pupils with reading disabilities become students with reading disabilities. In order to meet the needs of students with learning disabilities attending institutions of higher education, these institutions offer various adjustments for students who have been diagnosed as having a disability. The assessment is the key determining factor in deciding whether a student will benefit from a text-to-speech output accommodation. A student who has difficulty decoding multisyllabic words, loses his or her place on the page, or has difficulty comprehending printed text may benefit from text-to-speech output.

The Ashkelon Academic College offers assessed LD students enrolled in the EAP program the opportunity to complete their English requirements. Students formally diagnosed as learning disabled are entitled to accommodations. The accommodations offered to these students include the following:

a. A modified version of the text. This means that the original text of the article to be studied is rearranged in a different way. It shows a number of paragraphs followed by the questions referring to them, another set of paragraphs followed by a question or questions and so on. This helps LD students better focus on their assignment.
b. Time extension.
c. Use of TextAloud for listening to the text and related questions.

Edith Gotesman

Aim of the Project

The pilot study aimed at examining whether employing blended learning could facilitate the understanding of English texts of LD students and improve their reading comprehension abilities, thus leading to their becoming autonomous learners.

Methodology

Two groups of assessed LD students participated in the pilot study. The sample group consisted of 20 students enrolled in the special course for LD students, and the control group consisted of 7 assessed LD students who were entitled to the same accommodations but chose not to be part of the special course. Each group undertook five reading comprehension exams during the annual course. The exams varied in terms of level of difficulty, length of the text, and vocabulary. Students took the first exam at the beginning of the annual course, and the last exam was the final exemption test at the end of the course.

Discussion

The 20 students whose teaching and learning process took place in the computer lab used TextAloud for class assignments on a regular basis. In order to be able to practice the material taught in class and complete homework assignments by using the reading software, the teaching and learning process was supplemented by e-learning. LD students had access to the learning materials and the TextAloud program available online. They benefited from blended learning: frontal teaching, use of AT, and e-learning. The 7 LD students in the regular courses did not have a computer or a laptop for listening to the text in class. They benefited from the reading of TextAloud only when they took the final exam.

The teaching and learning process took place in a computer lab. Each student had access to a personal computer. Using blended learning as a teaching and learning strategy, face-to-face teaching and learning was combined with the use of AT. The instructor taught LD students traditionally, providing explanations of the reading strategies and explaining new vocabulary. The students' independent learning followed in the second part of the lesson. They put on their headphones and used TextAloud in order to listen to the text of the article. The instructor supervised, answered questions, and provided immediate feedback and technical assistance.

The software assists LD students to decode by reading aloud the text copied into the program window. The program's features allow each student to choose the preferred "natural voice" of a male or female reader, to adjust the speed and pitch of the reading, as well as go back and forth through the text as needed. Students benefit from individual work. They can concentrate better listening to the text through their headphones. They listen to the text and questions and can go back and forth, listening again and again, to parts of the text. The students work at their own pace, and they choose the voice that sounds better to them. All the students appreciate the option of reading-speed adjustment. They can adjust the reading speed according to their individual needs.

How did we solve the problem of listening to the texts at home, when doing homework? In the past, students would download the trial version of TextAloud and work at home, but the artificial computer voices the free trial version provides were not clear enough to them. The solution we came up with was to work online from home. Students virtually connected to the desktop of the college main computer by using their username and password. In this way they could use the college-purchased version of TextAloud and listen to the text being read by more natural voices.

Findings

The 27 students in the pilot study took five exams during the academic year 2010–2011. The results of their exams were statistically analyzed. Table 29.3 presents the means and standard deviations of the scores on the exams of the students in the specialized class. The results point to a significant improvement in the students' scores over time, $F(4, 76) = 11.6$, $p < .01$, $n^2 = 0.38$. A subsequent Bonferroni test indicated a significant difference between second and third exams and the last exam.

In addition, a comparison between the results of the LD students in the special class with those of LD students in the regular classes (Figure 29.3) indicates that although both groups showed a gradual improvement in exam scores, students who attended the special class appeared to achieve greater improvements. That is, while no significant differences between groups are found in the scores on the first exam, $t(28) = -0.207$, $p = .84$, significant differences are found in the scores on the exemption exam given at the end of the course, $t(28) = 1.5$, p .144.

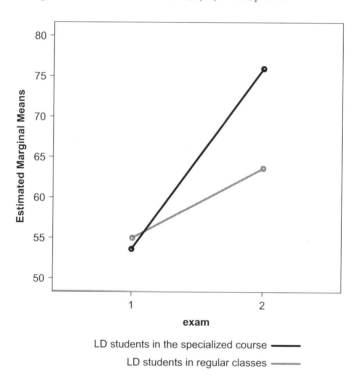

Figure 29.3 Estimated Marginal Means of MEASURE_1

Table 29.3 Mean and Standard Deviation of Exam Scores of LD Students in Specialized Class

	M (N = 20)	SD (N = 20)
2nd exam	53.60	13.869
3rd exam	56.45	13.987
4th exam	69.10	11.675
5th exam	63.10	11.787
Final exam	76.15	17.064

Table 29.4 Comparison in Means of First and Final Exams

	Dyslexic Students in Regular Courses	Dyslexic Students in the Special Course
1st exam	(13.13) 55	(14.98) 53.7
Exemption exam	(26.5) 63.6	(16.5) 75.96

Conclusions and Recommendations for Further Research

The pilot study aimed at examining whether employing blended learning could facilitate the understanding of English texts of LD students and improve their reading comprehension abilities, thus leading to their becoming autonomous learners.

Overall, the results point toward a tendency of improvement for both groups. Nevertheless, while both groups benefited from participating in the course as shown by their improvement in reading English academic texts, those students who took part in the special course were able to make greater progress. It appears that the use of blended learning including the use of assistive technology and e-learning best suited the students' needs and provided the necessary tools to supplement the face-to-face teaching. The use of the computer for reading texts in class helped students to understand the lesson better, increase their participation in the lesson, and be better prepared to read articles in their individual field of study. Moreover, participating in the special course provided students with the opportunity to learn, apply, develop, maintain, and generalize new reading strategies, leading to improvements in their reading fluency. This resulted in better grades and motivation to read articles in English.

The 20 LD students in the sample group benefited from TextAloud, which assisted them in bypassing their reading disability. The LD students in the regular class had to rely mainly on the instructor's help during the lesson for reading and comprehending the texts, which in turn put them at a disadvantage because the instructor's attention focused on the majority of regular students.

Students' access to TextAloud at home assisted them in doing homework assignments on their own. This enabled them to practice the various strategies and new vocabulary. LD students who attended the regular classes did not have access to the text-to-speech program from home. Consequently, completing their homework assignments was much more difficult, often leading to frustration and neglect to complete their assignments.

When asked about their experiences with blended learning, most students in the control group expressed satisfaction with the level of instruction as well as the multitude of teaching media, stating that the use of AT and e-learning greatly contributed to their accomplishments in the course.

More importantly, students claimed that their ability to "handle texts on their own" had also helped in boosting up their self-esteem, proving their ability to succeed in the academic studies despite reading difficulties.

An interesting point to mention was the way students related to the software. They responded differently. Some of them could not do without the reader and used the software all the time. Others used it only when they really did not understand difficult words they were trying to read by themselves. All of them acknowledged the advantages of the reader over the tapes they had used in high school: easier movement in the text, possibility to enlarge fonts, ability to arrange text according to individual preferences, ability to adjust the speed/pace of reading, and ability to choose the voice of the reader (male or female) which best suited their needs. The fact that students were able to use the reader by working online from home did contribute to their success. Students realized that the software could help them read in order to understand the texts studied during the course, and they could also benefit from the features of TextAloud later in life.

Nonetheless, some caveats should be mentioned that future implementation of AT and e-learning should take into consideration. Some students pointed to the lack of inflection and intonation of the reading program, which slightly impaired their understanding. They would rather listen to human voices, to a real person sitting across them and reading to them. In addition, instructors observed that some students found it hard to multitask while working individually during the lesson.

We need follow-up research on a larger population of LD students and a longer period of time. We consider using more varied research tools by adding interviews and case studies in order to observe individual variation. Research carried out thus far on e-readers indicates that, as is often the conclusion in educational research, individual variation merits greater attention than mere examination of group means (Hecker et al., 2002). The effectiveness of e-readers appears to be highly dependent on individual student traits.

The present study shed some light as to the contribution of blended learning in improving the reading comprehension of LD students. It provided them with the appropriate learning environment and the necessary tools for maintaining an open and flexible learning environment. Educators should not hesitate to integrate technology features into instruction for students who struggle with academic tasks. These approaches can support learning by building literacy, language skills, and independence.

Resources

www.resourceroom.net/readspell/ida_texttospeech_Elkind.asp
www.readplease.com
www.textaloud.com
www.ldonline.com
http://www.greatschools.org/special-education/legal-rights/968-matching-assistive-technology-tools-to-individual-needs.gs
http://www.academia.edu/259746/A_Framework_for_Web-Based_Learning

References

Anderson-Inman, L., Knox-Quinn, C., & Horney, M. A. (1996). Computer-based study strategies for students with learning disabilities: Individual differences associated with adoption level. *Journal of Learning Disabilities, 29*(5), 461–484.

Anderson-Inman, L., Knox-Quinn, C., & Szymanski, M. (1999). Computer-supported studying: Stories of successful transition to postsecondary education. *Career Development for Exceptional Children, 22*(2), 185–212.

Ashton, T. M. (2005). Students with learning disabilities using assistive technology in the inclusive classroom. In D. Edyburn, K. Higgins, & R. Boone (Eds.), *Handbook of special education technology research and practice* (pp. 229–238). Whitefish Bay, WI: Knowledge by Design.

Bonk, C. J., & Graham, C. R. (2004). *Handbook of blended learning: Global perspectives, local designs.* New York, NY: John Wiley & Sons.

Dalton, B., Winbury, N. E., & Morocco, C. C. (1990). "If you could just push a button": Two fourth grade boys with learning disabilities learn to use a computer spelling checker. *Journal of Special Education Technology, 10,* 177–191.

Dziuban, C., Hartman, J., Moskal, P. (2004). Blended learning. *EDUCAUSE Review, 7.* Retrieved from https://net.educause.edu/ir/library/pdf/ERB0407.pdf

Edyburn, D. L. (2004). 2003 in review: A synthesis of the special education technology literature. *Journal of Special Education Technology, 19*(4), 57–80.

Elkind, J., Cohen, C., & Murray, C. (1993). Using computer-based readers to improve reading comprehension of students with dyslexia. *Annals of Dyslexia, 43,* 238–259.

Hecker, L., Burns, L., Elkind, J., Elkind, K., & Katz, L. (2002). Benefits of assistive reading software for students with attention disorders. *Annals of Dyslexia, 52,* 244–272.

Higgins, E. L., & Raskind, M. H. (2000). Speaking to read: The effects of continuous vs. discrete speech recognition systems on the reading and spelling of children with learning disabilities. *Journal of Special Education Technology, 15*(1), 19–30.

Khan, B. H. (2001). A framework for web-based learning. In B. H. Khan (Ed.), *Web-based training.* Englewood Cliffs, NJ: Educational Technology Publications.

Kahn, B., (2005). *Managing E-Learning Strategies: Design, delivery, implementation and evaluation.* Englewood Cliffs, NJ: Educational Technology Publications.

Okolo, C. M., Cavalier, A. R., Ferretti, R. P., & MacArthur, C. A. (2000). Technology literacy and disabilities: A review of the research. In R. Gersten, E. P. Schiller, & S. Vaughn (Eds.), *Contemporary special education research: Syntheses of the knowledge base on critical instructional issues* (pp. 179–250). Mahwah, NJ: Erlbaum.

Raskind, M. H., & Higgins, E. (1995). Effects of speech synthesis on the proofreading efficiency of postsecondary students with learning disabilities. *Learning Disability Quarterly, 18,* 141–158.

Raskind, M. H., & Higgins, E. L. (1998). Assistive technology for postsecondary students with learning disabilities: An overview. *Journal of Learning Disabilities,* 31, 27–40.

Raskind, M. H., & Higgins, E. (1999). Speaking to read: The effects of speech recognition technology on the reading and spelling performance of children with learning disabilities. *Annals of Dyslexia, 47,* 251–281.

Siegel, L., & Smythe, I. (2004). Dyslexia and English as an additional language (EAL): Towards a greater understanding. In G. Reid & A. Fawcett (Eds.), *Dyslexia in context: Research, policy and practice* (pp. 132–146). London, UK: Whurr.

30

Supporting Student Engagement in E-learning in a Resource-Constrained Institution

Experiences From Makerere University

Michael Walimbwa

Introduction

The purpose of education is the deliberate transmission of knowledge, skills, and values. Agenda 21 of the Brundtland Report (Brundtland, 1987) identified education as an essential tool for achieving sustainable development and highlighted some of the areas of action for education. These include quality of education and reorientation of existing educational programs. Many higher educational institutions all over the world integrate learning technologies called Information and Communication Technology (ICT) and electronic learning (e-learning) in an attempt to attain quality education. E-learning, though ambiguous, means the delivery of all or parts of the course content in a virtual-learning environment (Rytkønen & Rasmussen, 2010), involving the use of Learning Management Systems (LMS), computer networks, and many other learning technologies. According to this research, e-learning encompasses learning that uses learning technologies and information networks: the Internet, an intranet or extranet, and electronic systems, whether wholly or in part, for course delivery, interaction, evaluation, and/or facilitation. ICTs have become so popular that they are getting local names—for example, TEHEMA (Technologia eHabari Mawasiliano) in Kiswahili (Walimbwa, 2010).

Makerere University, established in 1922 as a technical school, is one of the oldest universities in Africa. In an effort to improve the quality of training and reorient educational programs, and increase the growth of student enrollment, Makerere University has brought about the desire for instructional innovations, including blended e-learning approaches. Makerere University has gone through a number of transformation innovations in its teaching, learning, and research. The University started integrating learning technologies and e-learning in 1997 and has had a number of LMS, including, Blackboard, KEWL, and, currently, Moodle. In the past, some courses have been taught with a blended delivery approach. In my first year of teaching, I uploaded a course for teacher trainees called Educational Technology, which had 20 enrollees; the second year attracted 70, and the third year attracted more than 300. Over these years, an attempt was made to find out the types of learning support the students who enrolled in the course needed. This was done so that future students were given more access to learning materials electronically on the LMS and operated more effectively in a digital learning environment. It was expected that this would have a multiplier effect and would convince others that working on the electronic learning platform was exciting, interesting, and something for everyone.

Notably, different tools exist in an electronic learning environment with specific reference to an LMS, including, announcements, discussion boards, chat rooms, forums, wikis, resources, grades, backups, and digital drop boxes. The tools enable trainees to interact more or less like in a lecture-room environment that mimics face-to-face sessions. Other available learning technologies include iPads, smartphones, digital libraries, videos, and podcasts. The classes I handled had the same experiences and kept bringing up almost similar difficulties in their attempts to engage in e-learning and use the LMS. The assumption is that the few students who currently use technology for learning are knowledgeable and have access to the tools. Those who are not effective in a digital learning environment needed to be taught these skills so they would be proficient and their use of technology for learning would increase.

Essential to a digital learning environment are the following skills, as adapted from Tilbury and Wortman (2004):

- Envisioning—being able to imagine the best of what you are doing.
- Critical thinking and reflection.
- Systemic thinking.
- Building partnerships (even with the people we interact with electronically).
- Participation in decision making.

These skills, applied according to the contexts of different students and the integration of ICT in teaching, learning, and research, are instrumental in the move toward the reorientation of training and the attainment of quality learning and education. This is the reason why Makerere University, amid resource limitations, is investing in ICT capacity building. In the face of globalization and the ICT revolution, academics in institutions of higher learning are increasingly concerned with the need to make their activities competitive amidst the information age that may bring out a well-rounded graduate.

Research has shown that the appropriate use of learning technologies, e-learning and ICT, can catalyze the paradigmatic shift in both content and pedagogy that are at the heart of education reform (Bransford, 1999). Designed and implemented properly, learning technologies and e-learning promote the acquisition of the knowledge and skills that empower students for lifelong learning, an aspect for which is advocated by Fullan (2007). When used appropriately, e-learning, especially computers and Internet technologies, enable new ways of teaching and learning rather than simply allowing teachers and students to do what they have done before in a better way (Walimbwa, 2011). These new ways of teaching and learning are underpinned by constructivist theories of learning and constitute a shift from a teacher-centered pedagogy, characterized by memorization and rote learning, to one that is learner centered and flexible, with access to teaching and learning materials. Therefore, the learner is provided with more functional education and training experiences.

One of the greatest hardships endured in the provision of education in sub-Saharan Africa is the large numbers of students and limited resources. Learning technologies promise to reduce this and to open access to knowledge in ways unimaginable. ICT, out of which come learning technologies, has the potential of increasing the quality of training, reorienting programs, and eventually attaining transformation of educational experiences for learners. World Bank (2002) says that ICT greatly facilitates the acquisition and absorption of knowledge, offering unprecedented opportunities to enhance educational systems and widen the range of opportunities for learners. The problem, however, is in deciding which learning technologies to use. The choices are based on technological possibilities rather than educational needs (Shaheeda, Ng'ambi, & Czerniewicz, 2007); the introduction of ICTs, most especially in an African context, at different levels and in various types of education, is therefore very challenging. The question, however, is, do the key tools in learning technologies empower the learners with skills, as Tilbury and Wortman (2004) asserted?

The important questions here are as follows:

a.   What are the critical competencies in using learning technologies?
b.   What is the level of utilization of learning technologies in a given course?
c.   Does the use of learning technology have an impact on the acquisition of skills?
d.   Which kind of framework should be in place for effective integration of learning technologies?

Methodological Issues

This study adopted action research, including program evaluation approaches. The approaches were undertaken by using qualitative data collection methods, focusing on students involved in using learning technologies, evaluating the current competencies and strategies, and participation in training and their perceptions about how technologies were integrated into their training. The study adopted the content analysis approach. At the same time, data were collected about the current availability and utilization of ICT in comparison to traditional methods of teaching and learning, as perceived by the trainees.

Regarding instrumentation, text analysis and interviews were key for this study. A variety of texts were consulted to get a deeper understanding of using learning technology. Text was treated as a source of data in its own right. Among others, these included student–student and lecturer–student communications using LMS tools, like chats. These communications include questions, discussions, and so forth. Students who had previously used learning technologies were interviewed. The questions they asked during their study are still on the LMS and were studied in detail to get a glimpse of what their needs may be and how they perceive learning with learning technologies.

The collected data were edited, checking for consistency, completeness, and accuracy. After all the answers to the items were recorded, the responses were summarized, categorized, and coded into themes for analysis in order to draw conclusions from the results. Data, being purely qualitative, were analyzed thematically by identifying salient issues.

The Structure of Makerere University and the Teaching System

Makerere University has about 30,000 students. The largest numbers are on-campus students. The College of Education, where this research was conducted, has about 5,000 of the entire university student population. This research was done on two groups of second-year students in the course called Educational Technology. Each group consisted of about 300 students, making a total of 600 learners. The normal face-to-face interaction with these students was two hours per week. This was different in the virtual learning environment, where students chose how long they should use the learning technologies, depending on their motivation and interest.

Competencies in Using Learning Technologies and the LMS

Useful knowledge is inclusive of practical skills through learning by doing and training that may include ICT (Crede & Mansell, 1998). As already stated, a limited number of learning technologies are used in Makerere, with the most widely used being the Moodle LMS. Moodle is an open-source e-learning platform, designed to help educators create online courses of high qual-ity. The design and development of Moodle is guided by social constructionist pedagogy (Tuomi, 2006). A quotation from Ghandhi, at the top of the Makerere University LMS, says 'Learn as if you are to live forever, live as if you were to die tomorrow'.

The implication of this statement is very demanding on everybody who claims to learn by using learning technologies, including the LMS. It requires one's dedication and commitment. Moodle provides the tools to learn 'like you will live forever'. This means it has all it takes for a student to learn, and that one must multitask while using the learning technologies. In my opinion, the new generation of learners has these traits, so learning technology provides a better learning environment for them. Other learners must be trained on these skills to increase their success when using technology.

Shaheeda et al. (2007) cited a number of challenges in the education systems, including large classes, curriculum design, language issues, and academic preparedness. These challenges run across most institutions in sub-Saharan Africa. It is in an attempt to respond to these challenges that one needs the skills—access to technology is necessary, but it is not enough, because, in addition, it is always necessary to provide training to empower the University's faculty and staff with skills regarding the use of ICT, as most of the students are more skilled in them than are the faculty (Balasubramanian et al., 2009).

Yuan, MacNeill, and Kraan (2008) noted that educational institutions the world over have been using digital technologies for a long time. For Makerere's case, learning technologies were experimented with first in 1997. More than fifteen years down the road, one would imagine that the need for basic competencies and skills-sets in the use of digital technologies at this institution is now an issue of the past. This is not actually true. The problem comes from fast-changing technologies. In many cases, institutions have accepted to be fashionable, and change as tech-nologies change. The speed of technological change is too fast to enable a stable and substantive utilization of the technology in teaching and learning, therefore, there is a constant need to learn new technologies.

Level of Utilization of Learning Technologies and the LMS

When learning technologies came into existence, there was a lot of excitement. This has been similar to the excitement generated during changes of emerging technologies. Students sent messages to friends, family, and colleagues to share their excitement and support for the use of technology in learning. In fact, most students were very excited, to the effect that some sent personal e-mails and short messages, in congratulation for moving one step into the technologi-cal arena. Students use learning technologies liberally for personal purposes, even when they are engaged in an educational activity (Balasubramanian et al., 2009). The rate and frequency at which messages were received indicated that motivated students were frequently utilizing the learning technologies and LMS. They would send a comment immediately after a unit of some material was uploaded.

Table 30.1 represents the numbers of courses delivered using learning technologies, on the former and current LMS. It shows the number of students on the LMS and the number of courses uploaded to the LMS. The details of how some of these students and courses were operating on the LMS and the kind of difficulties they faced is still scanty. In a currently running project report, it was found out that most of the courses are not more than a shell, containing little or interactive content (Rytkønen & Rasmussen, 2010). To go beyond this, Crede and Mansell (1998) argued that new skills are needed to be able to use LMS creatively, which would include the use and integration of multimedia content.

Table 30.1 Makerere University Strategic Plan 2008/09–2018

Mode of delivery	Dual
Computer Access points	7,838
Computers/laptop numbers	6,200
Students on LMS	• 34,040 on Blackboard • 2,784 on KEWL • 200 on TUSK
Courses on LMS	• 1,034 on Blackboard • 283 on KEWL • 3 on TUSK • 720 on Moodle

It is this encouragement that showed the effectiveness of a blended delivery system. Therefore, the Educational Technology course was delivered in two modes—the normal, instructor-led classroom course, which also used other learning technologies, and the course delivered solely through the technology available on the LMS. It was evident that the capacity to use the LMS was underrated because there were more student users than anticipated. These students, however, went to the LMS to download notes that had been given in class, a sign that not enough creative work had been done. The weakness was that the notes uploaded on the LMS were exactly the same as those given in class.

At present, some lecturers are 'digital immigrants' who may think that present-day students learn like they did—which is an assumption that is far from valid. But it is acceptable that many of the new teachers start by uploading static text materials and say they are giving electronic notes. But this type of noninteractive, nontechnologically-based learning demotivates the students, as they find only downloading notes simplistic. A student who had used powerful tools like chat rooms and discussion forums asked whether something more could be done. Indeed, this learner suggested that the notes be sent as attachments to their e-mails, so we could engage in further information sharing through chatting and discussion forums using learning technology.

By the time comments from students came in, little was known about the power of blogs, Twitter, and Google Talk as learning technologies. They would prove very useful tools in both synchronous and asynchronous interaction. These technologies actually increase the level of interaction and must be considered when designing learning materials. These tools are highly interactive and can be used to enhance instruction and learning. The challenge, however, remains with Internet speed and available bandwidth. This is, at times, limited and slow. For example, an e-mail, which is something expected to take seconds to send and receive, arrives hours after it is sent. The fact that students could use their own personal telephones to call and ask for guidance, with their hard-earned airtime, was sufficient enough to conclude that learning technology excited learners so much that they are ready to invest their own money for a more educational purpose.

Learning Technologies and the Acquisition of Skills

Some researches stress that the graduates of modern institutions must obtain knowledge, skills, and abilities that are relevant to the place of work, both nationally and internationally, meaning that they should have not only academic skills, but they are also required to have problem-solving skills, reflective abilities, willingness to learn, and a tendency of lifelong learning (Makerere

University, 2013). These skills require a shift to more learner-centered methodologies of teaching through using learning technologies and delivery of courses on an LMS. In fact, some researchers have argued that the use of the LMS is one of these strategies, because students improve their abilities to critically reflect on texts and arguments due to the written communication form (Tony & Sangra, 2011). However, there has been no tracer study done in relation to the acquisition of the aforementioned skills if other learning technologies are used.

As already stated, the Moodle LMS and other learning technologies are designed and developed on the basis of social constructionist pedagogy. The tools on the LMS, like chat rooms, discussion forums, and digital drop boxes, are obviously empowering in several ways, as they link with other learning technologies. For example, a learner is in the chat room with so many others, but they are enjoying a chat with a few individuals. Chat rooms have many issues being discussed, unlike forums. So it is the learner's responsibility to follow those discussions they must follow. This has taught them the skill of being focused on one particular issue, even if there are many issues to be followed. The argument is that learning technologies can reinforce human interaction and interactive learning, and, also, e-mails can be used to connect people with common knowledge (Crede & Mansell, 1998).

Regarding critical-analysis skills, students have no direct answers from others, nor do they respond directly to others. It is the responsibility of the individuals who are interested to learn how to conclude issues regarding the tone, frequency, and state of the test with which they are interacting. Sometimes in their searches they are not given material matching exactly what they are looking for, but they get many similar things. It is their responsibility to review the items critically and select the best resources. Even when they are using mobile phones as learning technologies, it was stated that students do not have much airtime. They resort to instant messaging, which is cheaper, but the messages do not give an entire answer. It is their responsibility to be more critical and add flesh to the sketchy ideas they may acquire through the use of learning technologies.

It is obvious that learning technologies are generally being used in research more widely than in the past (Balasubramanian et al., 2009). When looking for literature on search engines like Google, Bing, and Yahoo, students will key in the search terms. It is known that the literature that the student retrieves will not meet their specific context. It is up to them to envision themselves in that context and transform the literature for their own needs. There is enough information and knowledge to be shared on the Internet, but this remains useless to the learners unless it is transformed into their contexts for further action.

It has been argued that education through learning technologies and the LMS is transformational and will change learning trends. Tuomi (2006) argued that education and learning by using e-learning management systems will be integrated across a full lifetime of an individual, eventually getting to lifelong learning. This is another skill that is required by today's learners. The benefit is that the open-source materials used in this kind of education are revised to keep abreast with the trends. For those who need updated information as a practice, they will be able to get it. Because information is power, and today's economies are powered by information technology, the skill of keeping updated is very relevant (World Bank, 2002).

Using learning technologies and the LMS is mostly supported by the Internet and the World Wide Web (WWW). Many researchers claim that this kind of learning is not just about the use of portable devices but about learning across contexts (Sharples, 2007). The challenge now comes in the evaluation of such learning, where a number of studies show that the evaluation of this kind of learning may overlap with the design. In Makerere University's context, this may be a good strategy to force learners to attain life skills. In most cases, during face-to-face situations, they cram what has been given to them, produce the same in the examination, and forget about it, which isn't the case when using technology.

There are claims that today's learners are 'digital natives', good at multitasking and dependent on technology to interact and acquire information (Bennet & Maton, 2008). Though multi-tasking has its own negative consequences, it may be very necessary. Skills that lead a learner to multitask may be very relevant, and the tools in learning technologies and on an LMS being constructivist can easily equip learners with such skills. An example is an organization where the current learner will work as, say, a receptionist. He or she will no longer be able to afford to sit at the front desk and wait for people to be ushered in but will require skills for doing many things at the same time to meet the needs of the organization and its customers. This skill of multitasking is valuable both in the learning environment and in the workplace, and it is possibly first learned by interacting with an LMS.

Recommended Framework for the Effective Integration of Learning Technologies

It is clear that motivational factors play a big role in making students use learning technologies. Acquisition and inclusion of multimedia materials into learning technologies will give deeper motivation to the categories of learners using technologies. More time should be put into making the students acquire skills in the use of multimedia instructional materials that enable them to manipulate, interact with, and use them in any context in which they may be interested.

Indeed, more interactive content to enable acquisition of the skills will also go a long way in changing the face of the use of learning technologies. Like students said, they needed content that make them find out, not just notes using learning technologies. Learners need to learn, but learning happens if a learner is presented with a challenge, and not just spoon-fed ready-made materials. Improving support for learners who are using learning technologies will increase the number of students who use them. The support need is both technical and administrative. This means the people who give such support need to be well equipped in both the required technical and administrative areas.

Conclusion

Some modifications in the approach of integrating learning technologies are required. There is need to use the LMS in a blended approach first, before purely delivering courses online, as the technologies are themselves limited in sub-Saharan Africa. Again, students need to be introduced to these approaches in their first year, such that by the end of their programs they are very familiar with and used to using the LMS. Creating more support facilities is a must. The support needed is both technical and administrative. The support should be concentrated not only in major computer laboratories, they should be decentralized in even smaller ones. In addition to support facilities, the best practices for emulation of technology in learning needs to be identified. It is very difficult to fully understand how some faculties have successfully integrated LMS as a delivery method for learning interventions in the teaching–learning process. But lessons learnt by such faculties could go a long way in helping other faculty members who are attempting to use LMS-based learning to implement it faster, while being aware of the encumbrance. As noted, there are more trainees interested in using the resources, but the resources—computers, networks, and personnel trained in giving support services—are very scarce and needed.

References

Balasubramanian, K., Clarke-Okah, W., John, D., Ferreira, F., Kanwar, A., & Kwan, A. (2009). *ICTs for higher education: Background paper from the Commonwealth of Learning.* Paris, France: UNESCO.

Bennet, S., & Maton, K. K. (2008). The "digital natives debate": A critical review of the evidence. *British Journal of Educational Technology, 39*(6) 775–786.

Bransford, J. (1999). *How people learn: Brain, mind, experience, and school.* Retrieved from Wikibooks: http://en.wikibooks.org/wiki/ICT_in_Education/The_Uses_of_ICTs_in_Education

Brundtland, H. (1987). *Report of the World Commission on Environment and Development. General Assembly Resolution 42/187.* New York, NY: United Nations.

Crede, A., & Mansell, R. (1998). *Information technology for sustainable development: Knowledge societies in a nutshell.* Ottawa: International Development Research Centre.

Fullan, M. (2007). *The new meaning of educational change.* London, UK: Routledge.

Makerere University. (2013). *Makerere University strategic plan 2008/09–2018.* Kampala: Makerere University.

Rytkønen, M., & Rasmussen, P. (2010). *E-learning at East African STRAPA universities.* Copenhagen, Denmark: University of Copenhagen.

Shaheeda, J., Ng'ambi, D., & Czerniewicz, L. (2007). The role of ICTs in higher education in South Africa: One strategy for addressing teaching and learning challenges. *International Journal of Education and Development using Information and Communication Technology (IJEDICT), 3*(4) 131–142.

Sharples, M. (2007). *Big issues in mobile learning.* Nottingham, UK: University of Nottingham, Learning Science Research Institute.

Tilbury, D., & Wortman, D. (2004). *Engaging people in sustainability: Commission on Education and Communication.* Gland, Switzerland: International Union for Conservation of Nature and Natural Resources (IUCN).

Tony, B., & Sangra, A. (2011). *Managing technology in higher education: Strategies for transforming teaching and learning.* San Francisco, CA: Jossy-Bass.

Tuomi, I. (2006). *Networks of innovation: Change and meaning in the age of the Internet.* London, UK: Oxford University Press.

Walimbwa, M. (2010). Application of e-learning in teaching, learning and research in East African universities. In S. Mukerji & P. Tripathi (Eds.), *Cases on interactive technology environments and transnational collaborations—Concerns and perspectives* (pp. 360–372). Hershey, PA: IGI Global.

Walimbwa, M. (2011). *E-learning innovation in East Africa's higher educational institutions.* Saarbrücken, Germany: LAP LAMBERT Academic Publishing.

World Bank. (2002). *Constructing Knowledge Societies: New challenges for tertiary education.* Washington, DC: Author.

Yuan, L., MacNeill, S., & Kraan, W. (2008). *Open educational resources—Opportunities and challenges for higher education.* Bolton, UK: University of Bolton.

Glossary

Adult learners: For BBC Janala, learners from 15 to 45 years are defined as adult learners.

Affordances: Affordances are inherent characteristics or functions of an object (e.g., technology).

AirPlay: An Apple proprietary technology that allows users to broadcast audio, video, and images to compatible devices using Wi-Fi.

Apple TV: A small Apple device that when connected to a monitor, TV, or projector and Wi-Fi allows users to project (mirror) the content from their compatible devices using AirPlay.

Application (app): Software programs on mobile devices that connect users to Internet services; more commonly accessed on laptop and desktop computers.

Baseline survey: A survey/study/analysis conducted with the goal of identifying the starting points of a project/program.

BBC Media Action: BBC Media Action, formerly known as the BBC World Service Trust, is the BBC's international development charity, funded independently by external grants and voluntary contributions. The purpose of the organization is to use media and communication to reduce poverty and support people in understanding their rights.

Biometric authentication: Identification of humans by their physical characteristics, such as a fingerprint, voice, and face. The methods are used for computer system access control.

Cloud (based) computing: A style of computing in which computing resources are scalable on utilization demand. Web applications, data storage, and other IT-enabled resources can be delivered as services via the Internet.

Computer illiterate: Not understanding computers, and unable to perform simple tasks with them. The term also refers to those who do know simple computer-related terms or software applications, such as Microsoft Word.

Cyber café: A place where Internet access is available to the public for free or at a nominal charge.

Cyberculture: In much of a reflection on ICTs, the term *cyberculture* can clearly be identified as one of the frequently and flexibly used terms lacking an explicit meaning. Generally, it refers to (as the prefix indicates) cultural issues related to "cyber-topics." (e.g., cybernetics, computerization, digital revolution, cyborgization of the human body, etc.) and always incorporates at least an implicit link to an anticipation of the future. However, a more explicit understanding of the referent of *cyberculture* varies from author to author, and is often absent. A wide range of miscellaneous phenomena are referred to as *cyberculture*—the term can be used as a label for historical and contemporary hackers' subcultures and for the movement connected to the literary genre of cyberpunk, as an expression describing groups of computer network users, and even as a futuristic metaphor for various prospective or (as some claim) actually emerging forms of society transformed by ICTs. At the same time, the term refers to cultural practices of ICTs (or solely Internet) users or to past or current new media research and theory.

Developed countries: A country with a relatively high level of economic output and security. Some of the most common criteria for evaluating a country's degree of development are per capita income or gross domestic product (GDP), level of industrialization, general standard of living, and the amount of widespread infrastructure. Increasingly, other noneconomic factors are included in evaluating an economy or country's degree of development, such as the Human Development Index (HDI), which reflects relative degrees of education, literacy, and health.

Developing countries: A nation with a low living standard, undeveloped industrial base, and low Human Development Index (HDI) relative to other countries.

Digital artefacts: With respect to ePortfolios, digital artefacts are digital materials that a student has produced and then uploaded to an ePortfolio platform. Digital artefacts can take the form of images, written works, video, audio, assessments, research, or any digital material produced as a result of learning. The digital artefacts can be provided as a body of work produced over time that can yield information related to attained knowledge and skills.

Digital immigrant: A digital immigrant is an individual who was born before the widespread adoption of digital technology. The term *digital immigrant* may also apply to individuals who were born after the spread of digital technology and who were not exposed to it at an early age. Digital immigrants are the opposite of digital natives, who have been interacting with technology from childhood. Digital immigrants are believed to be less quick to pick up new technologies than are digital natives. This results in the equivalent of speaking with an accent when it comes to the way in which they learn and adopt technology. A commonly used example is that a digital immigrant may prefer to print out a document to edit it by hand rather than doing onscreen editing (definition from Technopedia).

Digital learning: A term used to refer to a broad array of information and communication technology–enhanced or enabled learning opportunities. Digital learning includes efforts to integrate and utilize ICTs in traditional and formal learning settings, such as schools, universities, and technical-vocational programs, but may also include less formal or collaborative learning situations.

Digital repository: A digital repository is a software solution for managing, storing, reusing, and curating digital materials. They are used by a variety of communities and may carry out many different functions and forms. Contemporary understanding has broadened from an initial focus on software systems to a wider and overall commitment to the stewardship of digital materials; this requires not just software and hardware but also policies, processes, services, and people, as well as content and metadata.

Drag and drop: According to dictionary.com, drag and drop is a common method for manipulating files (and sometimes text) under a graphical user interface. The user moves the pointer over an icon representing a file or objects and presses a mouse button. The user holds the button down while moving the pointer (dragging the file) to another place, usually a directory viewer or an icon for some application program, and then releases the button (dropping the file).

E-learning (electronic learning): An umbrella term that refers to all types of training, education, and instruction that occur on a digital medium, such as a computer or mobile phone. Electronic learning means that learning proceeds through utilizing ICT for academic purposes (i.e., for online tutorials).

Electronic mail account or e-mail account: An authorization that allows the sending of electronic mail messages over a particular system, such as one college's network.

English in Action (EiA): English in Action (EiA) is a 9-year (2008–2017) language education project aiming to develop communicative English language skills for 25 million people in Bangladesh.

ePortfolio: An electronic portfolio (ePortfolio) is a web-based platform that consists of electronic media and related digital material. The electronic platform acts as repository for digital material produced by students, individuals, or professionals. The digital artefacts can represent a progression of competencies, skills, or assessments related to the learning experiences. Accessing an ePortfolio can provide a student with the opportunity to reflect on his or her learning and therefore provide a knowledge that builds on his or her individual growth.

Face-to-face tutorials: A student learning support conducted through face-to-face.

Fixed broadband: High-speed data transmission through "non wireless" mediums (e.g., cables).

Flipped classroom: The flipped classroom is a form of blended learning in which students watch lectures online and work on problem sets with other students in class. This approach allows teachers to spend more time interacting with students instead of lecturing. This is also known as *backwards classroom, reverse instruction,* and *reverse teaching.*

Formal education sector: The education sector where a curriculum is set, and, based on that curriculum, education is provided by schools and universities.

Global online accreditation programs: A specialized collection of courses developed by credible international organizations in their specific field of expertise. They also offer an industry wide recognized accreditation to their participants. The Project Management Institute Global Accreditation and the Global Airport Management Professional Accreditation Programme are two examples of this approach.

Grid: The grid is a set of interconnected regions that form a kind of world.

Guru Pintar Online: A portal attached to the Universitas Terbuka (the Indonesia Open University) website that serves teachers in Indonesia and aims to facilitate the continuous learning of teachers through UT's open educational resources.

Holistic: Emphasizing on the "whole" and interdependence of something that has multiple parts.

iBooks Author: A free e-book authoring application developed by Apple Inc. Materials created in iBooks Author must be created using a Mac computer and can be published either as an interactive iBook for iOS devices or as a PDF.

iMovie: Apple's proprietary video-editing application.

Informal education sector: An education sector where education is provided outside standard school.

Information and communication technology (ICT): Technologies that that provide access to information through telecommunications (Internet, cell phones, wireless networks).

Integrated-skills approach: A linguistic pedagogical approach designed to teach language skills together. Students will study reading, writing, listening, and speaking in an integrated classroom rather than studying each skill separately.

International Telecommunication Union (ITU): United Nations specialized agency for information and communication technologies.

Internet landscape: Overview of indicators that can map Internet technology and its users in a country or community.

Internet penetration: Percentage of total population of a country using Internet.

Kbps: Kilobits per second (8 kilobits = 1 kilobyte).

Keynote: An Apple proprietary presentation application similar to Microsoft's PowerPoint.

Learning management system (LMS): A software application that allows for the delivery and tracking of e-learning courseware. The LMS is a powerful tool for consulting companies that specialize in staffing and training, extension schools, and any corporation looking to improve continuing education of its workforce. Its impact has been felt mostly outside of traditional education institutions, although the same technological and market forces are dramatically changing today's classroom as well. Current trends in technology and business favor the increase of collaborative, web-based applications, user-oriented design, and other features that are often grouped together under the term "Web 2.0." By further inverting the traditional forms of interaction between instructors and pupils, and enabling a large amount of content to be created and managed more easily, the future of LMS appears to be dynamic.

Learning outcomes: Learning outcomes are the result of a learning activity (or activities) and objectives.

Learning support services: Student support provided by Universitas Terbuka (the Indonesia Open University) that includes face-to-face and online tutorials, online supplementary learning materials, dry laboratory, online test exercises, a digital library, an e-bookstore, and online examination.

Mailing-list-based tutorials: A tutorial administered by a tutor using the mailing list.

Manhattan Virtual Classroom (MVC): An open source of a web-based Learning Management System (LMS) platform.

Mashup: Mashup is a web application that combines data and/or functionality from more than one source. The main characteristics of a mashup are combination, visualization, and aggregation.

Massive open online course (MOOC): A massive open online course (MOOC) is an online course aimed at large-scale interactive participation and open access via the web. In addition to traditional course materials, such as videos, readings, and problem sets, MOOCs can provide interactive user forums that help build a community for the students, professors, and teaching assistants. MOOCs are a recent development in distance education.

Microblog: Microblogs allow the insertion of text up to 140 characters, in chronological order, and can receive comments from various people.

Mirroring: Mirroring allows users of AirPlay-enabled devices to display media from their devices onto other AirPlay-compatible devices, such as Apple TV.

Mobile broadband: Data transmission through a mobile operator's network.

Mobile operator: Organization providing cellular technology services for mobile phones (telephony, mobile broadband, short message service, etc.).

Moodle: Acronym for Modular Object-Oriented Dynamic Learning Environment; is a free software e-learning platform, also known as Learning Management System.

Multiplatform: Usage of multiple media to achieve a single goal.

National media survey: A survey conducted by AC Nielsen Bangladesh for mapping the media usage behavior of the country's population.

Navigation: Process of going through a website.

Navigation pane: A set of navigation links organized to the left or right side of a web page so that users can access important web pages with a single click.

Nonnative speakers: People whose mother tongue is not English.

Online courses: Courses offered to students by using Internet.

Online tutorials: Student learning supports conducted through the Internet.

Open educational resources (OER): Freely accessible, usually openly licensed documents and media that are useful for teaching, learning, educational assessment, and research purposes. Although some people consider the use of an open format to be an essential characteristic of OER, this is not a universally acknowledged requirement.

Open-source software: Open-source software provides free code to be transformed by the users.

P2P: Peer to peer connects computer to computer for file exchange.

Page-to-page browsing: Browsing through one page from another by clicking on links. For example, in Google, one needs to browse multiple pages to see the search results.

Perpetual beta: Perpetual beta is the keeping of software at the beta development stage for an extended or indefinite period of time. It is often used by developers when they continue to release new features that might not be fully tested.

Progress bar: A component in a graphical user interface used to visualize the progression of an extended computer operation or website.

Prototype: An early sample or model built to test a concept or process or to act as a thing to be replicated or learned from.

Radio button: A radio button, or option button, is a type of graphical user interface element that allows the user to choose only one of a predefined set of options.

Region: A region is an area of 256 x 256 meters. It can be run locally or on a grid.

Regional Offices of UT: UT offices that are located throughout the country and that are responsible for carrying out the daily operational activities, including registration, face-to-face tutorials, and examinations.

SCORM: Acronym for Sharable Content Object Reference Model; is a collection of standards and specifications that defines communications between e-learning content and a learning management system.

Scrolling: The continuous movement of information, either vertically or horizontally, on a video screen.

Self-motivational learning: The process of reflective learning entails the active participation in one's own learning by means of emotional, behavioral, cognitive, and environmental resources that contribute to achieving learning goals. The act of self-motivation in learning contributes to strengthening study skills, monitoring one's performance, and can lead to a positive impact on academic outcomes. This process encourages behaviors, goal setting, and attitudes towards learning experiences through mentoring from teachers or tutors.

Smartphone: A category of mobile devices with computer-like functionality. These devices sport complete operating systems and have a platform for application developers. Smartphones have larger displays and faster processors than so-called feature phones.

Social media: Forms of electronic communication (e.g., websites for social networking and microblogging) through which users create online communities to share information, ideas, personal messages, and other content (e.g., videos). Social media is Web 2.0 technology that is primarily used for connecting people and creating user-generated content (individually and in groups).

Social networking software: Social networking software provides support for groups of people to interact collaboratively, sharing information and resources.

Socio–economic class: Socio-economic class is defined by the profession/occupation and education of the chief wage earner of a household. It ranges from SEC A (at the top end) through to SEC E.

Streaming media: Video or audio content sent in compressed form over the Internet and played immediately, rather than being saved to the hard drive.

Tablet PC: A table or slate-shaped computer device with a touch screen, speaker, microphone, and camera.

Target audience: Set of people for whom a product or service is targeted.

Teachers' and students' e-readiness: A readiness of teachers and students to implement e-learning from various aspects.

TEHEMA (Technologia eHabari Mawasiliano): A Kiswahili synonym referring to information and communication technology.

Transformative learning: Transformative learning can best be described as a learning process that involves a fundamental change in perspective. Transformative learning is the process of effecting change through a frame of reference. The theory is grounded in the premise that learning creates change and through reflection can have an impact on one's subsequent learning experience. In 1978, Jack Mezirow formulated the concept of transformative learning. Mezirow noted that as his students' understanding of their personal, cultural, and social histories grew, so grew their ability to modify assumptions and expectations of learning.

Umbrella brand: A brand name used by a range of different but related products.

User test: A qualitative research method where potential and existing users of a product are exposed to a prototype of a product and then asked in-depth questions to discover their opinion.

Virtual Reading Room: a digital reading room learning environment.

Visit: An interaction, by an individual, with a website consisting of one or more links.

Web 2.0: Web 2.0 is the term given to describe a second generation of the Internet that is focused on the ability for people to collaborate and share information online.

Web analytics: The measurement, collection, analysis, and reporting of Internet data for purposes of understanding and optimizing web usage.

Web supplements: Course material supplements designed to provide students with current and up-to-date content to enrich the learning materials, such as the Universitas Terbuka's (the Indonesia Open University) OER.

Widgets: A piece of code or a shortcut to a larger application; widgets are the interactive elements that are made available in iBooks Author that allow the iBooks to be interactive.

Workflow: a sequence or process that students complete to achieve intended curricular outcomes.

Index

Note: Page numbers followed by *f* indicate a figure on the corresponding page. Page numbers followed by *t* indicate a table on the corresponding page.